'What is the goal? A house that is like the life that goes with it, a house that gives us beauty as we understand it — and beauty of a nobler kind that we may grow to understand.'

ELSIE DE WOLFE

COCOON

CREATING HOMES WITH HEART

ALI HEATH

MITCHELL BEAZLEY

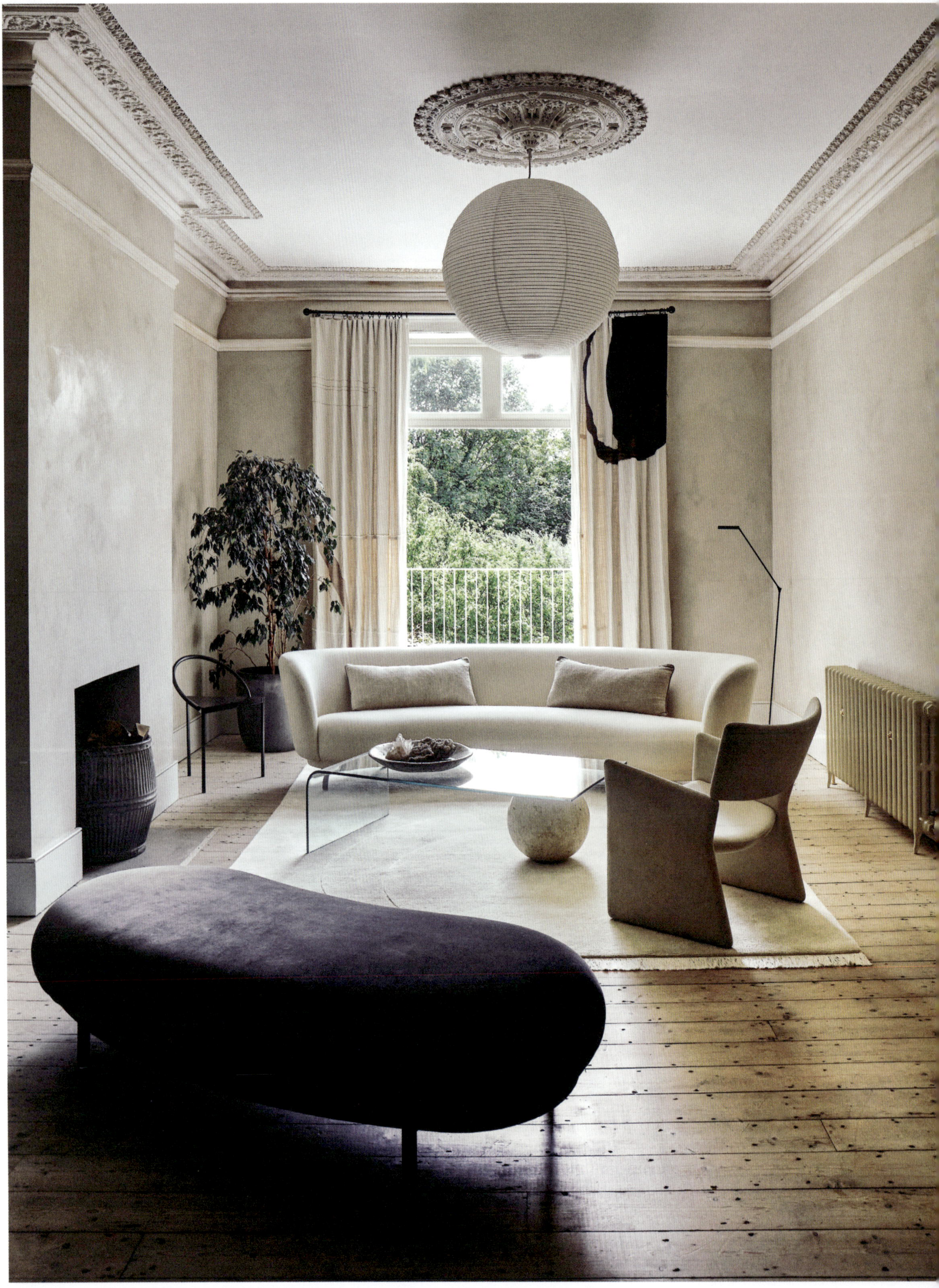

CONTENTS

Introduction 7

COCOONING 10

What is a Cocooning Home 12

The Alchemy of Home 14

Balancing Head & Heart 16

Design Manifesto 18

Dream Boards 20

My Home Love 24

A Room of One's Own 28

Nomadic Cocooning 36

FEELING 40

Spaces & Connections 42

Materials & Sanctuary 44

Rituals & Reflection 48

Light & Shadows 50

Objects & Stories 52

Entertaining & Bonding 54

Love & Togetherness 56

LIVING 60

Waterside Edge 62

Architectural Escape 76

Remote Getaway 90

Fabric House 100

Holistic Retreat 112

Inner Sanctum 124

Botanical Oasis 134

Urban Sanctuary 146

Country Idyll 162

Reimagined Bakery 176

Rural Haven 188

Valley Hideaway 200

Things I Love 215
Sources I Love 216
Thank You 218
About the Author 219
Index 220
Dedication 222
Homeowner Credits 223

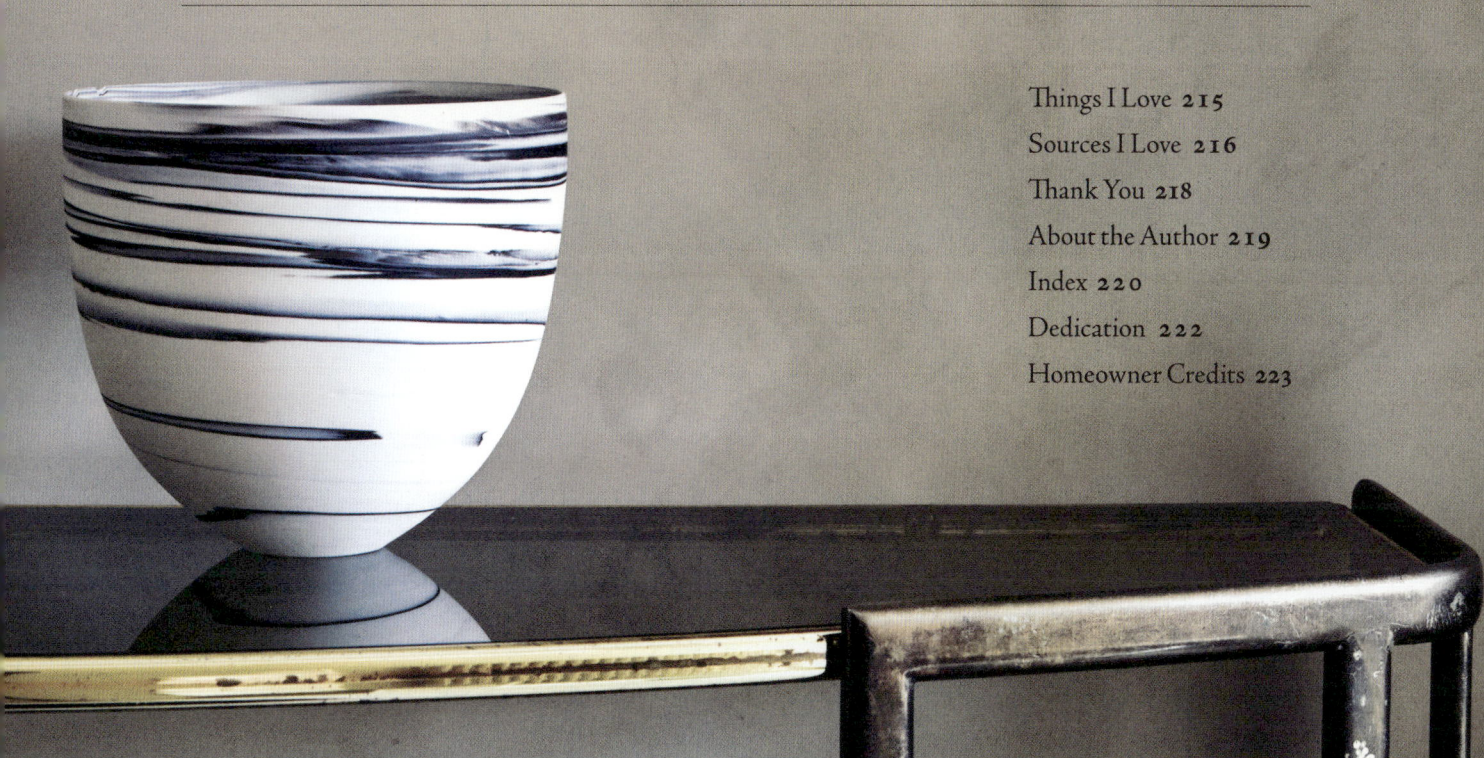

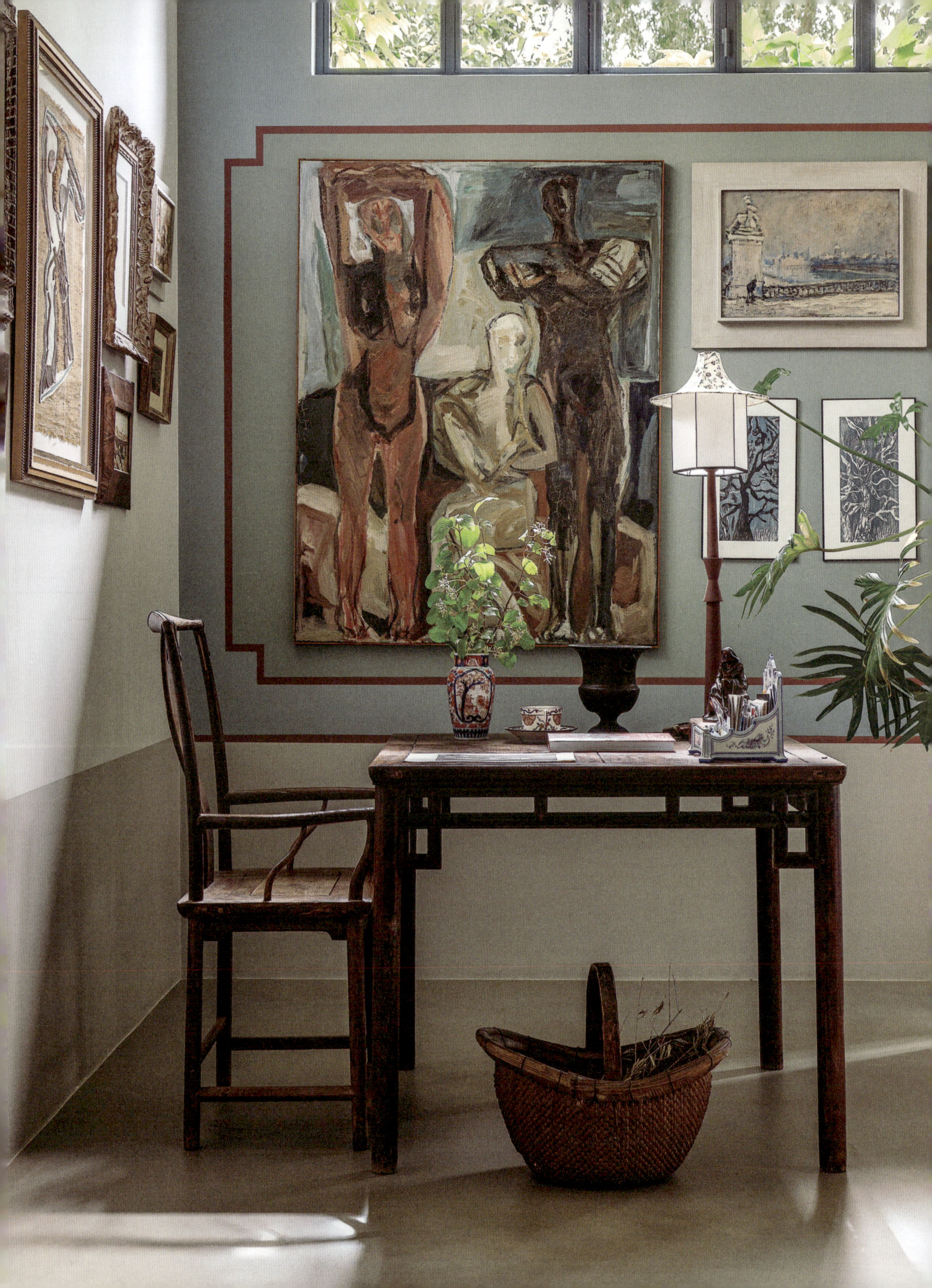

INTRODUCTION

'Cocoon' is a word that resonates deeply with me, encompassing the idea of home as a sanctuary. On the one hand, it describes the place to which we withdraw, where we can shelter from life's storms and escape the craziness of the fast-paced world we live in. But on a more soulful level, it speaks to the importance of creating a space that feels personal and nurturing. During our lifetime, if we are fortunate to connect with our home on both levels, the imprint of those feelings and memories will remain forever.

While my earlier books, CURATE and CREATE, were intended as style and design masterclasses that encouraged you to tell your own story and to create freely, COCOON is more focused on the human touch. And on how listening to our hearts can transform and heighten our experience of a nurturing home.

The way we live and work is changing at lightning speed – high tech, increasingly virtual and more polarizing than ever before. Consequently, the need to disconnect and to immerse ourselves more meaningfully within the spaces to which we are connected, and with those we care about, has never felt more important.

Looking back, I realize that the idea of retreat has fascinated me since I was a child: from the coziness of my tiny, floral-papered bedroom and elaborate dens created under deck chairs, to the prized, fully decorated doll's house made by my dad, which would transport my mind to other worlds. Our childhood spaces are our first encounter with the power of imagination and possibility and are a great lesson in miniature (both things and places), gaining immense importance in our thoughts.

Throughout the course of our journey through life, the experiences and people we meet along the way – inevitably some good, some bad – shape how we choose to create a home of our own. I have lived in our current family home with my husband and children for the past 23 years, and while my style may have evolved, the joy I find in spending time here with them has remained constant. The idea of 'home as our temple' rings true for me. It is a place that speaks to my heart, where I feel connected to my family and where we can all be ourselves without worry or judgement.

In today's media, we are fed many ideals of how a home should look. My design approach, at home and for clients, comes from a more human perspective. Instead of asking, 'What look should I create?' I prefer to flip the question to, 'How do I want to feel here?' This realigns our emotional connection with home, moving it into a space that balances head and heart decisions.

'Emotional' is a word that conjures up feelings of drama for some. But within our homes an emotional reaction to our surroundings is everything. When we place heart at the centre of our choices, we create meaningful encounters – something that goes way beyond the architectural and visual. It's why we remember the sound of our dog's eager footsteps as we come home, the scent of a log fire, or how a worn banister feels in our grasp. It's the joy of being surrounded by people and things you love, reminders of occasions that made you happy, and moments of the unexpected – such as the fall of the light, the life-affirming escapades of our children or the touch of treasured fabrics. This patchwork of life calls to our heart and our imagination and connects with our need for warmth and intimacy.

For me, the idea of cocooning is not about going off-grid or shutting down (although, for some, isolation can drive positive creative outcomes); and it is not an emotion triggered purely by seasonal changes. It is about the ongoing feeling of a space that supports and comforts our happiness and well-being. Whether we are living on our own or with family, our homes, no matter what their size, should be a safe harbour from where we expand our own colourful horizons – and open our minds curiously and creatively.

The creatives I was drawn to feature in this book have all embraced their own idea of sanctuary at home – each of their stories as different as they are special. Their design choices do not revolve around formulas, science or rules, but are heartfelt journeys that are immensely personal. A few of the homes that I share with you mark the next chapters for a couple of people featured in my book *CREATE*, while others belong to creatives who have been on my radar for many years. From a magical one-room home at the back of a London shop to a completely private island escape, this book has taken me on a journey across the islands of Ibiza, Mallorca, Tasmania and the Outer Hebrides; to the cities of Florence, London, Melbourne and Paris; and to the rural English countryside in Devon, Surrey and the Cotswolds.

I hope this book encourages you to listen to your heart and to create a home that makes you feel alive. Our stories are personal and our homes are a reminder of all that makes us who we are, and all that we dream of being. A home is never just four walls and formulaic decoration – it is a private escape and an 'imaginarium'.

With much love, Ali x

In a world where nothing is ever quite enough, our home and the way it connects to our heart, really is everything.

cocooning/

WHAT IS A COCOONING HOME

A SHELTER – where basic human needs are satisfied. A place to survive, live and feel safe.

AN ESCAPE – where you can quieten the noise, away from the outside world.

A NEST – where we love ourselves, feel loved romantically and give love to others.

AN ANCHOR – that underpins our need for authenticity, community and privacy.

A SANCTUARY – that nurtures space for rest, well-being and equilibrium.

A CANVAS – for our ideas, self-expression and creativity.

A MEMORY BOX – that holds stories of the past, present and future.

A HAVEN – where nature and sustainability are valued, both inside and out.

A PLACE – to connect to oneself, with family and friends, and the new global village.

A HARBOUR – from which to venture in your imagination, virtually and increasingly nomadically.

A RETREAT – to return to, where we can feel happy, fulfilled and comfortable.

A REFUGE – that heightens the connection with all our senses.

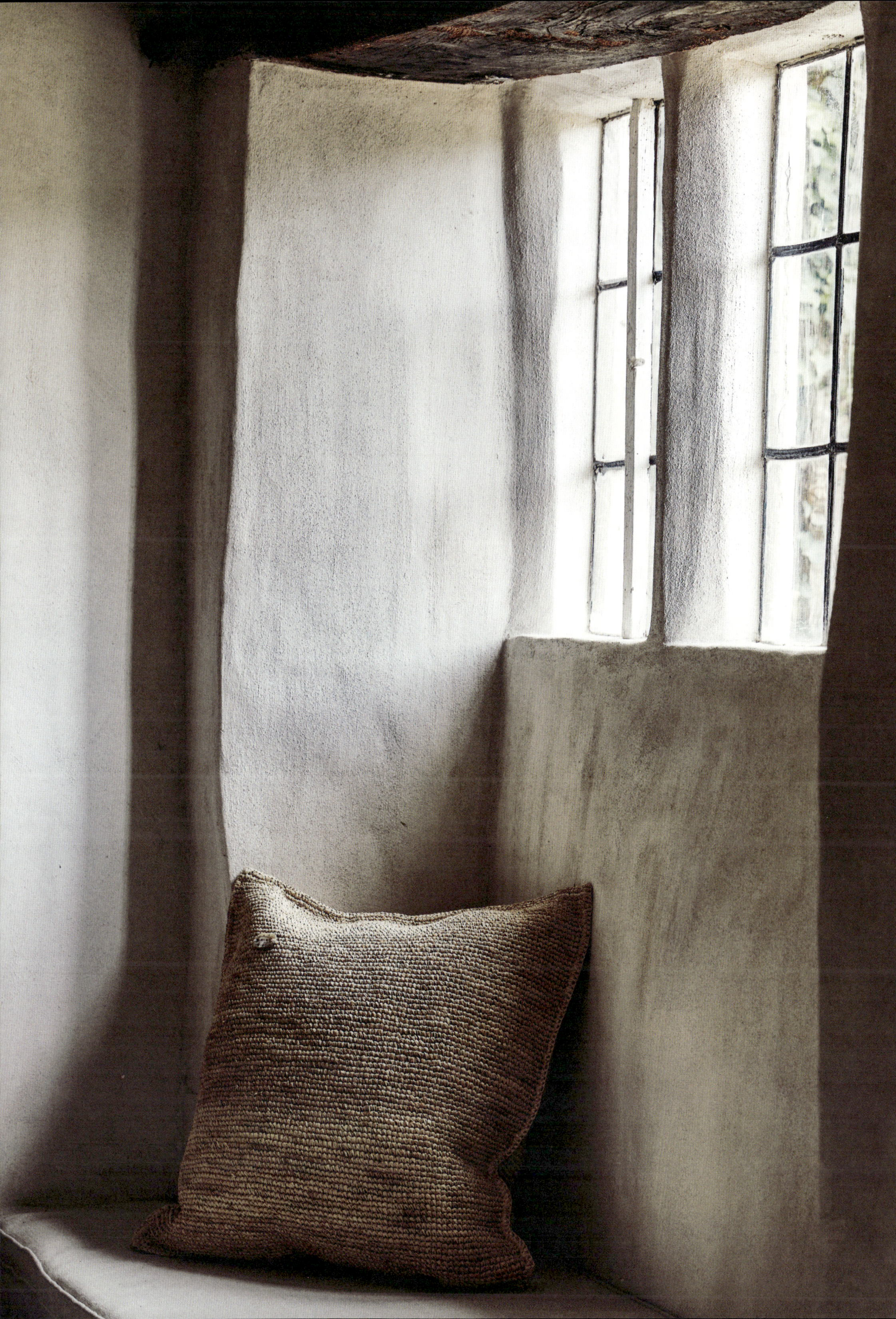

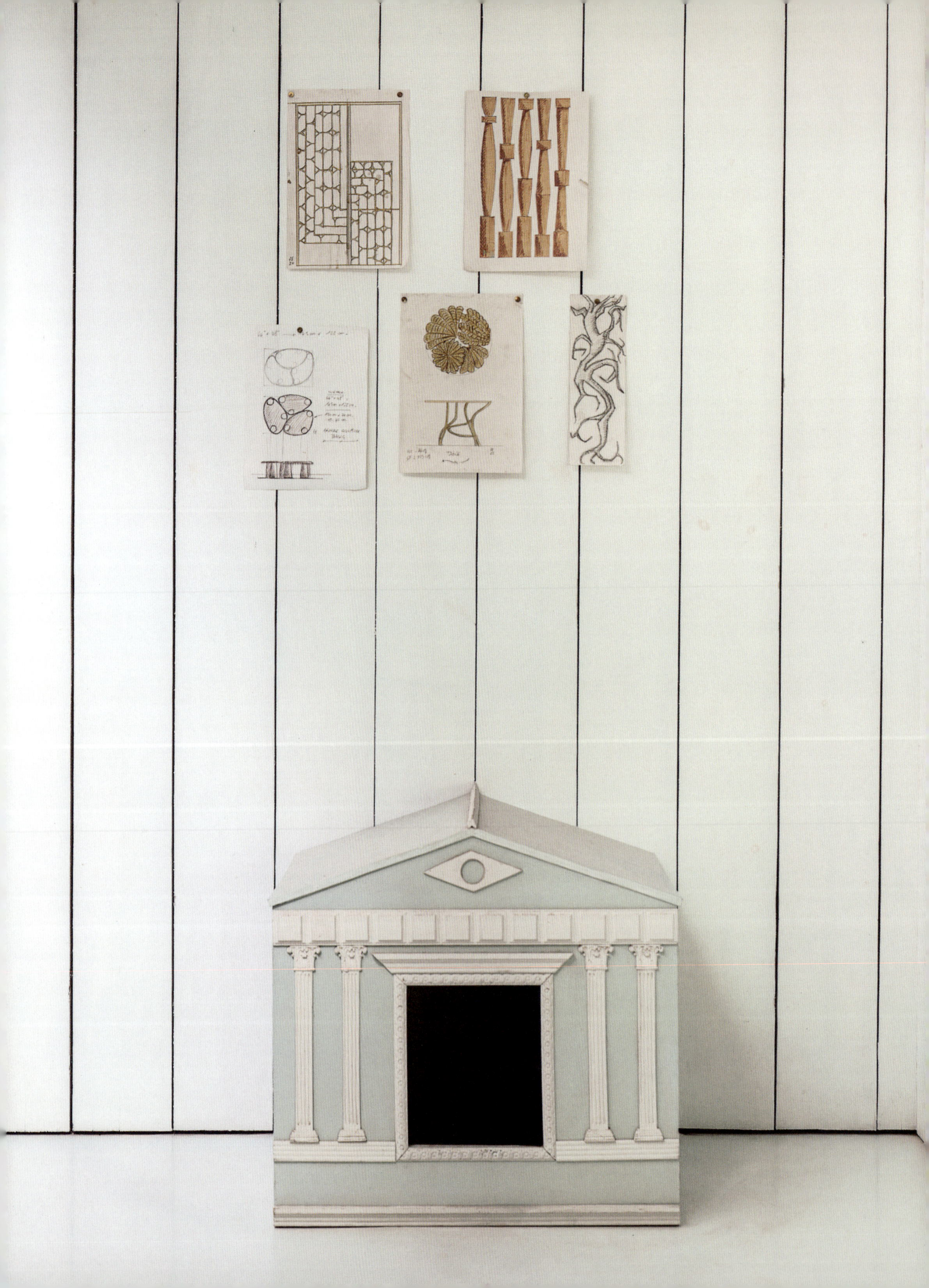

THE ALCHEMY OF HOME

Instead of adapting to the energy in our spaces, influence and shape that energy.

Back in the mid-1990s, I discovered the work of trend futurist Faith Popcorn in her book *The Popcorn Report*, in which she predicted the growth of cocooning at home and the 'craving for safety in an uncertain world'. Over the past 30 years, her TrendBank has continued to measure how this idea has and will evolve. And now, with societal shifts such as the COVID-19 pandemic, climate change, hybrid working, geopolitical unrest, the rise of social media, online shopping, digital entertainment and the advancement of AI, our reasons for cocooning have continued to evolve dramatically.

Psychologist Abraham Maslow created Maslow's hierarchy of needs in the 1950s. This five-tier model highlights our individual needs, ranging from the physiological (breathing, food, water, shelter, clothing, sleep), through to safety (security, health, employment, home), love and belonging (friendship, family, intimacy, connection), self-esteem (confidence, achievement, respect, individual needs), and self-actualization (morality, creativity, spontaneity, acceptance, purpose, meaning, curiosity and inner potential).

With modern lifestyle changes, this humanistic approach has become increasingly relevant to how well we live. The new luxury no longer revolves around functionality and materiality. Instead, it is focused on how things make us feel and the quality of our interactions and creativity. This challenges us to consider where we live, why we use our rooms in the way we do, and how our spaces could be more in tune with our needs. As well as what criteria our choices are based on, what brings us comfort, how we entertain, how we choose to work, and how we connect more closely with ourselves, other humans and the natural world.

At times, we draw the walls of our homes closer like a protective nest, while at others they provide the freedom we need to breathe and grow. This balance blends a desire for armour and adventure, reality and imagination, isolation and revitalization. We morph our spaces to suit our requirements, and our home becomes ever-changing – a place where everything is a possibility.

There is a lot of research taking place around the Default Mode Network and its impact on brain activity, including work by neuroscientist Dr Vossel. The DMN is a system of connected brain areas that show increased activity when a person is not focused on what is happening around them. Believed to be the neurobiological basis of the self, it is the place that processes incoming sensory information when you are quiet. An area between the nodes in our brains where we connect the dots and make sense of the world. Active when we are awake, this network kicks into default mode when we are not focused on demanding activity and puts us on autopilot. This enables us to engage in introspective activities such as daydreaming, mind-wandering and contemplation of the past and the future. Curiosity and imagination can alter our mind, body and behaviour dramatically, and trusting our intuition can make us feel more vital and creative within our homes.

It's why I think it is important to maintain the idea of a dream home, a place that one day we may rent, buy or build. It stops our idea of home feeling inert and ensures our imagination keeps firing. When we are children, our imaginations are totally free and we have no understanding of why, when or how we imagine. However, as we mature, our ability to dream can often slow down or stop, as logical and scientific thinking pushes creativity aside. Remember, things don't have to exist to give us pleasure; they can also be happy creations in our head. Staying connected to our childhood superpowers is a gift.

BALANCING HEAD & HEART
Invigorate how your home feels by bringing together the rational and the emotional.

HEAD	HEART
Physical	Psychic
Think	Feel
Theoretical	Cryptic
Rational	Emotional
Logical	Illogical
Predictable	Dreamlike
Displaced	Protected
Mature	Childlike
Trend-led	Authentic
Perception	Reality
Sensible	Inquisitive
Blinkered	Intuitive
Academic	Imaginary
Safe	Brave
Technological	Human
Public	Intimate
Tentative	Daring
Rigid	Comforting
Disconnection	Connection
Dissatisfied	Satisfied
Temporary	Longevity
Greed	Satiated
Shutdown	Revitalized
Expected	Wondrous
Ego	Curiosity

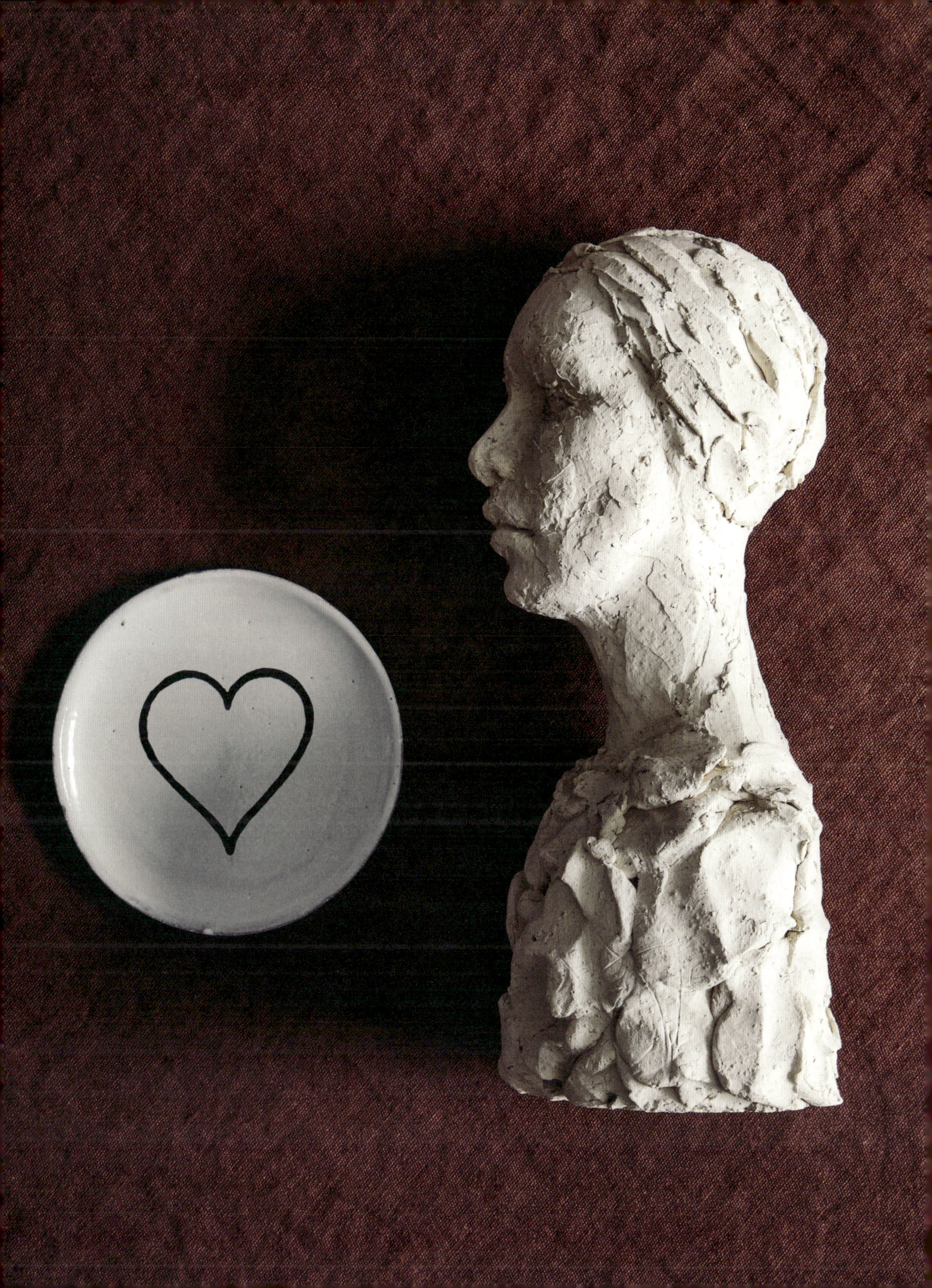

DESIGN

Your heart speaks the truth. Listen. Creating a cocooning home begins with a reality check. It starts with your feelings, then the rest is down to lifestyle, choice, budget and a sprinkling of personal magic. Return to the points outlined here when you are feeling overwhelmed – or shut your eyes, point and see what advice you land on. The chances are it might just be the prompt you need.

Which words express how you want to feel. Most people never stop to consider this, but it has a major influence on the design outcome.

How does your home currently feel. What needs to change? What works?

What homes do you love. Look to films, history and real life.

What stage of life is your home at. Is it a classic beauty, a bit rough around the edges or in need of a total overhaul? Let the bones of the house guide your decisions.

What styles do you like. Classic or contemporary, bohemian or Scandi, modern rustic or colourful, minimalist or maximalist? Research and decide what appeals.

Impact of travel on your style. What resonates and what has influenced your look?

Decide on your sourcing values. Local/global, mass-produced/handmade. Establish your criteria, then ensure supplier values align.

Establish your 'why'. It focuses the mind and keeps choices on track.

Natural materials cause a sensory reaction. Combinations of materials are often more resplendent. Choose wisely and always sample your selections.

Treat temperature as a design tool. It impacts our physicality and psychology. Some materials add warmth, while others, such as steel, lower the temperature.

Surround sounds. From nature, the location, passing traffic, structural creaks in the house and family life. Imagine taking out each noise – how would your home feel without them?

MANIFESTO

What makes you feel cocooned. Consider intimacy, comfort and scale.

Simplify the palette. Decide on your colours and anchor choices consistently. Successful paint schemes balance one dominant and one subordinate shade.

Comfortable, not precious. Bring together a balance of old and new, refined and rustic, rough and smooth, to avoid rooms feeling too precious or formal.

Surround yourself with things you love. They encourage belonging and nostalgia.

Create calm with order. Built-in, freestanding or hanging, good storage is key.

Learn to value 'being' and not 'chasing'. Create a look you can evolve, not replace.

Blurring of spaces. Multifunctional rooms create flexibility.

Clean air, ventilation and scent. Pay attention to how your choices make you feel.

Consider movement. The flow of the space should guide, stimulate, stop and intrigue you.

Light is everything. Optimize the wonder of natural daylight, embrace the shadows and choose artificial light sources for extra illumination. More is always better.

Realities of life. Disabilities, special needs, dementia and other illnesses will require different approaches at home. Adapt spaces to ease care needs, heighten the sensory, and to ensure there's also space for the caregiver to retreat.

Consider the exterior. Do you want this to blend in unassumingly, or stand out and catch the eye? Allow passers-by to glimpse in or maintain your privacy?

Be rebellious. There are no rules as to what lives where or what room does what.

Never hanker for what you don't have. A home is only as good as the feeling within, regardless of the view.

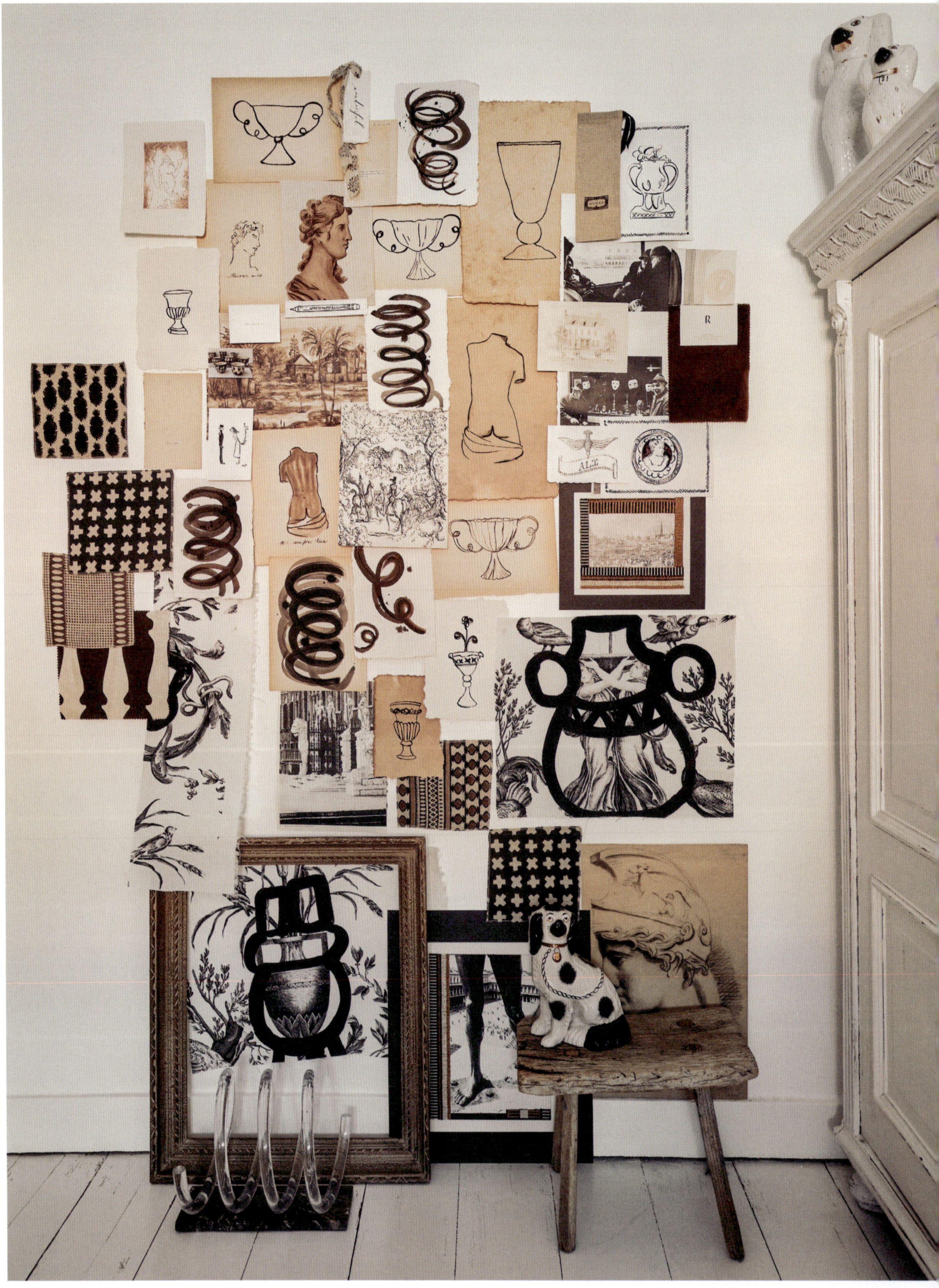

DREAM BOARDS
The most powerful muse will always be our own inner child.

Mood boards – or, as I like to think of them, dream boards – are a great way to capture the essence of what you wish to create in your home. They should be ever evolving and provide you with the freedom to play, think big and imagine. We are all creative and there is no single way to create a mood board.

Decide on the format. Flat-lay trays work well for concepts, as you can add 3D pieces to help tell the story. Wall mood boards are great for 2D inspiration.

Observe, add to and consider. Always a work in progress, keep evolving your ideas.

Source, photograph, collect daily. You never see things when you're looking for them.

Be curious – ideas come from near and far. A wall texture, washed-up pebbles, shell formations, ripples in the sand, plant shapes, graffiti, paper fragments, paintings, art, legends, mythology.

Consider all genres, not just interiors. Observe the connections between fashion, travel and lifestyle stories. The cut of a skirt, the gaze of a statue, the palette of a landscape can all trigger new thoughts and ideas.

Consider perspective. Look up, look down. It's amazing how this changes the view.

Light is magical. The way it catches an object or space is fleeting. Always try to capture the feeling you are hoping to recreate on camera.

Revisit your feelings. Look through the photos overflowing on your phone – they act as a reminder of how places, people and things make you feel.

Dream boards are meant for play. Keep them fluid before refining and focusing.

Interior designers are no different to you. Our curious eye simply looks everywhere and at everything.

CREATIVE WALLS Mood board at home in my office. Sculpture by Malene Birger.

PAGES 22–23 STORY OF THINGS A flat-lay mood board created at home with collected tear sheet inspiration, heirloom treasures and special finds from Pentreath & Hall, Ginny Sims, Lukas the Illustrator, Nām, and Ricardo Fontales.

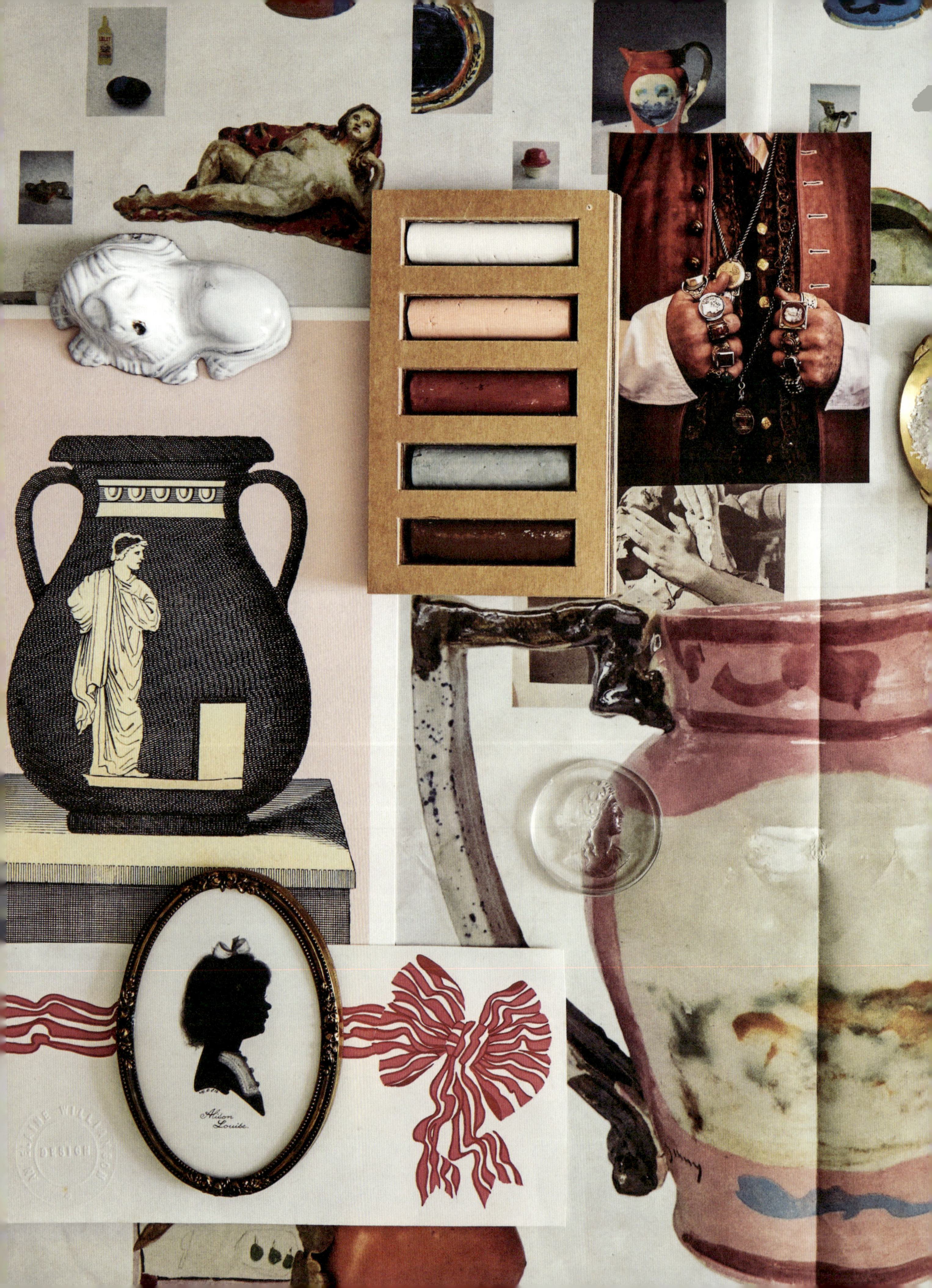

Alison
Louise
DESIGN

207 CENDRE BLEU
006 BLEU PALE
003 BLEU CERULEUM
016 GRIS VERT
205 VERT MOUSSE
045 VERT MOYEN
044 VERT ÉMERAUDE
230 ROSE INDIEN
025 OCRE DE CHAIR
232 FEUILLE MORTE
001 BLANC

MY HOME LOVE
Places that speak to the heart warm your soul.

When we moved to our house, it felt as if it had been waiting for us. Welcoming us in, keeping us safe, holding us as we have created a nest for our family and moved through many stages of life. We had no idea how precious this house would become and how much love we would feel within its walls.

Our home has become the place that anchors us as a couple, where we have raised our children and cherished our first dog, and from where I established my studio. It's where we came home to after a miscarriage and the loss of both our fathers. And where we share love, tears, laughter, parties and lively get-togethers. As custodians of this 285-year-old Georgian house, it's also where we feel connected to the history of our beautiful town. Twenty three years of the same, but each year different. I never thought we would stay this long, and who knows how many years we will remain, but as a family our roots are permanently entwined here.

I find the idea of creating my own sanctuary to be a much-needed escape from the world. Anyone who is also an introverted extrovert will understand the importance of home and the need for retreat. There is no place I am more me, which is a gift, as I am immensely aware that a happy home is not a given for everyone and this is why our imaginations are so important.

With a curious eye for beautiful things, I have filled once-empty rooms with many personal treasures. The process not so much about collecting – although the collections have grown – but more about responding to feelings of love for the objects discovered and introduced, and the sentimental letters and precious mementoes saved.

Design updates have been slow, rooms continue to change role, and displays move all the time, but the pieces that make their way in have retained a sense of permanence. I love my family for bearing with all the creative iterations.

Spaces have not been overthought but instead designed for simplicity and for family and friends to be together. In winter, our beautiful dog is always the first to secure his spot by the fire, while in summer, with the doors flung open, he follows the sun around the garden and is always by my side as I write. Some things have become worn around the edges, as we have let go of the need for perfection, and comforting stacks of books, which will one day have a permanent place, continue to climb. I like to think of our home as a reminder of what's important to us, and as the years go by, I realize that this home is what has enabled so much and from where so many seeds of life and possibility have grown for us all.

People worry about becoming empty-nesters when their children leave home, but I've found that our nest is the constant to which our children keep returning. Sometimes it's empty, but often it's full – of them, their friends and ours around a table or together in the kitchen and garden, listening to stories, recalling past events and, as parents, feeling proud of what they've become.

In between those more hectic days, the quiet moments of calm have become something that my husband and I look forward to, not dread. Our cocoon keeps evolving, the story gets richer, and new ideas for us as a couple and as individuals keep incubating. Yet, at their core, the love and feelings we've nurtured here for years remain alive. A series of moments – real, precious and sentimental. I guess the reason home feels like home.

NATURAL FINDS Treasured antique coral and sea holly, bought on summer vacation in the Île de Ré, off the west coast of France, are curated on our living room shelf – reminders of happy family days.

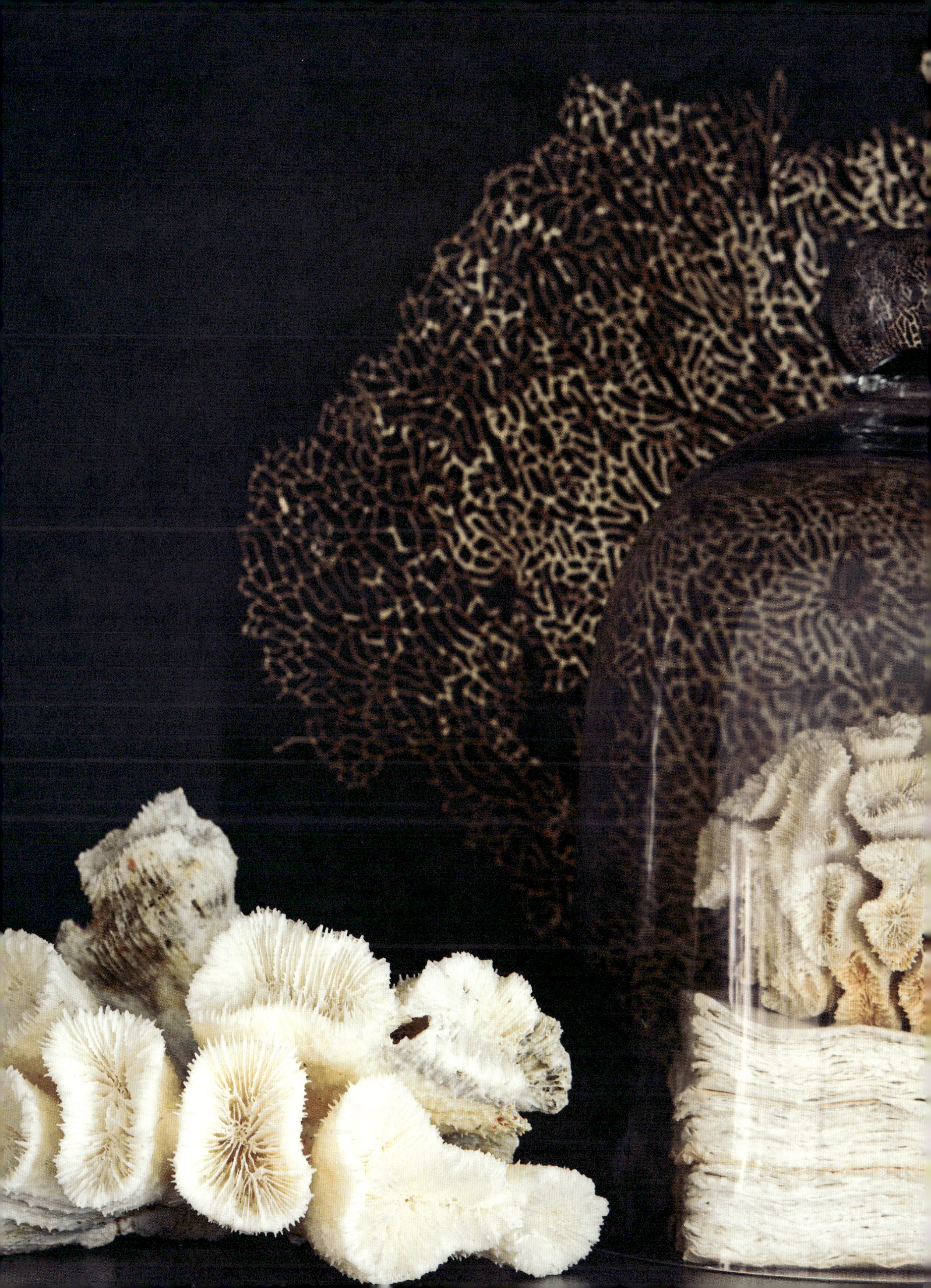

COCOONING ESCAPES When working with my client, Banchory Farm, in Scotland, on the interior design of their boutique holiday cottages, comfort and sanctuary are of paramount importance in the design process.

Let the beauty of what you love be what you seek and what you create.

A ROOM OF ONE'S OWN

Many of us now work from home, some or all the time, but the idea of a space dedicated just to you can still be an elusive idea. Unless you have an excess of guest rooms, or empty children's bedrooms suddenly ripe for change, then most of us can find ourselves chasing the light – working from the dining room table, a nook on the landing, at the kitchen island or even in bed. Whatever the location, creating a sense of occasion around where you spend your day helps to make it feel enticing. Whether that involves lighting a candle, filling a vase with flowers or placing an ideas box next to you. Irrespective of your setup, I think it is good to dream about the ideal for when circumstances change. And if you want to dream big, take inspiration from the pages that follow, which showcase Betty Soldi's creative Florentine studio. It's all the proof we need that a room of our own is always a good thing.

MAKE AN ENTRANCE Situated in a former 1801 *limonaia*, Betty Soldi's design studio was historically used to shelter revered lemon trees. Striking plasterwork curtain fringing frames the rose-covered entrance.

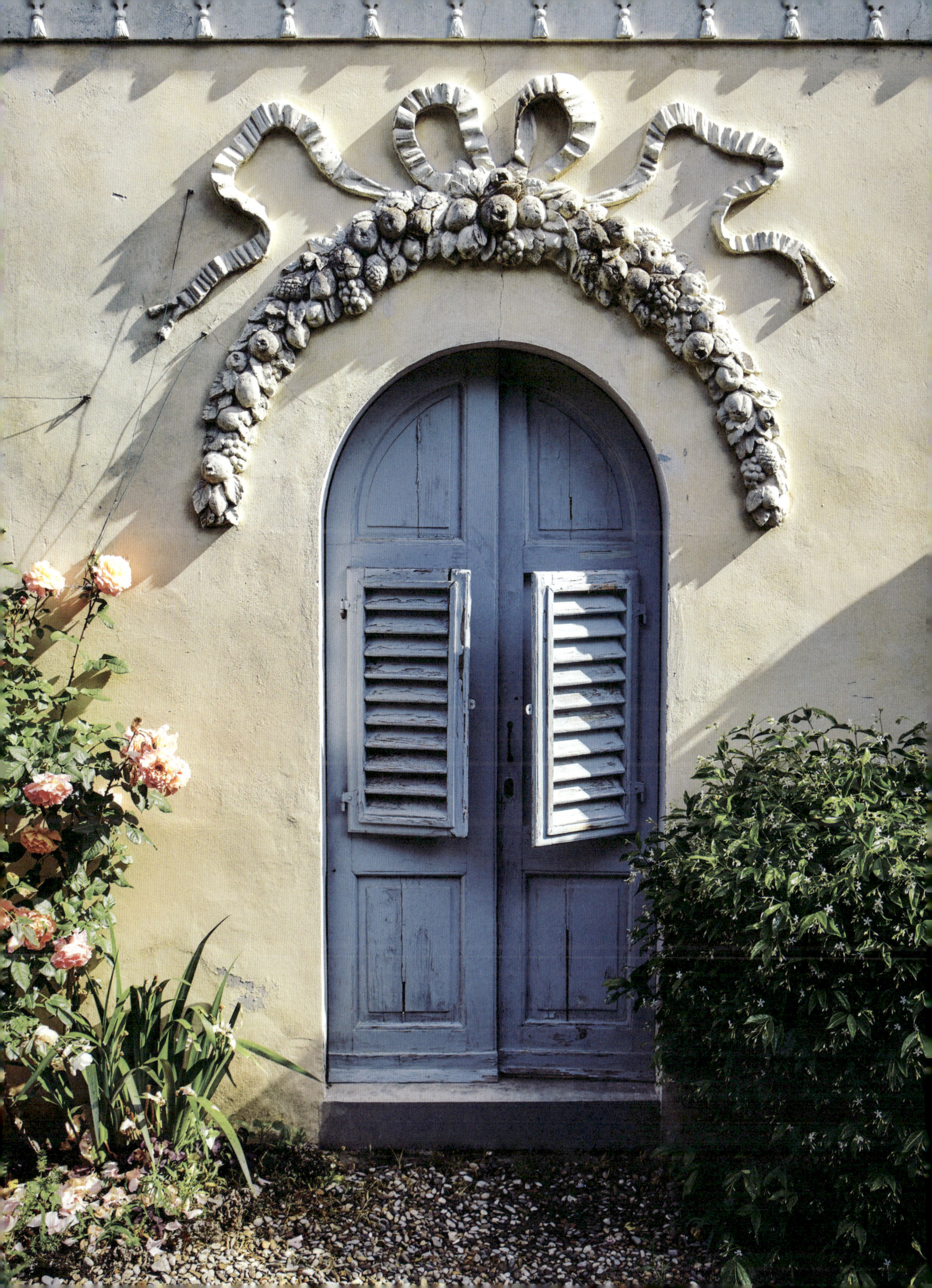

TRULY ITALIAN ROOTS

AFFINITIES
Ernst Haeckel
Art Forms in Nature

Gustave Doré
FANTASTICO

stargazing

ARTISTIC RETREAT
Betty Soldi / Inkspired Creativity

Born into a Florentine family, who have produced handmade fireworks since 1869, Betty Soldi left for England with her family at the age of eight, where she was educated. After a gap year in Florence studying art history, she returned to London to study Design and Visual Communication – training in the principles of Bauhaus architectural script before overlaying her own Renaissance-inspired strokes. Now, creating 'fireworks with ink'. For ten years Betty worked externally for Fortnum & Mason, then returned to Florence, where she opened a design studio and concept store, before pivoting as an artist and expanding her ink creations to encompass more diverse formats. Betty's Florentine studio is enchanting. I hope you enjoy stepping into her creative cocoon as much as I loved immersing myself in her magic.

Describe your studio. It is in the grounds of the Corsi garden – the first English garden to be created in the city, in the 19th century. My studio is nestled within an 1801 *limonaia* – a decorative pavilion historically used to shelter revered lemon trees. Raised above road level, the garden is situated opposite the Boboli Gardens, in a hidden quarter of Florence.

What first drew you to this space. Working just around the corner from home, I had been desperate to create in a space with more light. Peeking into this garden, like everyone else who passes, I called to the universe and a few months later the garden's studio fortuitously became available to rent. As soon as I step into my studio, I say hello and ask how it is doing. I feel very connected here and acutely aware of my senses, which enhances my creative practice. It is such a joy to spread out and return the next day with everything still in place – at home, things were always tidied away.

Describe your walk from home to the studio. Before arriving, I always pop down the road, say hello to our greengrocer, take my daughter to school, and then stop off for a 'coffee with wings' (to take away) – picking up fruit, flowers or something lovely on my way.

What do you see, hear and feel as you open the gates. From the moment I open the gates, I step into a different way of being, as you would through meditation or travel. The gardens are a dreamscape but also urban – I love the contrast between entering a quiet oasis juxtaposed with welcoming the city sounds of passing vespas, beeping horns and shouting workmen. I am immediately aware of nature and notice every detail – flowers opening, colours changing, petals falling, stems and tendrils advancing, and our resident fluorescent-green South American parrots chirping in the trees above, rather like little pterodactyls.

What makes the garden so special. It unravels with secret mazes, hidden corners and a wonderful *pensatoio* – a decorative curved wall and bench, built as a place to contemplate and look up at the stars. Alive with fragrant roses, jasmine, wild daisies and topiary, there is a plethora of sculptural planters, fountains and quiet resting places, as well as historical terracotta muses, statues and stone lions that act as guardians of this magical garden. To get lost here is to find yourself and your thoughts.

Describe the exterior of your studio. Exquisite plasterwork curtain fringing frames the two original rose-covered entrances, which flank a central run of four sets of glazed doors. Historically, taking the lemons inside and the decorative detail outside was a way of honouring the connection and respect between nature and the handcrafted.

Tell me about the interior of your studio. From spring through to the arrival of winter, the doors are flung open to the garden, with butterflies and bees coming in and out all day. I enjoy the gentle breeze and the warm air and follow the light as it moves around. The symbiosis of nature coming in while we look out is important to me. The back wall of the studio integrates a stretch of wall built in the 1400s by Cosimo I de' Medici and is the backdrop to my collection of books and inspirations, displayed on timeless modernist shelves by Dieter Rams for Vitsœ. These 'story' shelves are coordinated by colour and combine treasured reference books and materials alongside objects I love.

Describe the furniture choices. Furniture has been discovered along the way: eclectic vintage chairs, a Saarinen table from my home in London, a precious marble tabletop found by my partner, Matteo, and a black wooden table with a wonderfully patinated surface. A precious antique chandelier, fairy (string) lights and a mirror from my friends at Retrouvius, in London, add sparkle. It is a magical space that encourages you to imagine the impossible.

Do you have any daily rituals. First, I make tea, arrange some flowers from our local market or simply cut a few roses from the garden outside – that interaction with the garden is sacred. Every day is different. In my calligraphic discipline we are taught that control is everything. For me, the magic lies in precisely the opposite. Remaining curious and allowing wonder to strike: the best ideas flow.

Has the studio affected your creativity. Surrounded by light, my art has flourished and become more tendril-like and 'swooshy' in feel. There has been an expansion in my style and the formats I work on, which has more to do with letting go, intuition and release than with technical skill. When I sit in the studio with my back to the shelves, I feel my history is behind me. This enables me to look out to the present, feel inspired and encourages new ideas to emerge.

How does the space affect clients. Clients visibly relax and exhale when they arrive, realizing that there is another way to be productive outside of a formal office environment. This type of space is rare – it is an immersive experience that ignites and inspires, and ideas always feel as if they are swirling, waiting to be found. To be here is to trust in my intuitive process, to share strengths and to be open to ideas. If we don't push, there will always be a 'What if I fall?' mentality, but if we do push, then outcomes change to 'But what if I fly?'

Does your studio feel cocooning. In spring and summer, with the doors wide open, I feel nurtured by the vibrant view, sounds, scents and touch of nature. In autumn and winter, it is about the promise of warmth inside – radiators on, scented candles burning, hands wrapped around a warm cup. And all year I feel very grounded standing on simple terracotta floors, sat directly on top of the earth. *Sentire* is a beautiful verb in Italian, meaning 'to feel'. The same word is used for all the senses – and I think that is rather brilliant because it is about the subtleties of one thing and how everybody's interpretation of that is different. That's what the studio is – a sanctuary for me, but also a unique experience for so many others.

ALL IN THE DETAIL Betty's studio shelves burgeon with inspiration and creativity. A simple rose from the garden is used alongside more traditional ink pens to bring inky words to life.

SAPONE

MASSIN / LETTER AND IMAGE
Elisenda
SOLDI

Betty Soldi
Light tomorrow with today!

DRUON

EF5744 ANTIC PAINT AVORIO-ROSA 38
1X360F F45 SPAZZOLAT SCARLATTO 37½

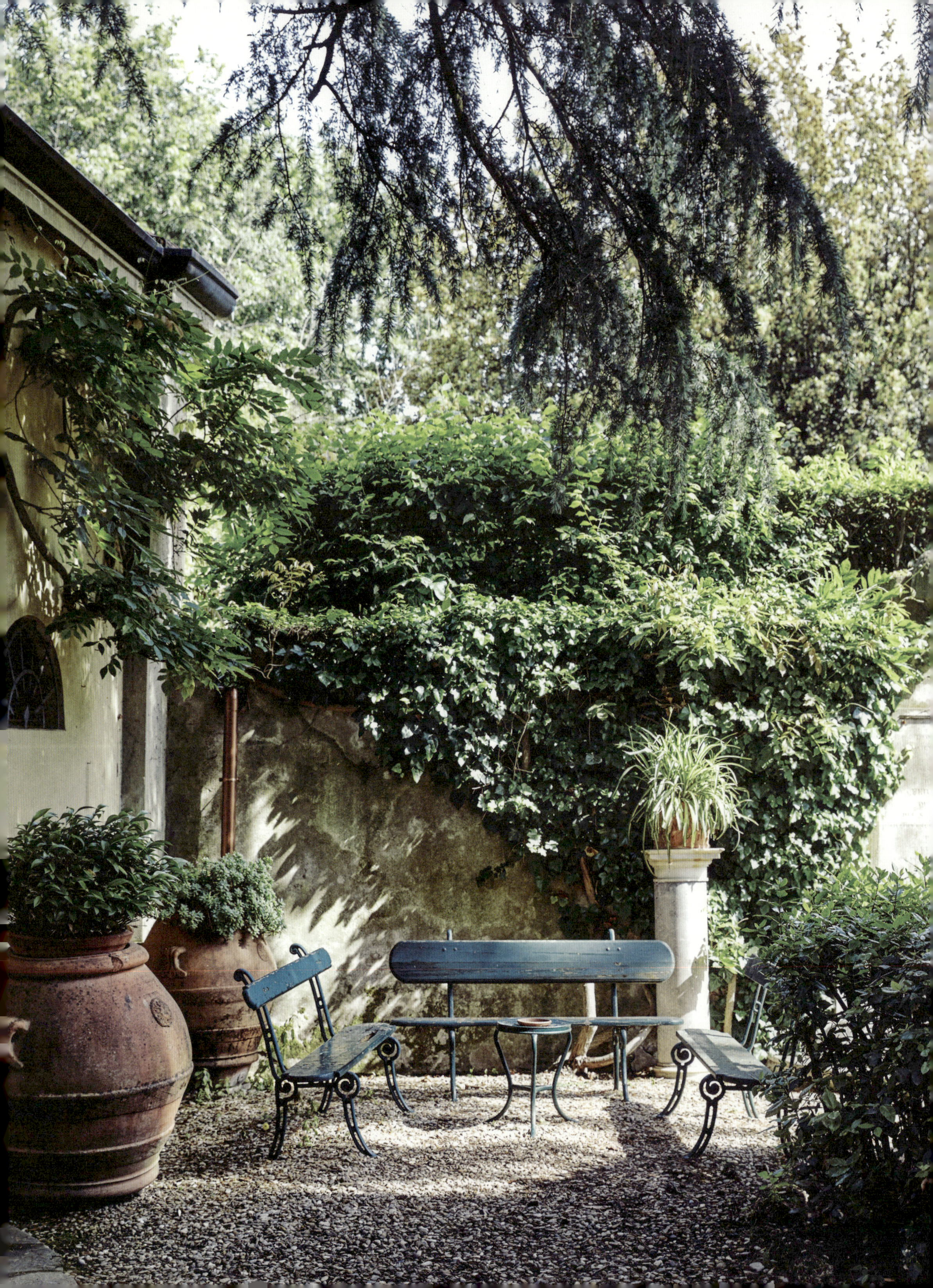

GARDEN VISTA The garden surrounding Betty's studio provides daily inspiration to both her and visiting clients. The glazed studio doors open along the length of the building and encourage an indoor/outdoor feel.

NOMADIC COCOONING

Technological advances mean that many of us no longer need to be anchored to one place and can now work efficiently from anywhere in the world. This has encouraged a new breed of 'nomads' to shake up secure, corporate lives in big cities, in favour of freedom, travel and experience. No longer buying into the concept of home ownership, car purchase and possessions, many people want to be free of debt and feeling weighed down by excessive monthly commitments. Choosing instead to use their money to fund joint work/travel dreams to many far-flung corners of the world.

This change celebrates putting 'self' and emotional needs first, and lets go of ego, 'ought-to-do' lists and a fear of venturing into the unknown. The opportunity to experience the world, not as a tourist but as a local for longer periods of time, encourages us to unite with new global communities, to cocoon ourselves in alternative cultural landscapes, and to explore our individual creativity with renewed freedom.

Australian entrepreneur Samantha Wills has touched my heart over many years since the launch of her book *Of Gold and Dust*, which charts the path of her compelling entrepreneurial journey from kitchen table startup to cult, multi-million-dollar jewellery business. Making the decision to close her business at the peak of its success in 2019, she has continued to evolve – as a writer, creative, mentor and business ambassador. Last year, she packed up her life in New York and embarked on a 12-month nomadic work/travel trip with her partner. I hope her wanderlust story inspires you as it has me.

To know where you belong, you must first be brave enough to risk the idea of adventure.

WANDERLUST

Samantha Wills / Writer & Creative

Your wanderlust triggers were… After living in New York for nine years, I spent the COVID-19 pandemic back home in Sydney. When our borders reopened, I eagerly returned to New York, expecting to pick up where I'd left off, but didn't anticipate how much we had both changed. I found myself writing in my apartment each day, increasingly aware of my exorbitant monthly rent. After spending eight glorious weeks travelling in Europe, I realized that my total spend was less than just my New York rent for the same period. I decided to spend my money seeing the world and enhancing joint work/life experiences – seeing new places, tasting different foods and learning new languages.

Leaving New York was… Easier than I anticipated! I loved my apartment and how I had decorated it, but was excited for the adventure ahead.

Items packed to remind you of home… I pick up a jar of Vegemite wherever I come across one! Other than that, I don't have sentimental things in my suitcase. I keep the sentiment for my emotional baggage!

Favourite places travelled to… I LOVED Mexico City. From the food to the creative scene, it was truly magical. I immersed myself there creatively – I took a pottery class and went to all the museums and galleries.

A cocooning home for you means… Having a space that supports my creative practice, as creativity is the essence of my being. This is more related to the space and setup than the aesthetic. A simple table and chair act as nomadic anchors for me and make any space feel cocooning. Mixing bowls or couch cushions often improvise as computer stands, but the space keeps me grounded and ensures I show up for my creativity and my core self every day, even when on the move.

Criteria for choosing Airbnb stays… Natural light and ideally a four-seater dining table are my must-haves for a creative setup. Everything else is a lovely-to-have!

How travel has changed your idea of home… It has shown me that home is an emotion – where your nervous system feels good.

What wins out: experiences or possessions… Experiences, without a doubt. Possessions feel like a burden when living out of a suitcase. This year has been a powerful detox and reset my shopping habits away from the quick dopamine hits of 'add to cart'.

Most magical moments on this trip… Visiting Taman Beji Griya Waterfall for a tranquil purification ceremony in the Ubud rainforest, in Bali, was a particularly beautiful, rewarding experience. We ventured through caves and waterfalls, offering traditional tributes to the Balinese gods. At the end of the ceremony, you stand under a massive waterfall and scream into it, releasing all your worries and fears for the gods to take away.

Your work is now all about… Storytelling. The vehicle for this used to be jewellery and now it is through more traditional mediums – book pages and screen.

What travel has taught you creatively… That creativity meets you wherever you are. It is inherently within all of us, and if we show up for it, it will find us, no matter where we are.

What your days look like… My days have a familiar structure: wake up, work out, grab a coffee, then work. However, travelling has shifted my mindset – I don't take locations for granted, knowing we're only there for a short time. It makes me appreciate every moment.

Highs and lows of working on the move… The highs are fantastic – it's like being on a permanent working vacation! The lows are few…but I have missed a familiar community. Friends have joined me in different parts of the world for a few treasured weeks at a time, but departures bring tough goodbyes.

Making this year work financially means… New York prices can jade you, so travelling has been cost-saving compared to living in New York! My work is very project-based – so having the freedom to manage my diary and location has always been paramount. When I started my first business at 21, I gave up the big backpacking trips, while all my friends were uploading their adventures to Myspace. I was consumed by building my jewellery business, hoping the sacrifice would be worth it. It's not lost on me. I have a lot to thank 21-year-old Samantha for being able to live this way now.

Life priorities that have shifted… Less stuff, more experiences. I used to see financial purchases, like designer bags, as rewards. Now, all the money spent on items that are just gathering dust (and probably mould) in a storage unit seems so disconnected from what I value. The little moments along the way now feel like the real rewards, and thankfully they don't require any storage space!

Advice to aspiring nomads… If you have the funds saved or can work on the go, just make the jump and give it a try. It's such an energetic reset for the soul.

What's next… I am writing my third book at the moment and hopefully working on some film projects soon. Bali is home at the time of doing this interview, but I have no idea where we will be in three months' time, and, for now, not knowing is a really lovely feeling.

feeling/

SPACES & CONNECTIONS
Home is not a place, it is a feeling.

Home is where all life begins and sets forth, and if we are lucky, it is a place that warms the heart and brings us comfort and the chance to daydream. Our spaces are precious and the connection we feel, which others experience when they visit, is powerful. They provide a glimpse into our soul, our creative passions, and how we choose to live. They connect us to past history, our memories, and to a future that we hope is a bright one for the next generation. I think if you choose for your home to be one filled with joy and curiosity, those emotions become rooted in how your own family run with life.

Later in the book, when I describe the homes of the featured creatives, I imagine that at some point a description will encourage you to recollect a personal place you have lived in, or perhaps an intimate memory of your own – far removed from what I write on these pages. Those feelings and recollections of home are your story and no matter how many lives have shared the same walls, those emotions are yours alone. Soulful, timeless and non-erasable.

'You pile up associations the way you pile up bricks. Memory itself is a form of architecture.'

LOUISE BOURGEOIS

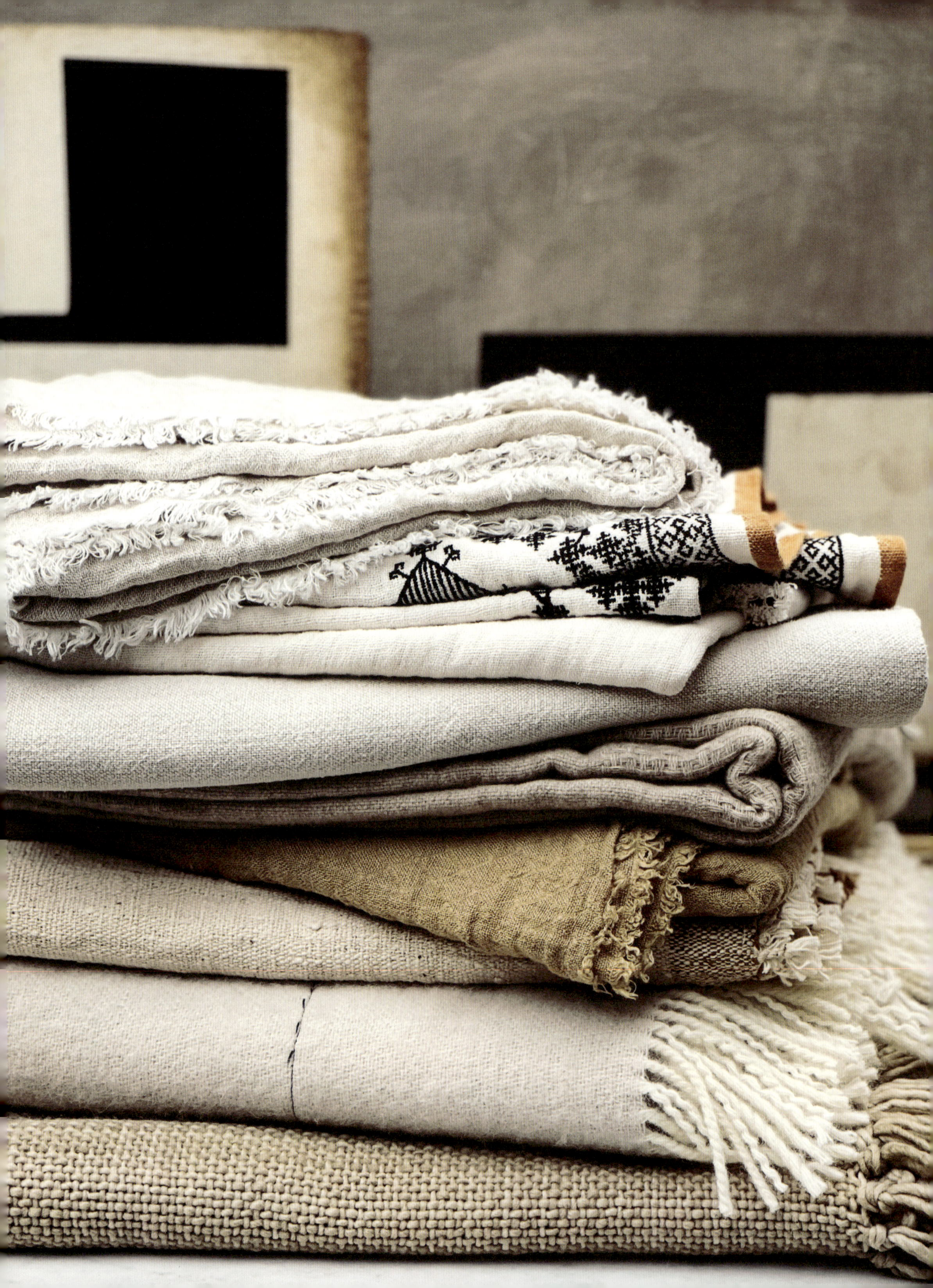

MATERIALS & SANCTUARY
Create a home you never want to leave.

Choose regenerative and sustainable. Placing these design choices at the heart of your home encourages a greater feeling of sanctuary and the chance to nurture a positive legacy.

Health and well-being. Only choose materials that you want to stroke, hold, smell and use. Non-toxic supports. Synthetic is never good. Always ask questions about the origin and journey of materials.

Touch is essential for us to feel nourished, calm and loved. When surfaces, walls, furniture and textiles feel good, so do we. They stimulate nerve endings and heighten comfort.

Go barefoot before you buy. Understand how materials, such as wood, concrete, stone, marble, terracotta, natural sisal, coir, rush or wool, affect your senses and enjoyment of home.

Bathrooms should feel reviving, not clinical. Sensual, luxurious finishes create a feeling of escape.

Curves soothe. Known as the 'preferred curvature effect', extensive psychological studies show how curved shapes stimulate areas in the brain that trigger relaxation and calm.

Handmade and handcrafted warm the soul. Never underestimate the power of objects made by hand.

Textile weight and weave add intimacy. Layer wool, cotton, sheepskin, cashmere, mohair – the more natural the layers, the more cocooning the feel.

Keep spaces intimate. Plump sofas to hunker down on, comfortable chairs to take in the view and inviting beds to cozy up in.

Earth matters. Textiles are enjoying a resurgence. Specialist craft knowledge is being celebrated once more. Skills that were almost lost are now becoming part of the sustainable solution.

Learning from nature. As raw materials become more endangered, the value placed upon new technology pioneers and new material frontiers will continue to grow.

Close your eyes. Tune into what appeals. This is not just about the visual, but what moves you emotionally, too.

From overconsumption to a reality check. To heal our greed culture, we must become content with less and calm our addiction for always wanting more.

Home should be the escape. When we feel supported by our choices, it helps us to relax and make more discerning life decisions. You are your home, so take care of yourself.

LAYER UP At home I have an obsession with textiles and I am always collecting handmade natural throws to layer on beds, chairs and sofas. The more layers you use, the more inviting the space.

NATURAL ALWAYS MAKE SENSE

Invest in beauty and your home will continue to get even better with age.

WOOL

Natural fibres – *to weave*
Cashmere blankets – *to wrap*
Cozy sheepskins – *to comfort*
Vintage blankets – *to restore*
Textured hangings – *to inspire*

LINEN

Bedsheets – *to relax*
Soft pillowcases – *to imagine*
Decorative tablecloths – *to celebrate*
Antique textiles – *to cherish*
Handstitched clothing – *to nurture*

WOOD

Heirloom furniture – *to love*
Outdoor huts – *to dream*
Handmade paper – *to reminisce*
Chopped firewood – *to warm*
Worn floorboards – *to feel*

STONE

Weathered tables – *to welcome*
Reclaimed sinks – *to refresh*
Old flagstones – *to ground*
Antique plates – *to share*
Carved statues – *to remember*

PLASTER

Patinated surfaces – *to soothe*
Curved walls – *to envelope*
Light fittings – *to glow*
Raw materials – *to stimulate*
Bespoke moulds – *to create*

MARBLE

Island countertops – *to prep*
Candleholders – *to entertain*
Repurposed slabs – *to serve*
Carved plinths – *to display*
Traditional bathtubs – *to unwind*

BRASS

Artisan tapware – *to appreciate*
Oversized showerheads – *to revitalize*
Light switches – *to elevate*
Handcrafted cutlery – *to connect*
Bespoke finishes – *to soften*

SLOWCRAFT MEETS HIGH TECH

Hemp houses – *to survive*
Re-invented materials – *to sustain*
Bamboo packaging – *to reduce*
Natural bioplastics – *to reimagine*
Knitted bridges – *to re-engineer*

TEXTURAL HEAVEN Top row: Stone sink, home of Louisa Grey; my linen press; daily sage rituals at home, smudge sticks brought back from the Menorca Experimental. Middle row: Textural layers in Anna Unwin's home, Ibiza; my master bedroom layered in textiles by Caravane, Mulberry Home and antique textiles from Atelier AH; artful display shelves, Satellite Island. Bottom row: Olive trees and terracotta pots lend a Mediterranean feel to our courtyard; natural materials at play in Tom Cox's guest cottage; scent rituals, Anna Unwin, Ibiza.

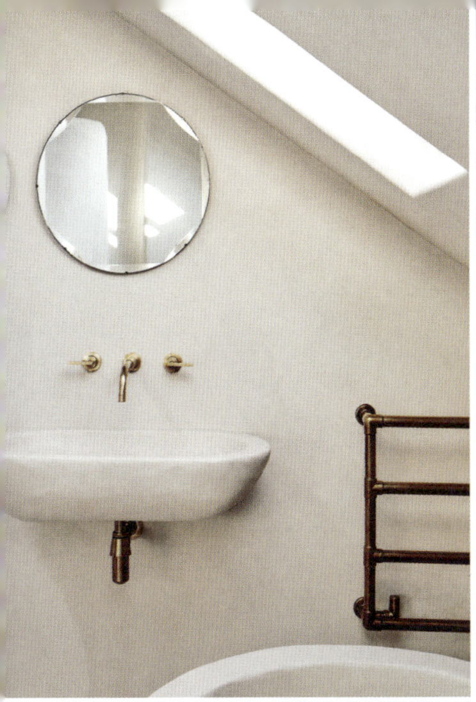
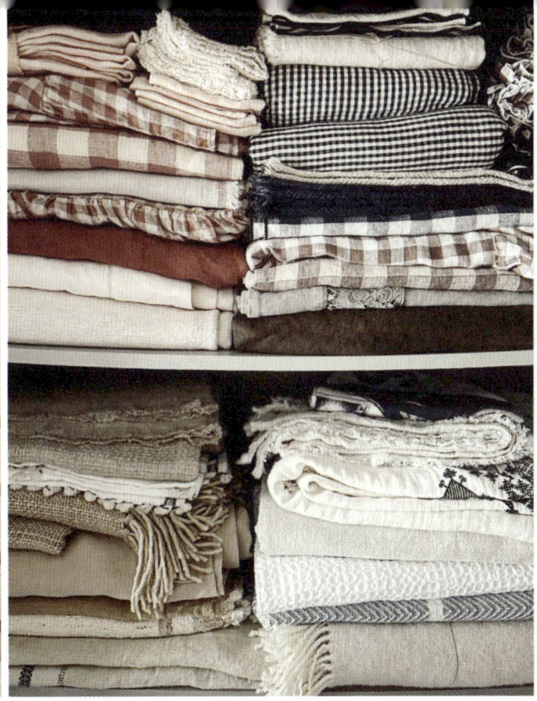
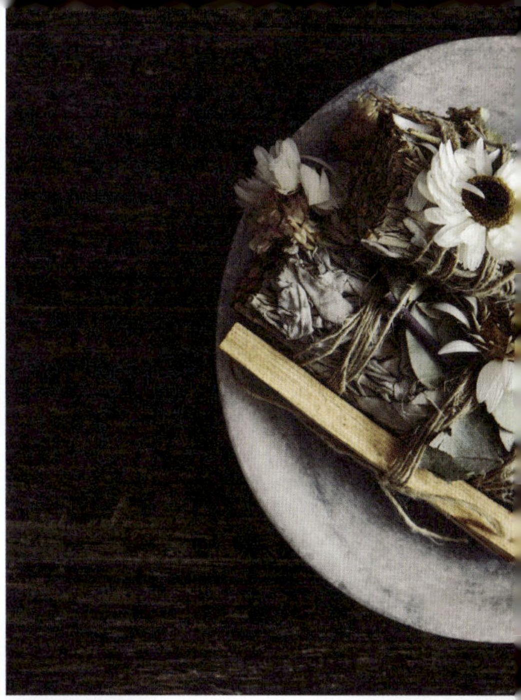
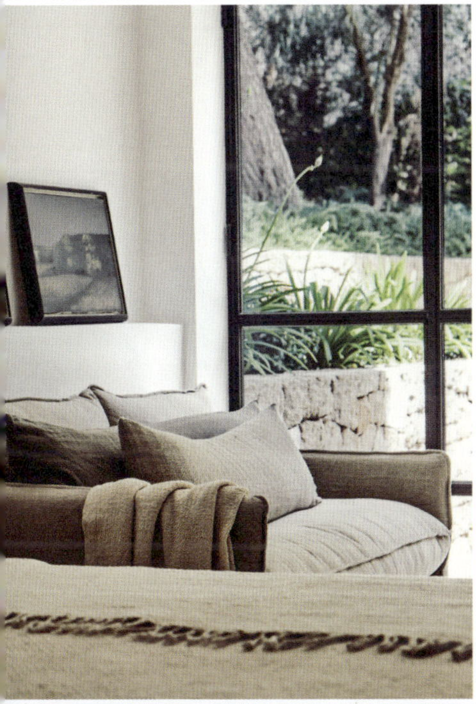
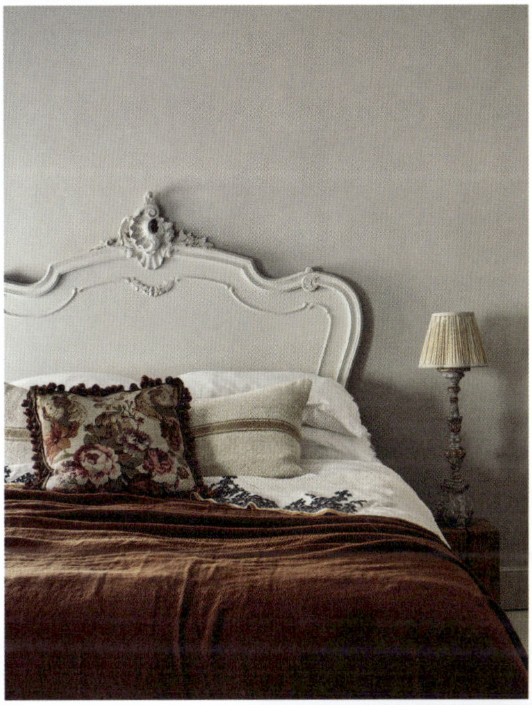
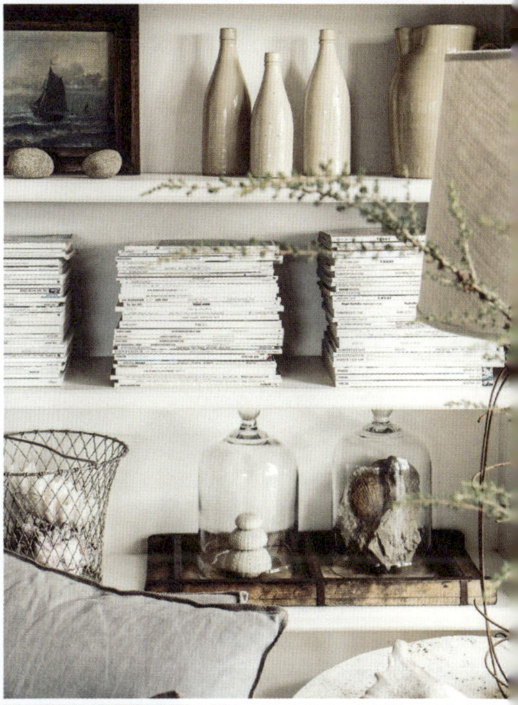
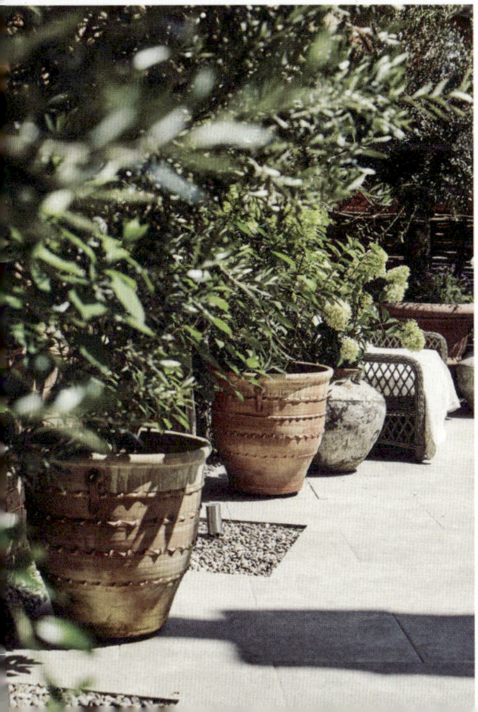
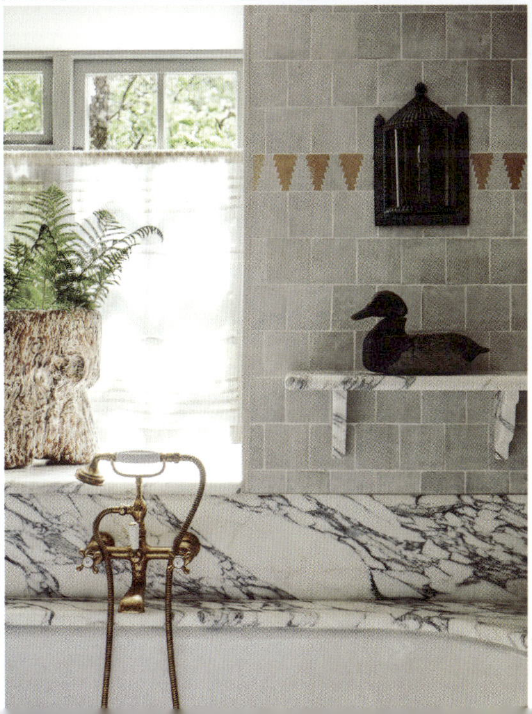
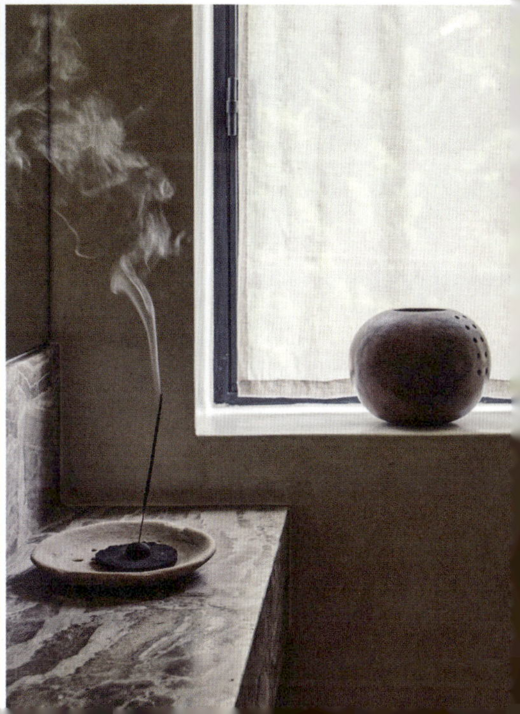

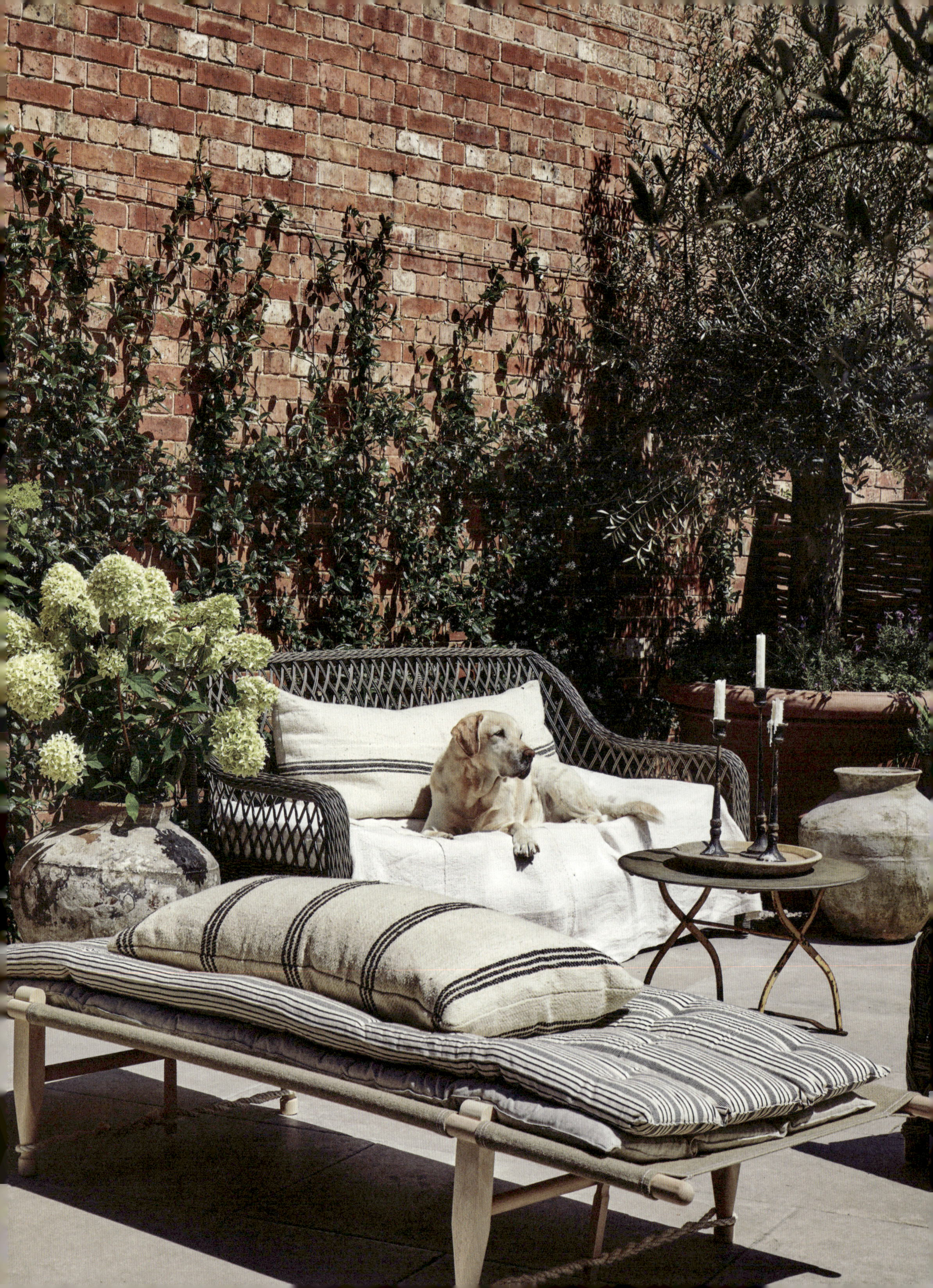

RITUALS & REFLECTION
Choose happiness at home and it will radiate within your family.

We seem to move from one major news story and disaster to the next, and so our need for calm to counter the chaos is ever more important. This is not about making light of world issues, but simply a survival technique that we all need to settle our thoughts and to refocus our minds. Making time for rituals and reflection is not a luxury; it is vital.

A simple act of occasion. Rituals don't have to be big, dramatic gestures. Just a gentle pause for reflection, a time to say thank you, and to pass forward thoughts of kindness and hope.

Anticipation of the day ahead. The hours before anyone else awakes feel like a gift. There is great value to be found in appreciating the slow moments when everyone feels compelled to go so fast.

Turn your face to the sun. Allowing the sunshine to touch your skin first thing in the morning for at least ten minutes balances your circadian rhythm. Walk the dog or potter in the garden with your skin exposed for a much-needed burst of vitamin D.

Nature nurtures. Appealing to all our senses through sound, light, shape, temperature and texture. Whether sweeping the garden, walking barefoot in the sand or lying under the stars, each interaction is a form of meditation, encouraging you to slow down and to tune into something higher.

Countering our 'smart' choices. As a society we believe we have evolved 'smartly' on this planet, but watching the sun rise and set acts as a reminder that our 'smart' choices have come at a real cost – and we must all help preserve the future.

Immersive soundscapes soothe. Whether in nature, or through music, sound baths and silence.

Wired for art. Research shows that just one or more experience of art a month can extend your life by ten years. Productivity at the expense of creativity does not make us happier.

Power of scent. The aroma of familiar fragrances is calming and comforting. Whether by burning candles, cleansing the house with sage or setting a fire, the effect is cocooning.

Unwind and detox. Mix essential oils and magnesium salts into your bath water to help you relax. Dim the lights, play some tunes, let your mind wander.

Hang out, hug, lay on the grass, cuddle on the sofa. Don't feel guilty for chilling on your own, or with your children, loved ones and animals. Every kiss, embrace and minute you spend together transmits visceral feelings of safety, love and comfort.

Go with the flow. Our energy is guided by the flow of our daily focus and rituals.

Listen to your intuition. It can be powerful if we allow it to be. The most important factor is to believe in it.

ENERGY GIVERS ✧ *Sun on the skin, sea air, thunderstorms, swimming in the rain, intimacy, family hugs, dog cuddles, goodnight kisses, laughing with friends, smiles from strangers, first snowfall, rest, sleep, music, creative thinking, new adventures, faded photos, art, film, theatre, books.*

LIGHT & SHADOWS
Turning the ordinary into the extraordinary.

Light gives us energy and lifts our spirits. It is one of the most important factors in making a home feel welcoming, but often one of the last things to be considered.

Seasonal changes. Observe how light changes the mood, contrast and warmth. In summer, light increases our serotonin levels and happiness; in winter, our circadian rhythms slow down, as the light decreases, which can impact our mood and how we feel.

Optimize natural light. Leave windows free of heavy window treatments and position curtain drops on the outer edges of windows. Simple linen voiles and half-height café curtains will create a softly diffused atmosphere.

Use light to your advantage. Follow the path of the sun throughout your home and utilize spaces accordingly as part of your daily routine.

When task lighting is needed, avoid brightly lit. Use dimmer switches to control the light intensity, so spaces remain cozy.

Candlelight adds magic. It flatters rooms, people and objects, and creates a relaxing, romantic mood.

Light show. If you are lucky to live with a view, the ever-changing joy of sunrises and sunsets can transform our outlook on the world. Open your home to that stage and let the light in.

Darkness enhances light and vice versa. Opposites attract and in turn stimulate our minds to think more intimately and creatively.

NATURAL HIGLHIGHTS The movement of light enhances the look and feel of beautiful objects. In the home of Anna Unwin (see page 76), a simple pestle and mortar becomes a sculptural piece of art, caught beautifully in the shadows.

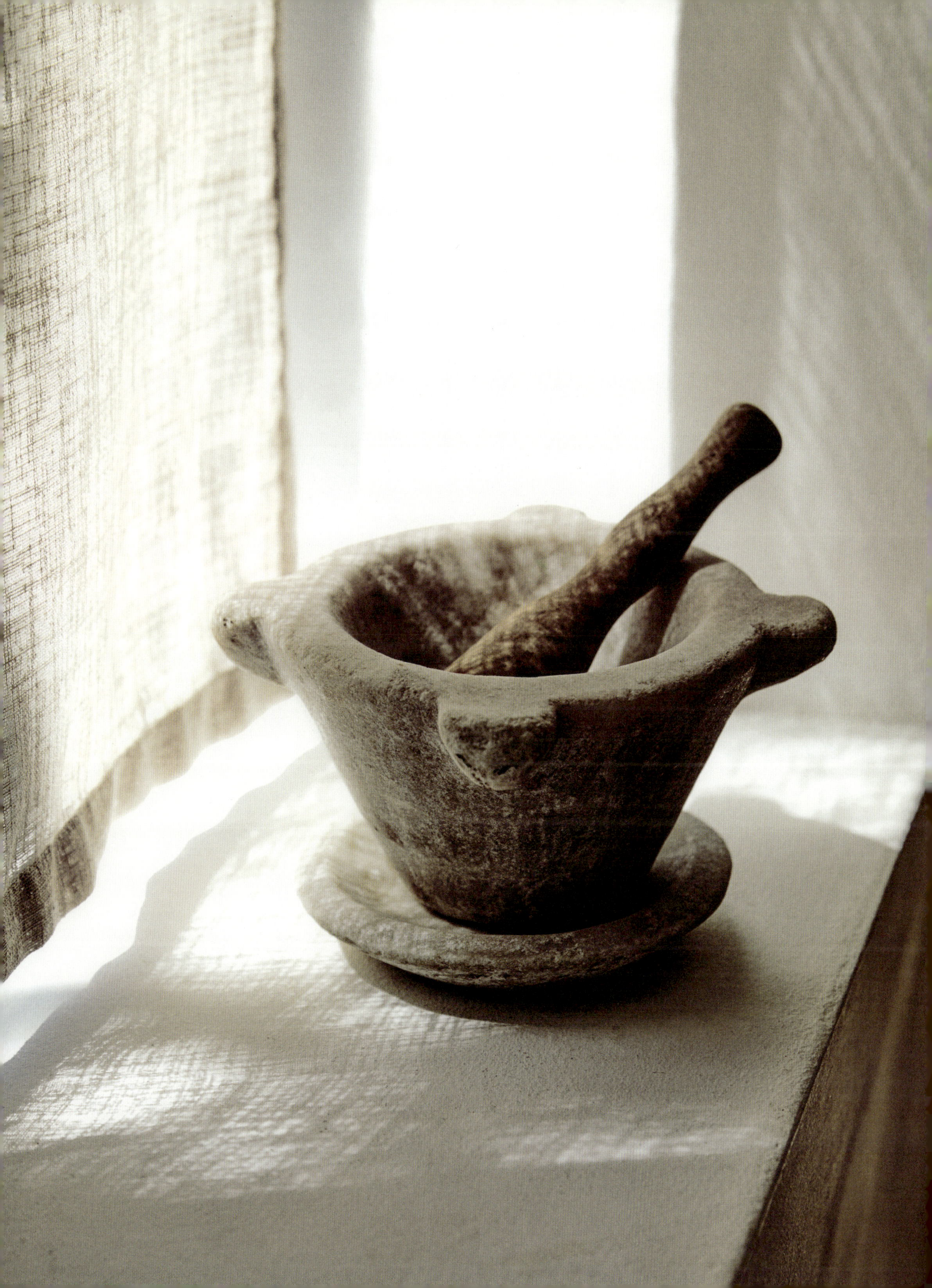

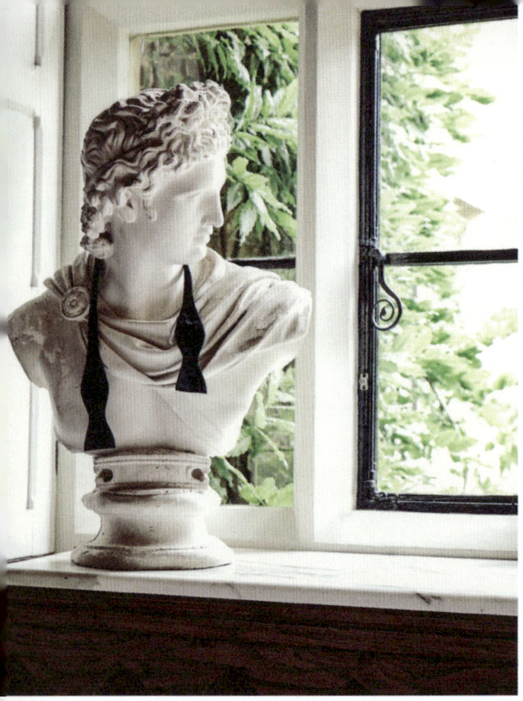
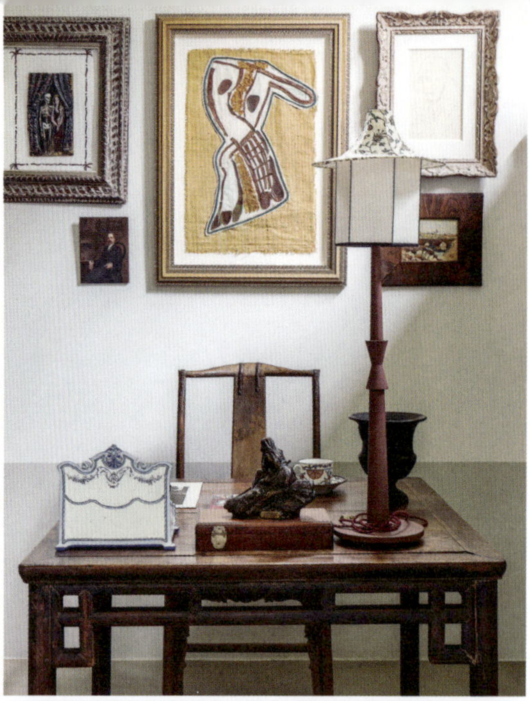
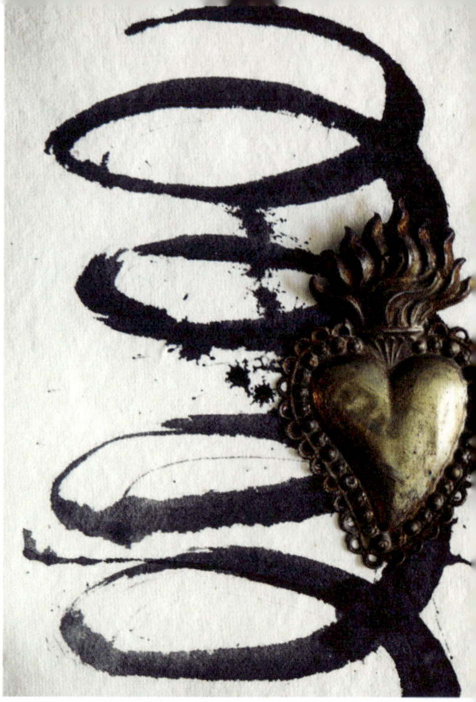
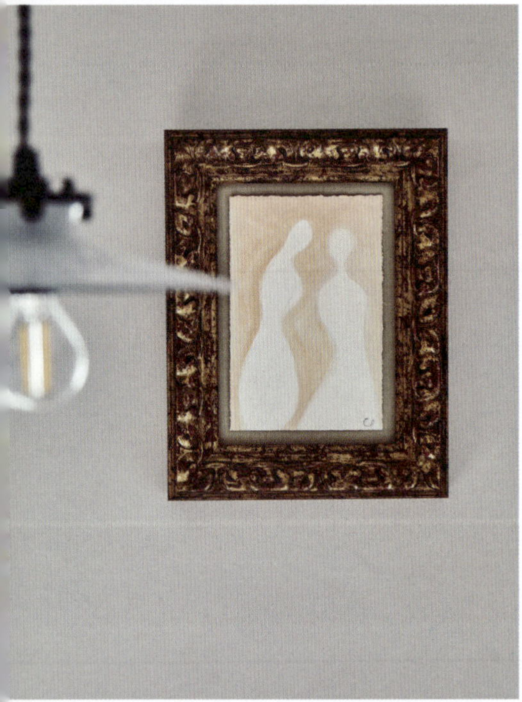
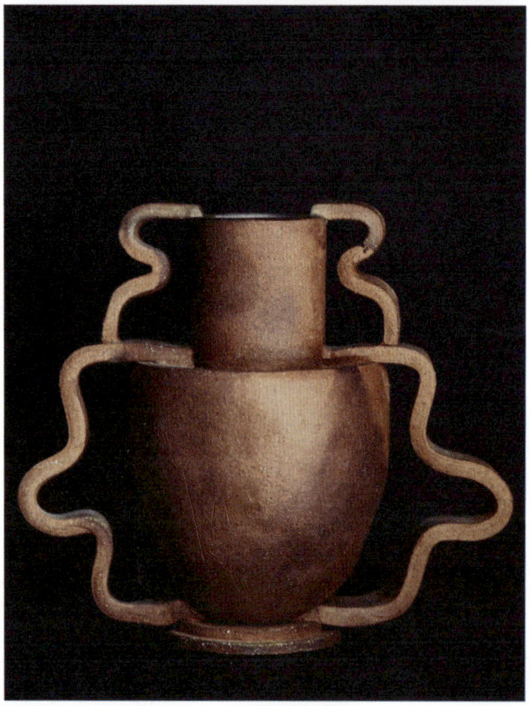
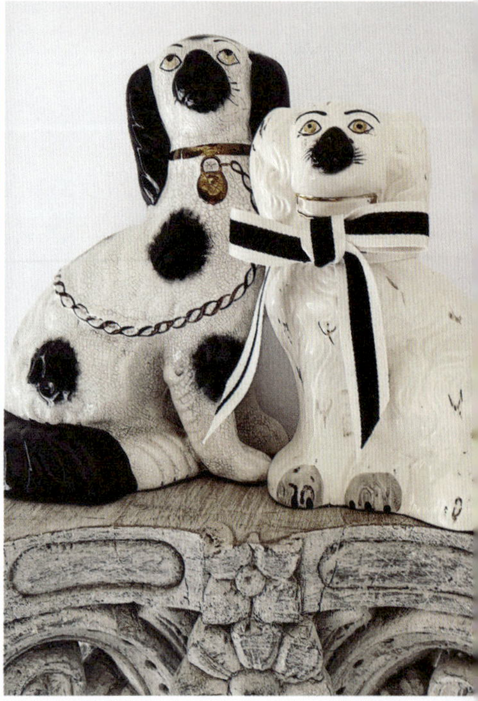
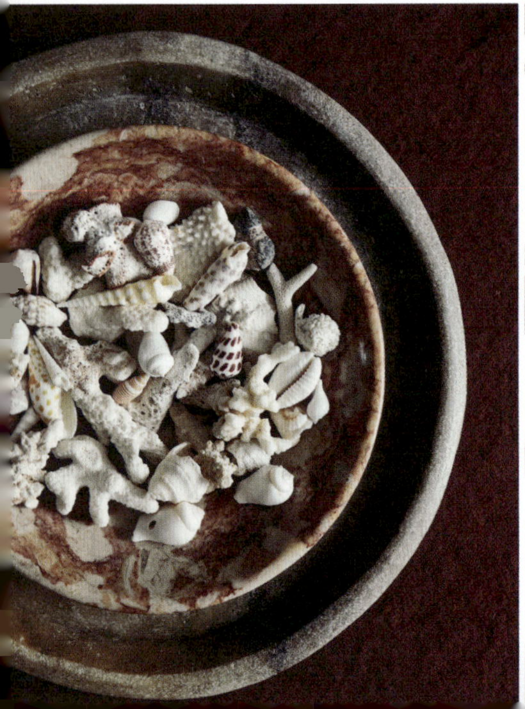
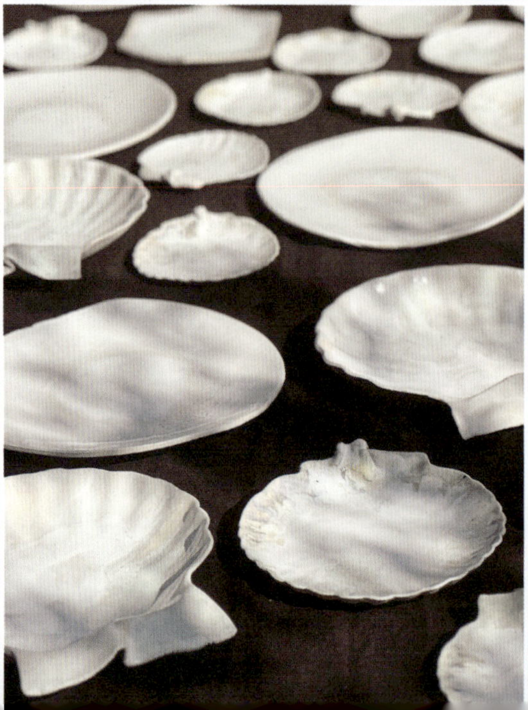
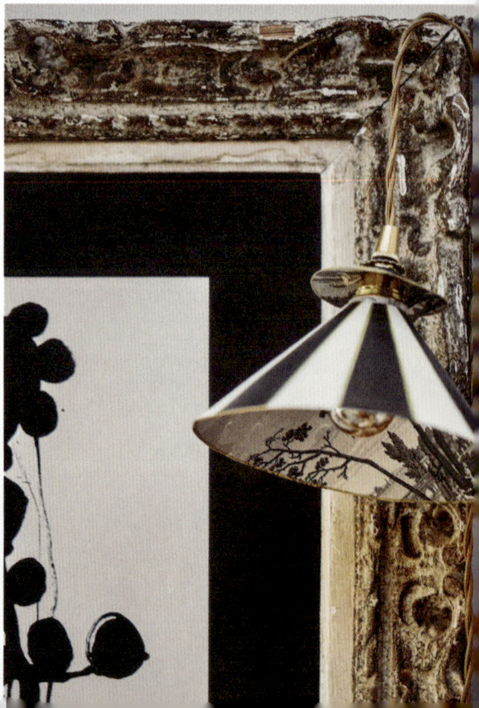

OBJECTS & STORIES
Create beauty around you to revitalize your soul.

Every object we choose for our homes comes with its own story. Celebrating what it is you love about each piece is powerful and provides a unique insight into why we gravitate towards collecting certain things. Beauty is never absolute, and the cryptic reasons why we all find something attractive are a combination of many elements that touch our senses.

Collecting is not a science. Feather your nest only with the things that speak to your heart. It's about humanity, not vanity.

Immense happiness can come from the smallest of objects. When something resonates, the feelings it conjures can be intense. Value is not monetary.

Collections evolve. There are no time limits and no piece must be perfect.

Simplicity encourages versatility. A humble wooden footstool can provide a coffee table, display surface or occasional seat.

Add your own backstory to objects. It's a way for those we share our homes with to make sense or fun of the things we find captivating. Stay true to you – what's frivolous to one person is gold to another.

Spontaneity of thought. Change things up, move objects around, and allow fresh inspiration to strike.

Tip the balance. Mix old, new and handmade. The combination makes your home feel welcoming.

Books offer escape. Read the magic and get lost in the imagery. Reading is a powerful way to switch off, recalibrate and imagine. Transform your cocoon into a much larger universe – even if only in your head.

A FEW OF MY FAVOURITE THINGS Top row: Antique bust, home of Tracey Appel; personal collections, home of Marianne Evennou; antique ex-voto and artwork, Atelier AH. Middle and bottom row, collections at home: Artwork by Caroline Popham; terracotta vase, TROVE by Studio Duggan; antique ceramic dogs, Atelier AH; seashells, collected on holiday; plates, Elvis Robertson; artwork by Malene Birger in an antique frame and light from Aroundfiveoclock.

ENTERTAINING & BONDING
Breaking bread together keeps us connected.

Just as making a home is the result of lots of ingredients, so too is the preparation and enjoyment of a meal often a vital part of what makes a house a home. My husband is the creative when it comes to cooking and his passion for food consciously shapes the flow of our day and the way we interact as a family. He would never consider himself a creative, but the way he makes food is an artful act of love.

With the rise of cocooning, socializing at home has taken on a new dimension for every age group, and our kitchens, dining rooms and gardens are becoming embedded at the core of our homes once again. Intimate and private, in place of overcrowded and public.

Old-school rituals are as popular with the young as older generations, and they are now just as likely to spend time creating a beautiful tablescape. The wonder of craftmanship and well-made, quality design is being increasingly recognized, from talented independent artisans, to high-street stores and designer websites – with brands such as Zara Home reinstating the value of the handmade, and independent companies like ABASK shining a light on exceptional craftmanship and design.

Meals are when conversations are shared, important decisions made, meaningful relationships cemented and problems solved, and where time together becomes sacred. At home, a delicious Sunday roast is the most looked-forward-to occasion of the week, and as important as any aesthetic detail in our home. A ritual that encourages us to sit together: as a couple, a family or with a table full of friends.

Entertaining is about making memories – whether it's a crazy party or simply a chance to spend time together, with no pomp or ceremony. Conversations enjoyed, supper when it happens, and nothing overthought. Precious moments that become permanently etched on your home and in your heart.

TABLE MUST-HAVES ✧ *Oversized linen tablecloths and generous napkins, sparkling glassware or handmade ceramic beakers, beautiful cutlery and handcrafted plates. And for parties, preferably my favourite Saint-Germain cocktail (see opposite) to get things started. Cocktail recipe discovered at Il Palazzo Experimental in Venice.*

Saint-Germain

40ml (2½ tablespoons) Hendrick's Gin
15ml (3 teaspoons) Saint-Germain Liqueur
15ml (3 teaspoons) elderflower cordial
25ml (5 teaspoons) lime juice
3 slices of cucumber
1 egg white

First, shake without ice, then again with ice. Double strain before serving. Finish with a lime twist.

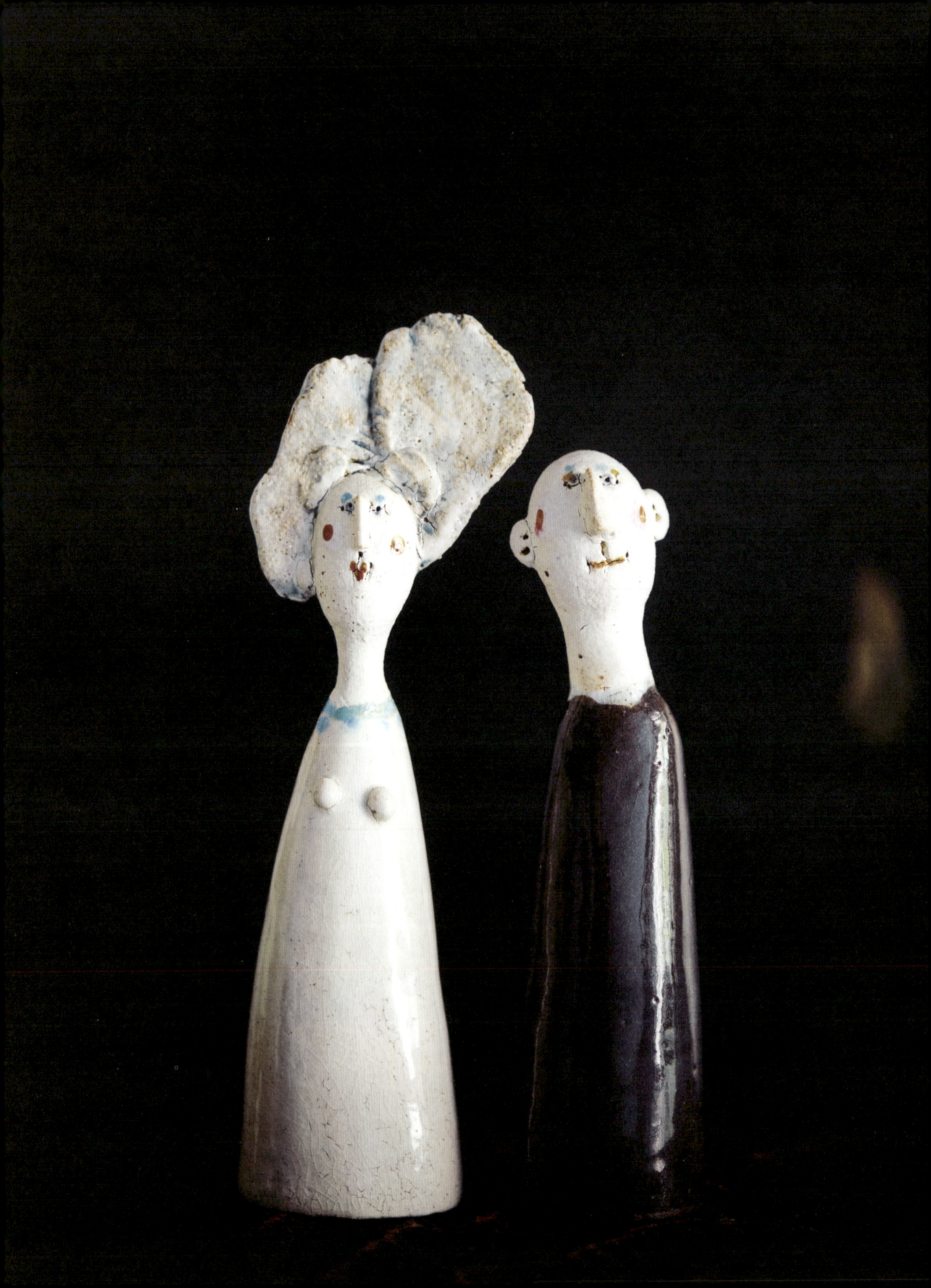

LOVE & TOGETHERNESS

Be the reason someone still believes in magic.

Love is an emotion that we hope to give and receive – in a romantic relationship, with our family and friends, and most importantly to ourselves. With love we thrive, but it needs to be worked at, talked about, looked after and celebrated. If we create the right environment at home for it to breathe, we all flourish.

Cocooning celebrates the idea of togetherness and time-out. Work hard, yes, but play hard too. Connect, then disconnect. We need to give more weight to the power of authentic relationships, in-person conversations and time to just 'be'. Reposition the pursuit of doing nothing in our minds from something perceived as lazy to a necessity that gives our bodies and thoughts some time to recharge.

As a society we are faster, more advanced and more technologically agile than ever before, yet emotionally teetering on the brink, with more single-person households, increased solitude and greater levels of anxiety. Younger generations are losing the ability to flirt effortlessly, and to know how to give and receive compliments. The swipe-left culture has become the norm and the magic of old-fashioned courtship is diminishing. Will AI robots become the more dominant love and friendship forces of the future? Or will society embrace the need for greater human connection once again? The choice is in our hands.

As families and within extended communities, I feel we must teach those social skills to the next generation or risk the possibility of dehumanization and burnout. It's a balance, but home is the place that can help uphold those values. Sunday was historically a day of rest for a reason. Learning from our elders and each other is a way to enrich our wisdom and improve our knowledge. Understanding the importance of meaningful relationships will enhance respect.

Yet at the same time, traditional household norms are changing. Despite our worries, not all single-person households are lonely and not everyone who lives in solitude is isolated.

Many individuals are actively choosing the freedom not to marry or have children, or to have them without a partner. And not everyone feels the need to embrace the idea of a permanent home. Whatever our life choices, we should respect each other in those decisions.

It is never a given that home is a happy place, but always remind yourself that your start in life does not have to define your outcome. A nurturing home is something we all deserve, and we can all create. It is about letting go of the past, loving yourself and finding the space – no matter how small – that allows you to feel safe and nurtured. Sadly, feelings of love and togetherness don't always come from your immediate family, but they can be emotions fostered within a wider circle of friends.

Change is advancing quickly, and the need to balance progress and connectivity is essential. By focusing more on our human needs, we give our souls the chance to catch up with our hurried lives. Or, more importantly, we encourage our busy lives to slow down and reconnect with our souls.

OBJECTS OF MY AFFECTION At home, my favourite 'Little Lady' and 'Little Man' ceramics by Jane Muir add decorative charm. Surround yourself with the things you love and your spaces will always feel warm and welcoming.

Architecture is not just to be enjoyed by the eye, but should be something that stimulates all of our senses and our imagination.

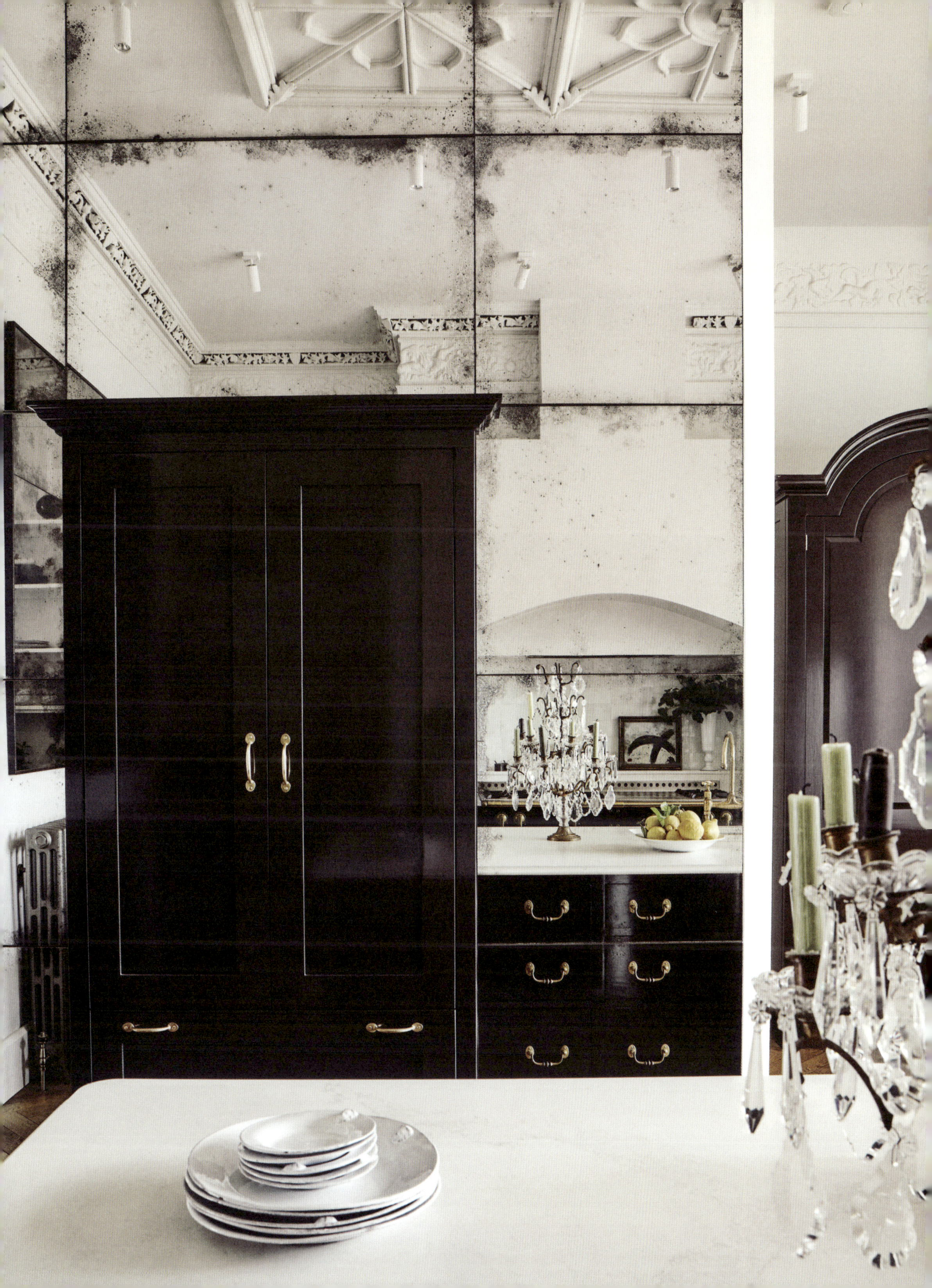

living/

WATERSIDE EDGE
Kate & Will Alstergren / Aquaculture

SITUATED IN SOUTHERN TASMANIA, IN THE D'ENTRECASTEAUX CHANNEL, Satellite Island is one of the last stops before Antarctica – an island, off an island, off an island. Accessible only by helicopter or private boat from nearby Bruny, it is a cocooning getaway that is the epitome of seclusion.

Owned by the Alstergren family, Kate and Will spend their time between here and Melbourne, enjoying the island with friends and their three grown-up boys, while also creating private getaways for small groups of up to eight guests. 'We inherited the island from Will's Norwegian Uncle Ian, who bought it in the 1960s. The cliffs reminded him of his childhood roots and the island became the one great love of his life,' says Kate. 'He lived a solitary life here, built a simple home, kept sheep, started a salmon farm and fostered his passion for painting and writing.'

As you approach, dramatic sheer sea cliffs, ancient blue gum trees and indigenous bush drop away to unspoilt pebble beaches and hidden coves. In summer, you can enjoy panoramic sea views, looking out over quiet, blue-green waters and the occasional sailing boat, while in winter the horizon extends to the snowcapped Hartz Mountains on the opposite side of the wide strait.

Kate has breathed new life back into the 34-hectare (84-acre) island – with the help of Australian stylist Tess Newman-Morris – artfully transforming the original home into a three-bedroom, wood-clad summerhouse and a former salmon shack into a two-bedroom boathouse. Sited directly at the water's edge, you can fall asleep with the side doors wide open, looking out to star-filled skies and the sound of the gently lapping sea. From the top of the island at Last Glimpse Point, rustic bell tents provide an unrivalled spot to watch the sun set and, on occasions, the dancing Southern Lights.

Inspired by their family's Norwegian roots and love of simple Scandinavian aesthetics, the interiors are understated and informal, with whitewashed walls against a muted palette of blue, grey and stone. Relaxed furniture, precious family antiques and organic materials encourage you to linger and unwind – think soft linens, relaxed cottons and sun-bleached woods, layered with sculptural foliage, calming beeswax candles and many natural treasures collected from around the island. A precious armoire is home to heirloom Nordic crystal, modern glassware, ceramics and antique silver cutlery, encouraging a sense of occasion every day.

A PLACE LIKE NO OTHER The two-bedroom boathouse at the foot of the cliffs sits on its own rock shelf at the edge of the world. A place where time stands still.

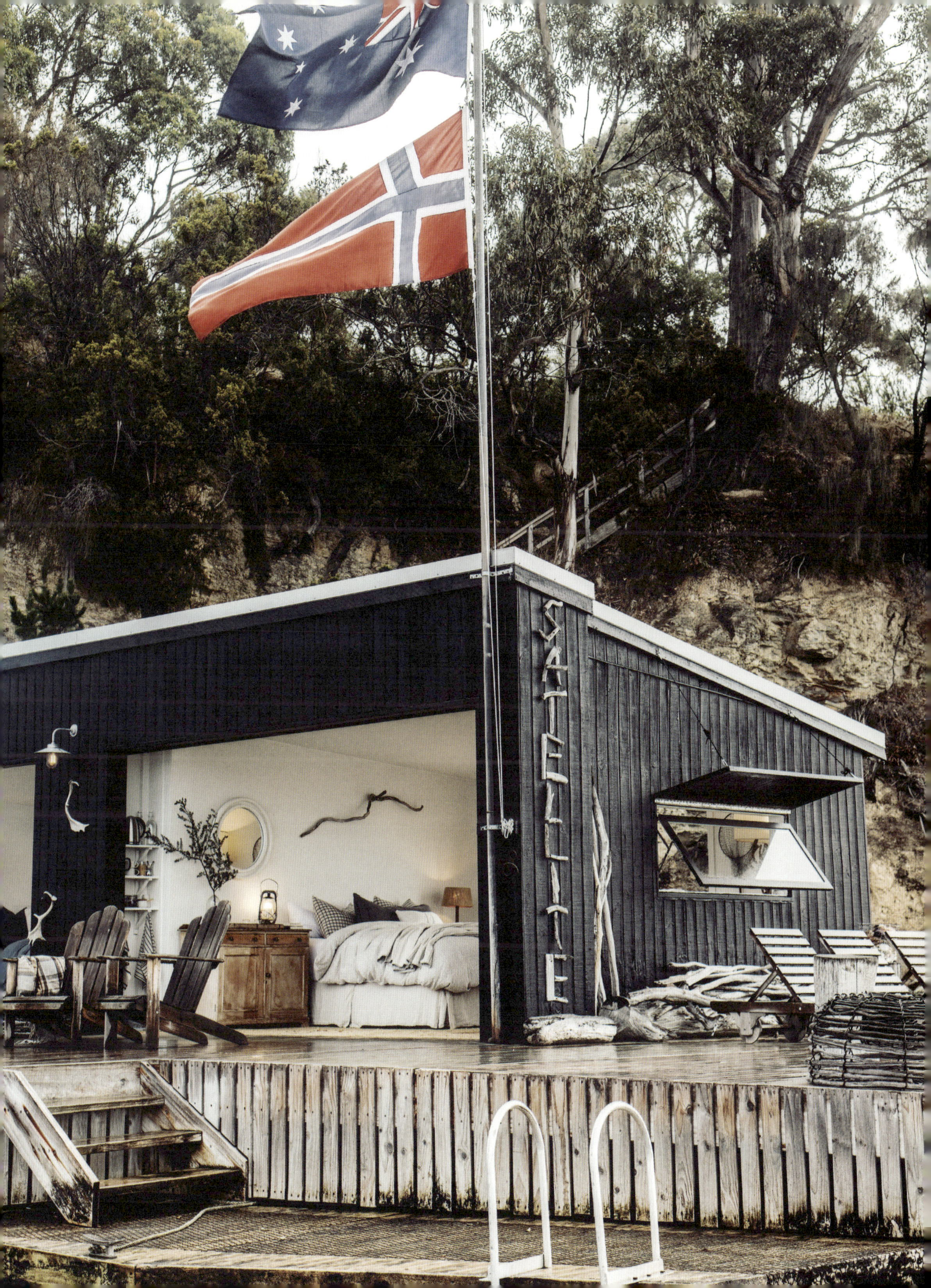
SATELLITE

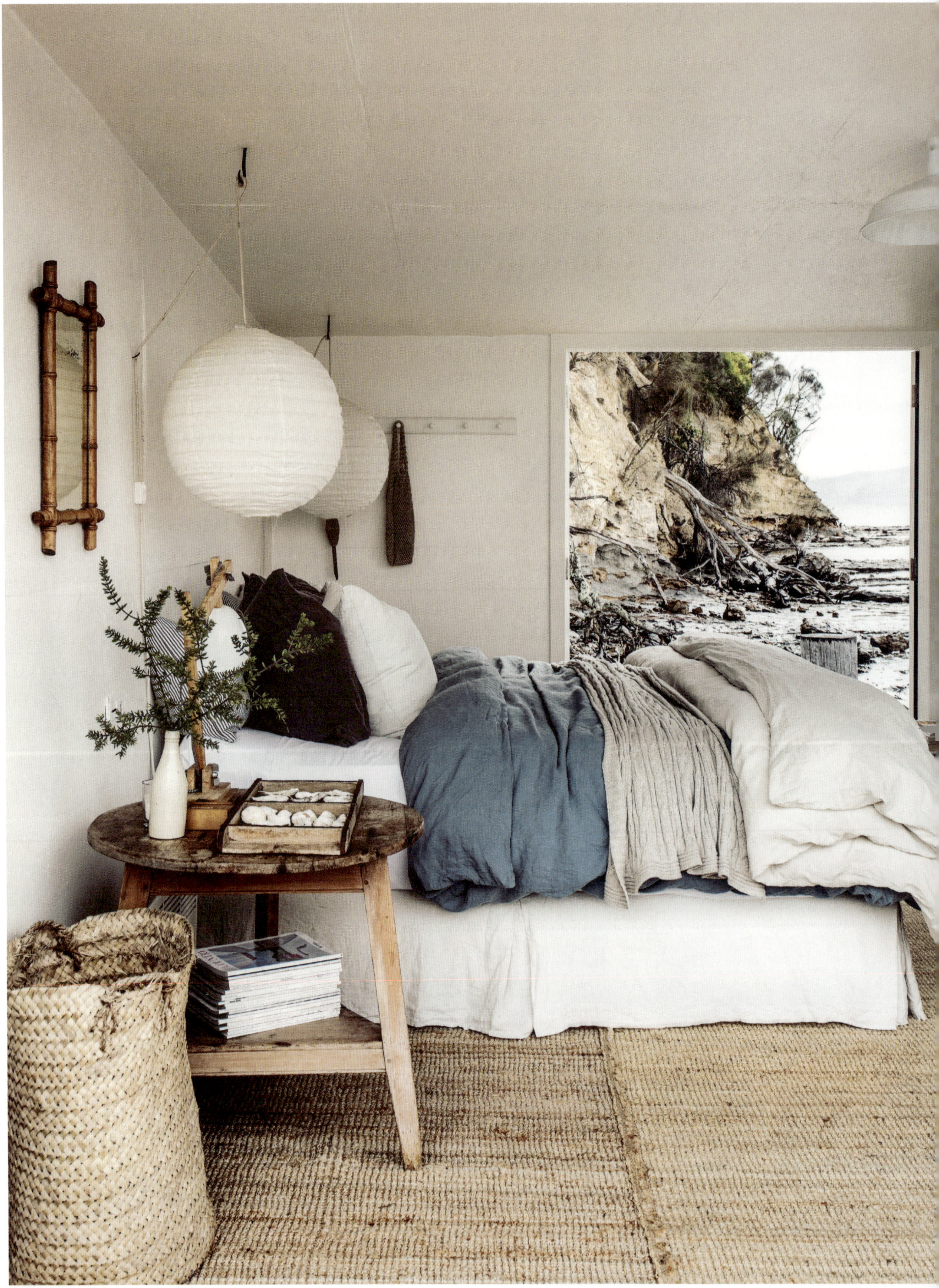

'For me, the idea of cocooning is allowing nature and our living spaces to merge as one,' says Kate. 'I wanted the interiors to feel like home and to make everyone who visits feel very relaxed. When you leave the mainland, you let go and become very present in the moment. Connected to each other within nature, but with the freedom to explore the island in your own unique way.'

More recently, Kate has continued to evolve the feeling of sanctuary, creating a new open-sided space for outdoor events and extended family gatherings. And with the help of gardener Fiona Brockhoff, she has further developed fruit orchards and vegetable gardens, and added a drought-tolerant garden with native plants around the house. With soft grasses, *Westringia* hedging, *Correa alba*, wonderful *Casuarina* trees, pink-flowered *Grevillea* plants and colourful *Banksia*, the new garden meanders down to a secluded outdoor bath area.

'New ideas always begin with family enjoyment in mind, to keep things natural and homely. The island is filled with memories of 21st birthdays, raucous Christmas stays and soon a wedding for our eldest son. We have poured a lot of love into this place – it feels like our fourth child, and Ian's spirit is very much alive here,' says Kate.

Days are spent by the water – beachcombing the ancient rock shelf, wild swimming and snorkelling, or enjoying *Pearl*, the family's old wooden boat (a gift from a friend), which hangs off the pontoon. 'The underwater world is magical and abundant. Dating back nearly 300 million years to the Permian period, it has a life force of its own. I love the wildness, free diving and pulling enormous abalone from the sea floor – finely sliced, they are delicious – and it's the same with the wild scallops and urchins. I have never forgotten the taste of my first ones here,' explains Kate.

Whether exploring the rugged landscape, reading by the water's edge, relaxing by an open fire or shucking wild oysters from the jetty, stays here are about slowing down. 'If you are lucky to experience the phosphorescence-rich waters at night, it feels like you are swimming among a thousand stars or in a sea of diamonds.

'Time stands still on the island, and we have learned so much immersed in its raw beauty. When people visit, they feel as though they have discovered a secret world – places like this are hard to find and for us there is nowhere more special.' ✧

WHAT DREAMS ARE MADE OF Early morning dips and morning meditations, then back to bed to watch the sun rise, with just the sound of the splashing waves as your playlist.

THE LITTLE THINGS Enjoy slow days exploring in the boat, catching supper, shucking oysters and relishing long, lazy lunches before spending quiet evenings by the firepit.

WATERSIDE EDGE 67

SUMMERHOUSE HAVEN
Calm interiors, comforting textures and everything you need to create wonderful memories from various cozy spots inside the house or on the outside deck (see page 70).

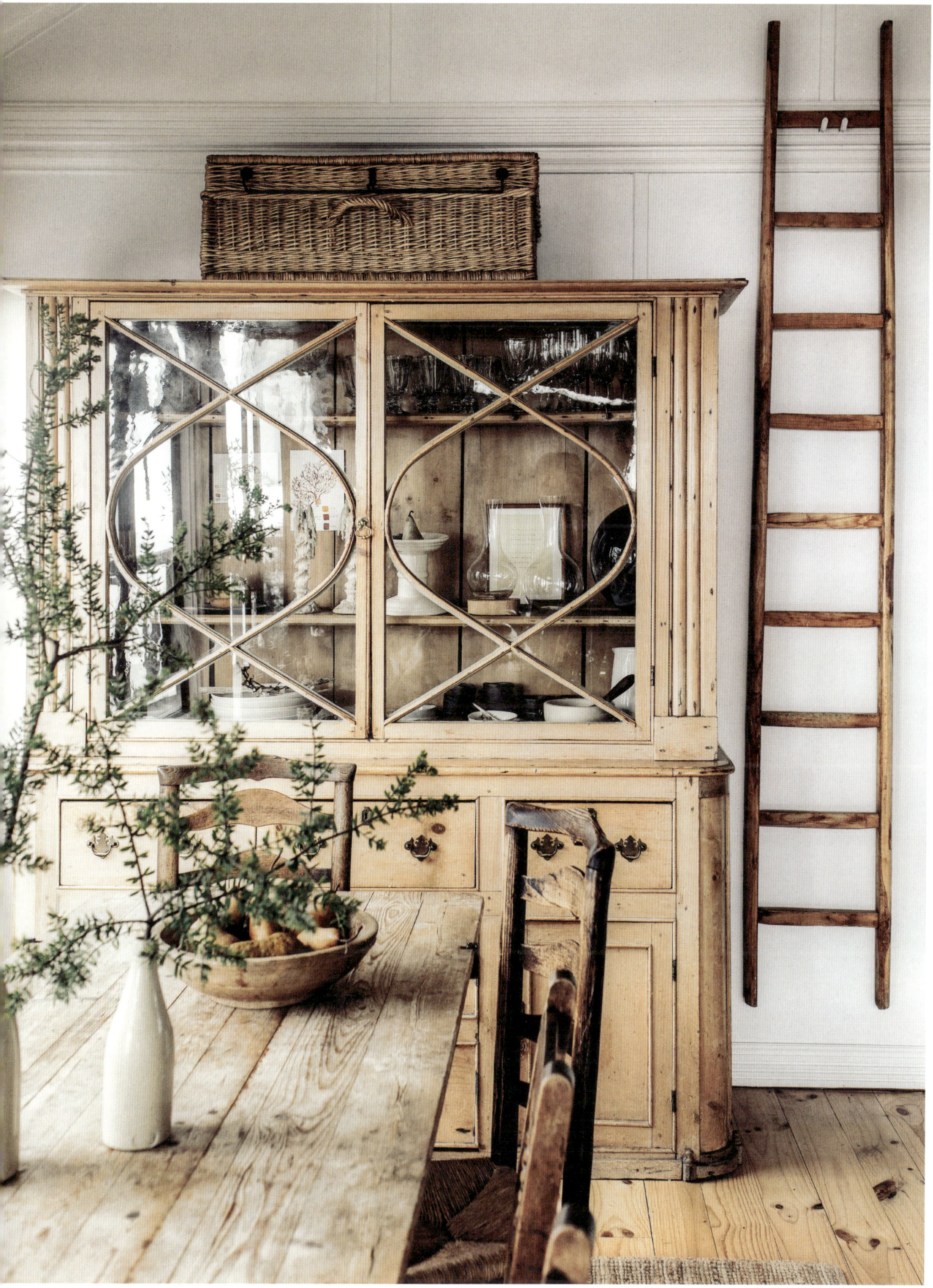

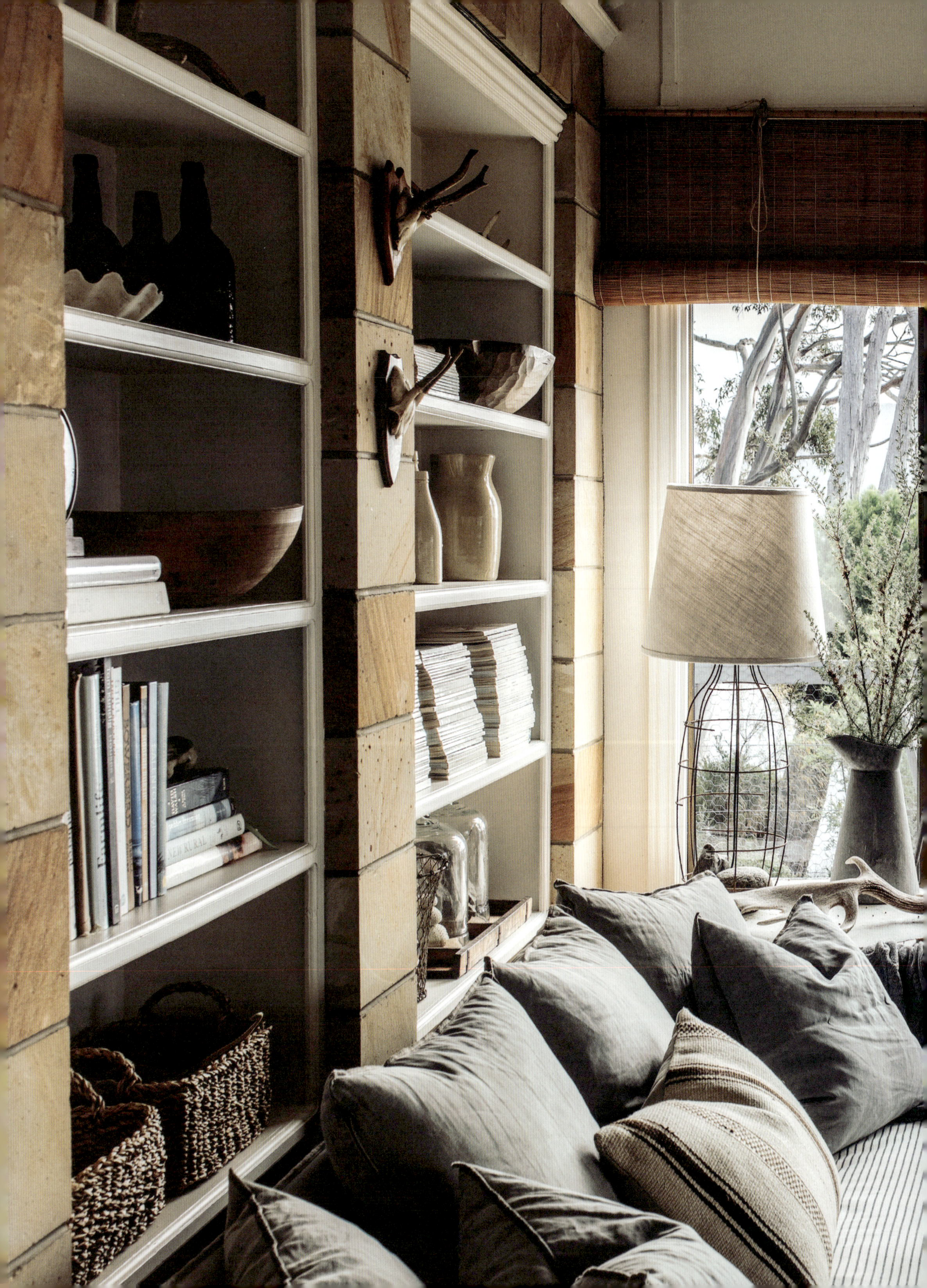

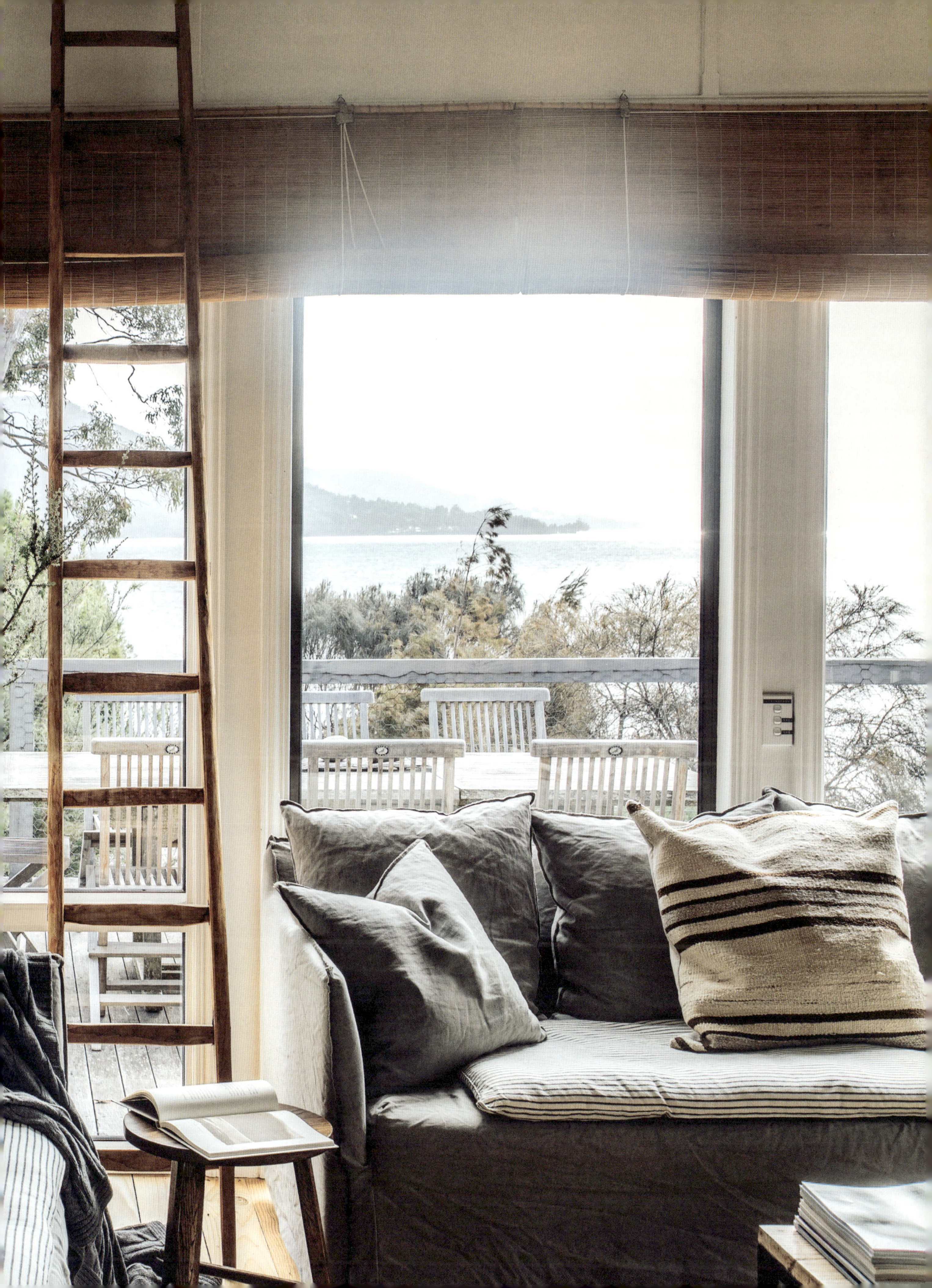

SOAK UP THE VIEW Watch birds soaring high overhead or lie back under star-filled skies, enjoying the hot, sea-water bathtub. The shower room at the boathouse looks out to the pontoon.

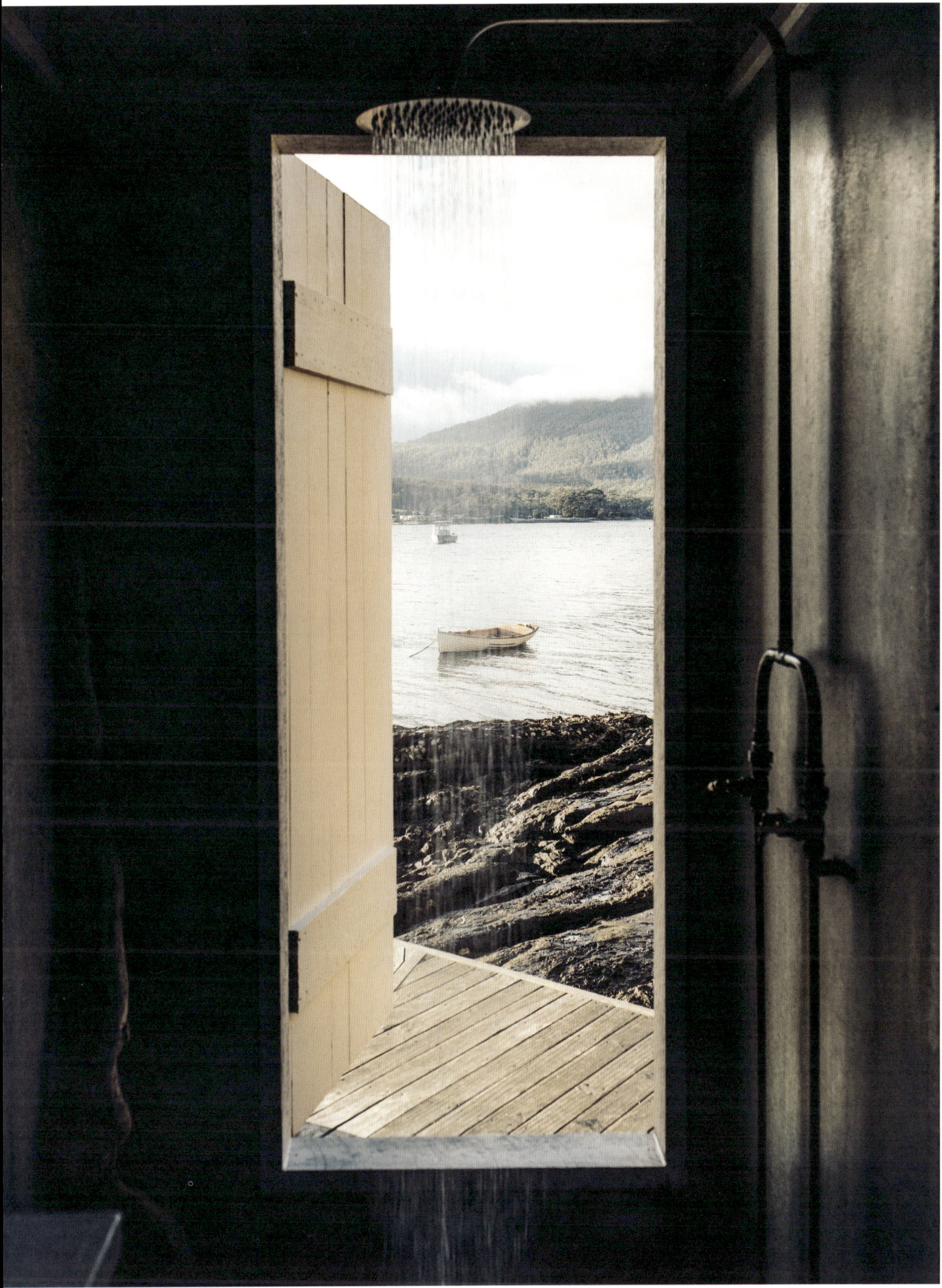

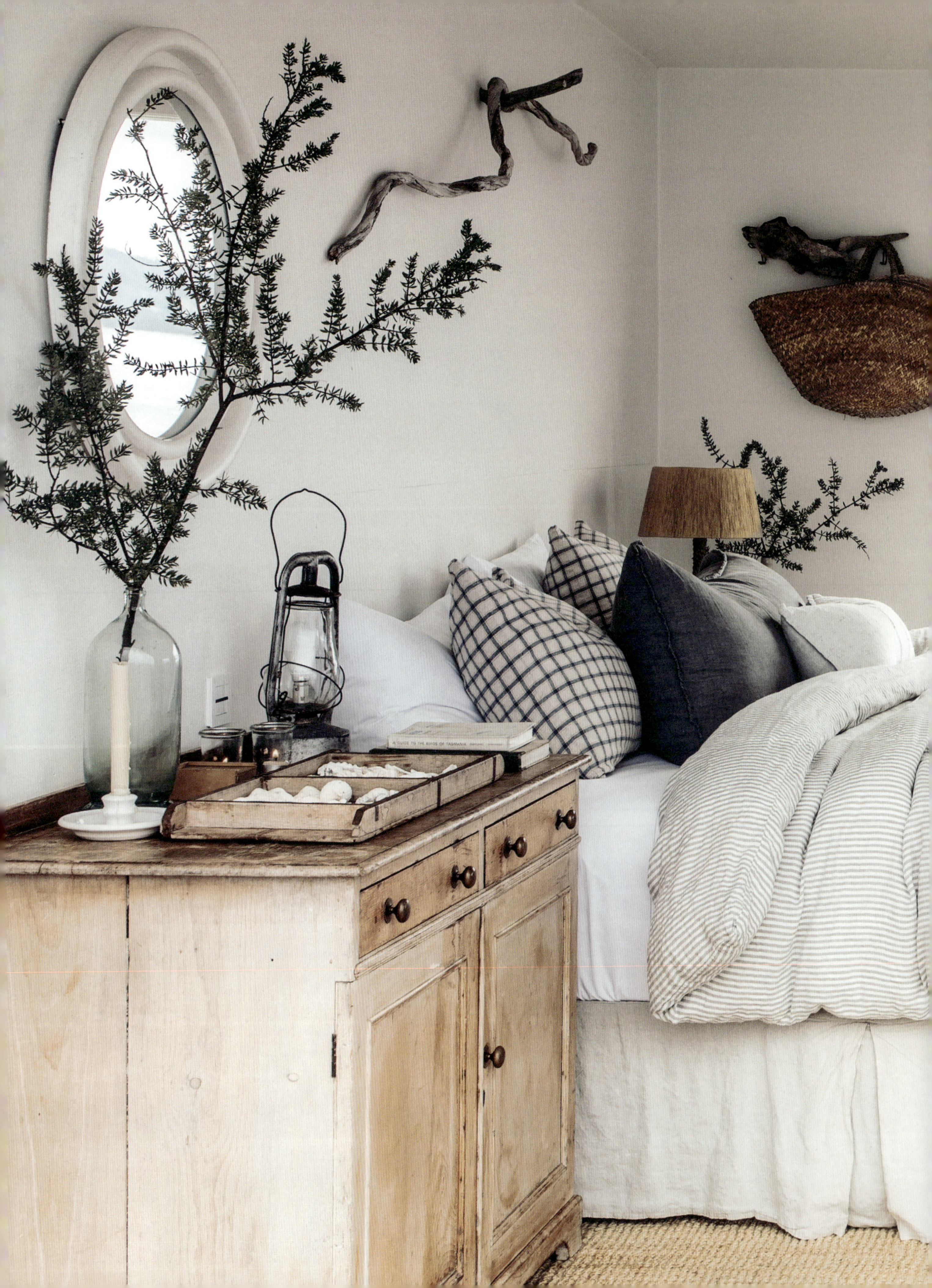

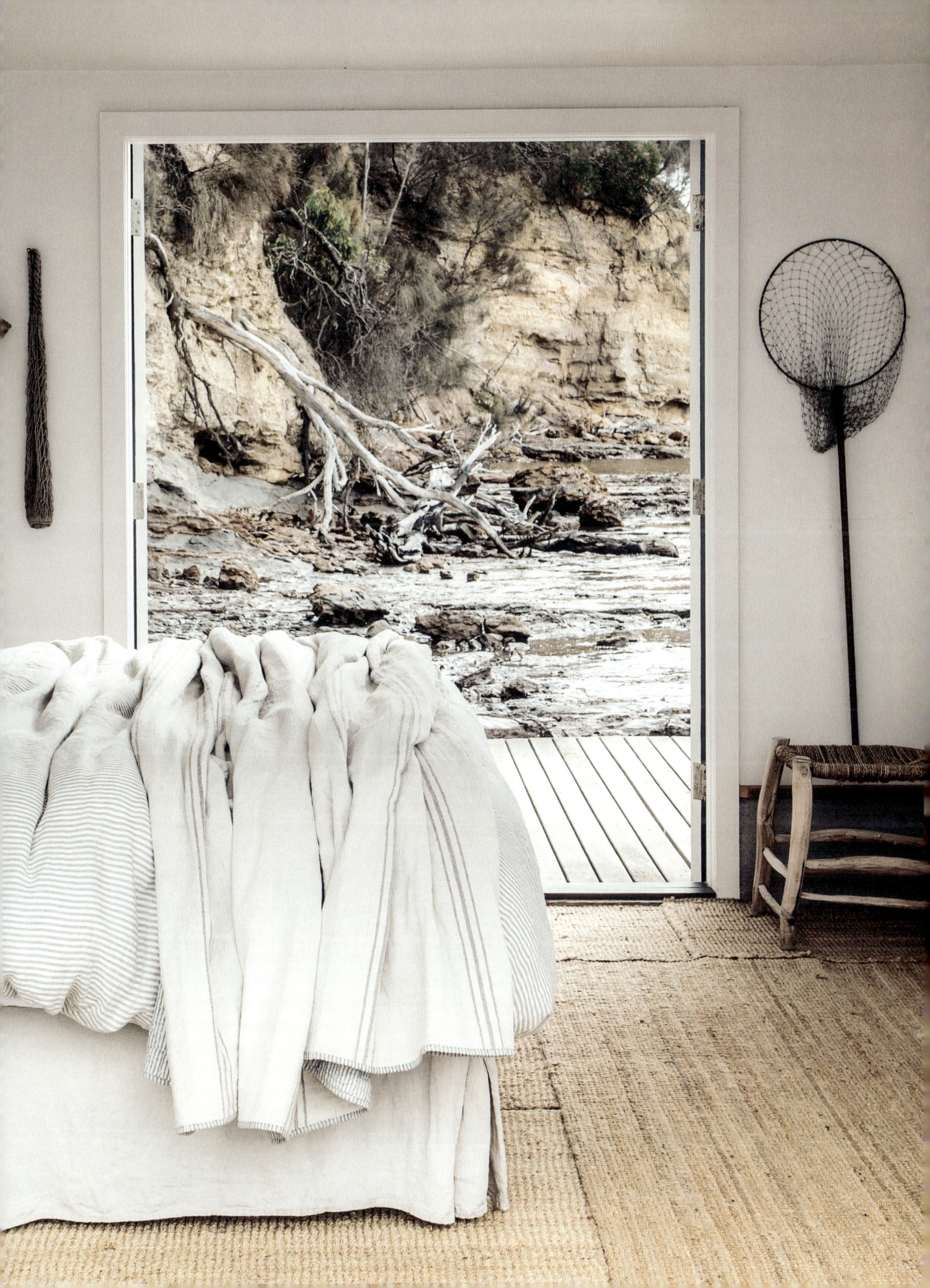

ARCHITECTURAL ESCAPE
Anna Unwin / Curator

AN ALCHEMIST BY NATURE, ANNA UNWIN'S CAREER HAS SPANNED SHOPKEEPER, stylist, jewellery maker, antique dealer and now fashion curator. With a fascination for things that catch her eye, whether through research or instinct, Anna is always on the hunt for fabrics, objects or furniture with that certain something. Her motto is 'recycle, reduce, reuse', and she is drawn to the character of time-worn materials, which can be repurposed into something new, or to beautifully patinated textures with a story to tell.

'The move last year to Ibiza provided a catalyst for change both at home and for work,' says Anna. The vintage furniture and decorative accessories that Anna was selling online switched to private archive sourcing. This allowed her to transition her focus to the creation of limited-run fashion and homeware edits – designed by Anna using vintage textiles and handcrafted by a team of artisan makers. Think oversized patchwork sheepskin gilets, cool Hungarian blouses and many other creative ideas quietly bubbling away.

'When the market catches up, I like to keep evolving. It keeps the direction fresh and satisfies my desire to create modern heirlooms, using recycled materials in a more contemporary way. Our new home has become a test bed for ideas,' says Anna.

Relocating from the UK, Anna and her husband Willie, along with their three teenage girls, have realized a long-held dream of living in Ibiza, where they have been coming for the past 20 years. 'The sale of our home in England aligned with the refurbishment of this house by a friend, and the time felt right to make the move,' Anna explains.

The Brutalist-style, three-storey, architectural villa, which is softened by fragrant bougainvillea and flowering jasmine, was built in the 1970s. Nestled within a gated community and a secluded garden, and surrounded by pine forests, cacti and tropical foliage, the house is centrally located, being within easy reach of beaches, towns and restaurants – this balances a desire for retreat with all that the island of Ibiza has to offer.

'We wanted the girls to enjoy experiencing a new way of life and being able to step away from a faster pace. The move has enabled us to slow down, reconnect and enjoy the comfort of home. Moving from a sprawling house, this feels very together –

LIGHT THE WAY Whitewashed walls, rustic stone and abundant shadowy light create a welcome approach to Anna's home through mature tropical gardens and borders filled with topiary.

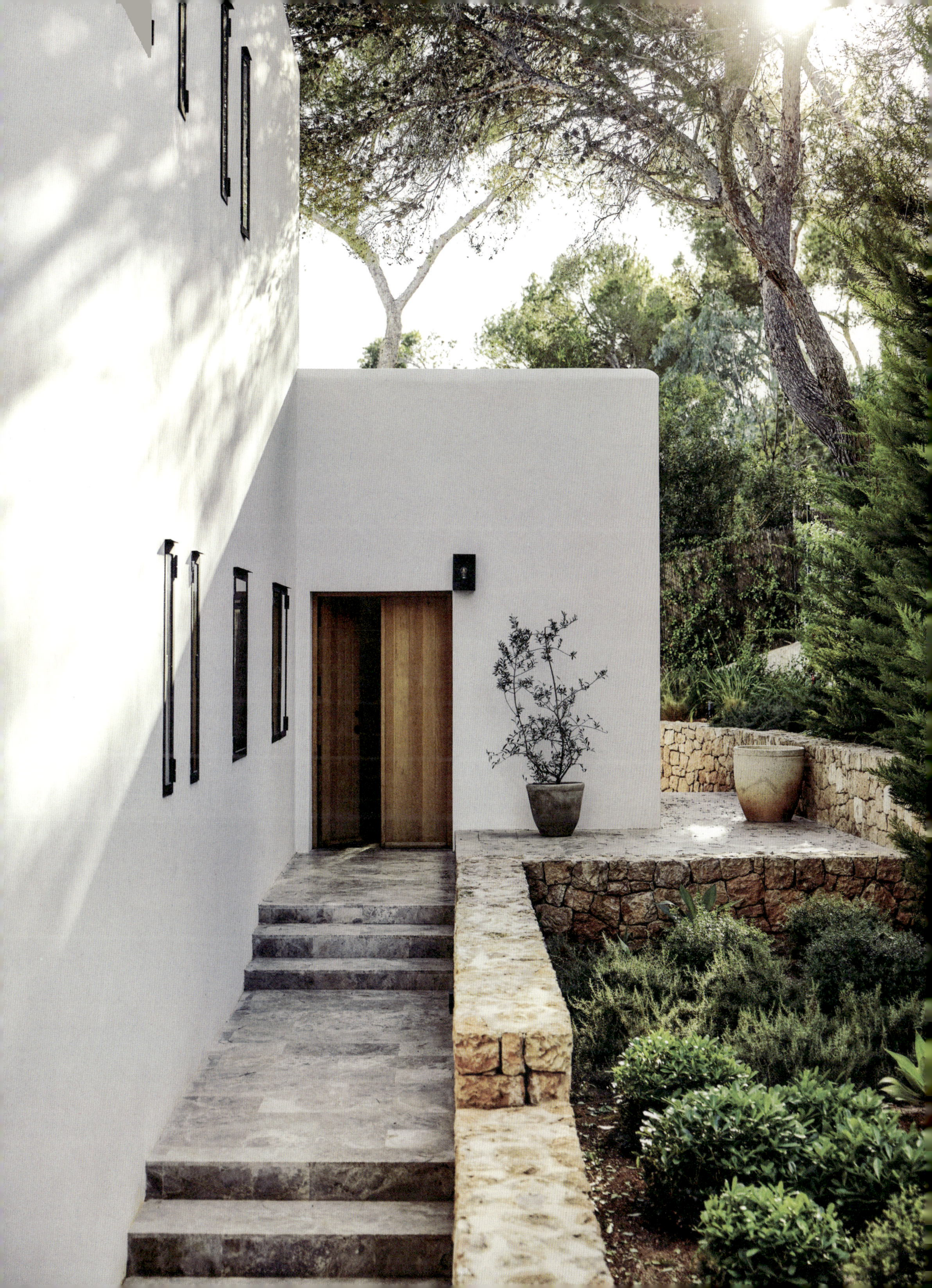

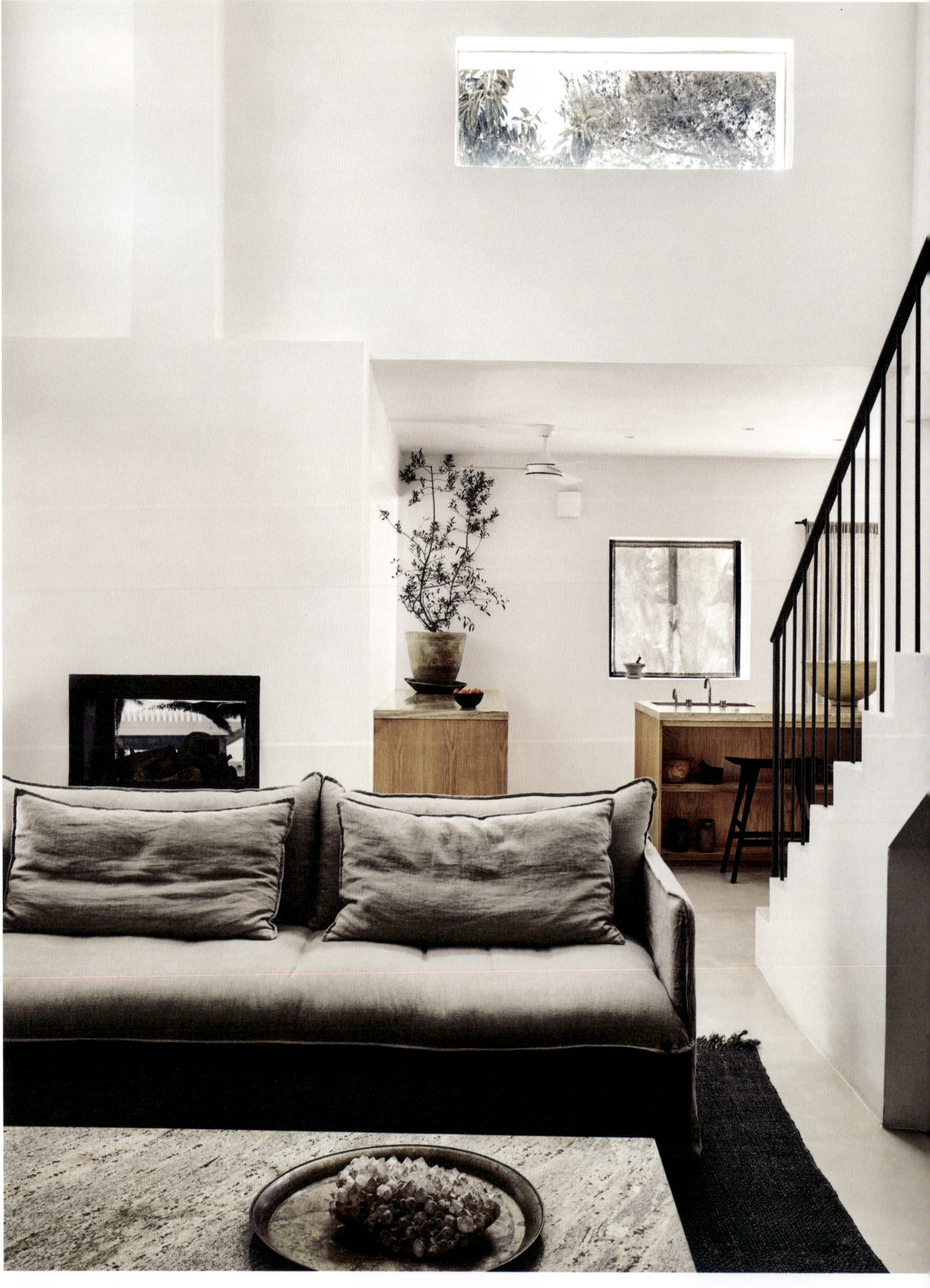

we use every room, but there is also space for retreat, with private bathrooms, balconies, outdoor entertaining areas and lots of quiet nooks,' says Anna.

Transformed from derelict and unloved to laidback and connected, the house is filled with a muted mix of old and new. Arranged over three floors, crisp whitewashed walls are offset by a palette of rich dark greens, soft sandy hues, warm naturals and inky dark woods, which reference the nuances of nature, the beach, and the rocky landscape that surrounds the house.

Timeless materials have been consistently layered throughout – with concrete floors, travertine kitchen finishes and elegant wooden cabinetry, alongside hand-forged curtain rails and tactile ceramics. In the bathrooms, sleek marble sinks and bespoke brass tapware add to the feeling of sanctuary and escape.

Authentic vintage textiles are curated as wall hangings, decorative cushions and inviting bed layers, which heightens the sense of comfort and contrasts intuitively with contemporary handmade rugs, simple upholstered headboards and deep, linen-covered sofas. Floaty voiles diffuse the light and enhance atmospheric shadows, while seamlessly connecting the interior and exterior. By the pool, 'Princess and the Pea' day beds, reinvented from sofas bought many years ago from Caravane, have added textural edge – providing the perfect resting spots after cool morning swims or late afternoon naps.

Anna's collections of earthy, gathered finds have been redefined here and bring a nomadic sense of warmth and nostalgia. 'True craftmanship stands the test of time and surrounding ourselves only with the things we love feels very comforting,' she explains. 'Island life has changed my idea of luxury – it's now just as much about buying locally made honey and incense as it is drinking from handcrafted cups.

'The move has given me the chance to rekindle my creative passion. Occasionally, we rent the house out for styling shoots and to private guests, but it has become a home that grounds us all. We feel very connected to this special place.' ✧

TEXTURAL LAYERS A bespoke linen sofa, a vintage coffee table from AU and a handmade Terra rug in 'Moss' from the House of Grey x Armadillo & Co. Ellipse collection add textural interest.

ON THE SURFACE Warm caramel-coloured marble and natural wooden cabinetry lend a tactile appeal to Anna's kitchen. A papier-mâché bowl sits alongside a rustic pot, sourced from local Ibizan markets.

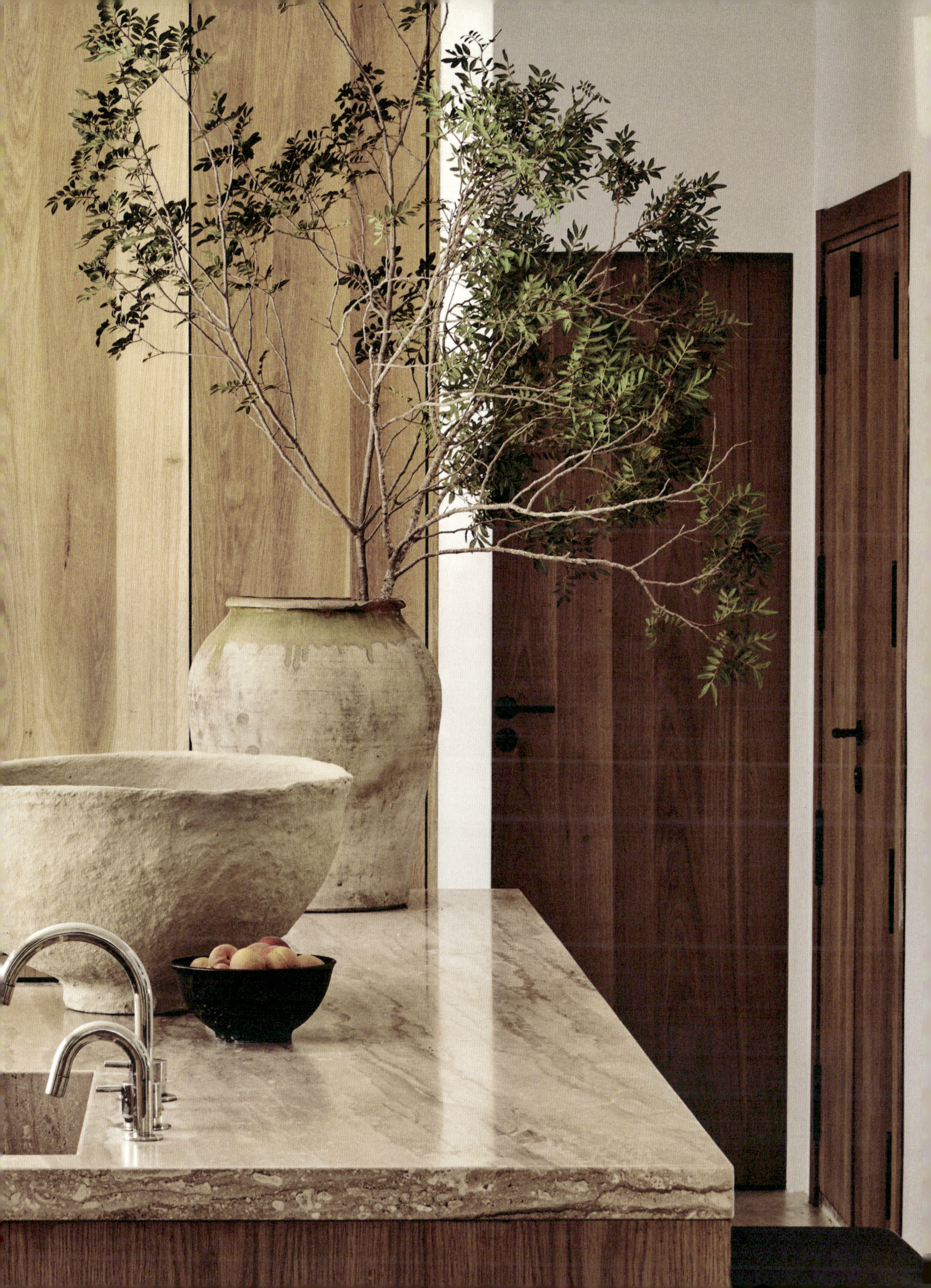

MONOCHROME EDGE
Contemporary furniture from Ethnicraft is offset by a handmade light from Chalk Path Studio.

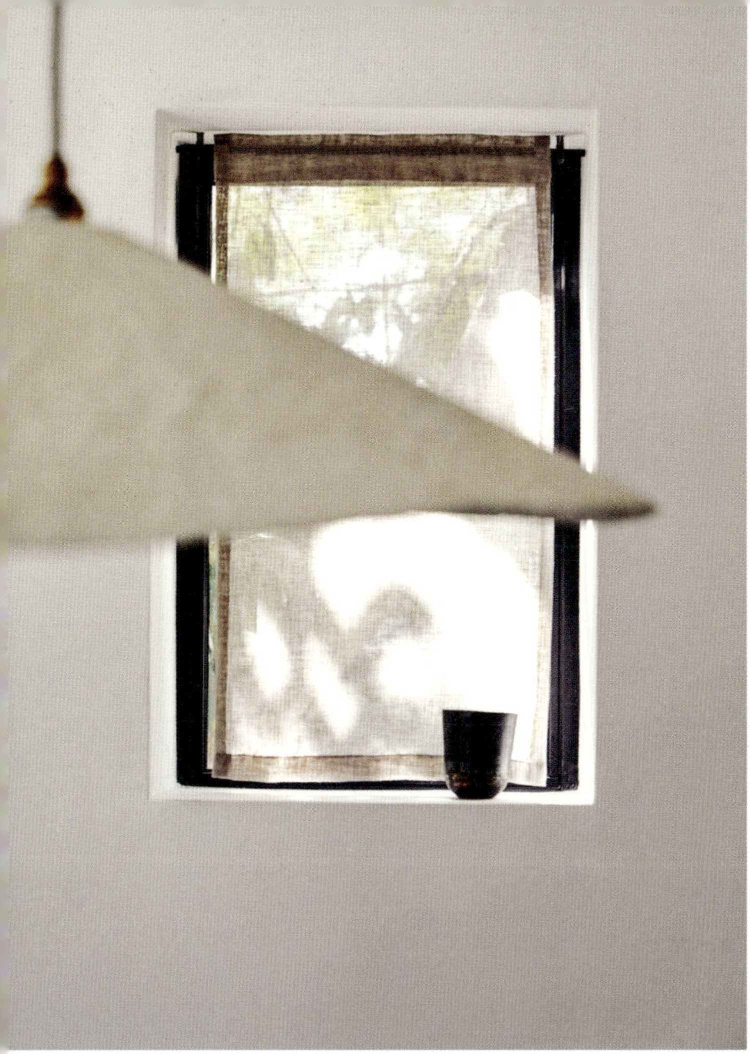
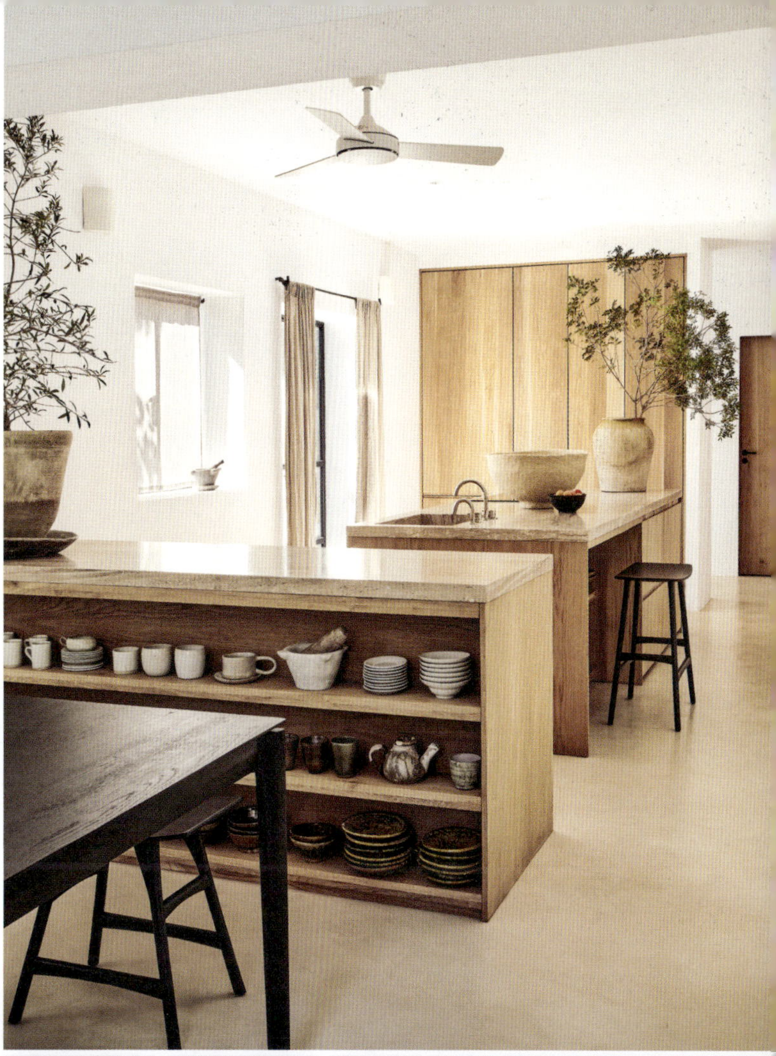
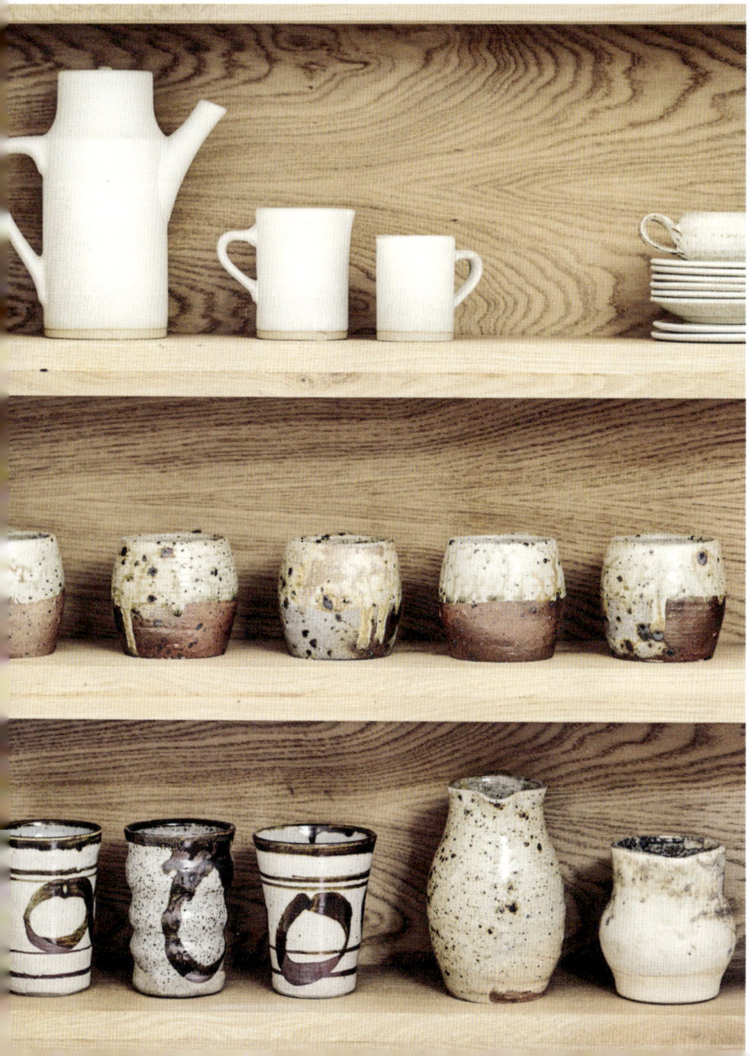
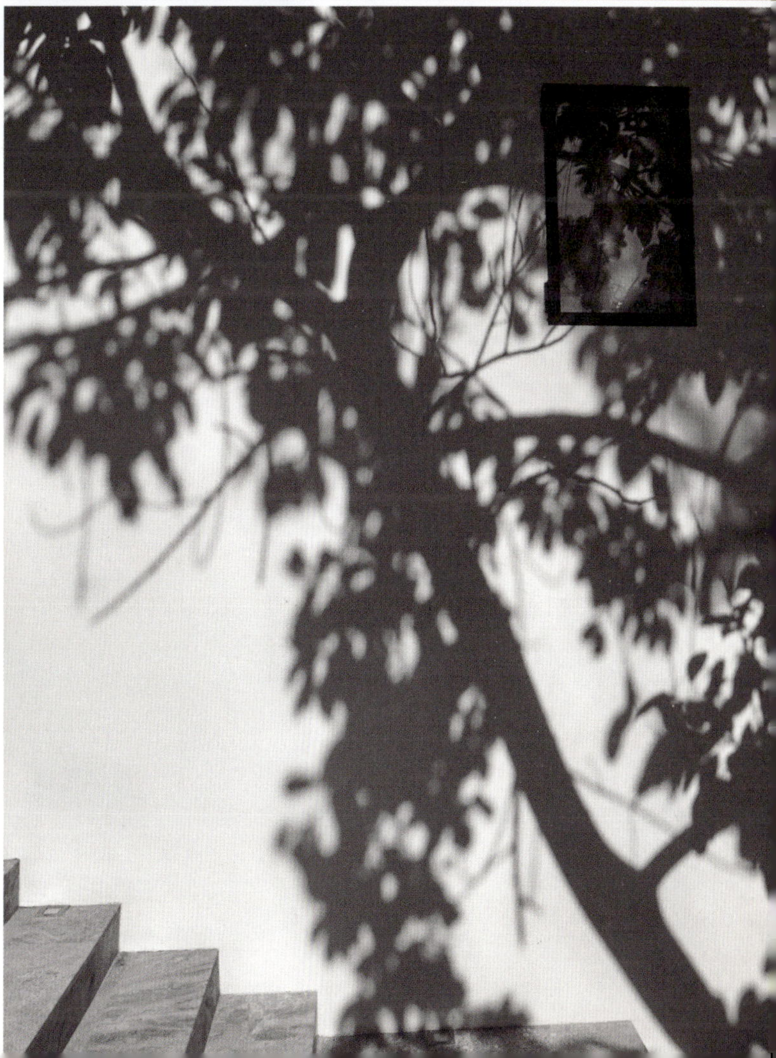

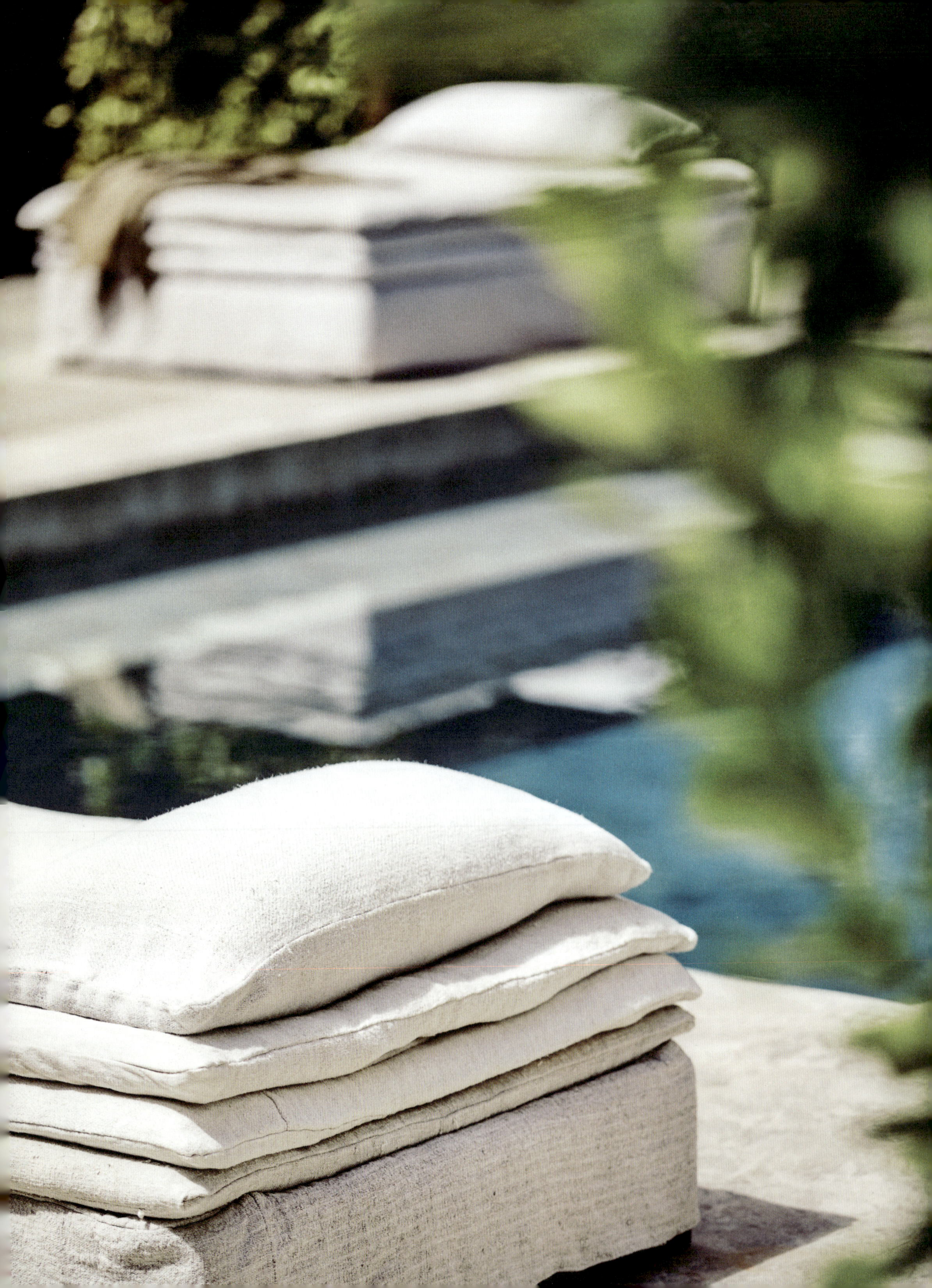

ARCHITECTURAL ESCAPE 85

CLEAN LINES Architectural nooks create cozy places to retreat and relax. Textiles from AU and Cultiver. Simple lime plaster walls are paired with Vola tapware.

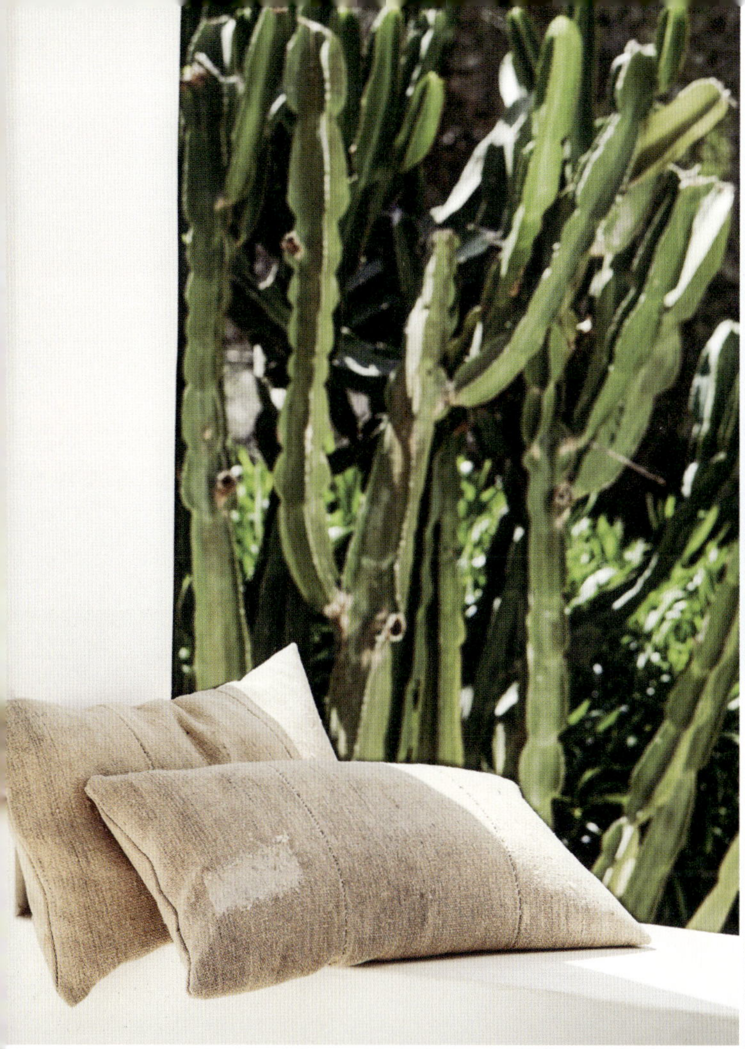
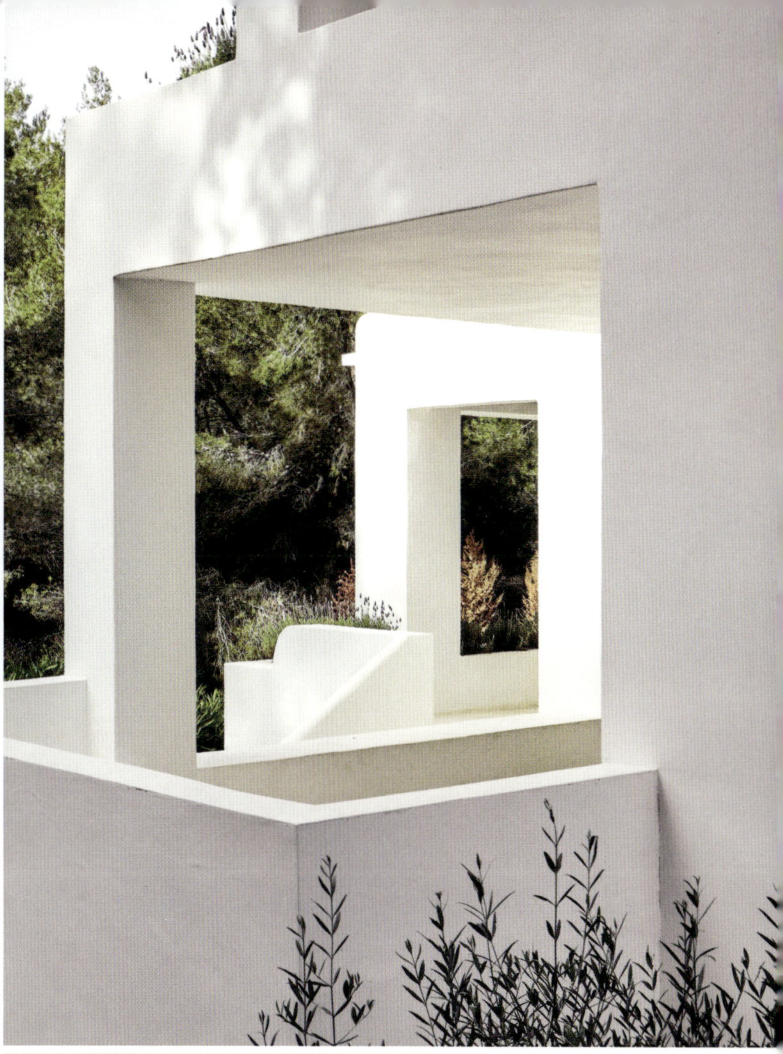
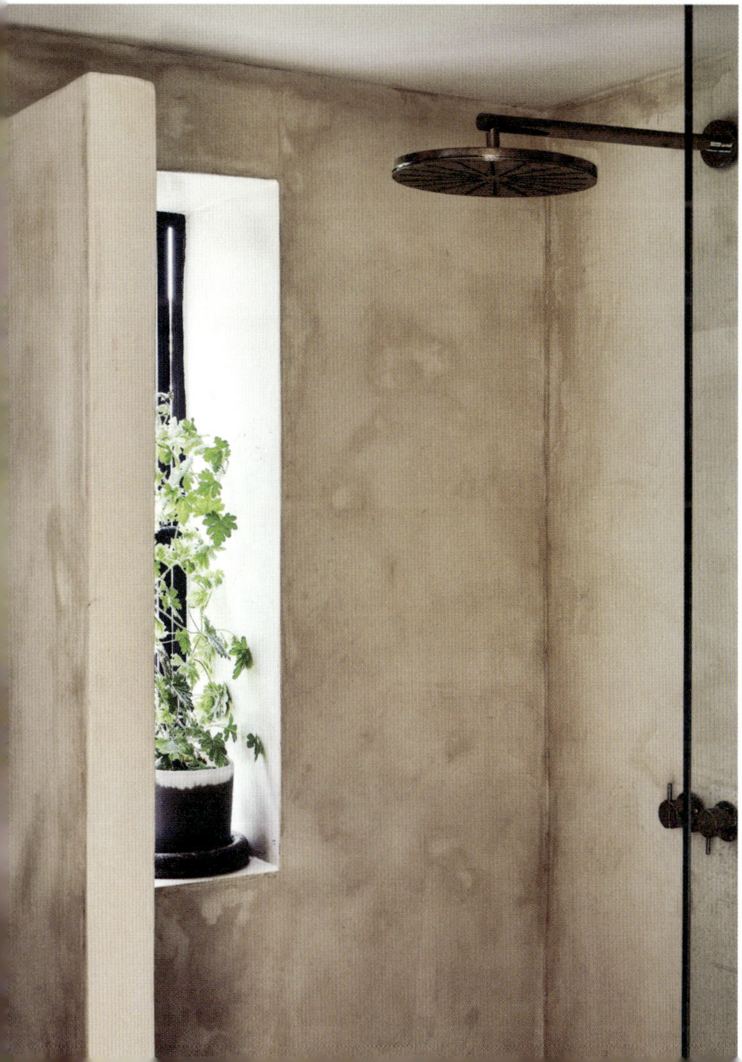
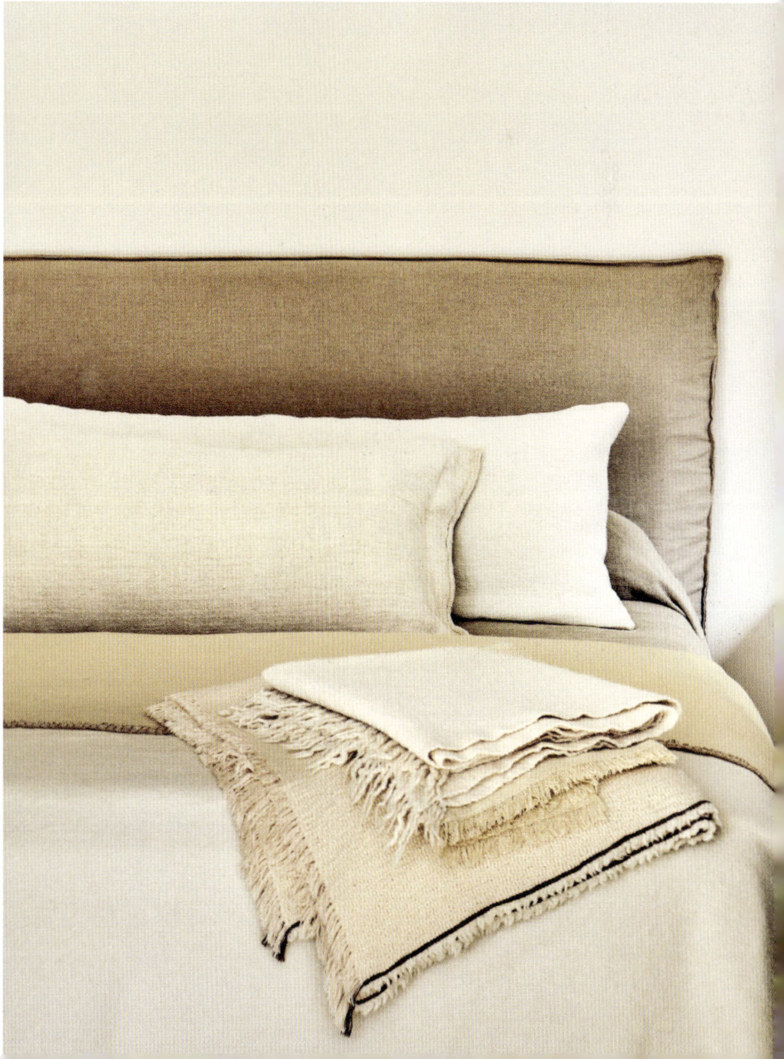

RESTFUL RETREAT In the master bedroom that adjoins to the lower courtyard next to the pool, a bespoke headboard and warm green and natural linen textiles create a sanctuary-like escape. Lime plaster bathroom walls and rich, dark wood surfaces in the en-suite bathroom add to the cocooning vibe.

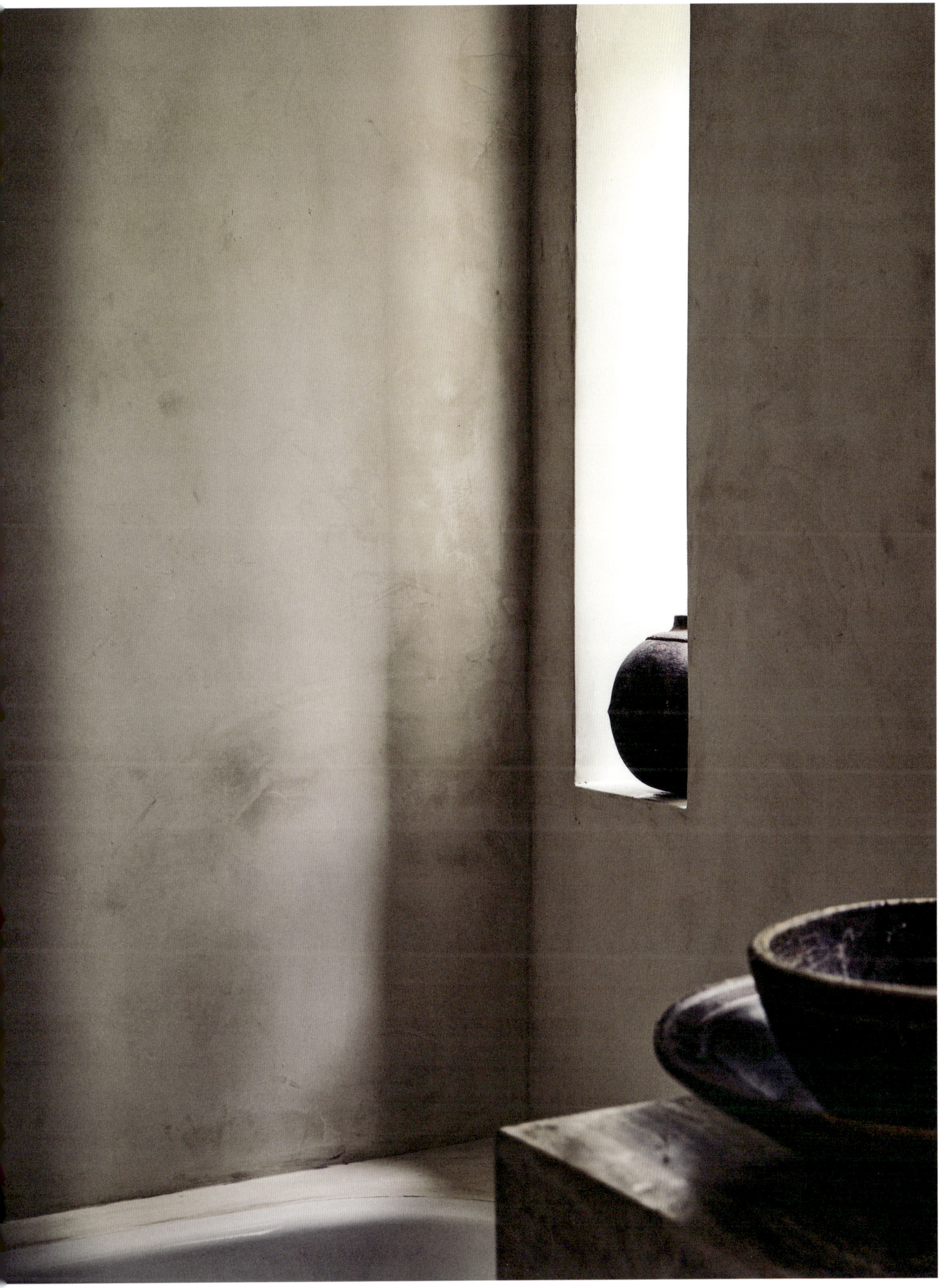

REMOTE GETAWAY
Kiki & Chris Hodgson / Designer / Farmer

FOR KIKI AND CHRIS HODGSON, SLOW LIVING SITS AT THE HEART OF NO.9, their Scottish Hebridean escape on the remote island of North Uist. A home that redefines the concept of luxury away from excess and ostentation to the simple and more bucolic.

Located on the wild coastline of Lochportain, their larch-clad, Scandi-style cabin is one of a few houses scattered along this isolated shore. 'I fell in love with the Hebridean islands as a child, spending every summer on Mull. Returning as an adult, Chris and I have explored many islands together, but were drawn to the magic here and the sense of well-being we felt, immersed in its unspoilt beauty,' says Kiki.

'Now in our sixties and having spent a lifetime running the family farm in North Yorkshire, we wanted to explore diversification opportunities that would bring together our love of design and nature,' Kiki explains. What started with the building of a luxury holiday let – The Grey Shed, next to their Yorkshire farmhouse – gave the couple the confidence to realize another long-held dream of creating a Scottish holiday home that could also be shared as a boutique bolthole.

With useable land very hard to come by, an online search during lockdown revealed a de-crofted plot – meaning the site could be switched from farming to housing. Unable to travel and relying on Google Maps, an impulsive offer was made and accepted. 'Our best decision – and we had a very emotional first trip to finally view our purchase, once we could travel,' says Kiki.

Working with Rural Design, an award-winning architectural practice on Skye, the couple replaced a uninhabitable 1970s dwelling with a new, off-the-peg, contemporary Scottish longhouse-design construction that came complete with glazing and cladding. Tweaking the specification, Kiki added a large glass panel next to the wood-burning stove to frame the early morning sunrise and incredible bay view; and removed plans for a third bedroom, which created space for a cozy dining area, a master en-suite and a captivating front-to-back sea vista as you enter the house. Opening the vaulted elevations in the heart of the home has also added immeasurable volume. 'Everyone is surprised at how spacious the cabin feels,' says Kiki.

'We wanted the design to blend with the vernacular and to enjoy unobstructed views of the sea and dramatic skyline – on a clear day you can even catch glimpses of the

> **SPACE TO BREATHE** Uninterrupted views, wild scenery and spectacular sunrises make waking up here very special. With windows on three sides of the cabin, the light casts a beautiful glow throughout the interior.

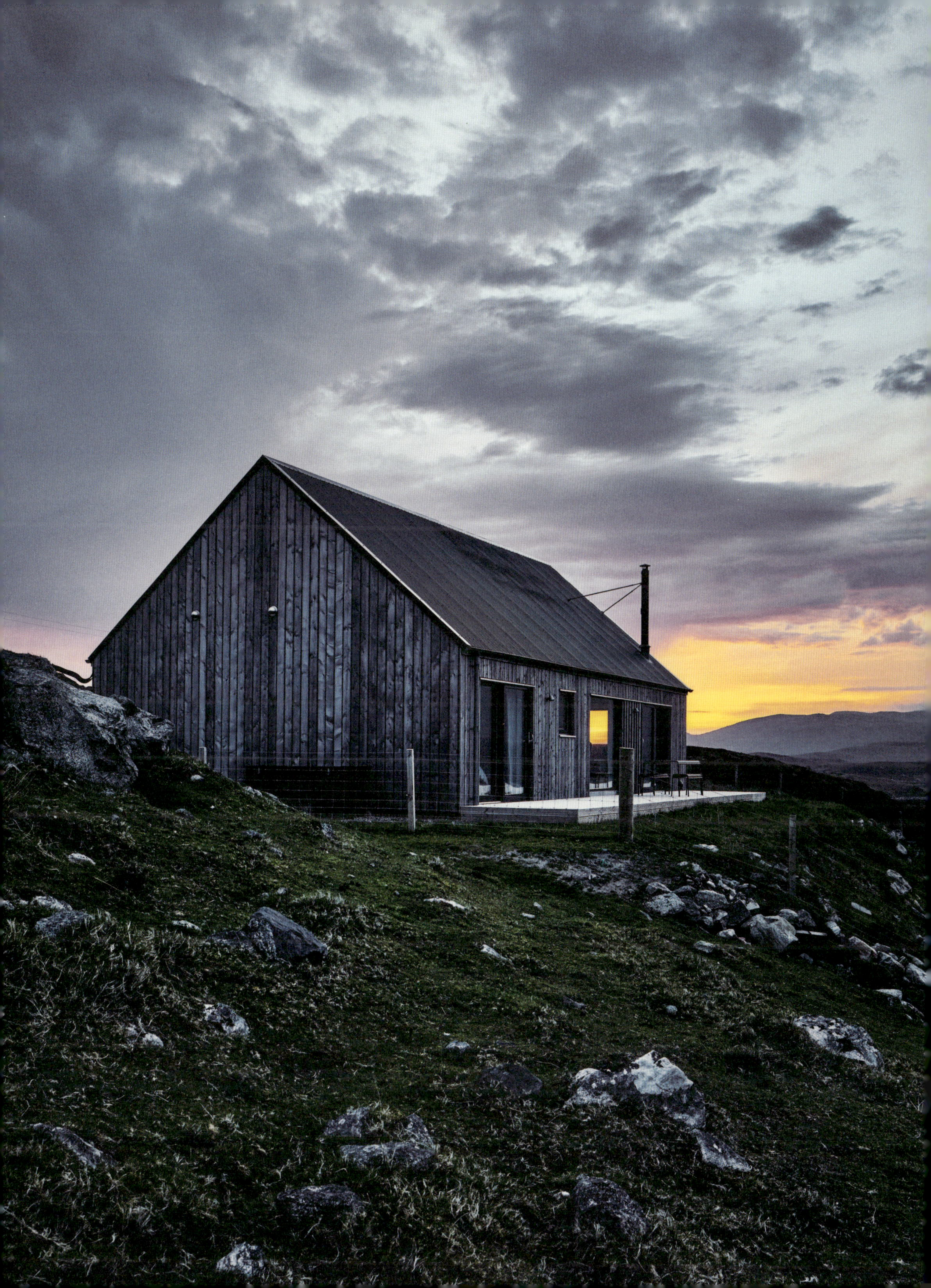

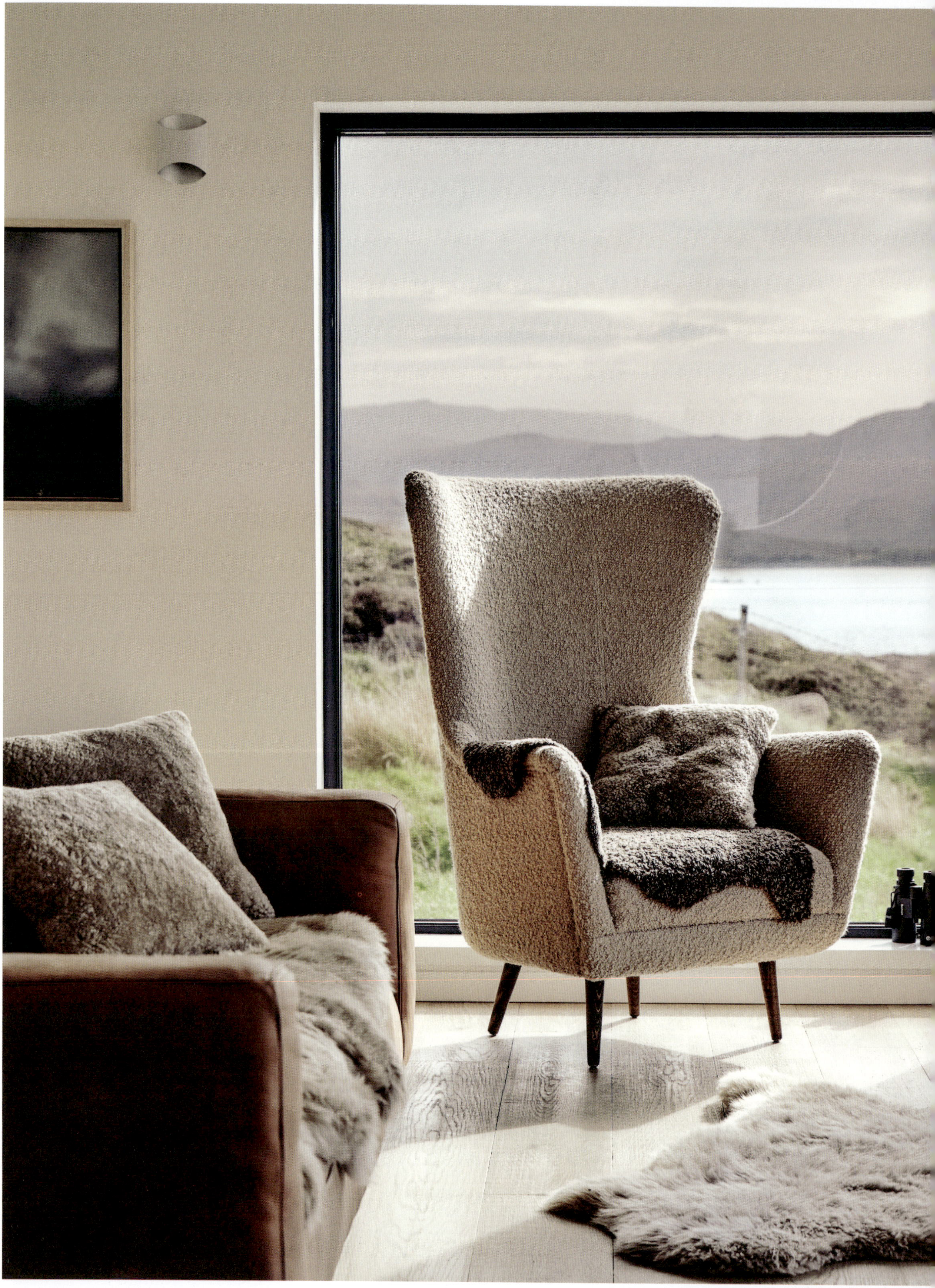

Isle of Skye and the mainland,' explains Kiki. Original stonework was repurposed for the foundations and the cabin named No.9, in a nod to the site's address, heritage and regeneration. 'Most houses on the island are given Gaelic names but we liked the simplicity of using the original number, as it felt like a mark of respect for the history of all the previous inhabitants.'

Super-insulated, with an air source heat pump, thermally efficient glazing, and a Mechanical Ventilation with Heat Recovery (MVHR) system that circulates the air supply and retains heat, the earthy-meets-refined, cozy cabin interior has been thoughtfully designed by Kiki. Taking design inspiration from calm, Scandinavian influences, and the palette of the surrounding natural landscape, simple whitewashed walls are offset by raw oak floors and handmade countertops created by Skye Stone Studios, using fragments of local marble set into resin.

Embracing the remote location, a Sebastian Cox kitchen from deVOL and a mix of contemporary and handmade crockery, displayed on well-curated shelves, have made the joy of preparing good food and the sharing of meals a memorable occasion at home – with the bonus of always having the best seat.

Throughout the cabin, textural materials enhance the feeling of welcome and sanctuary. Think comfortable beds, luxury bathrooms, a buttery leather sofa, soft sheepskins, natural linens, warm woollen blankets and tactile, bouclé-covered chairs that encourage you to cozy up, binoculars in hand, to observe the ever-changing view – alive with red deer, sheep, otters, dolphins, seals, seabirds, golden eagles and owls. Venturing out, you realize how raw and potent the island is – with just one small forest of pine trees, then miles of wild, deserted roads that come edge-to-edge with watery inlets, hidden bays and some of the most spectacular coastline and white sandy beaches you can imagine.

'When we arrive with our dogs and step out to the smell of wild thyme and the sound of seabirds, I can feel myself breathe out. It was important to us that the house trod gently on the landscape, and in return the island and its wonderful community have nurtured us. Time stands still here and soothes the soul.' ✧

STYLE & SYNCHRONICITY Large open windows, a calming palette and soft natural surfaces, in a mix of leather, bouclé and sheepskin, create a continuity of design that adds to the sense of calm and cohesion.

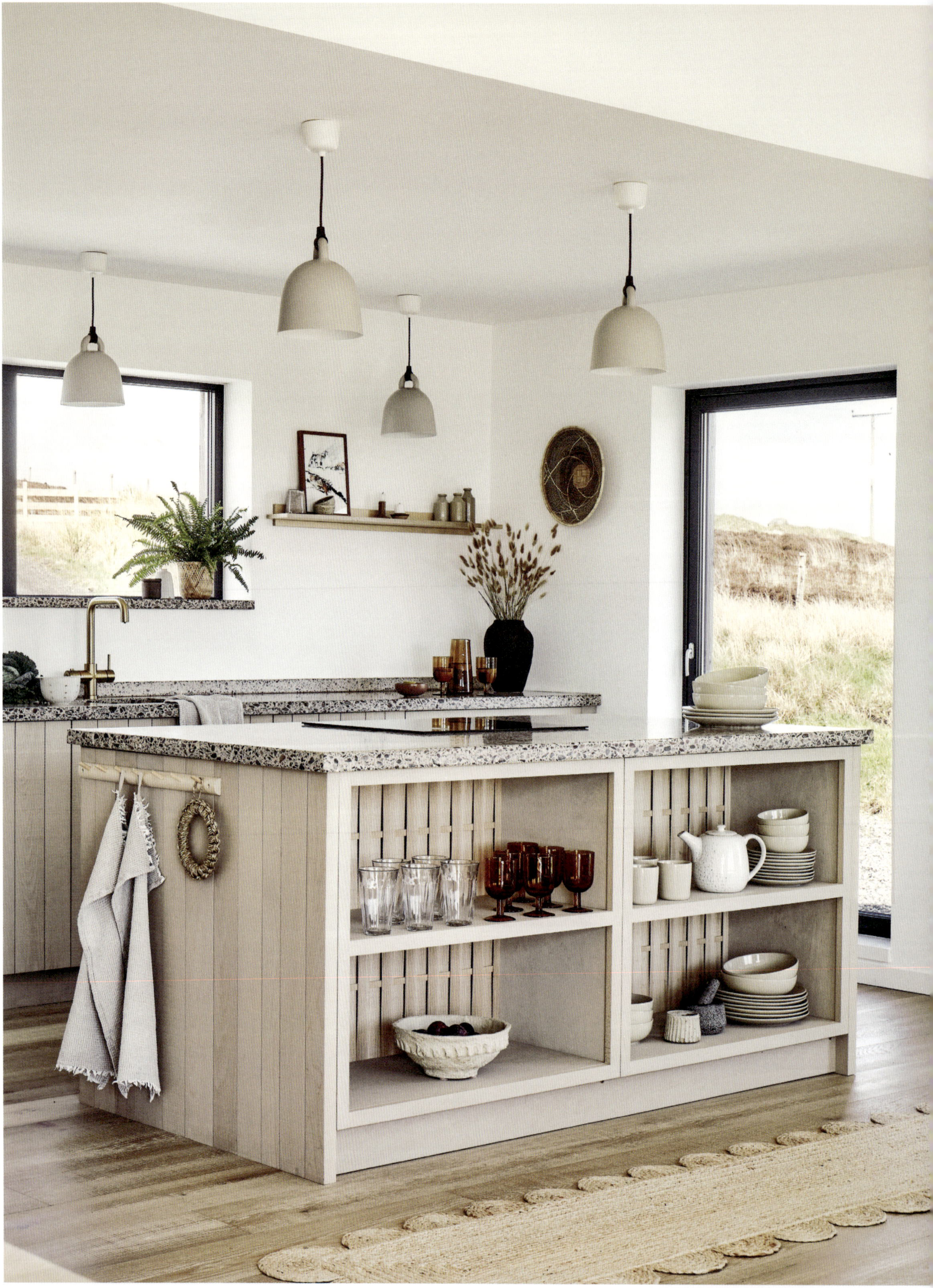

COZY UP The British-made wood-burning stove by Burley enhances the feeling of welcome. Open shelves create an opportunity for decorative display. Artwork by Ellis O'Connor.

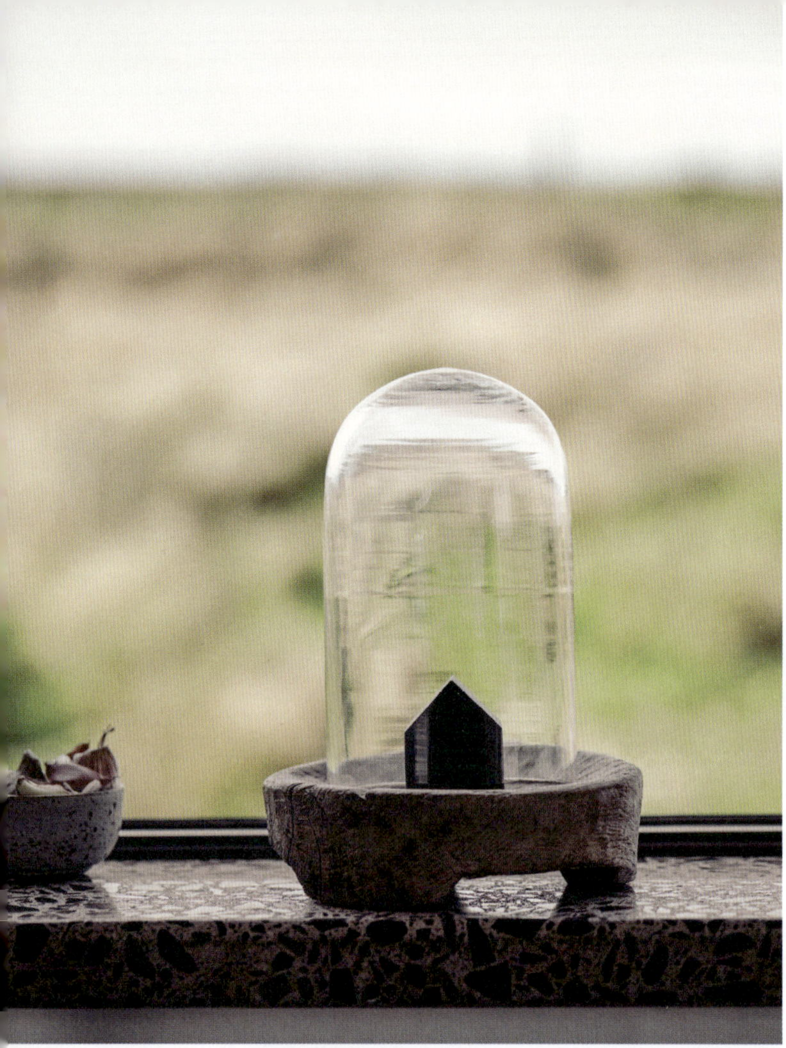

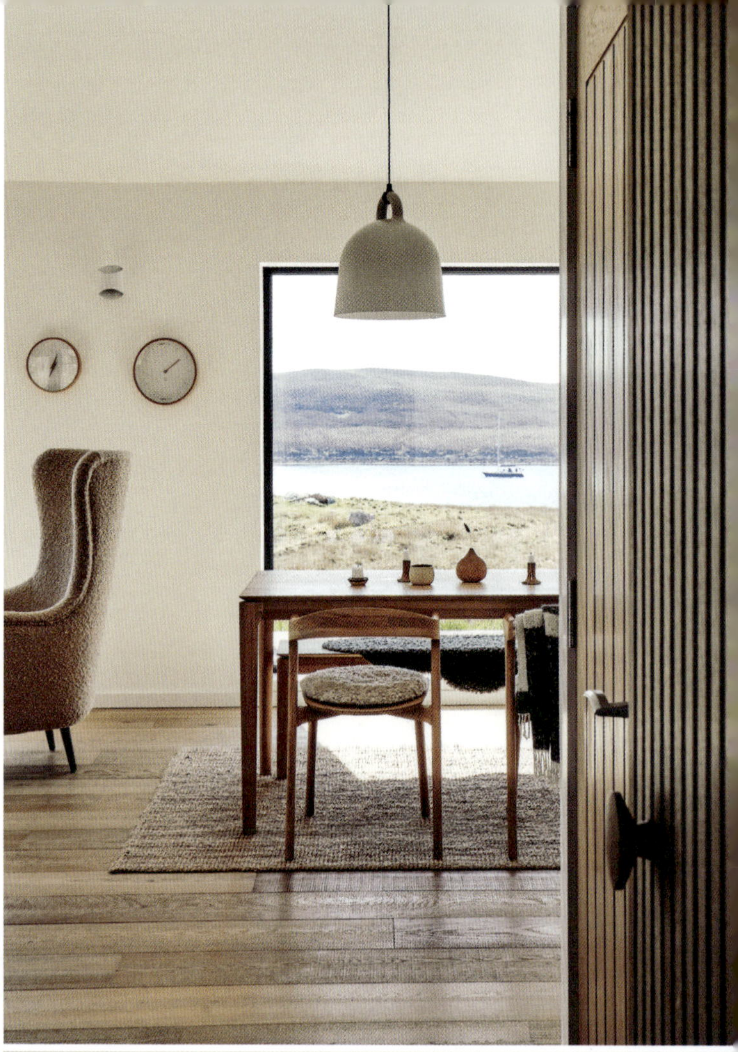

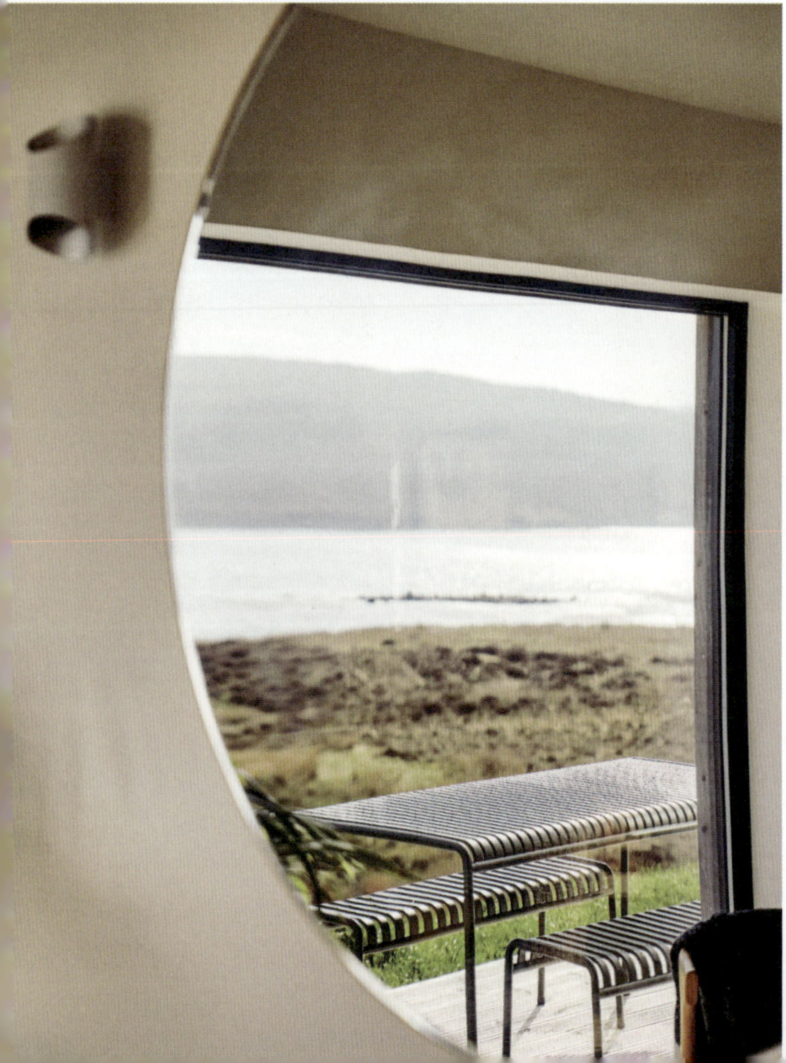

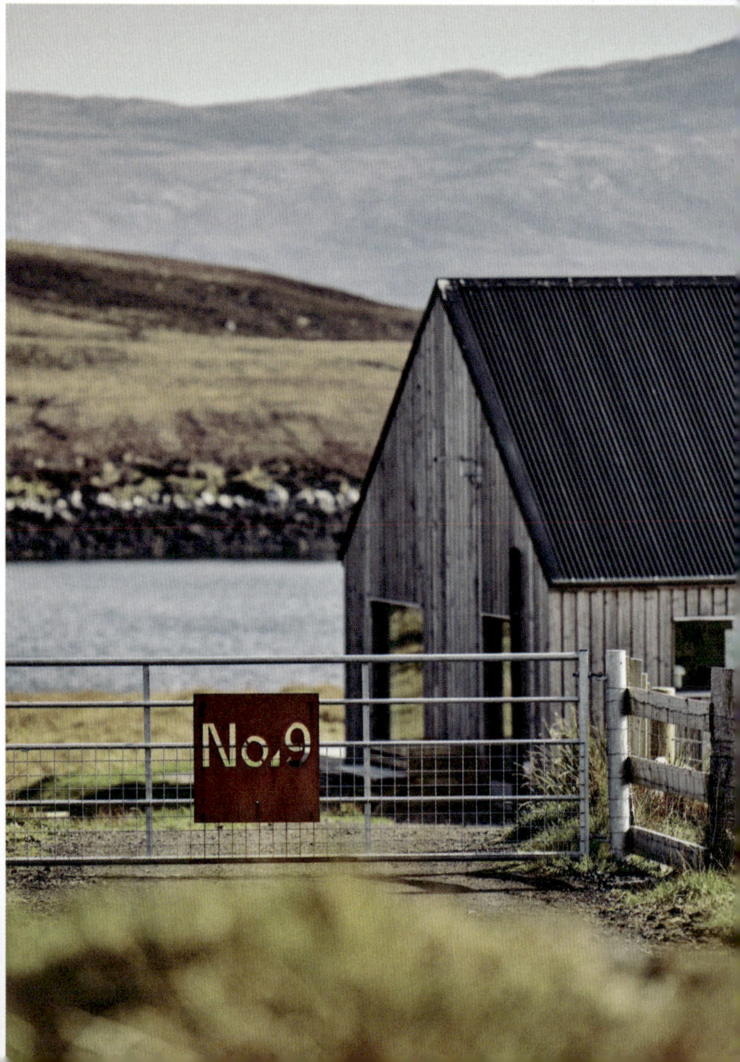
No.9

OUTSIDE IN As you enter No.9, the view extends behind the dining table (from Ethnicraft) straight through to the landscape beyond. Metal furniture from HAY (opposite, bottom left).

PAGES 98–99 QUIET REFLECTION From the master suite, unbroken views across the bay can be enjoyed. Artwork by Carol Douglas and Ellis O'Connor hangs above the chair and behind the bed. Treasures Kiki has collected from the island feature throughout.

REMOTE GETAWAY

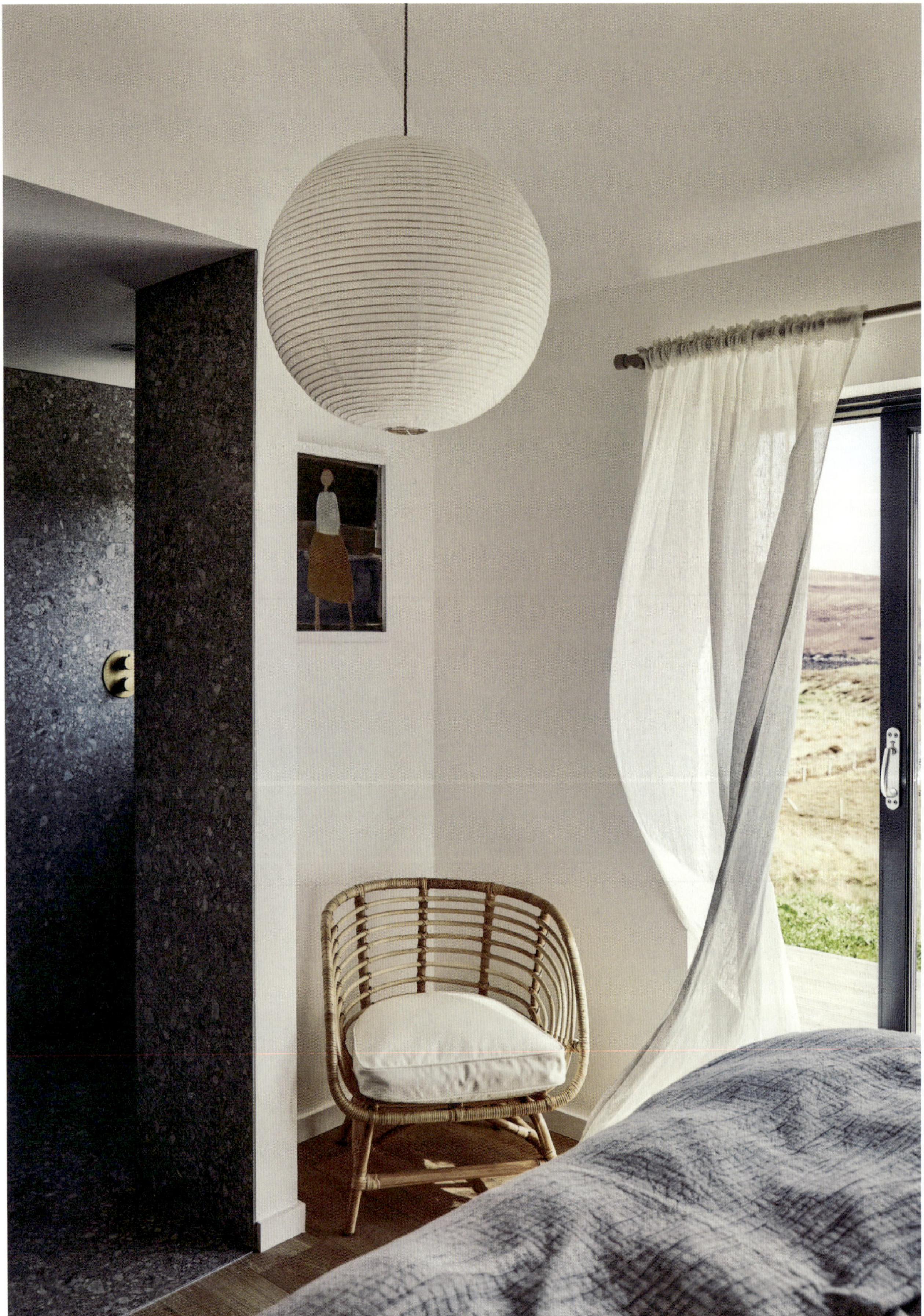

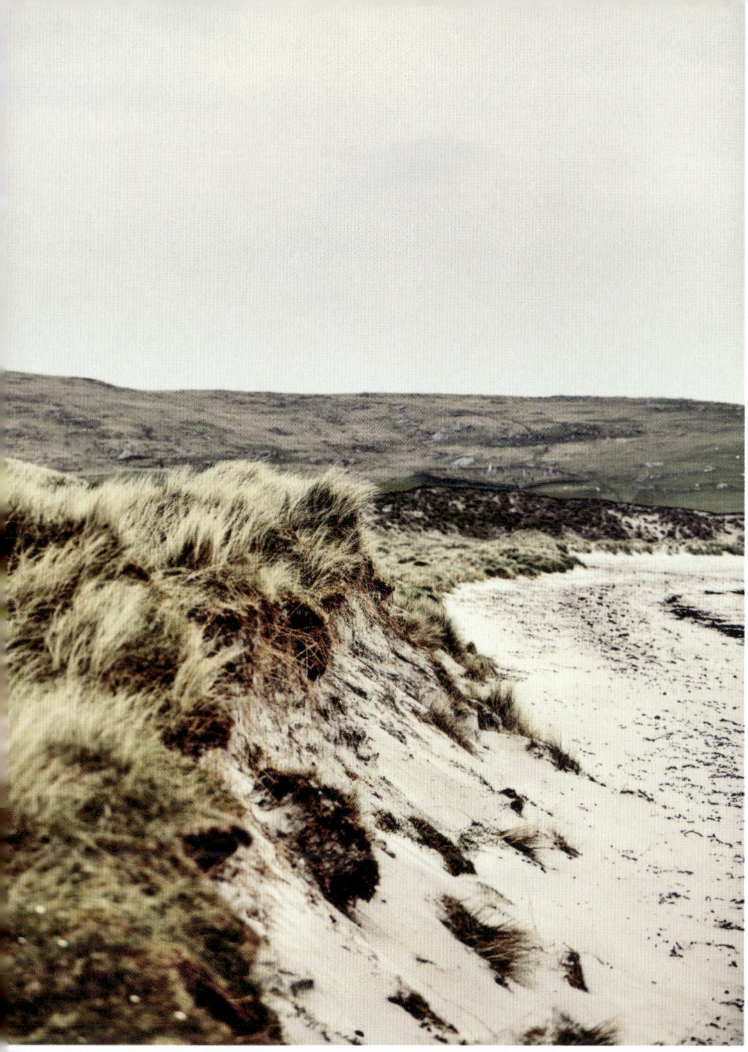
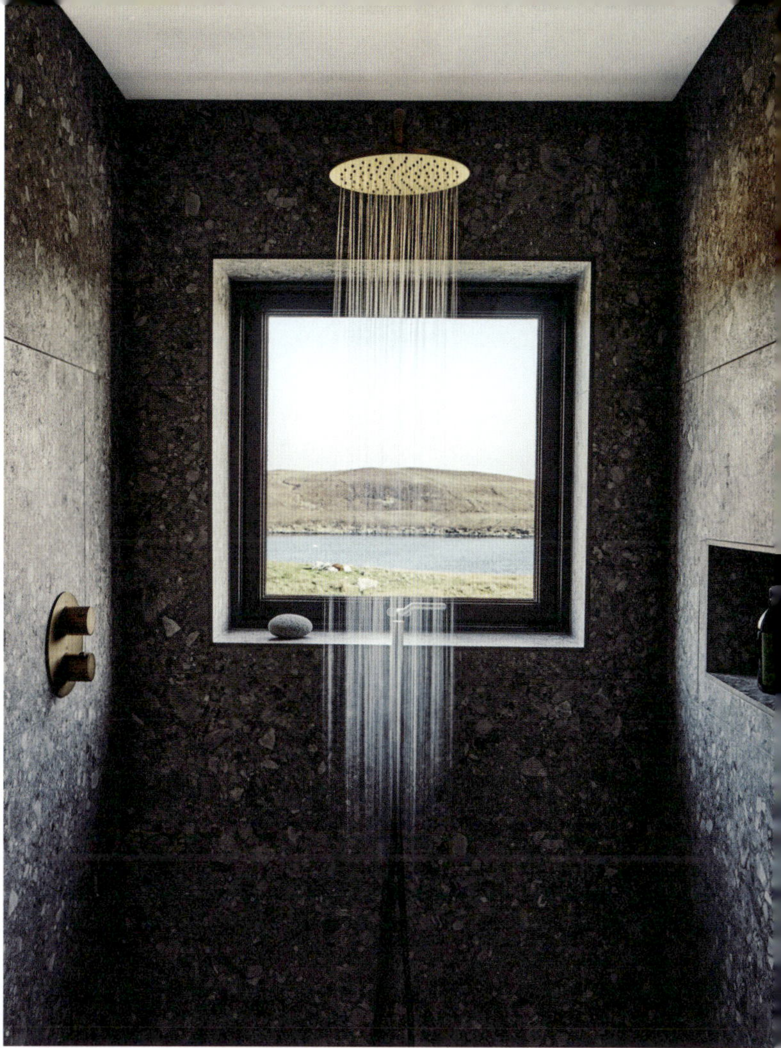
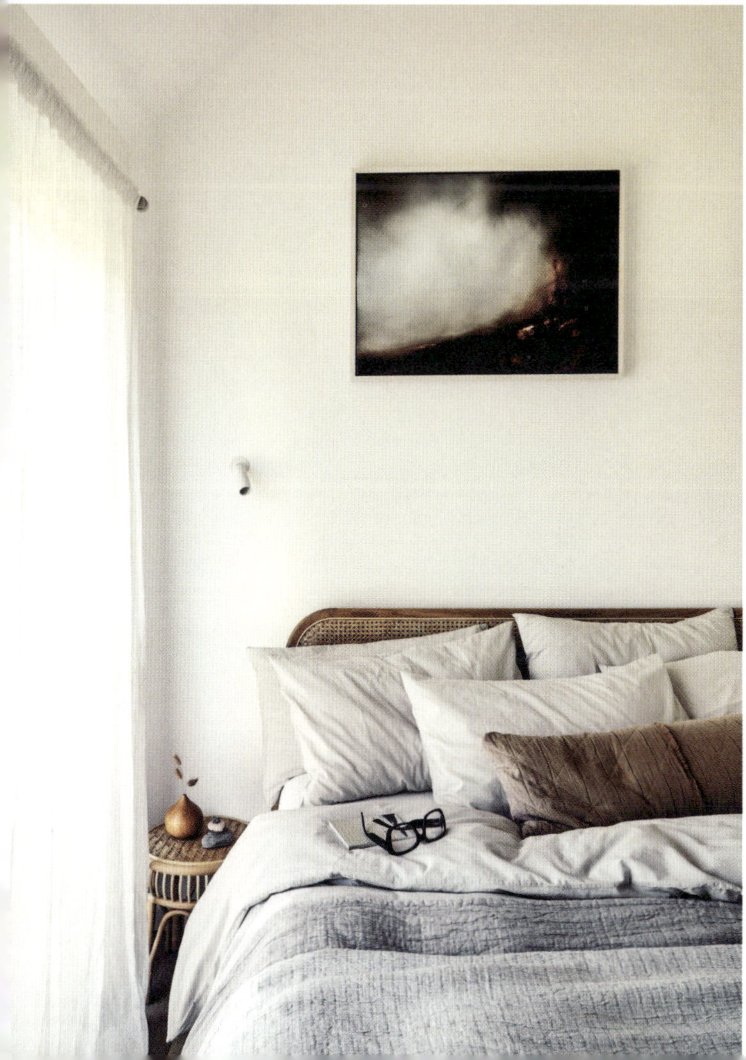
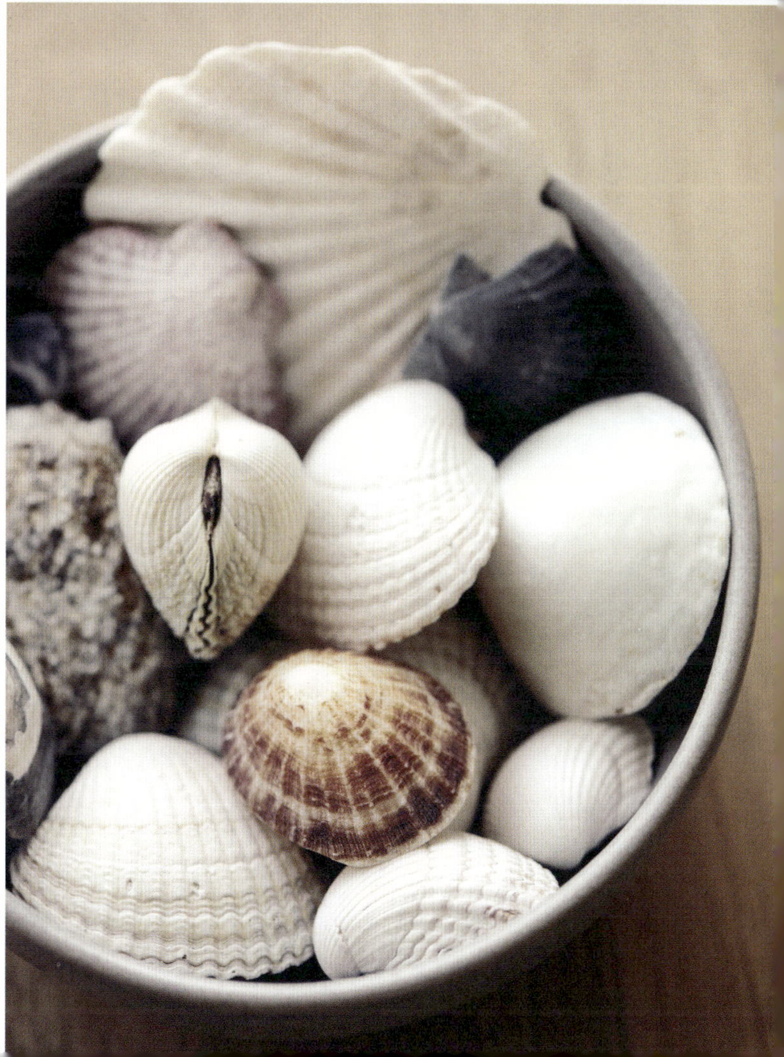

FABRIC HOUSE
Amanda Pickett / Interior Designer

IN THE COASTAL VILLAGE OF DEIÀ, IN MALLORCA, SCOTTISH DECORATOR and antiques dealer Amanda Pickett has added her name to a creative cognoscenti of writers, artists, musicians and interior designers who have succumbed to the charms of this world-heritage site, an hour north of the capital, Palma.

With a magpie eye, Amanda has turned a run-down 17th-century *casa de pescadores* (fisherman's cottage) into a creative studio where she can make, transform and imagine. And has become a go-to source for both designers and private clients, who share her affinity for the colourful and extraordinary.

Born in Scotland, Amanda came to Mallorca on a whim eight years ago, with her partner Gary Clarke, after the premature arrival of twin girls and in need of a change in scenery to recuperate. Arriving with all five of their children, a dog and a trailer full of antiques to sell, they fell in love with the bohemian vibe and the unspoilt, rugged landscape at the foot of the Teix mountains. Deià cast its spell, they married, and the rest is history.

As with many creatives before her, most famously Robert Graves, a local lady told the family: 'You don't choose Deià. Deià chooses you,' as Amanda explains, smiling. 'After a few months of being here, the opportunity came up to rent the same lady's home – we've lived there ever since.'

The couple opened a stand-alone antique and interiors business on the main street, but with lockdown, Brexit and the cost of importing antiques they shut up shop and moved their studio to a quieter part of the village. They shifted their focus to interior projects, the design and decoration of handmade beds and day beds, and one-off textile creations that have become synonymous with Pickett's House style – and a business ethic that values quality craftmanship and the restoration of old, or the transformation of the time-worn, into something new.

'I wanted the space to feel like an extension of home, a private sanctuary where I could create, but where our kids could hang out and run free with the dog after school,' says Amanda. With a workroom, relaxed living spaces, two bedrooms, a bathroom and a simple kitchen, the cottage-turned-studio spirals up to a magnificent rooftop terrace, with views of the 14th-century Sant Joan Baptista church, where you can listen to the sound of joyful bells. Surrounded by natural beauty and a rustic array

INSPIRED DESIGN This rustic 17th-century fisherman's cottage has been transformed into an engaging studio space. The scalloped sunshade and hanging panels are from Pickett's House.

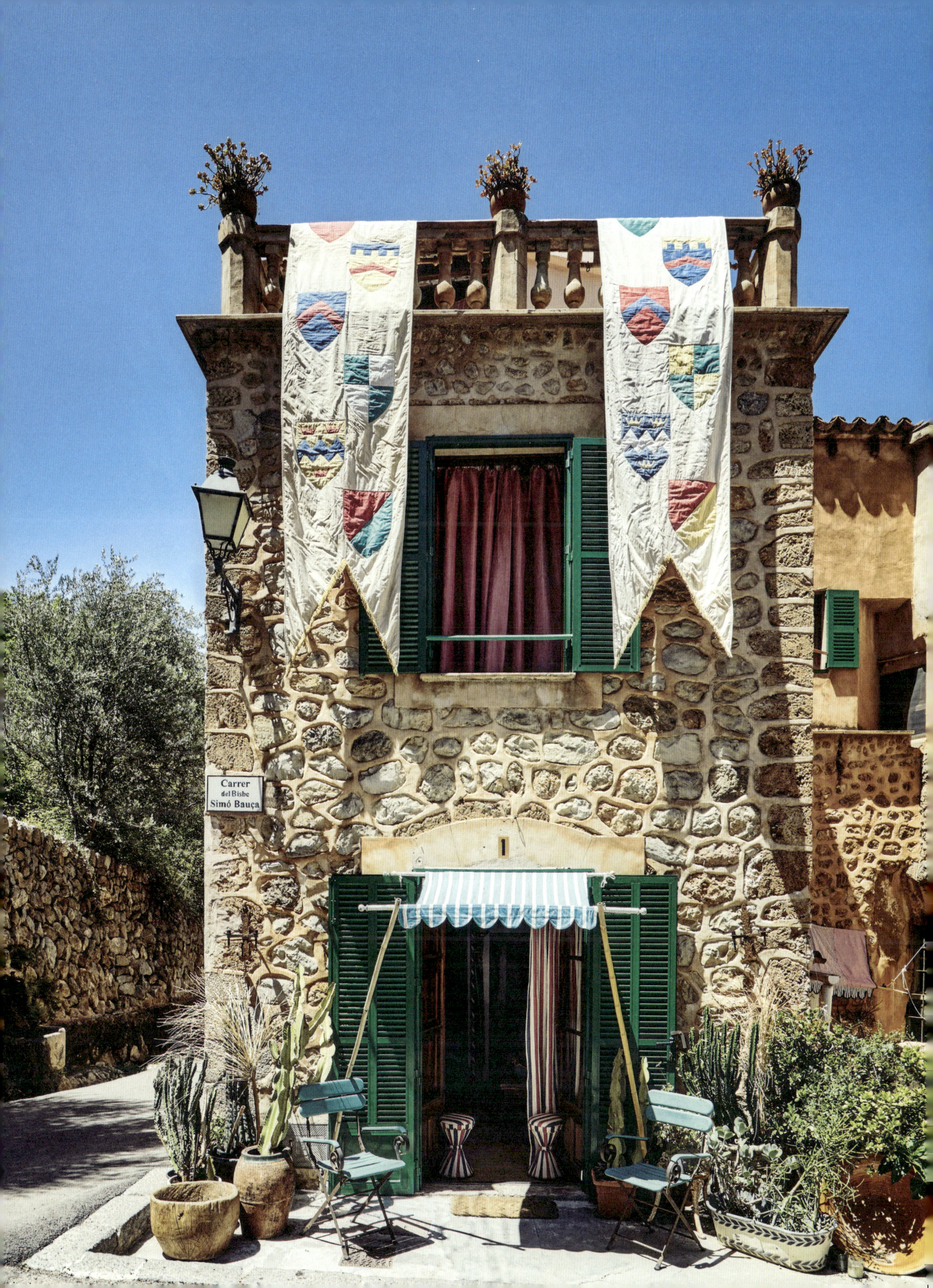
Carrer
del Bisbe
Simó Bauça

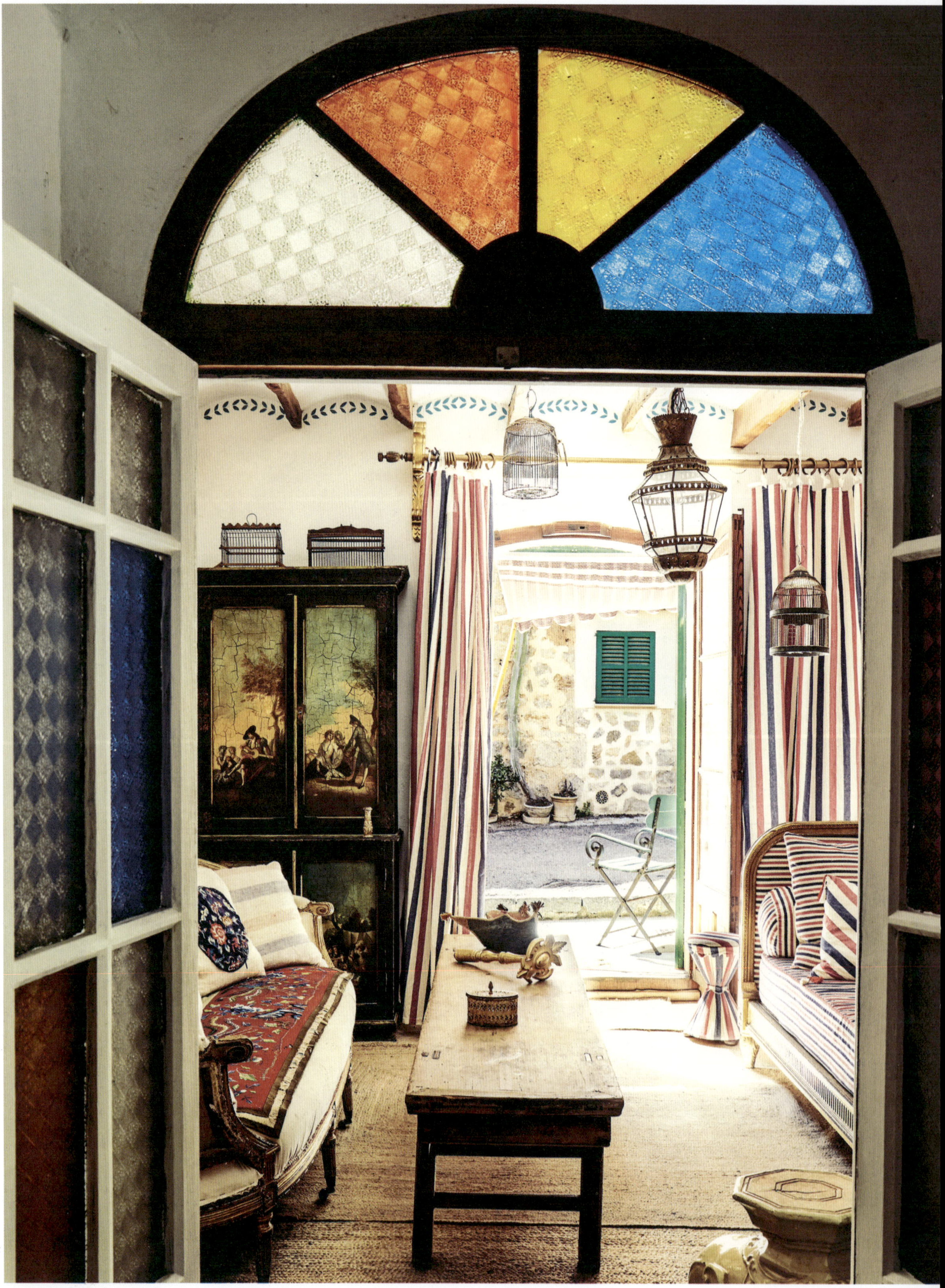

of 'Sóller-style, green-shuttered' properties, the turreted roof – adorned with Amanda's colourful, hand-stitched banners – adds to the quirky appeal. Encouraging her to do what she does best – make magic.

The restorative interior has become an incubator for design ideas, layered alongside an ever-changing collection of antiques. 'My father was a professional restorer who specialized in fine English, Georgian and Regency furniture – I have always gravitated toward pieces for both their beauty and backstory.'

Simple whitewashed walls, original dark wooden beams and an abundance of natural rugs form a restful backdrop to a profusion of colour and pattern. 'Stripes and scallops are my favourite motifs and appear a lot in my projects,' enthuses Amanda. And throughout the house they can be found embellishing fireplace edges, curtains and cushions.

A bold red, blue and white stripe, from Pickett's House's own fabric collection, adorns a 17th-century giltwood day bed – a seat where dreams have been played out for centuries and where conversations and music are shared daily. 'My designs are inspired by fragments of vintage fabrics collected over many years – everything comes with provenance.'

In the main living room, an 18th-century, hand-painted Dutch armoire is offset by new stained-glass-effect windows, created by Amanda – using jewel-like shades to brighten up dull, frosted panes. 'When the sun streams in, they bring the house to life,' she smiles. And similarly, naïve wall murals – including garlands, birds, animals and flowers – add an eccentric and colourful charm throughout the cottage. They were painted by Amanda and the twins, who share her creative DNA.

Many local treasures, like the ruby-red fabric in the front bedroom – used previously for outdoor fiestas and transformed into a fun, tented bed canopy – have found their way in and add to the idiosyncrasy.

'The cottage is our haven – it encourages us all to imagine. Life should always feel like an adventure – we have found that here.' ✧

RAINBOW EFFECT Amanda has added welcoming cheer to the cottage, painting frosted glass panes with vibrant colours. The antique day bed is covered in a Pickett's House ticking stripe that is woven locally.

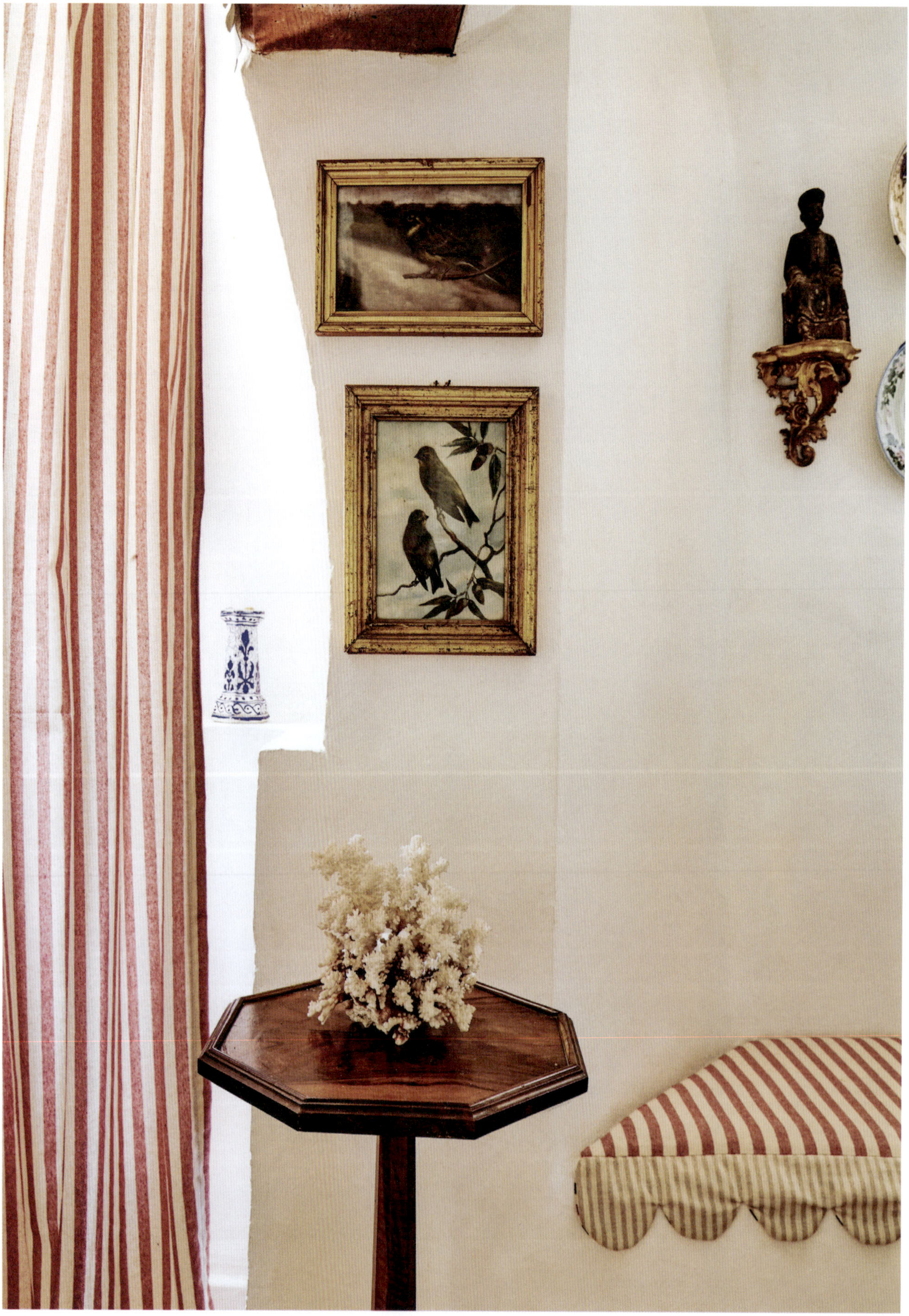

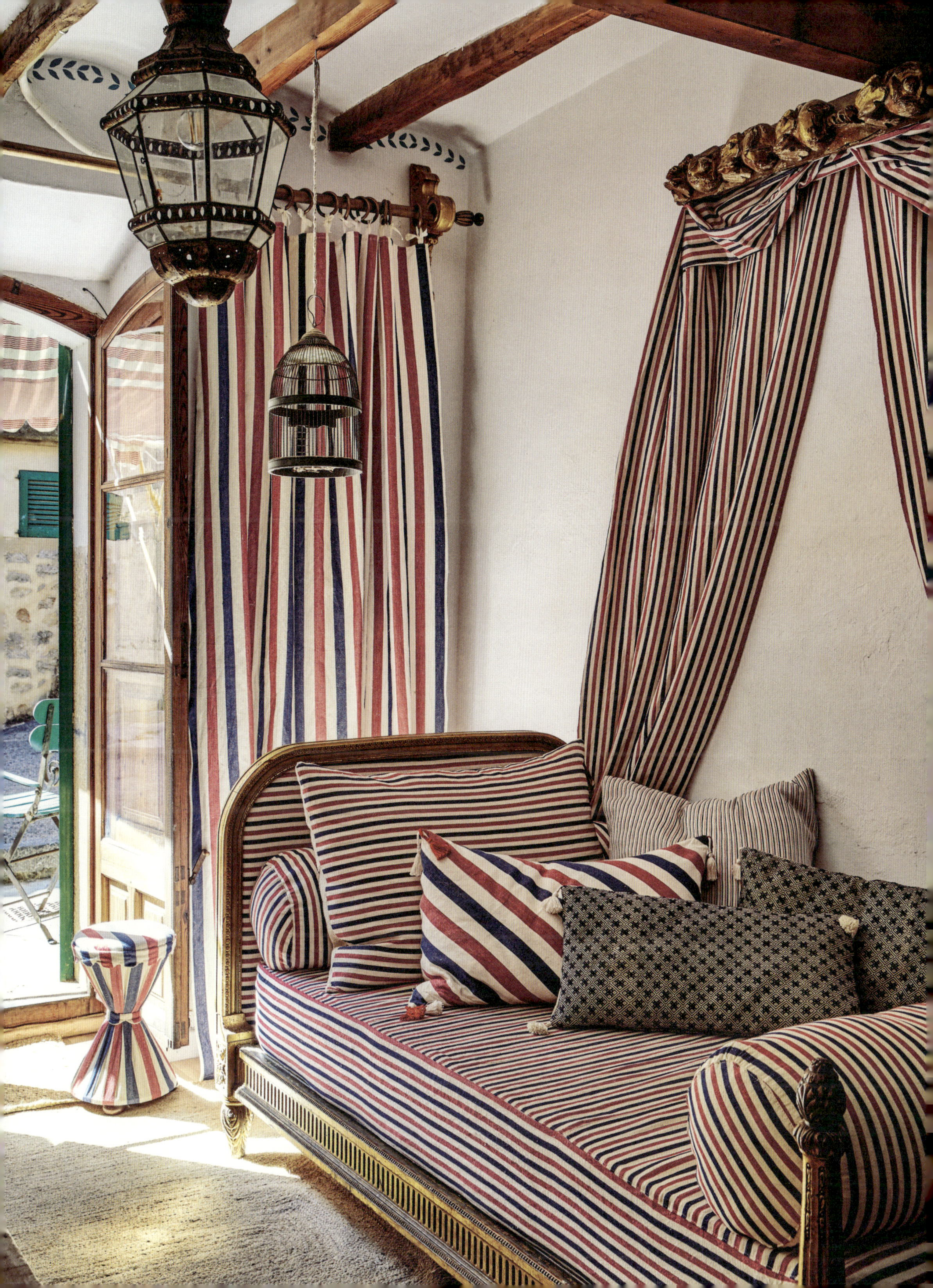

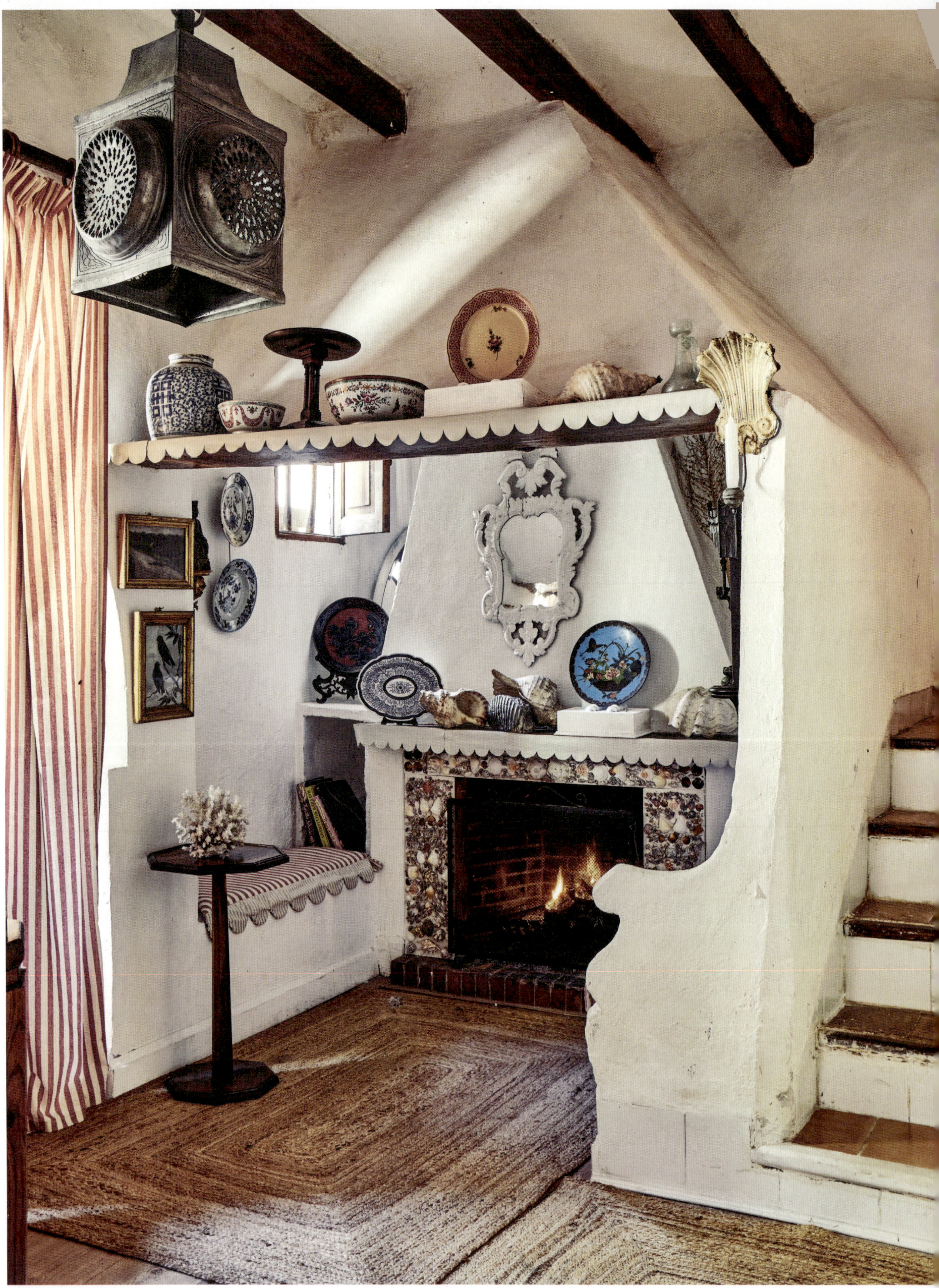

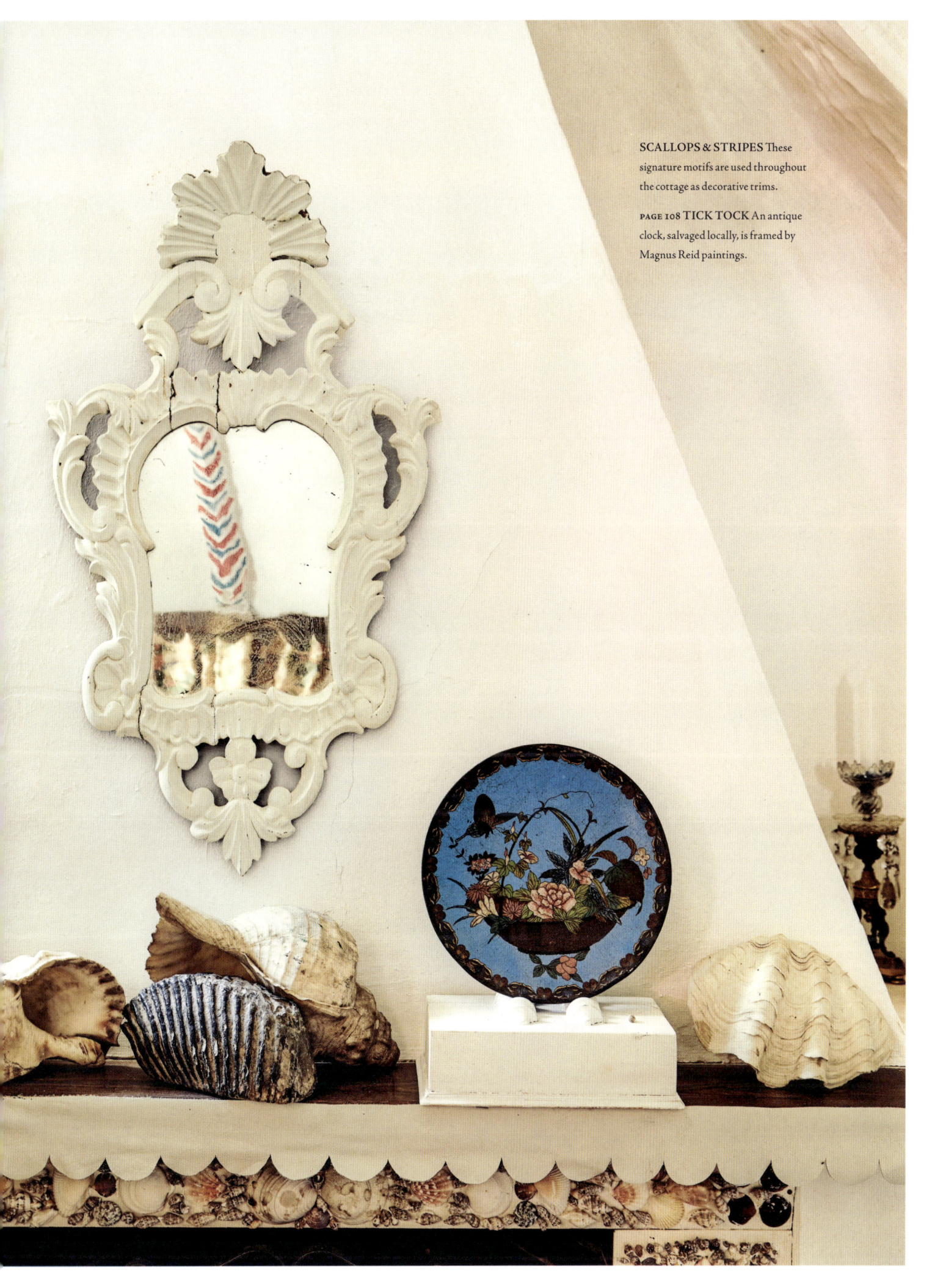

SCALLOPS & STRIPES These signature motifs are used throughout the cottage as decorative trims.

PAGE 108 TICK TOCK An antique clock, salvaged locally, is framed by Magnus Reid paintings.

108 LIVING

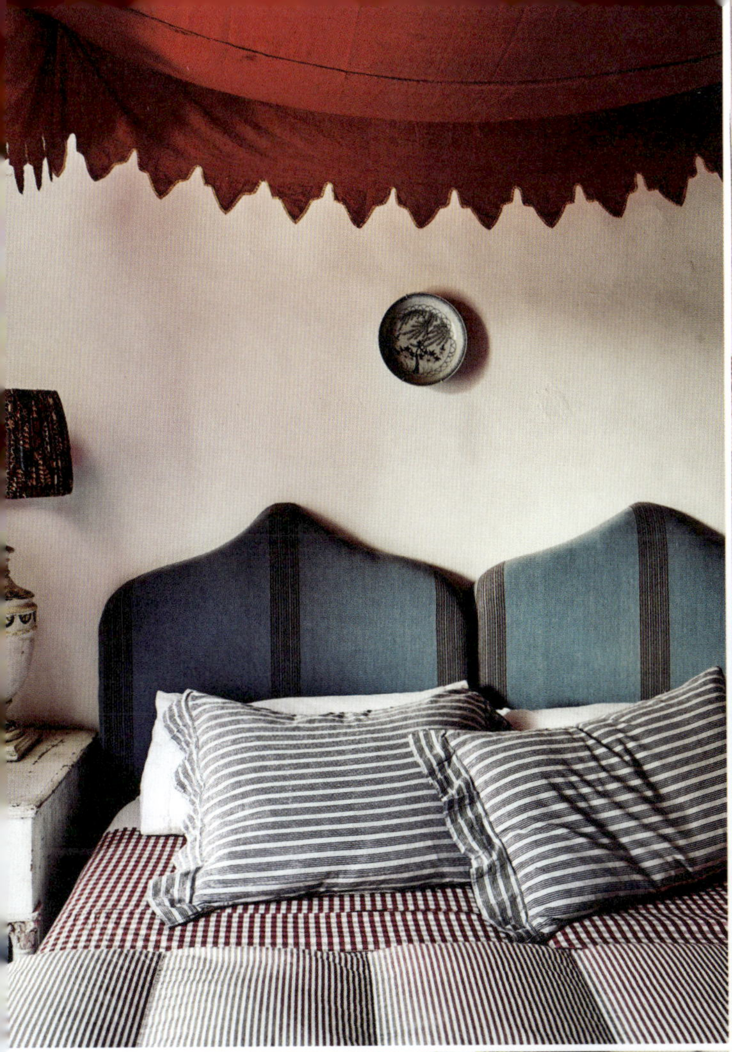
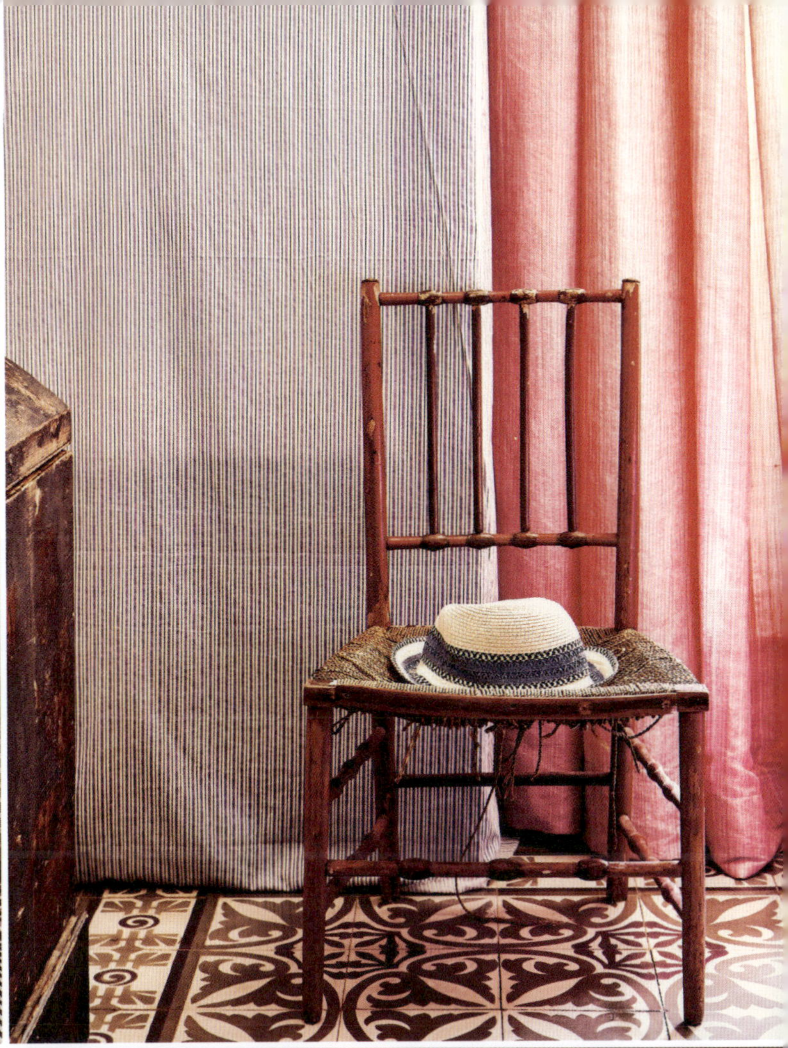
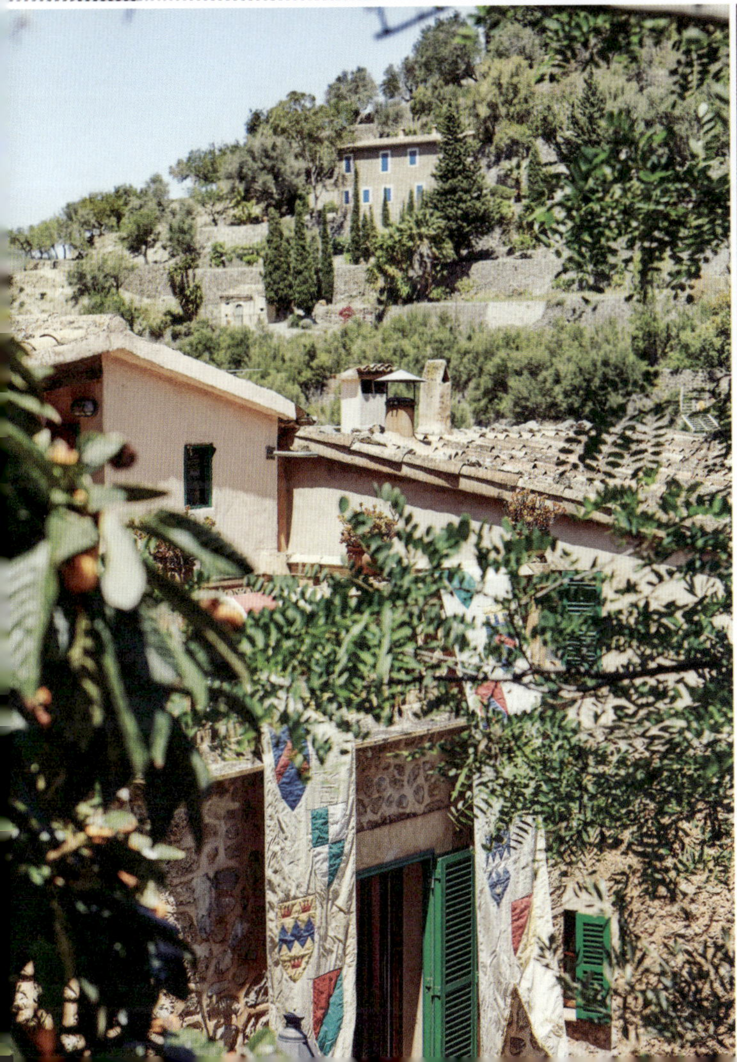
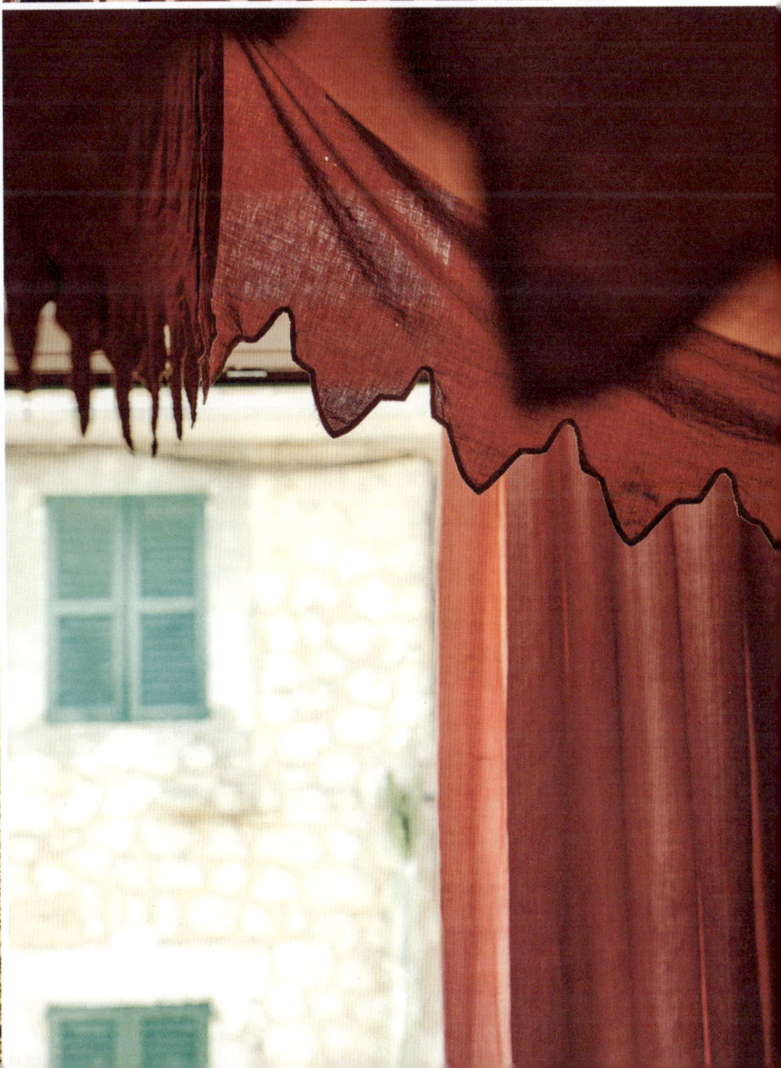

SWEET DREAMS A quiet top-floor nook is adorned with hand-painted murals. Outside, frilled gingham sun recliners provide the perfect retreat.

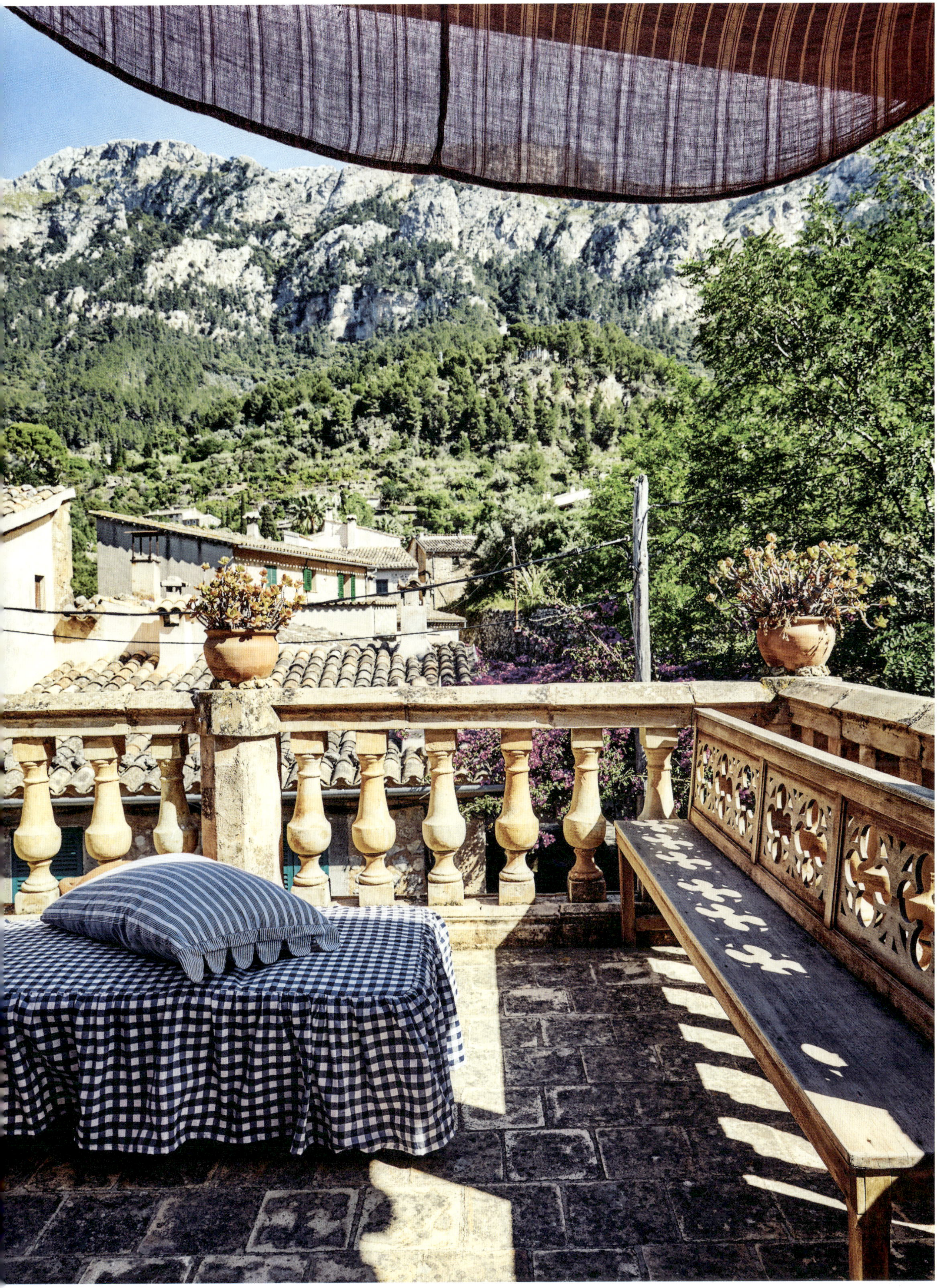

HOLISTIC RETREAT
Louisa Grey / Interior Designer

WITH THE REALIZATION THAT HAPPINESS, HEALTH, DESIGN ETHICS AND THE WAY we live and work all go hand in hand, Louisa Grey, founder of eponymous design studio, House of Grey, made bold life changes six years ago. Ending a relationship and selling her former house and studio, she eliminated stress and facilitated a desire to bring all facets of her life together at home. 'I wanted to balance quality family time with the ability to run my business from a holistic, open-house studio,' says Louisa.

Realigning her life and the idea of home as a place of daily sensory retreat, the move to this Victorian townhouse in London, with her 11-year-old son Huxley, shifted the paradigm that sanctuary spaces are somewhere we need to escape to. 'This is symbiotic of the way I live and design – if your home supports you, it will be somewhere you never want to leave. I describe it as Circular Salutogenic Design, a concept which nurtures personal and family well-being alongside healthy, ethical design decisions that prioritize the use of non-toxic and natural materials, which come from and can be returned to the earth,' says Louisa.

Having trained in weaving at the Chelsea School of Art, Louisa established a career as a successful interior stylist before founding her own design studio back in 2013 – after becoming disillusioned with the industry's waste and the throwaway media narrative, which perpetuated issues. 'The connection between my life experiences and home/work choices is inextricably linked,' explains Louisa. 'Having struggled to conceive, I followed a natural IVF path of lower hormones and acupuncture, which drew me towards more holistic health practices.

'I am hugely grateful to have given birth to Huxley, after my early perimenopause at the age of 36, and felt a growing need to be more informed about the impact of design on both the environment and our lives – which shaped the early foundations of House of Grey. I wanted to break new ground and design with passion and integrity. Combining quiet, understated luxury alongside conscious, healing choices,' continues Louisa.

Initially, Louisa pitched the idea of holistic design to various hospitality brands, but when no one saw the opportunity for positive change commercially, she decided to back herself and use her home to showcase how we can design and develop sustainably, while future-proofing the property. Working with a group of pioneering specialists who share her vision, across everything from wall finishes to the choice

INTUITIVE CALM The front reception room was designed by Louisa as a space to practise yoga, meditate and enjoy gong baths. Palus rug in 'Chalk' from the House of Grey x Armadillo & Co. Ellipse collection.

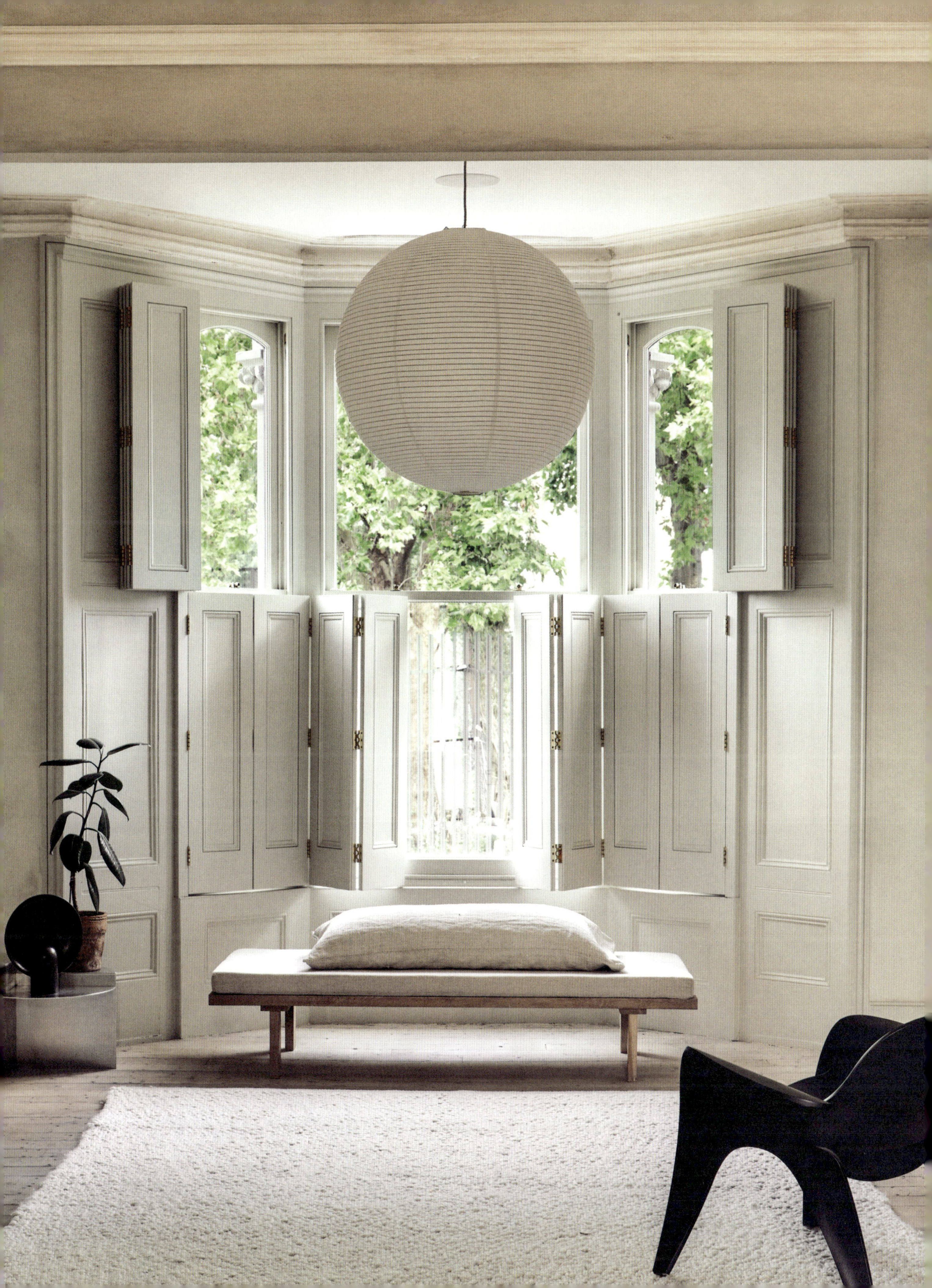

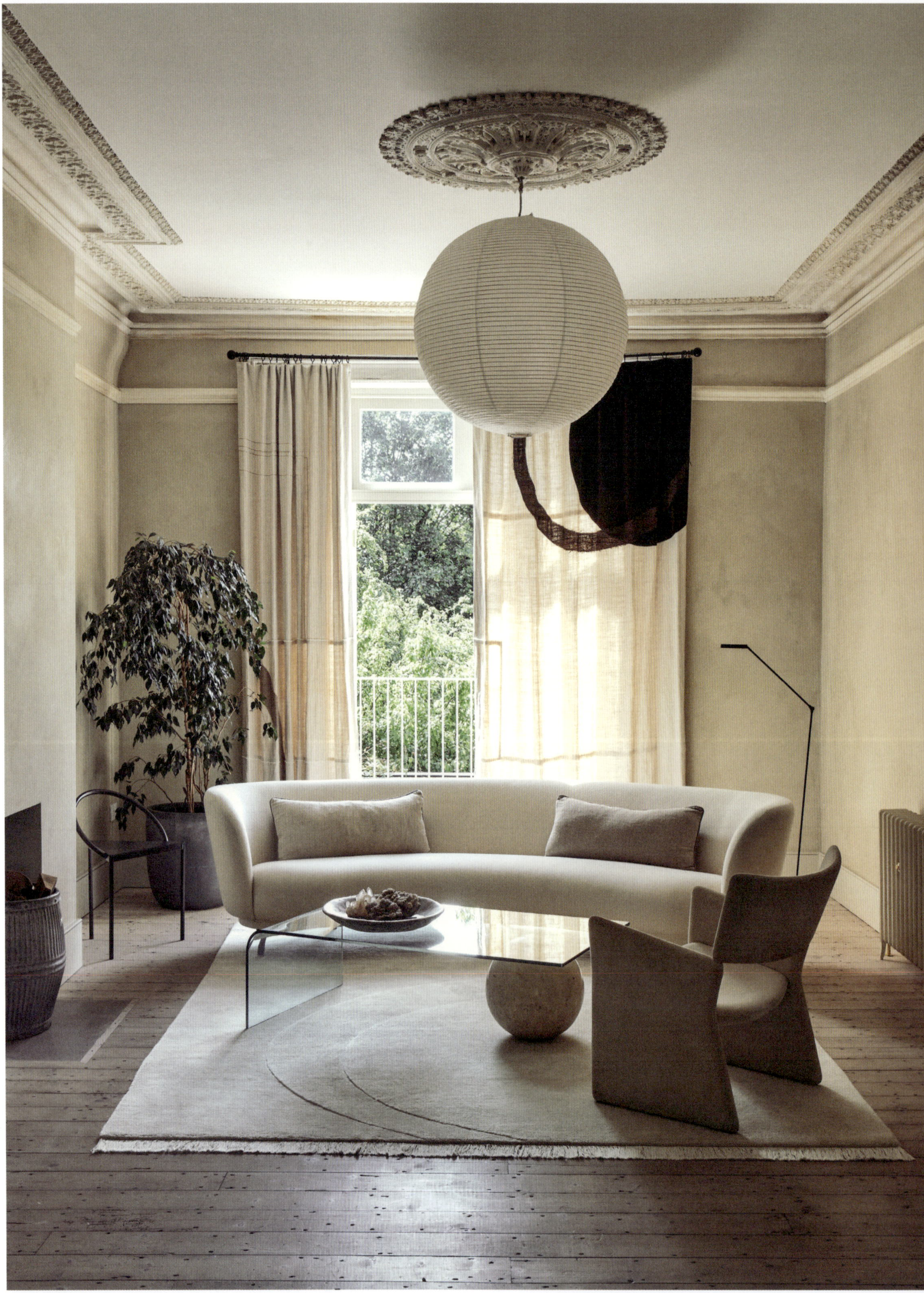

of furniture and appliances, Louisa has extensively researched every material and product used within her home. 'Choosing only toxin-free and natural, it has been great to work with the materials and experience them first hand,' she explains.

Previously divided into seven bedsits, the house was run-down, but after years of neglect all the original features remained. With a separate entrance for the studio, plenty of family space and a south-facing garden – with pear, cherry, apple and fig trees – the now restful atmosphere feels more Southern Italy than North London. Nurturing the bones and thermal efficiency of the house, the walls have been insulated in double-layer sheep's wool from Cumbrian company, Thermafleece; the roof retiled in British quarried slate; windows replaced with double-glazed timber frames; plastic pipes changed to copper for their antimicrobial qualities; and original floorboards patched with reclaimed finds from a former Harley Street site.

On the lower-ground floor, a new, light-filled kitchen and dining extension was created, with a wild green roof, that opens out to the garden. It is adjacent to a cozy snug that connects to the House of Grey studio. With exposed timber joists and gently curved, natural clay-plastered walls by Clayworks – that regulate humidity, purify the air and prevent damp – the cocooning aesthetic is a nod to the Puglian architecture appreciated by Louisa and a reminder of memorable travel experiences.

On the ground floor, elegant double reception rooms retain their traditional Victorian character, with original mouldings painstakingly restored and lofty walls painted in chalky, VOC-free limewash paints – collaborations with Bauwerk Colour and Graphenstone. Furniture choices are intentionally minimal, reflecting Louisa's desire for longevity and less, and always a mix of antique with new. Upstairs, luxurious, naturally filled, custom-made Vi-Spring beds and hand-trowelled limestone bathtubs and showers heighten the feeling of sanctuary and calm. Textural, handmade layers add to the sense of comfort and innovation – natural wool rugs created with ethical Australian company, Armadillo, and a bespoke 'Luna' collection of hand-thrown ceramics made by Romilly Graham for House of Grey.

'This has been a very personal journey, piecing together all elements of my life in a desire to connect health and happiness. So having a space that allows you to self-regulate and live in harmony with the sensory environments we create, and our wider planet, really does change our daily and long-term contentment.' ✧

ORGANIC SHAPES A Dandy sofa from Massproductions, a spherical HAY pendant light and a vintage coffee table from Anna Unwin add to the cocooning feel. Curtains designed by House of Grey and Nest Design.

116 LIVING

SPACE & SANCTUARY Dandy ottoman upholstered in Kvadrat Harald 3 fabric (opposite). Spade chair by Faye Toogood and Umbra wall hanging in Myrrh, by House of Grey x Armadillo Ellipse Collection (top left). Stairs by an antique mirror lead to the first floor (top right). Stairs to lower-ground floor (bottom left) and the family snug, adjacent to the lower-ground floor kitchen and office (bottom right).

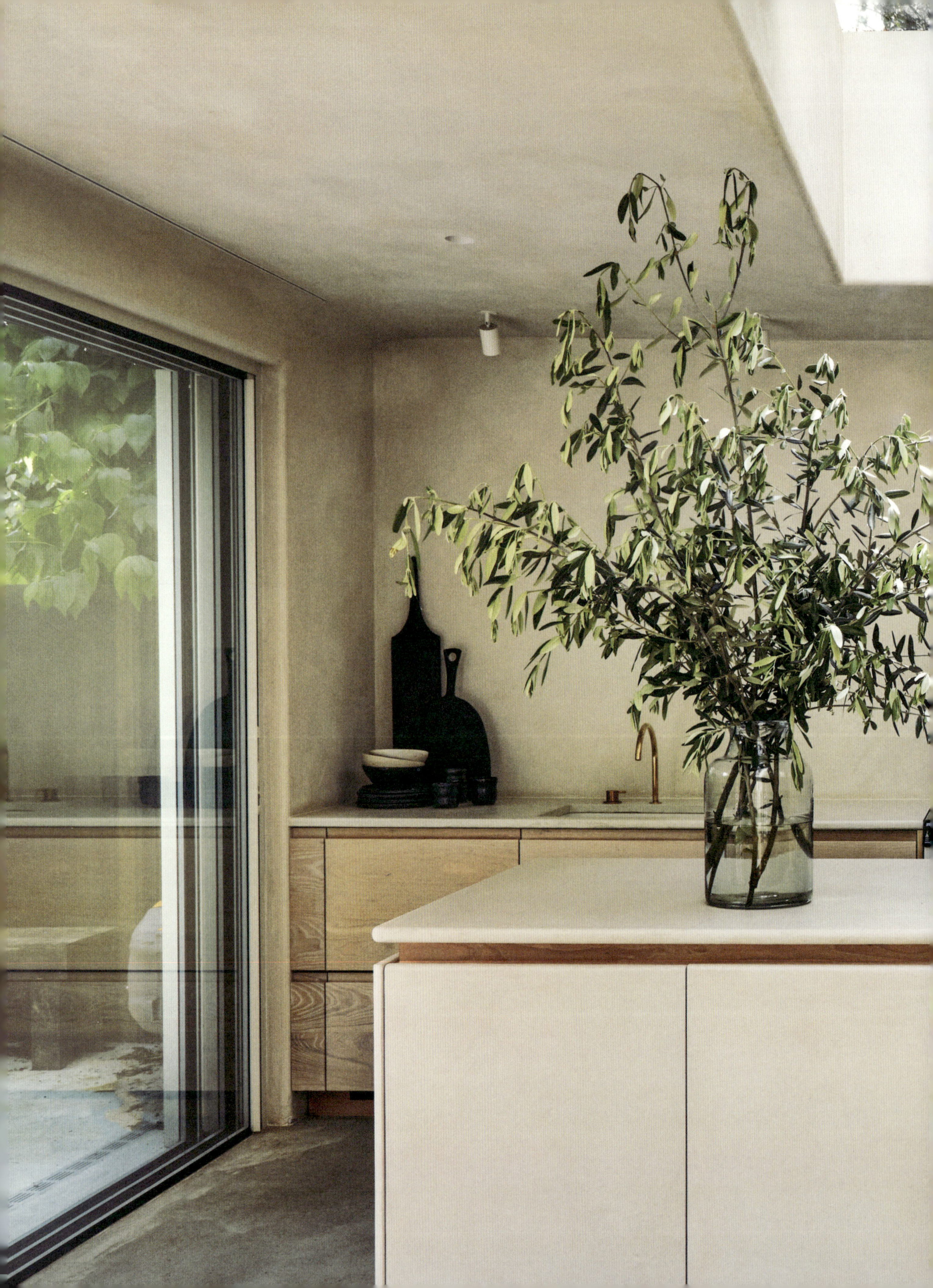

LESS IS MORE The kitchen was designed by House of Grey and produced by Finch Home Ltd. Set on wheels, the kitchen island can move, providing additional flexibility. Tapware by Vola, black oak cutting boards by Edward Collinson and painting by Christine Grey.

BEHIND THE SCENES Built-in kitchen cabinets, with integrated handles, were designed by Louisa in collaboration with Finch Home Ltd. Vintage table made by Louisa's architect-builder father. Pendant light by Chalk Path Studio. Bowls made by Louisa.

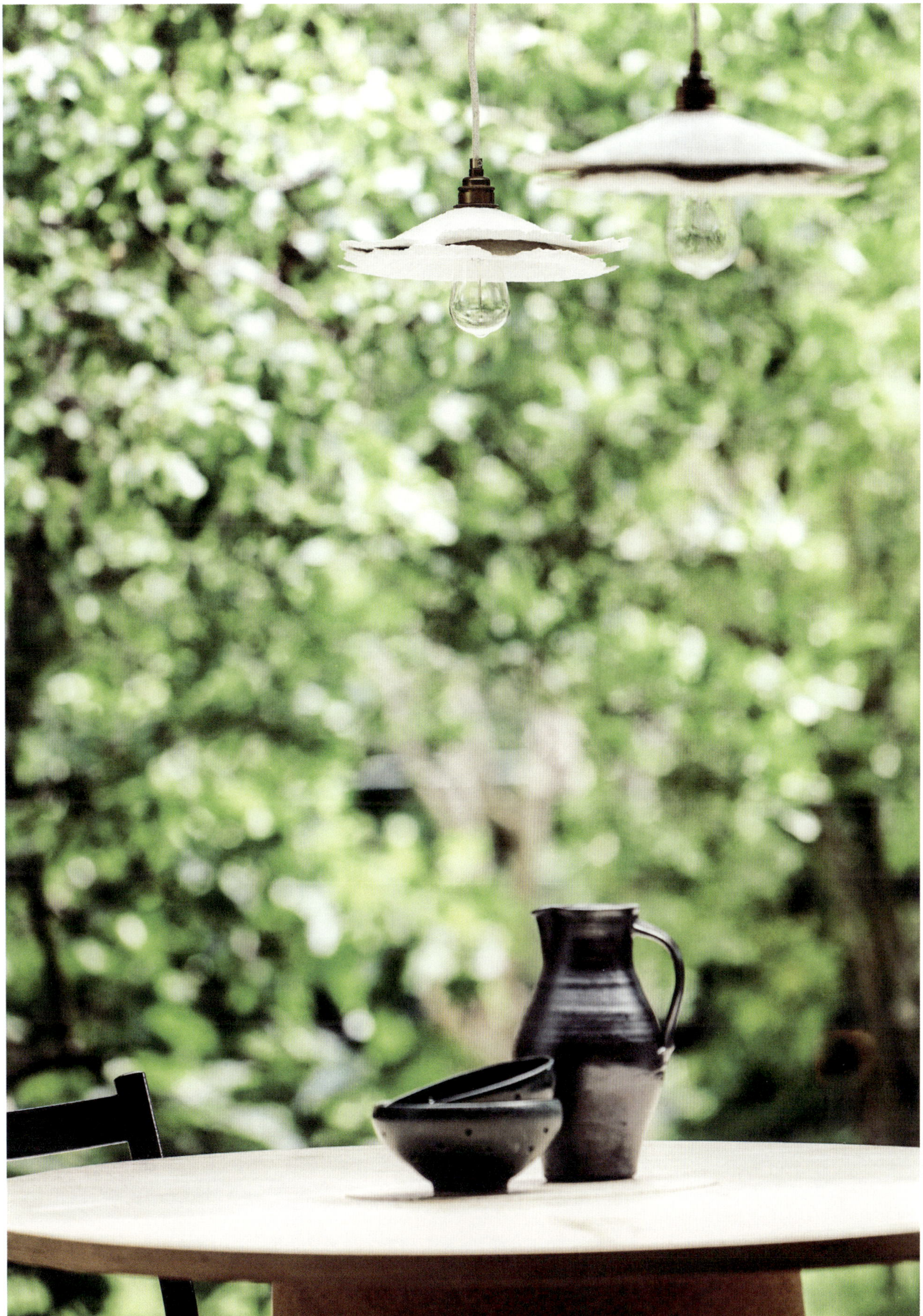

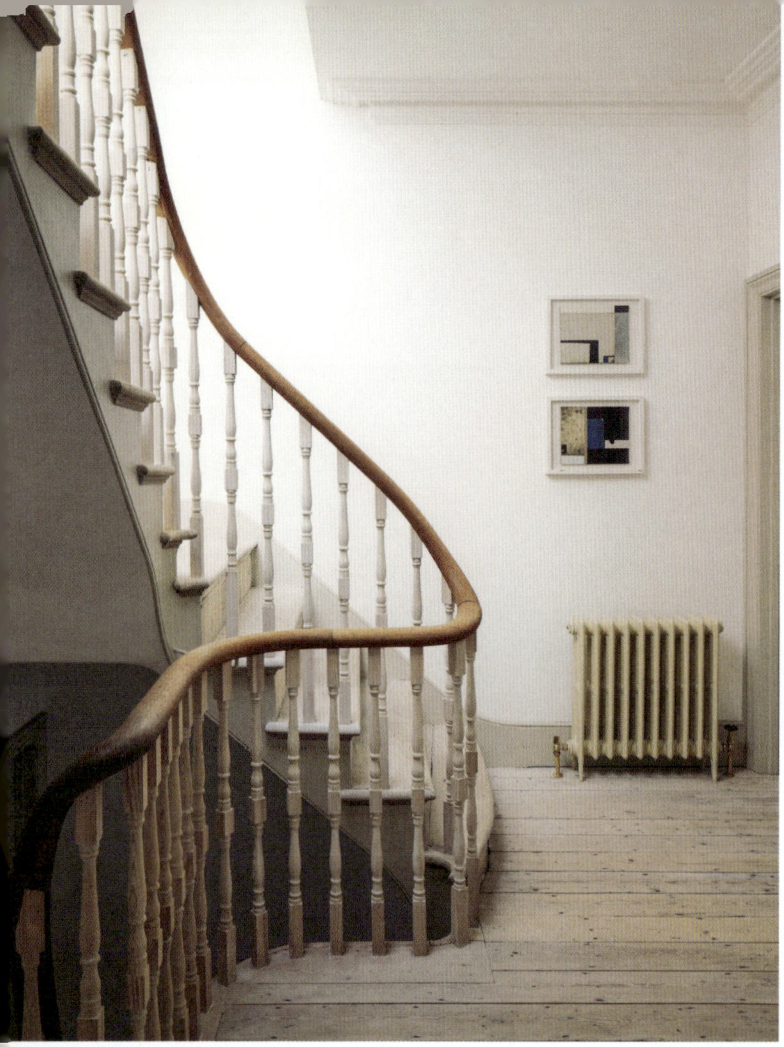
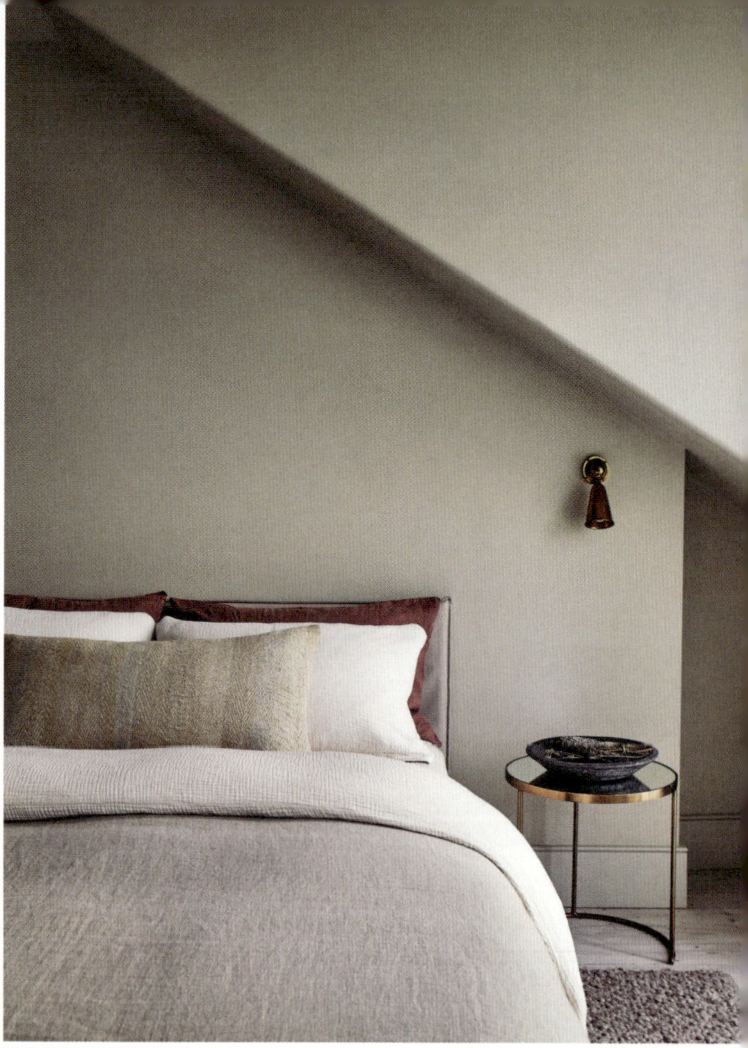
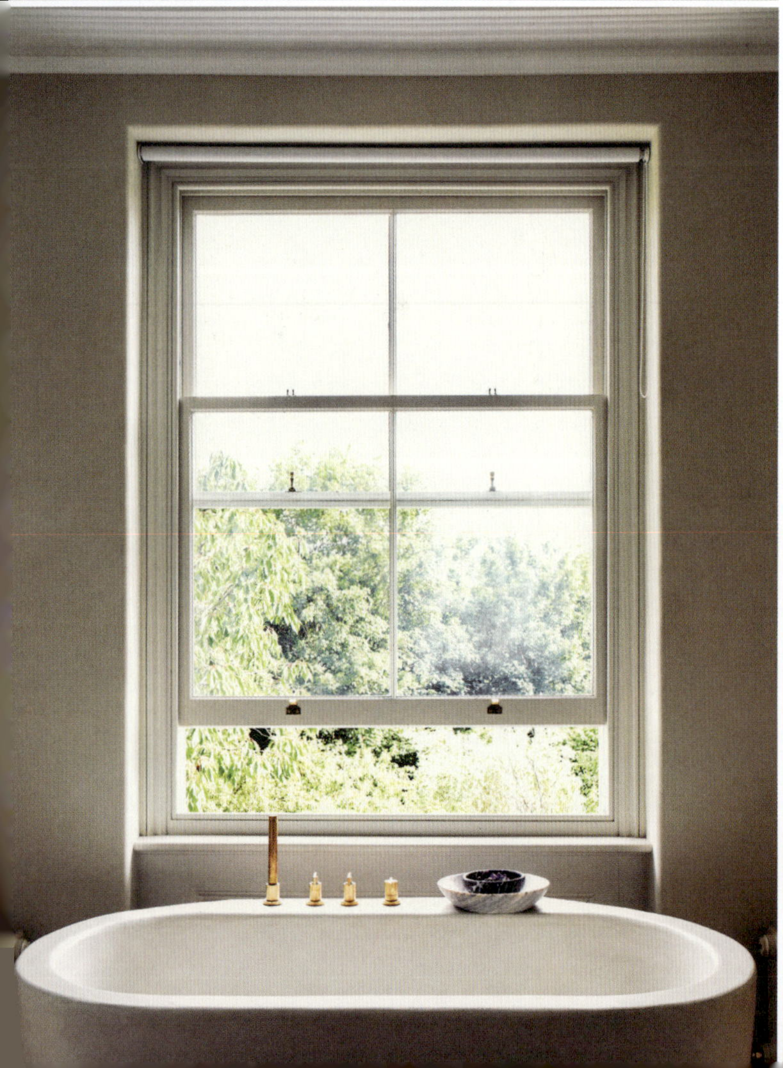
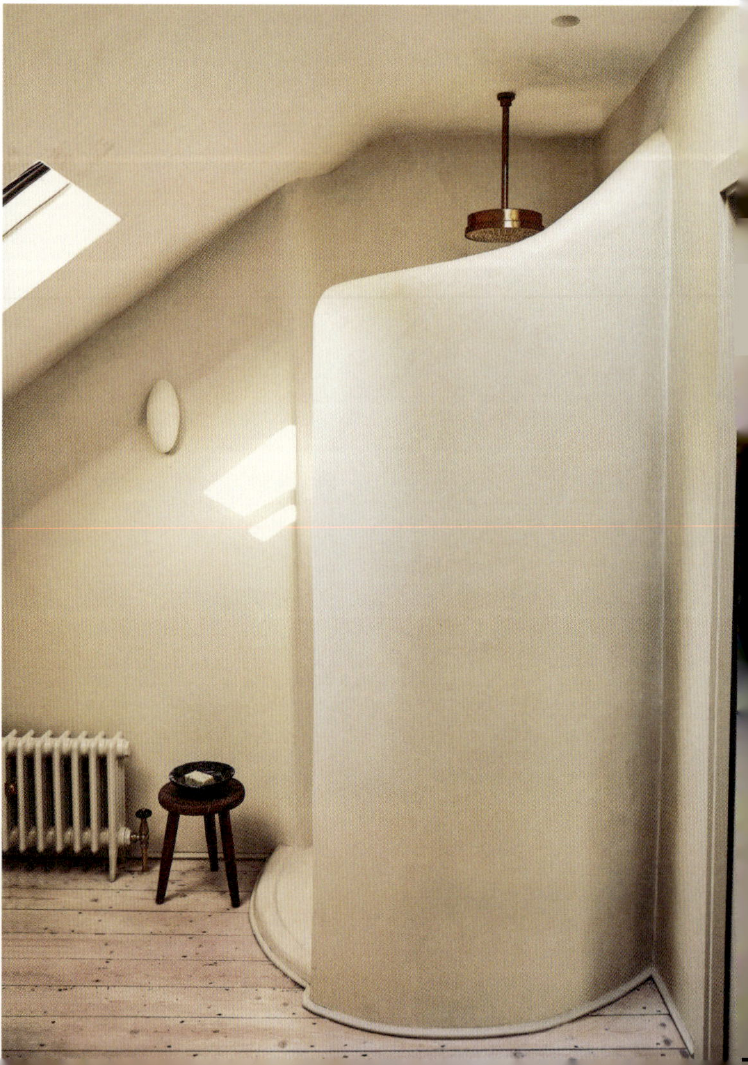

NATURAL VIEWS From the restful master bedroom (this page) glazed double doors open onto an en-suite bathroom that overlooks the garden (opposite, bottom left). Bathtub designed by House of Grey and finished in a specialist mineral material. The curved shower in the second-floor shower room was cleverly moulded in situ by Louisa and her builder (opposite, bottom right).

INNER SANCTUM
Katrina Phillips / Shopkeeper & Interior Designer

STEPPING OVER THE THRESHOLD AT THE BACK OF KATRINA PHILLIPS' LIFESTYLE shop on London's famous Portobello Road, you pass through heavy wooden doors into her creative haven – a former retail space and studio, transformed into an ethereal home, with a sensory mise-en-scène charm.

At the start of the pandemic, Katrina moved into the shop to reduce overheads and save the business. She now splits her time between London, Ibiza and Jamaica, working as a creative thinker for the Marbella Club, the Teranka Hotel and GoldenEye. Resisting any need to clamour for fame, Katrina's perspicacious mind and intuitive eye are held in high regard within the industry and also with private individuals – some of the best in film, fashion, music and theatre. Under the radar, her loyal, self-effacing charm – a mix of realist-and-dreamer, creative-and-academic – is a rare breed.

Artistic, inviting and peaceful, Katrina's London home balances the extraordinary alongside the functional. Cocooning nooks, complete with a roll-top bathtub, four-poster bamboo bed, traditional Aga and bespoke handmade sofa, add to the aesthetic and comfort. Reclaimed shelves are laden with collected ephemera, rare natural objects, family heirlooms, art, books, current projects and life's daily essentials.

With calming marble floors, bare whitewashed brick walls and layers of natural textures, the space invites quiet contemplation and silence after busy shop days, where rich conversation is part of the draw for customers. 'It feels very meditative here. Sometimes I enjoy the company of friends, or my partner Ben, but when he is away, I am happy living in rebellious isolation with a deck chair by Tracey Emin for company' – Katrina's self-confessed, inanimate soulmate, much like Tom Hank's Wilson in the film *Castaway*.

To understand Katrina's style, it's important to return to her roots. 'Back in the 1970s, conformity was not something I knew, growing up around the Portobello Road. My father was an actor turned self-made antiques dealer – the first to strip pine and source architectural antiques. Buying John Hardman's stained-glass and metalwork studio, he restored spectacular buildings around the world. In 1963, he leased this shop as an antiques store, and when he died, 20 years ago, my late mother encouraged me to take it on. With the business run into the ground without him and the estate under threat, sadly now gone, she wanted the spirit to remain,' says Katrina.

A CUT ABOVE Marble floors laid by Katrina's father using a patchwork of salvaged finds. In the shop, antiques, art, natural objects, fashion, the handmade and the intrinsically soulful are thoughtfully sourced, or created in collaboration with talented artisanal makers.

✱ PRIVATE BEYOND HERE ✱
RESIDENCIA

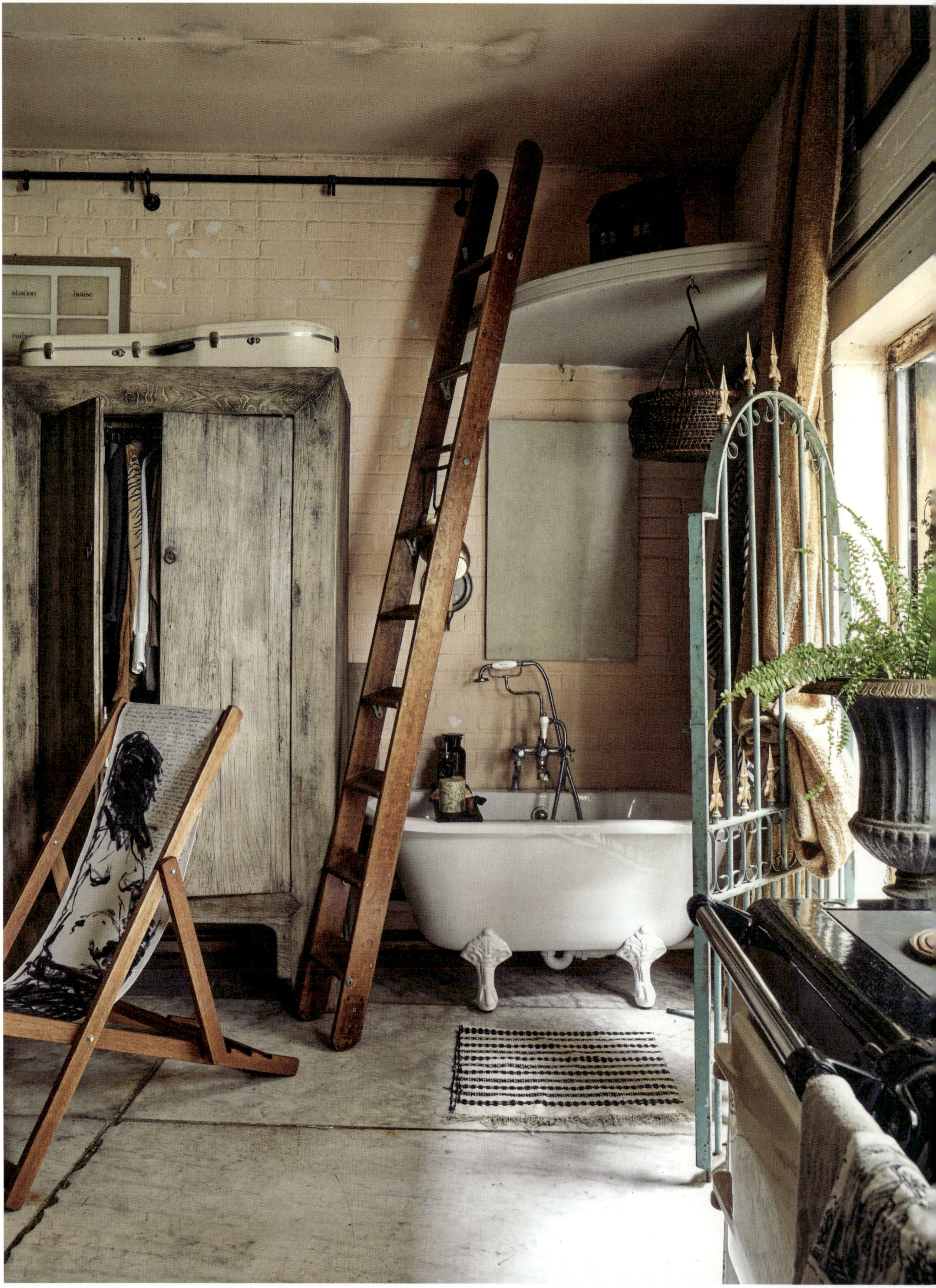
station
house

'One of six siblings, we grew up surrounded by other people's flotsam and jetsam, but on a theatrical scale – from enormous marble angels to pulpits and altars, never knowing what would appear next. It was like a magic act: pull back the curtain and anything was possible – the full contents of an old sweet shop, a garden full of ex-display reindeer from Selfridges, or at times no furniture at all,' explains Katrina.

'Mum's focus was to encourage our education and a separation from the mundane. Nurturing the art of conversation and an appreciation of words – we consumed books about adventurers and gardeners, wrote avidly and made time to draw.' Annual vacations were spent with maternal Scottish grandparents in Argyll – close to nature, enjoying proper picnics with cousins, pulling in boats with her grandfather (a fisherman), playing on the beach, helping family cook, make and mend, and collecting all manner of moss, lichen and rocks. 'We were taught to honour nature and the handmade, and endless stories were shared around the fire.'

After leaving school, Katrina lived on a Kibbutz farming avocados. 'It felt liberating experiencing more rustic homes, intuitively using old farm equipment as decorative art.' Similarly, reading Classics and English at Brown University, in Rhode Island, in the 1980s, America opened her eyes to another way of living and a new visual culture: whitewashed loft spaces without a hint of chintz, where conceptual African sculptures and shields cohabited beautifully alongside a Picasso or Andy Warhol painting.

Returning to England, with her first baby, Katrina set up a jewellery business and worked as a costume designer and journalist before completing a Masters in Playwriting at the University of Birmingham, sponsored partly by Tom Stoppard and Fay Weldon. Pitched as the next big female writer, under literary agent ICM, she was diagnosed with narcolepsy and shifted direction out of necessity, turning a part-time role with fashion brand Ghost into head merchandiser for 12 years, working alongside founder Tanya Sarne, before taking on the shop and building her own lifestyle store.

Katrina's sanctuary is an edit of her non-conformist life. A journey of finding self-acceptance, dedication through adversity, and a passionate love of creativity – in harmony with nature and rich with integrity. Her father's motto 'fortune follows the brave' feels indicative of her own path – one that will no doubt continue to weave compelling stories for years to come. ✧

STAGE SET The back door leads out to a light-filled miniature yard that neighbours a church. Reached through a decorative metal gate, draped with a warm ochre, deadstock Chanel fabric, this conjures a sense of going offstage.

128 LIVING

LIVE BEAUTIFULLY The kitchen table came from Katrina's family home – a reminder of characterful family life, lively political debate and fierce games of Scrabble.

PAGES 130–131 ONE MAN'S TREASURE A grass sculpture, inspired by Derek Jarman's Garden, from Jagged Art. The antique blue man by Johannes Hedegaard for Royal Copenhagen. A tall shelving system in the kitchen is layered with a lifetime of personal treasures and current projects.

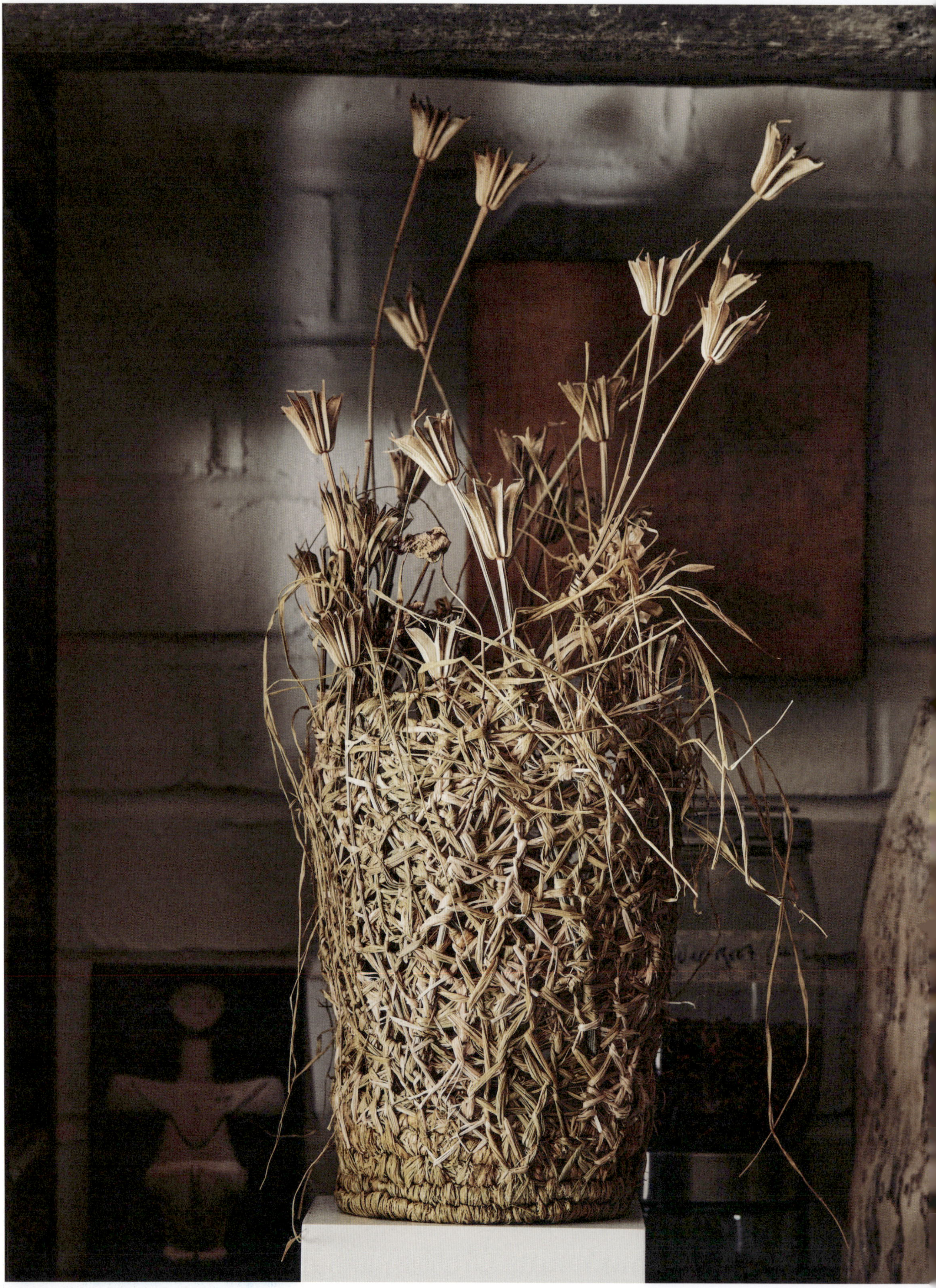

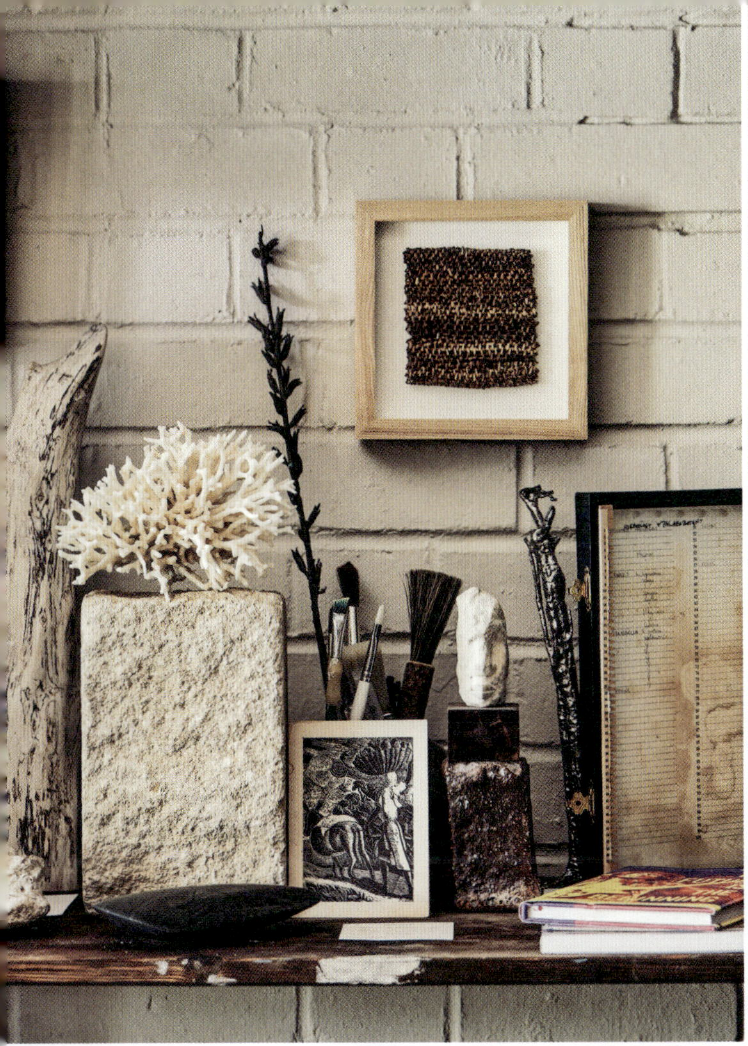
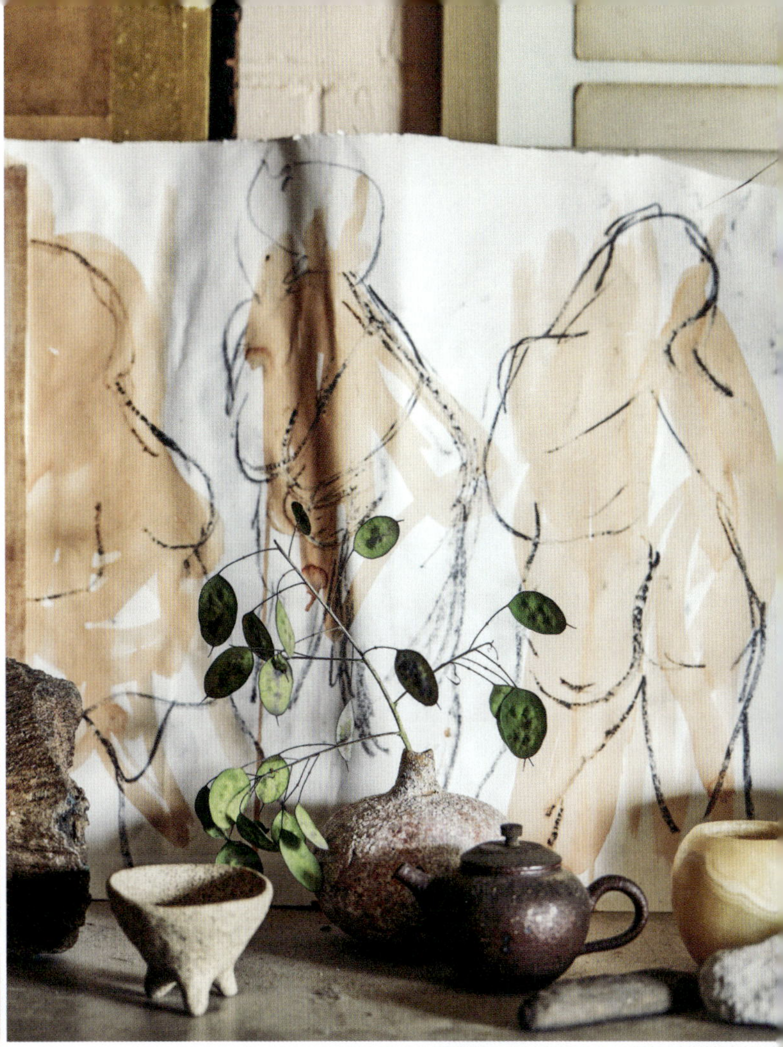
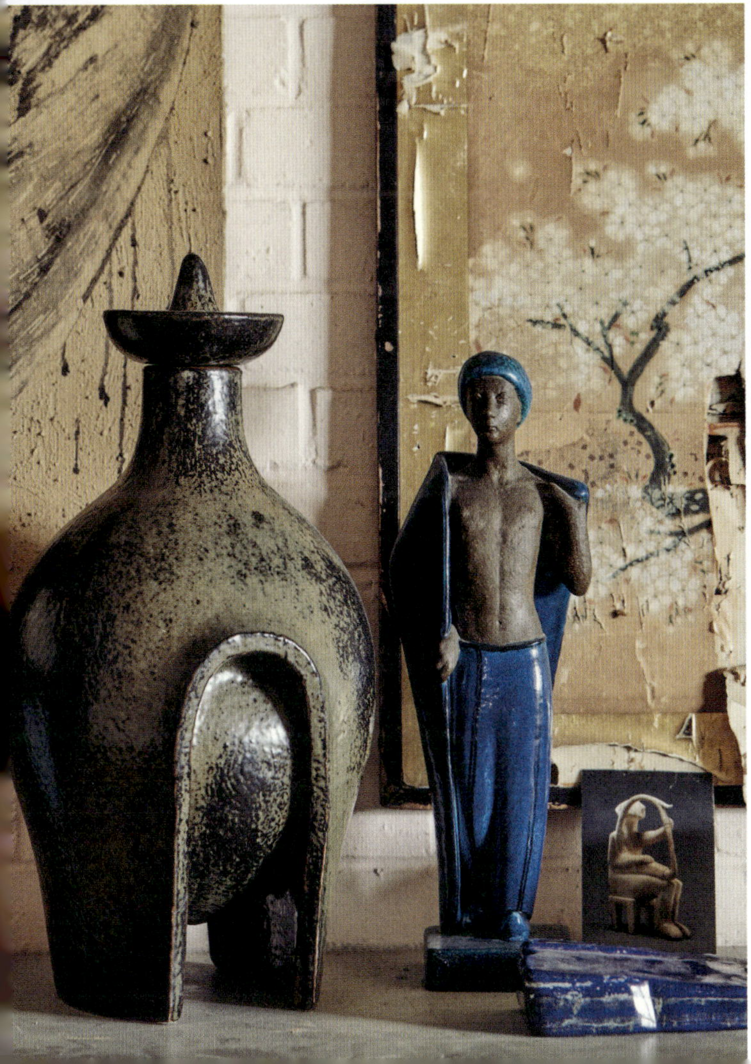
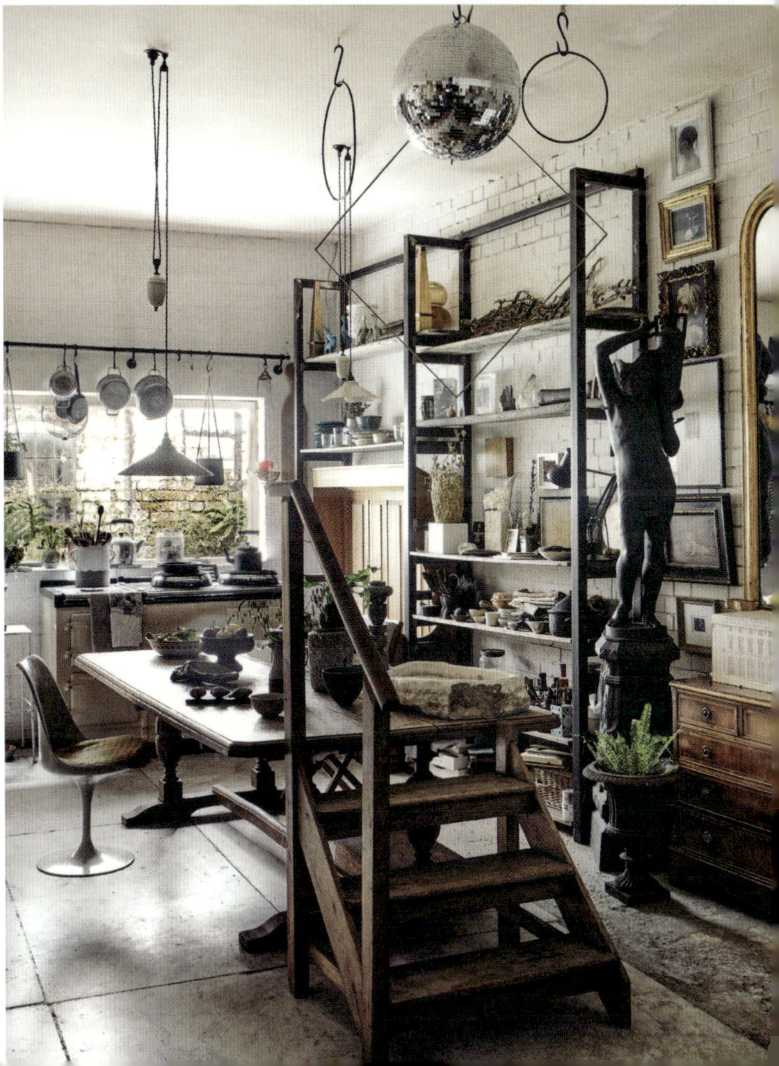

horse
garden
hay
flowers
cow
tree
lamb
oak
goose
fern
chicken
leaf
corn
station
house
railway
cottage
train
shed
ticket

WILD CARD Bespoke sofa designed by Katrina – frame by George Smith and the long cushion inspired by Christian Liagre. The Japanese screen is a reminder of Katrina's childhood, dressing up in kimonos gifted by Japanese clients. Framed 19th-century teaching cards, used with her own children, reflect a love of words. A glitter ball adds a touch of glamour.

BOTANICAL OASIS
Rob Mills / Architect

OVER THE PAST FIVE YEARS, I HAVE HAD THE PRIVILEGE TO GET TO KNOW Australian architect Rob Mills, founder of award-winning architectural practice RMA, based in Melbourne and Sydney, and to write about several of his personal homes and client projects. Hillside Residence, a recent RMA project, illustrates the power of collaborative client-architect relationships, and the brilliance that can happen when both parties come together as trusted experts.

The holy grail for Rob when designing homes comes from a place of perspective. Rob learned early in his architectural career to look down on the world from above and to see beyond everyday visual boundaries. Pushing his creative eye to reach into the unknown and to elevate connections between great land and dramatic architectural design. 'I am always searching for a heightened sensory experience and feeling of escape – where you can enjoy a view of the ocean or the sounds of the forest, or feel immersed in the wilderness. For me, that comes with the opportunity to create an exceptional living experience,' says Rob.

The owners of Hillside Residence purchased this prestigious plot, in Albury, New South Wales, and approached Rob to unlock the spectacular topography and design an intimate home for their family, embracing the expansive views of Albury's Botanical Gardens and the mountain ranges beyond. 'Founders of a large-scale construction business, the family came energized with a powerful desire to defy the possibilities of construction, along with the technical prowess to execute our bold ideas with precision', explains Rob.

The two-storey monolithic structure is anchored at the base into the sloping hillside, with retaining walls constructed from locally sourced stone. The upper level cantilevers out into the surrounding forest, creating the illusion of a home floating within mature treetops. The extended roofline and expansive terrace open into the main living area, creating an indoor-outdoor fluidity and also helping to reduce the heat load from extensive glazing – optimizing shade and comfort during warmer months.

Stepping inside, you enter onto the top-floor level – home to a kitchen, study, dining area, master bedroom suite and laundry room. On the second tier of the property, a signature RMA helix staircase, influenced by a David Chipperfield design in London, connects further family and guest bedrooms, along with a prized wine cellar and central elevator.

TREE HOUSE The outdoor terrace of this luxurious Albury home is set among the treetops, with views out to the Botanical Gardens. Landscape design by Eckersley Garden Architecture.

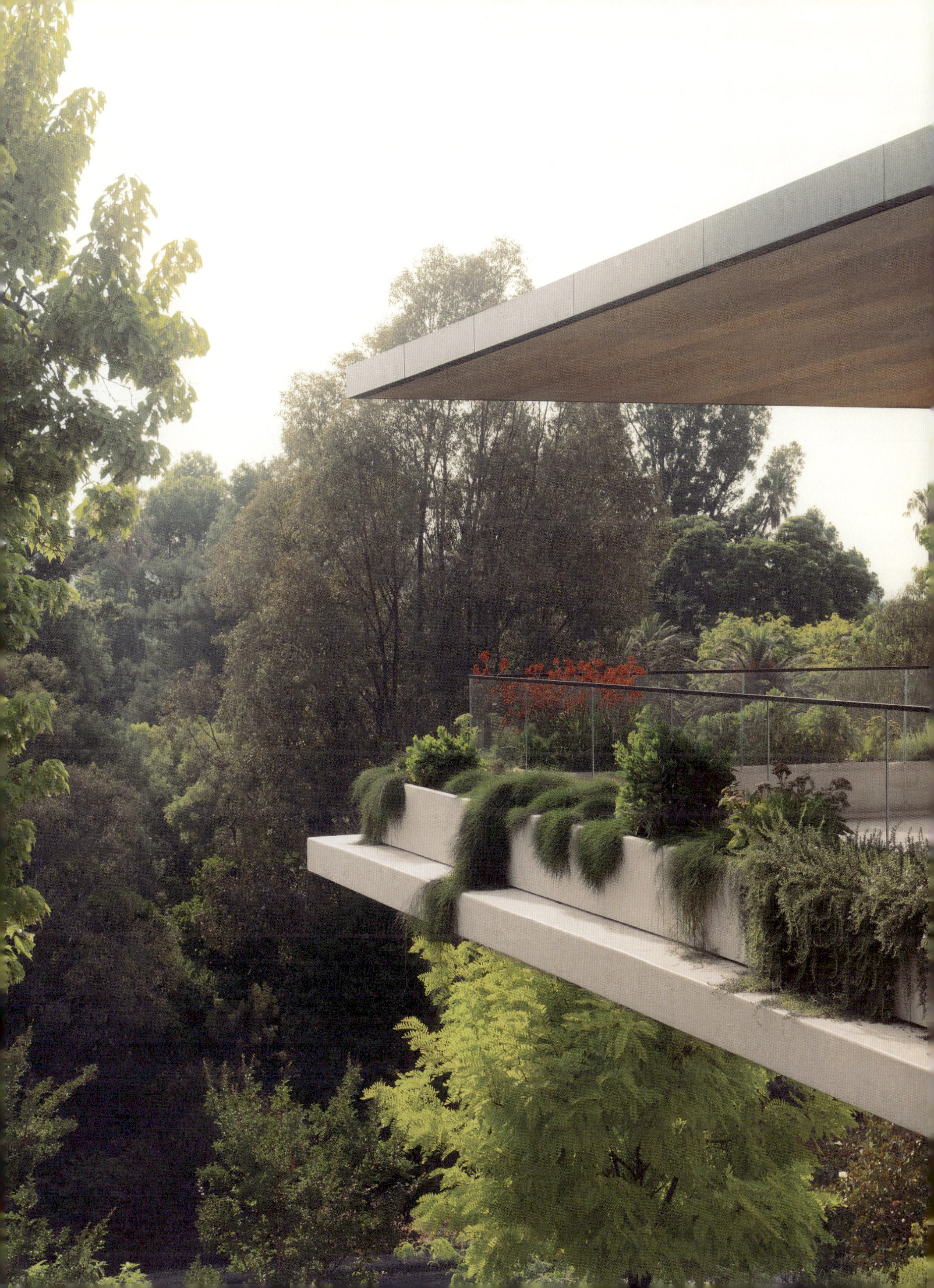

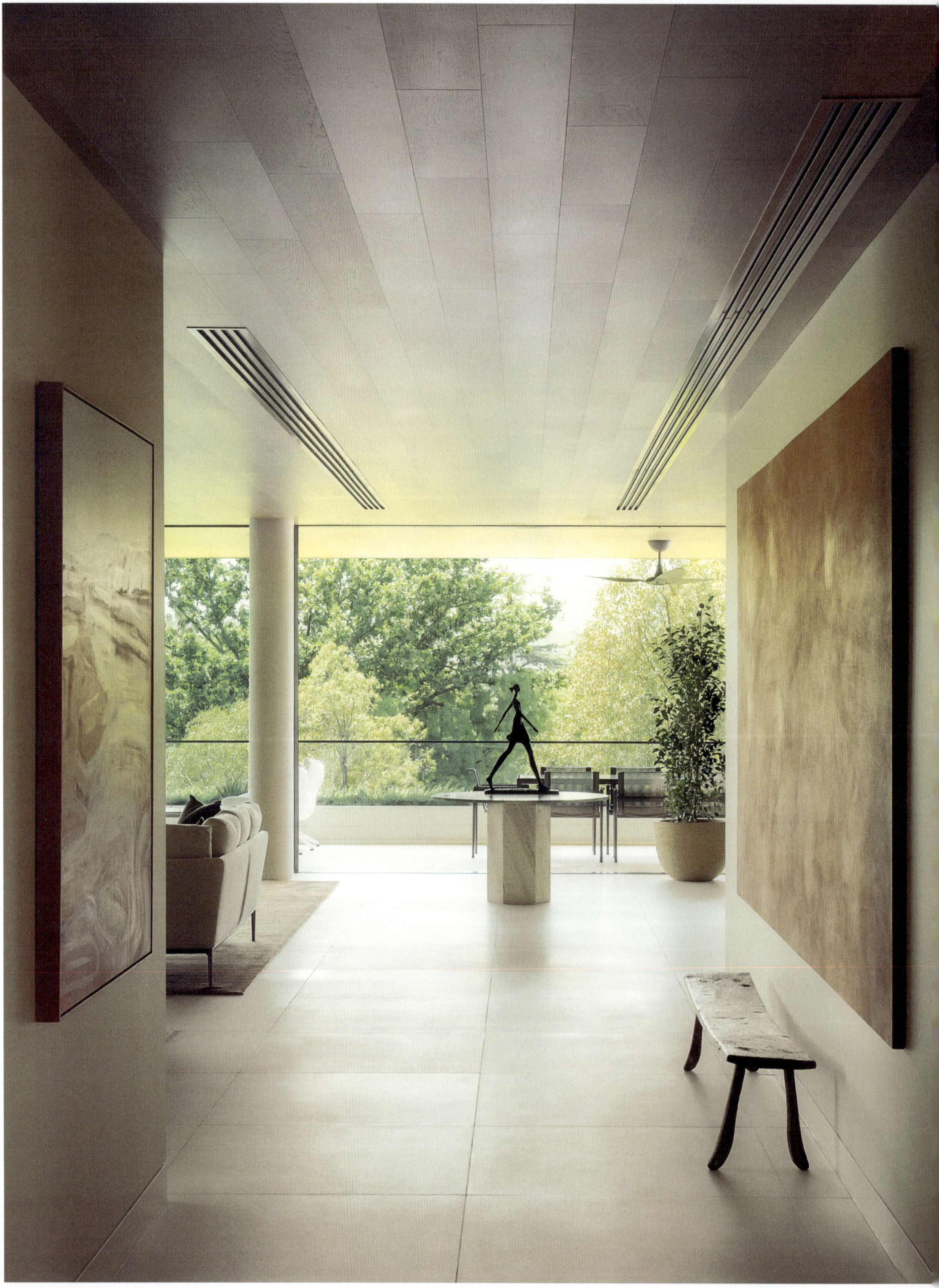

With the landscape as hero, a calming palette of natural materials was chosen to work harmoniously – timber-clad ceilings and cabinetry in American oak, natural limestone floors, quartzite kitchen surfaces, luxurious onyx bespoke bathrooms and undyed yak-wool carpets, that add a sense of comfort to retreat-style bedrooms.

The spatial layout is relaxed and flows seamlessly from the interior to the exterior, softening boundaries and connecting spaces. The linear kitchen – both functional and aesthetically beautiful – has a refined, quiet elegance, while the central study, cocooned within a glazed metal cube, sits proudly at the heart of the home. Designed as a space for peace and focus, it is positioned to connect with the interior and the ever-changing vista.

The owners chose to build furniture and decorative choices from scratch to suit the structure, and throughout, Louy Bell, head of interiors at RMA, has worked closely with them to create an intuitive interior that speaks to their confident, yet humble, sense of self. With space for the family to live, play and just 'be' – and without any need for the more ostentatious or showy. Bold pieces, such as the oversized Antonio Citterio sofa, for B&B Italia, invite togetherness, while a particularly well-placed corner chair by Patricia Urquiola offers a cocooning nook for quiet contemplation and to take in the view.

Earthy decorative finishes are inspired by the landscape and the family's extensive travels around Australia – think rich terracotta rugs, soft furnishings and paintings in burnt orange and warm ochre, buttery leather upholstery, natural linen lampshades, and decorative glass and marble vases from Michaël Verheyden. Abundant curved finishes gently soften strong architectural lines, across lighting choices, organic oak bowl displays and curvaceous, plant-filled terracotta pots that mirror the lush botanical gardens.

In 2024, this multi-award-winning project was awarded best residential interior in the Architecture MasterPrize – an award celebrating the best in international architecture. 'Human relationships and our connection to nature are as paramount as the buildings we create,' says Rob. 'This has been a truly collaborative meeting of minds, capturing the spirit of the owners. Surrounded by such beauty, there is a wonderful sense of nurture and sanctuary. A private world, in a place they love.' ✧

MEETING OF MINDS Project architect Ornella Altobelli's skill, experience and attention to detail cradled the design, while Louy Bell worked closely with the owners to build a collection of Australian and Indigenous art. The *Language of the Earth Coolamon* (2021) sculpture by Sarrita King sets the tone as you enter.

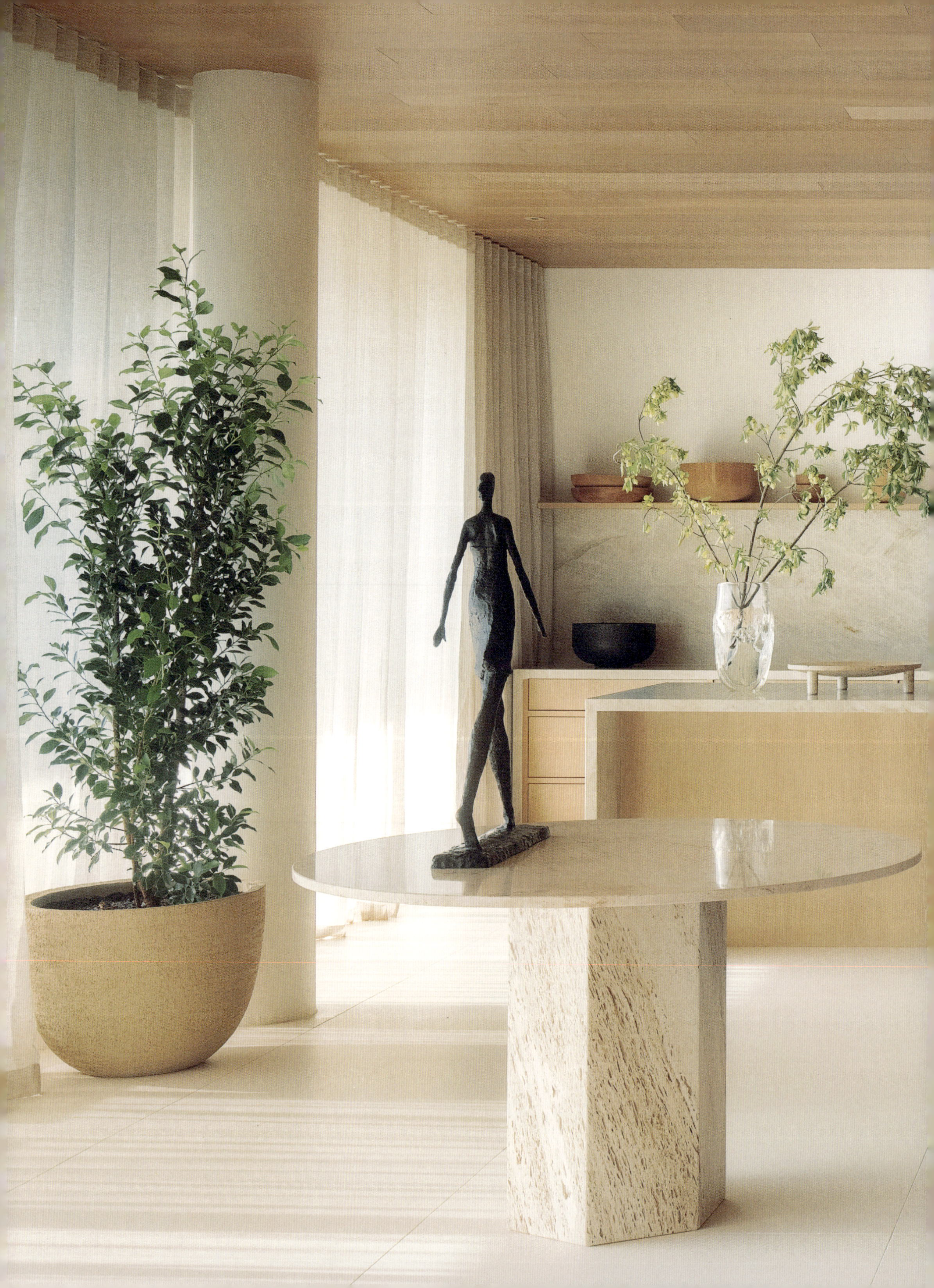

SIMPLICITY & STYLE The bespoke kitchen is central to family life, with an Epic dining table by GamFratesi for GUBI and comfortable Colette kitchen stools, sourced from Roberto Lazzeroni for Baxter from Space Furniture. Overhead Tubi pendant light from Articolo.

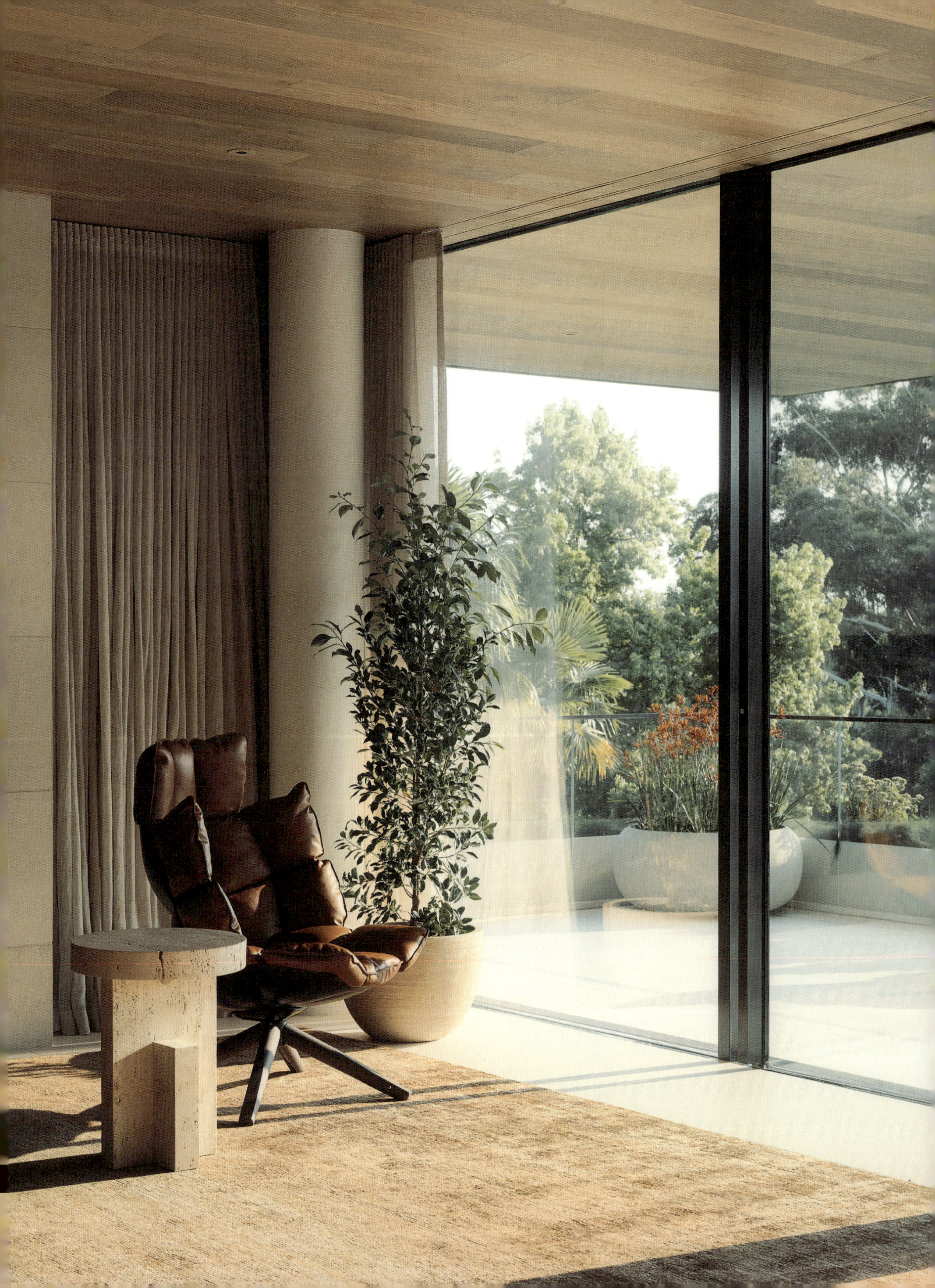

DESIGN CLASSICS An oversized sofa by Antonia Citterio for B&B Italia creates a cocooning spot for the family to enjoy time together. Twiggy floor lamp by Marc Sadler for Foscarini. Husk armchair from Patricia Urquiola for B&B Italia.

PAGES 142–143 **WORK & PLAY** The HETA table from Lowe Furniture and Caratos chairs by Antonio Citterio add richness to the dining area. In the study, a Baxter Bourgeois desk in leather and walnut.

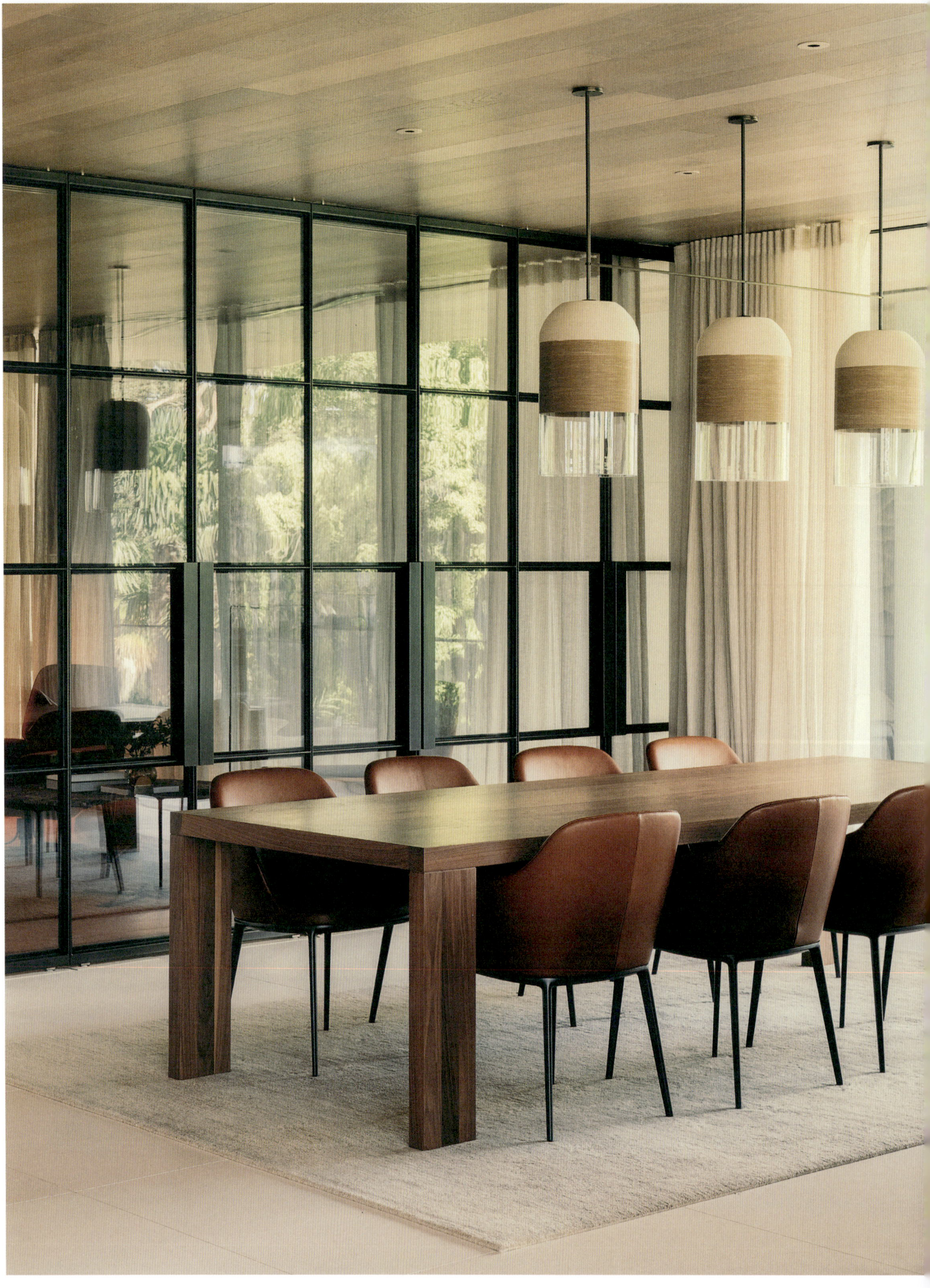

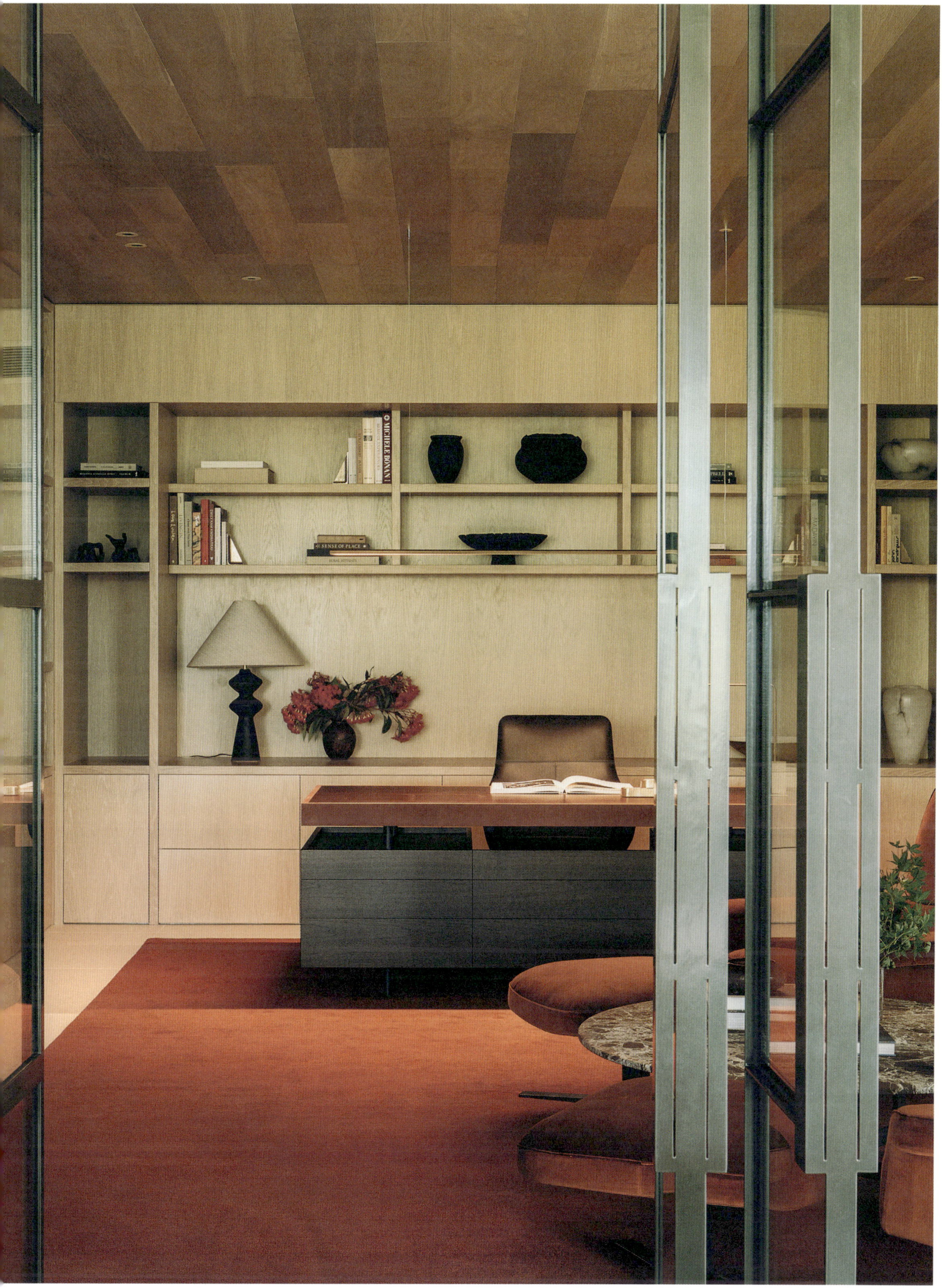
MICHELE BONANI
SENSE OF PLACE
RURAL RETREATS

GLASS HOUSES In the master bedroom, relaxing views heighten the feeling of calm and sanctuary. In the master en-suite, tactile onyx surfaces are layered with textural towels from Loom (opposite, top right), while in the walk-in closet a Calacatta Viola marble vase from Michaël Verheyden enhances the natural finish (opposite, bottom left).

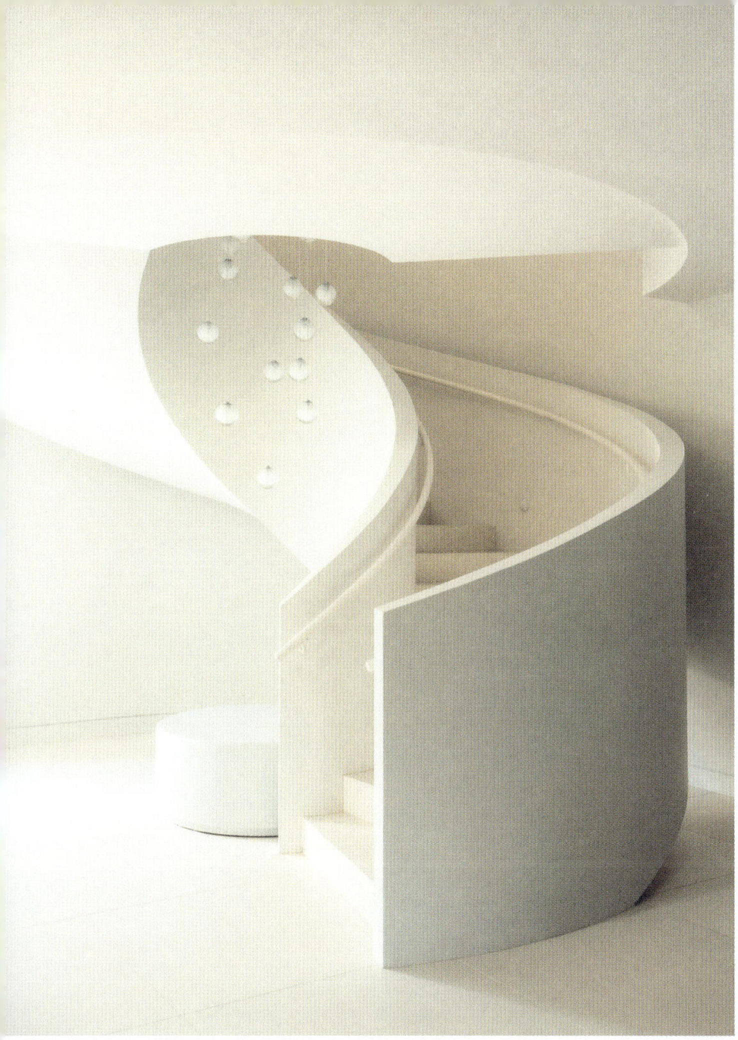
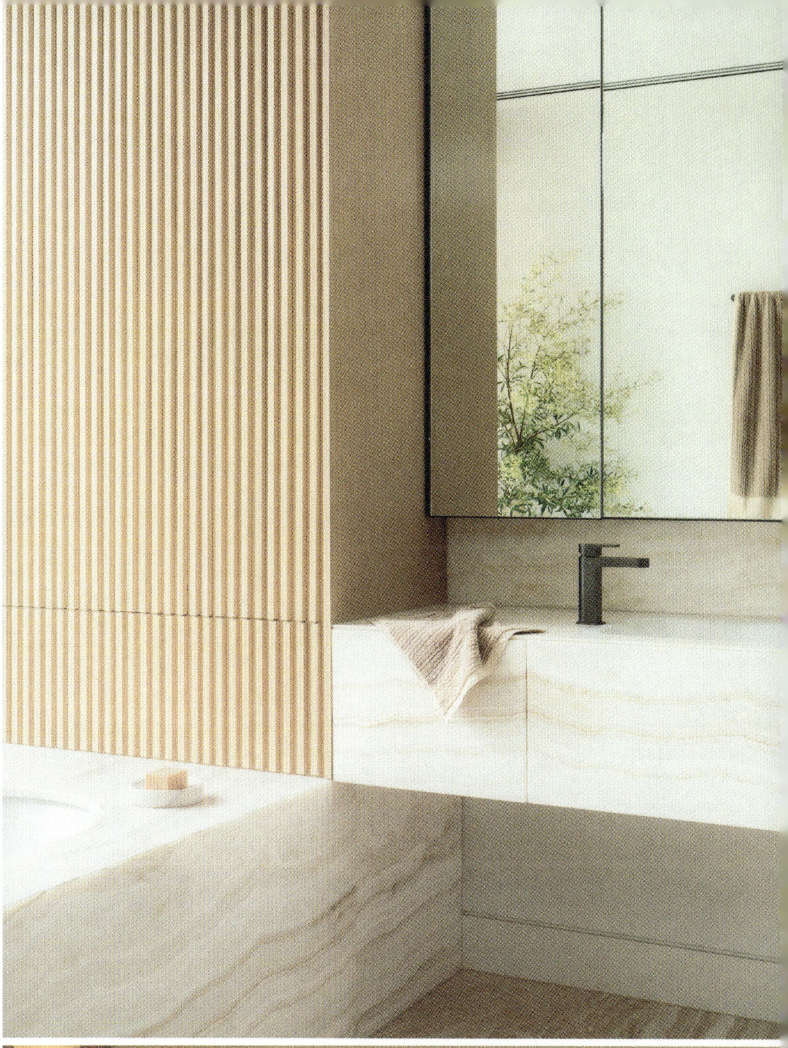
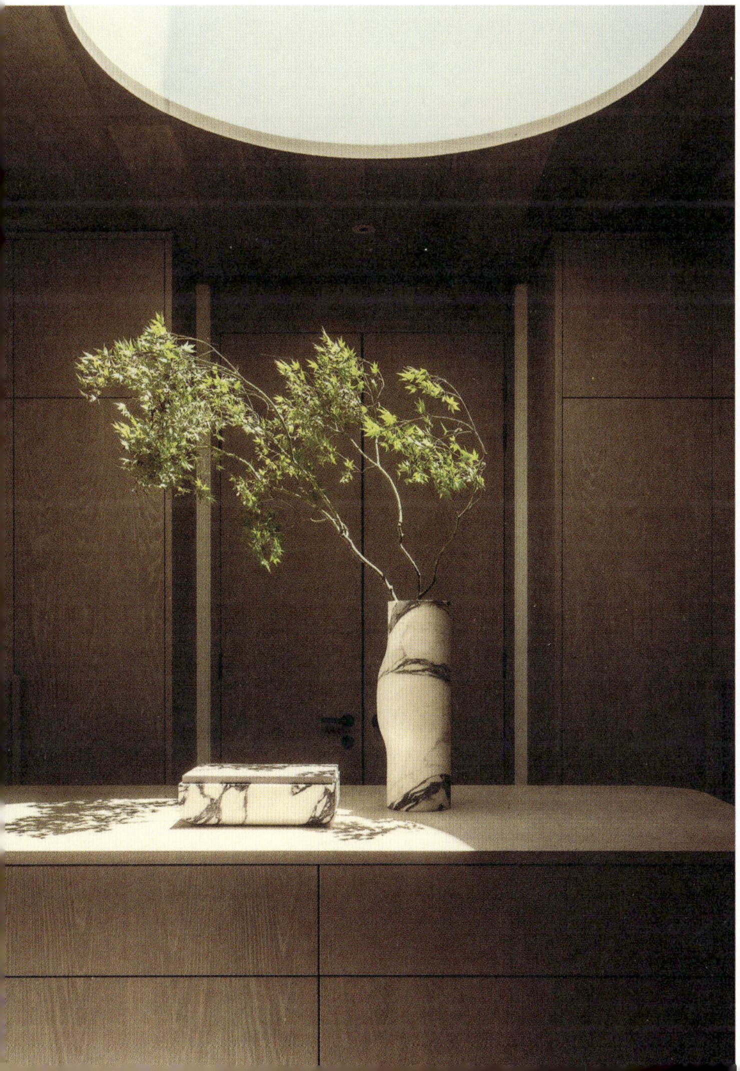
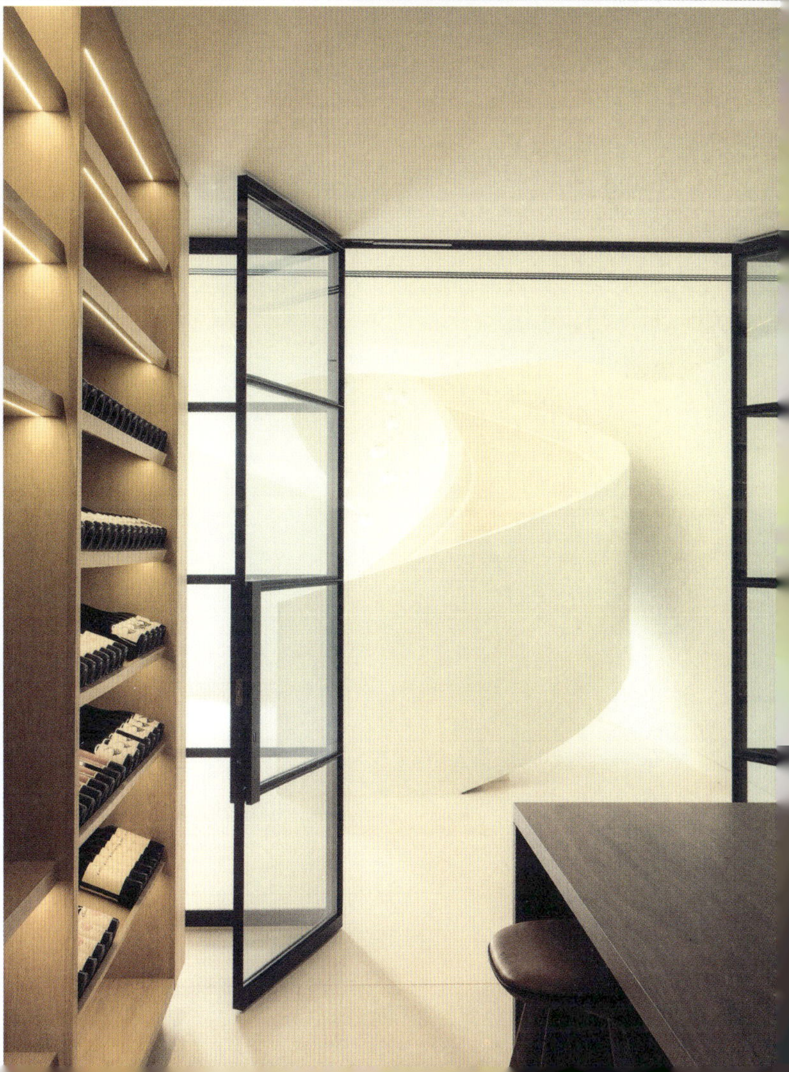

URBAN SANCTUARY
Marianne & Franck Evennou / Designers

SOMETIMES, CREATIVES ENTER YOUR WORLD AND THEIR UNIQUE TALENTS REMAIN firmly embedded within your memory. This is how I feel about the work of Marianne and Franck Evennou – Marianne, for her magical and atmospheric interior design eye, and her husband Franck for his fantastical creations as an artist, sculptor and furniture maker. Having included one of Marianne's beautiful projects in my last book, CREATE, I am thrilled to share their story.

Together, Marianne and Franck have transformed their home in Senlis – a quiet, medieval town, 45 minutes from Paris – from a run-down, single-storey former industrial bakery and butchery into a four-storey home-meets-studio. The 400-square-metre (4,300-square-foot) space was intended as a workshop solution for Franck, who was keen to increase the scale of his designs. But, after a few years an opportunity to purchase coincided with university for their boys, and the couple decided to sell their nearby 17th-century convent and to combine studio and home in this minimalist setting. 'It was an emotional time, but we were ready to let go of many antiques and possessions and to write a new chapter,' says Marianne.

'Working together on the architectural design and build, the space grew with us like a person. Starting as a raw concrete cube, with no garden or terrace, our plans were to keep the interiors modern and stark. Slowly, over time, we re-evaluated and added two upper floors, bought some land to create a lower-ground garden with an overlooking studio for Franck. And rebuilt a neighbour's workshop, enabling us to create an outdoor terrace on top, which connects to our living space through new floor-to-ceiling metal doors,' explains Marianne.

Best known for her ability to shape-shift the alchemy of diminutive Parisian apartments, Marianne's home offers contrasts in terms of its new proportions, yet mirrors her signature approach of turning a micro box into a vast macro world, through transformative spatial design and freedom of expression.

From street level you encounter a theatrical entrance with a hand-painted *trompe l'oeil* around an oversized mirror, hidden storage walls, and also a place for Marianne's bicycle: 'I believe that entrances should be showstopping and feel immediately protective and inspiring – they are the first connection between the outside and our inside world.'

MIRRORED REFLECTIONS A favourite Chinese desk and paintings reflected in the hallway mirror add an immediate sense of intrigue as you set foot in the inspirational entrance hall.

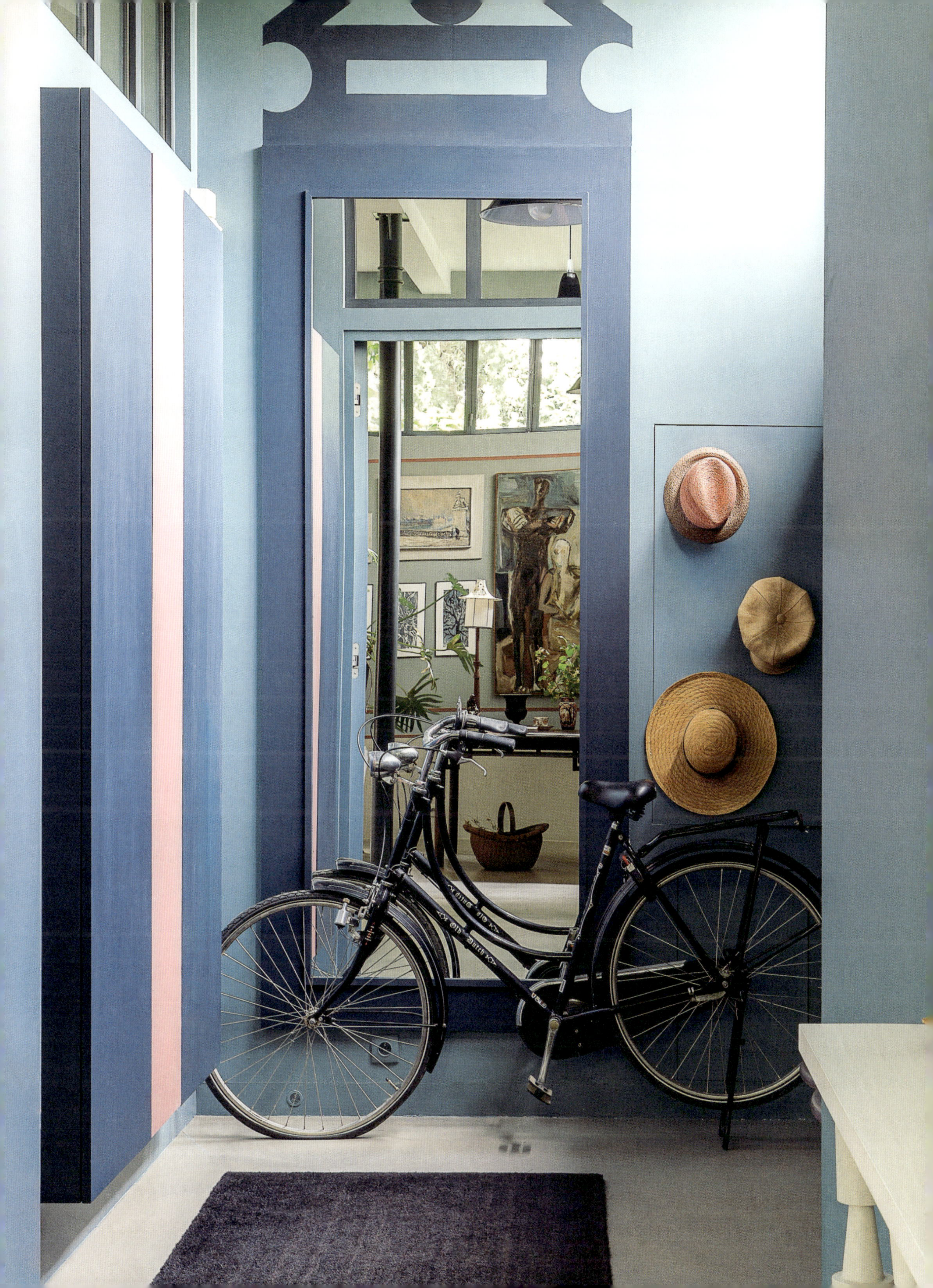

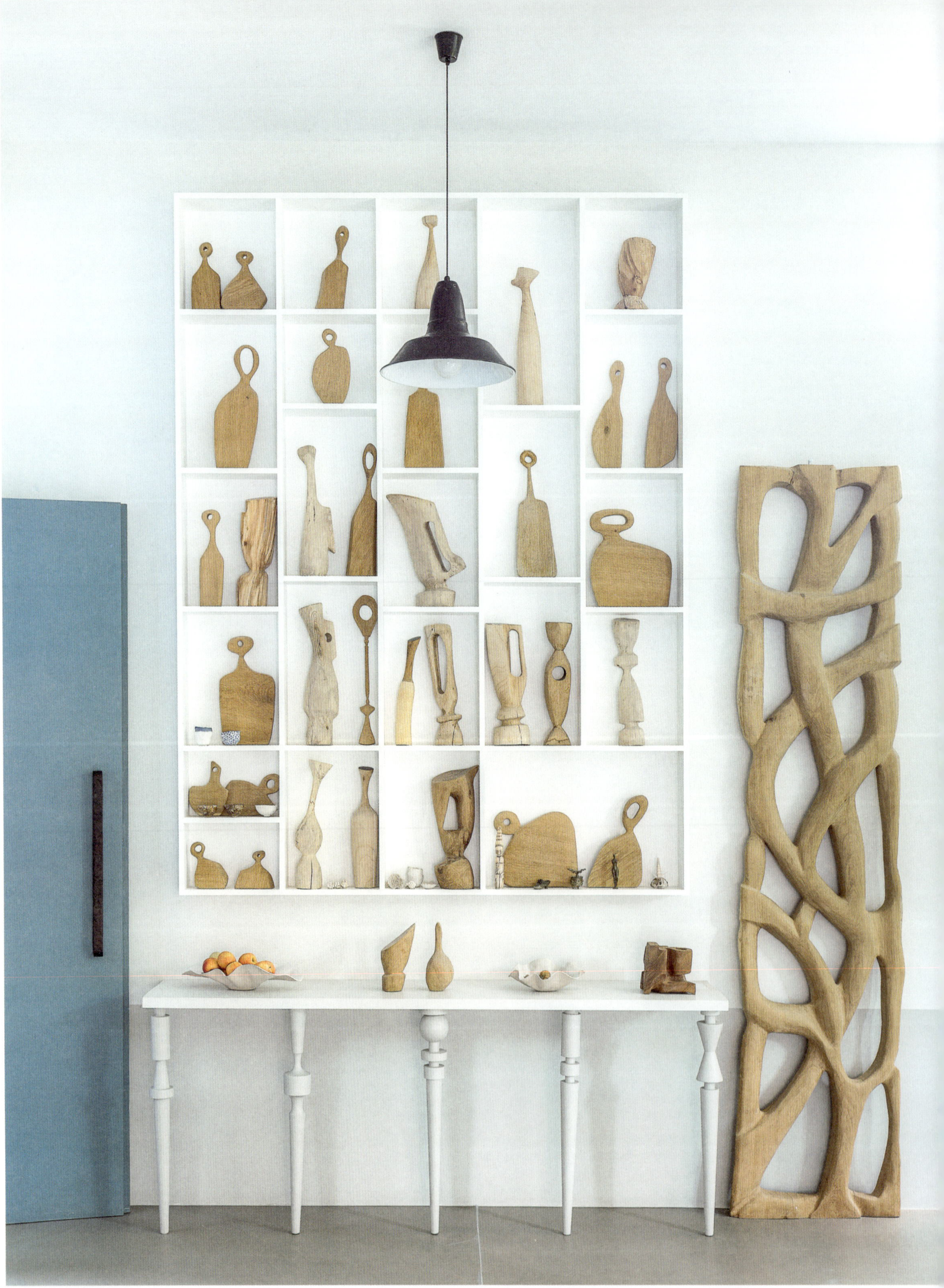

The lofty living space, 4m (13ft) high, is divided into atmospheric zones – a quiet writing area, opposite a cozy fireside nook where the couple read and listen to blues, and a bright seating space that looks out to the terrace and into the dining and kitchen areas through striking metal partitions. 'There is a depth to discovering new things behind glass separations. It changes the flow and adds drama and connectivity.'

Vast iron columns echo the industrial vibe and support a cocooning upstairs master suite and capacious studio for Marianne, where she has created compelling art nooks within the quirks of the original beams. There is also an adjacent guest bedroom, home to Franck's precious copper bath (see page 160), which has travelled with him since the age of 25, making its way in miraculously through new roof window cavities.

With light sources up high, the studio windows look out internally over the living area and connect to the heart of the house. 'With no windows facing the wider world, it feels as if we are at sea in an ocean liner – all on different levels, looking out and sailing through our own world of the imagination,' says Marianne. 'To dream, I like to keep the backdrop simple with calming whites, blues and soft grey shades. Franck is a minimalist and loves a peaceful white box to concentrate and relax, but the maximalist in me is slowly adding more colour to create depth and contrast.'

Raw materials in concrete, metal, glass and stone are offset by a mix of Franck's covetable work: dynamic wooden sculpture displays, oversized lighting and quirky brass and steel furniture shapes, along with personal pieces, such as their black-and-white plates and hand-painted monochrome tablecloth.

Throughout, Marianne has sourced select antiques and artisanal textiles that sit alongside more personal finds: think drawings by the children, paintings from grandparents, handmade ceramics by friends, flowers from the garden, books on every level, and unique pieces, such as the African fertility sculpture that illustrates their shared creative journey, which has unfolded over the past four decades. 'All our lives we have lived in smaller apartments. It is a luxury to have space and quiet.'

Their house celebrates Marianne's idea of home as an imaginarium: a place to live, create and find refuge from the wider world. A voyage of discovery, indeed – a memorable world that piques all your senses and honours the possibility of creativity when you remain true to yourself. ✧

ARTFUL DISPLAY The turned-leg table and display case, home to Franck's sculptures, were designed with Marianne. They show how slim furniture and oversized vertical profiles can add drama to narrower hallways and transitional spaces.

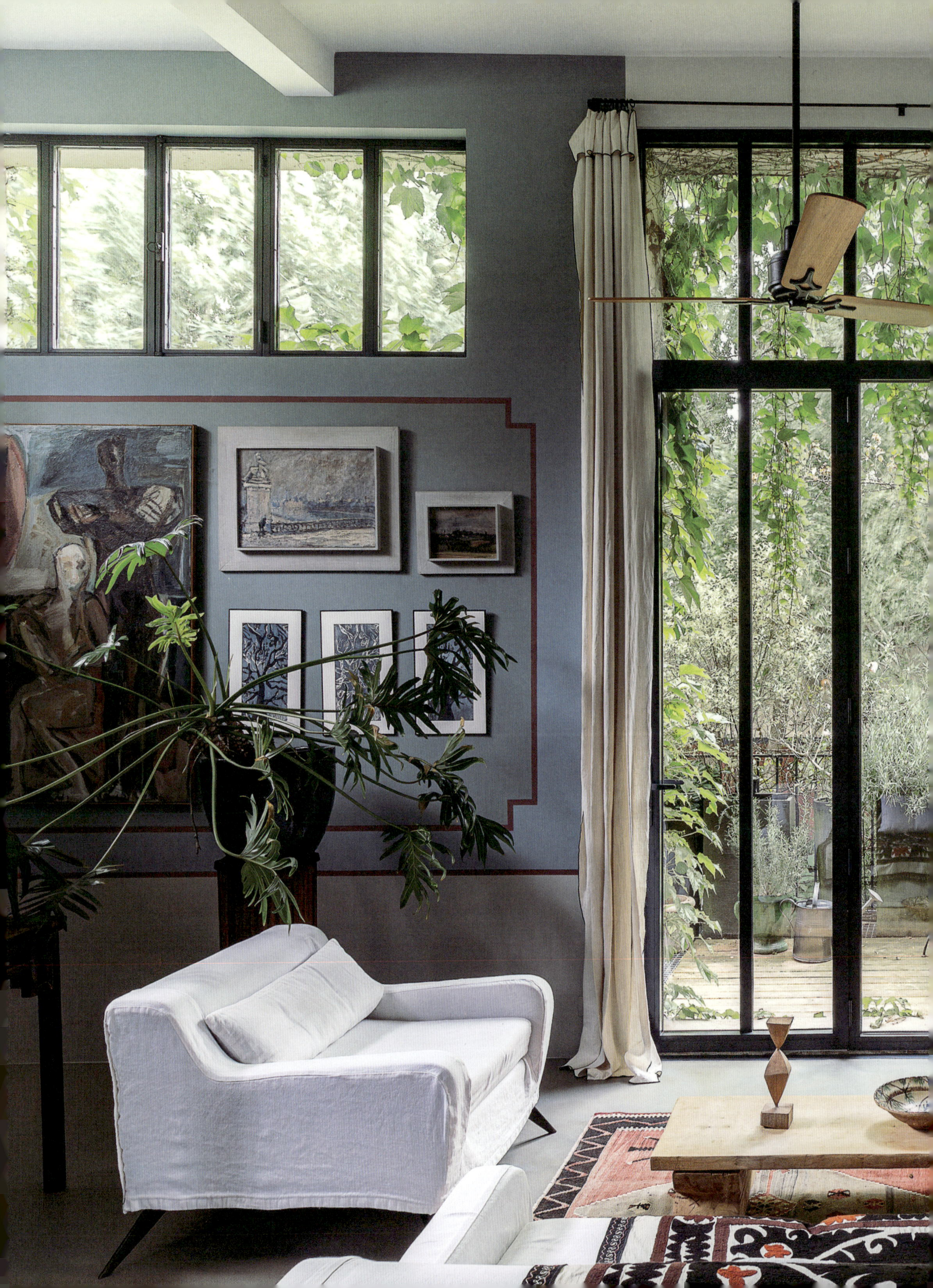

ROOM WITH A VIEW Multiple-level glazing opens up sightlines within the home – out to the garden, into the dining and kitchen area (see page 154), and from above in Marianne's studio down to the central living area.

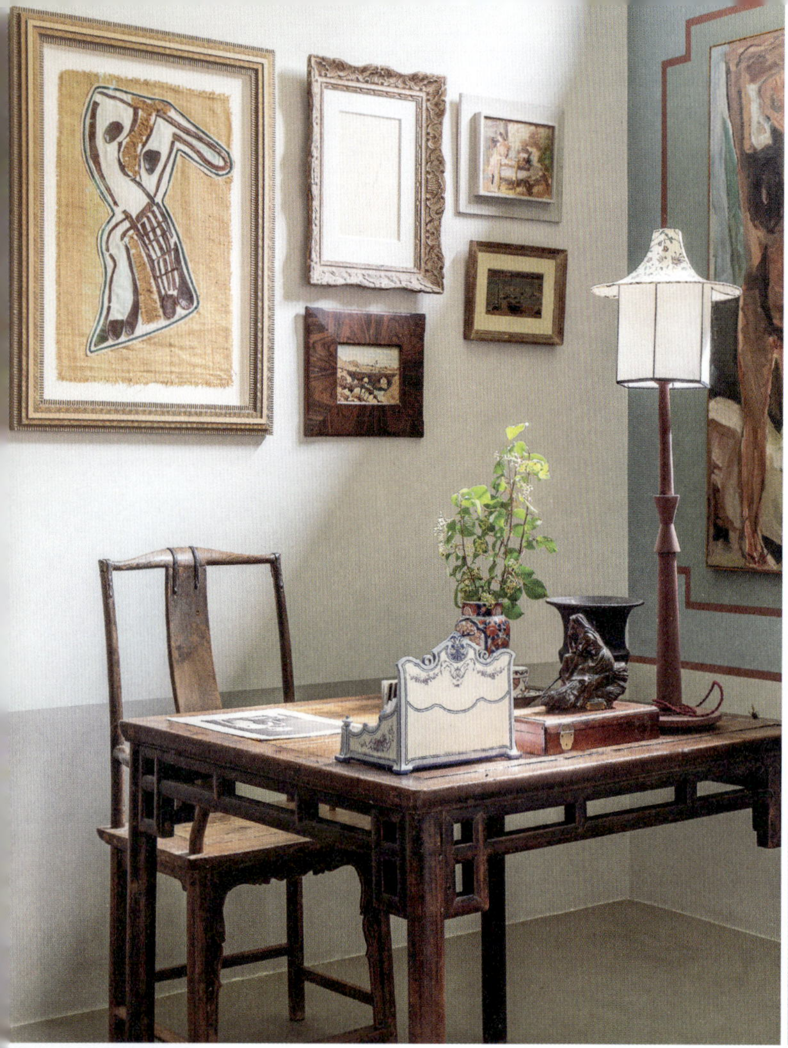
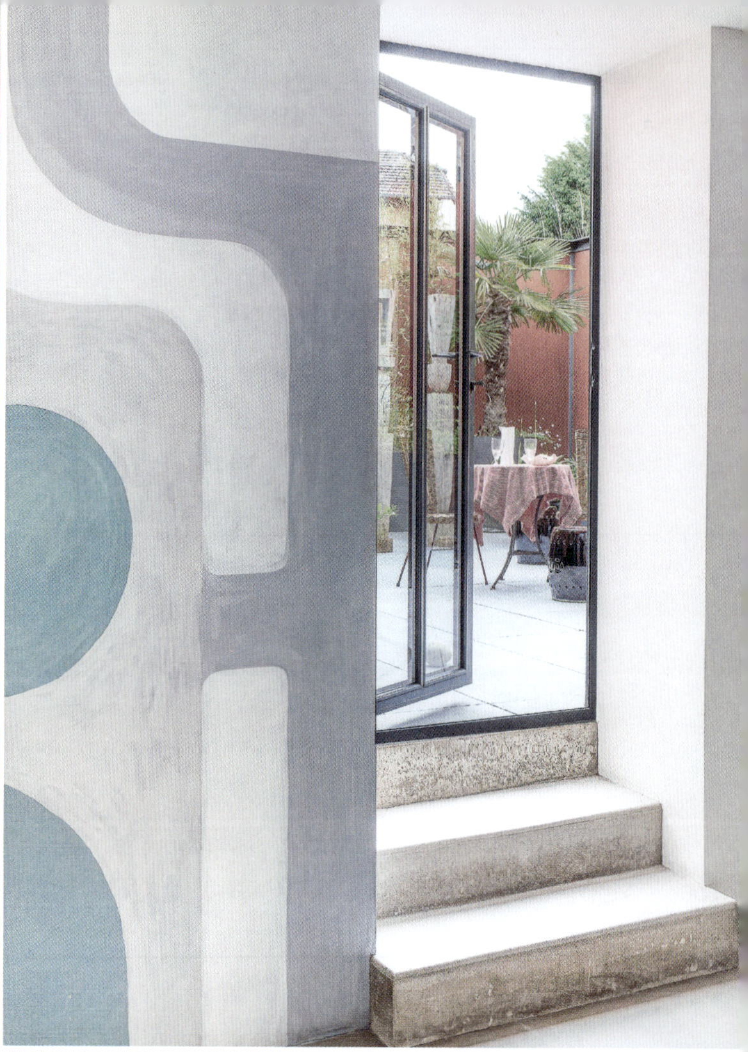
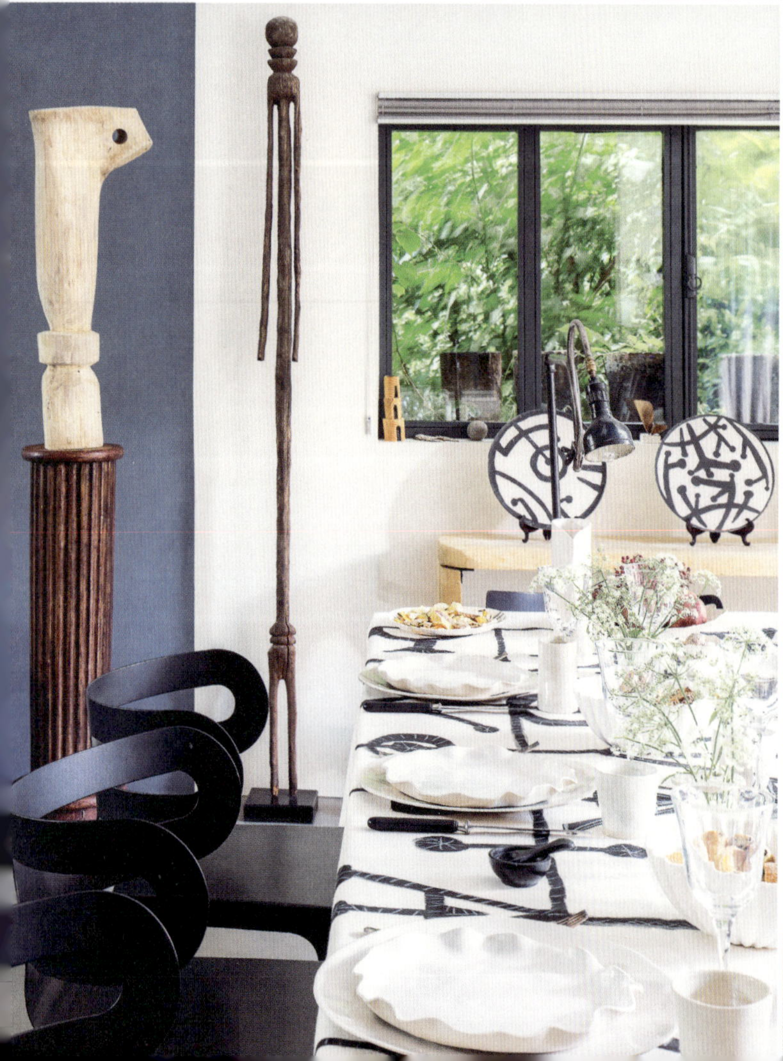
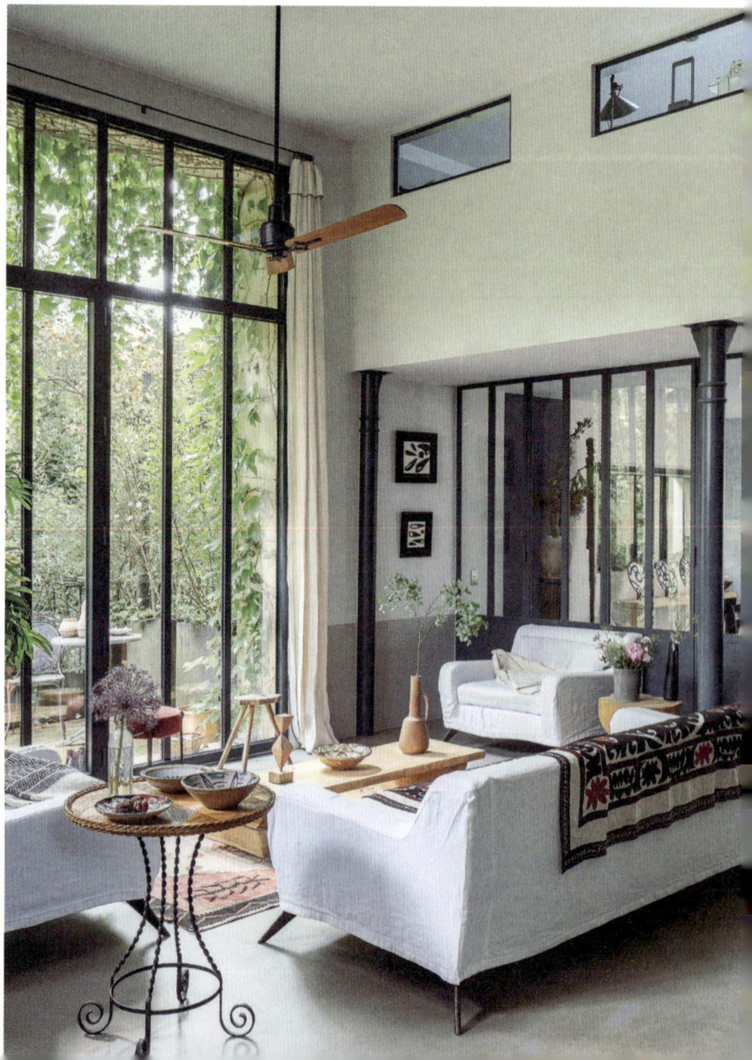

HANDMADE BEAUTY Wooden totems sculpted by Franck. Chinese desk found in Shanghai during one of his first exhibitions (opposite, top left).

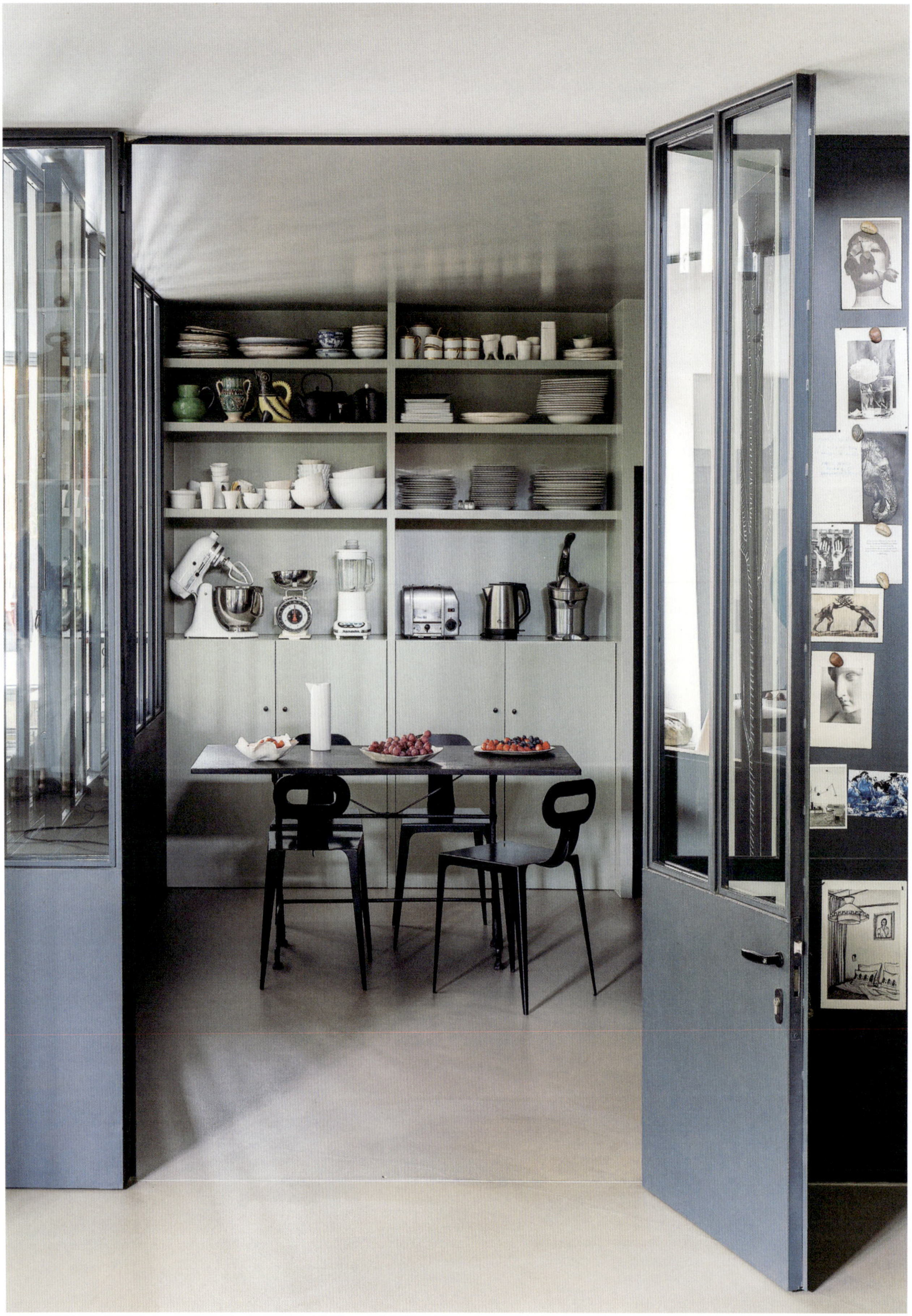

INSIDE OUT Custom-made kitchen by Schiffini. A metal bistro table with sentimental value – the couple's first purchase together at the age of 18 – is flanked by Franck's chair designs from 'La Famille Charles' collection.

BREATHING ROOM Bronze tapestry chairs and 'Twin' tables with bronze legs and slate tops, both made by Franck. Stairs next to the kitchen lead to Marianne's studio and guest room. Personal notes and mementoes are displayed on the outer kitchen wall.

PLAYING WITH SCALE In the master bedroom, gingham textiles, a bronze lamp by Franck and a treasured self-portrait of Marianne's grandfather add personality and warmth. An antique mirror reflects the dressing room, next to the bed.

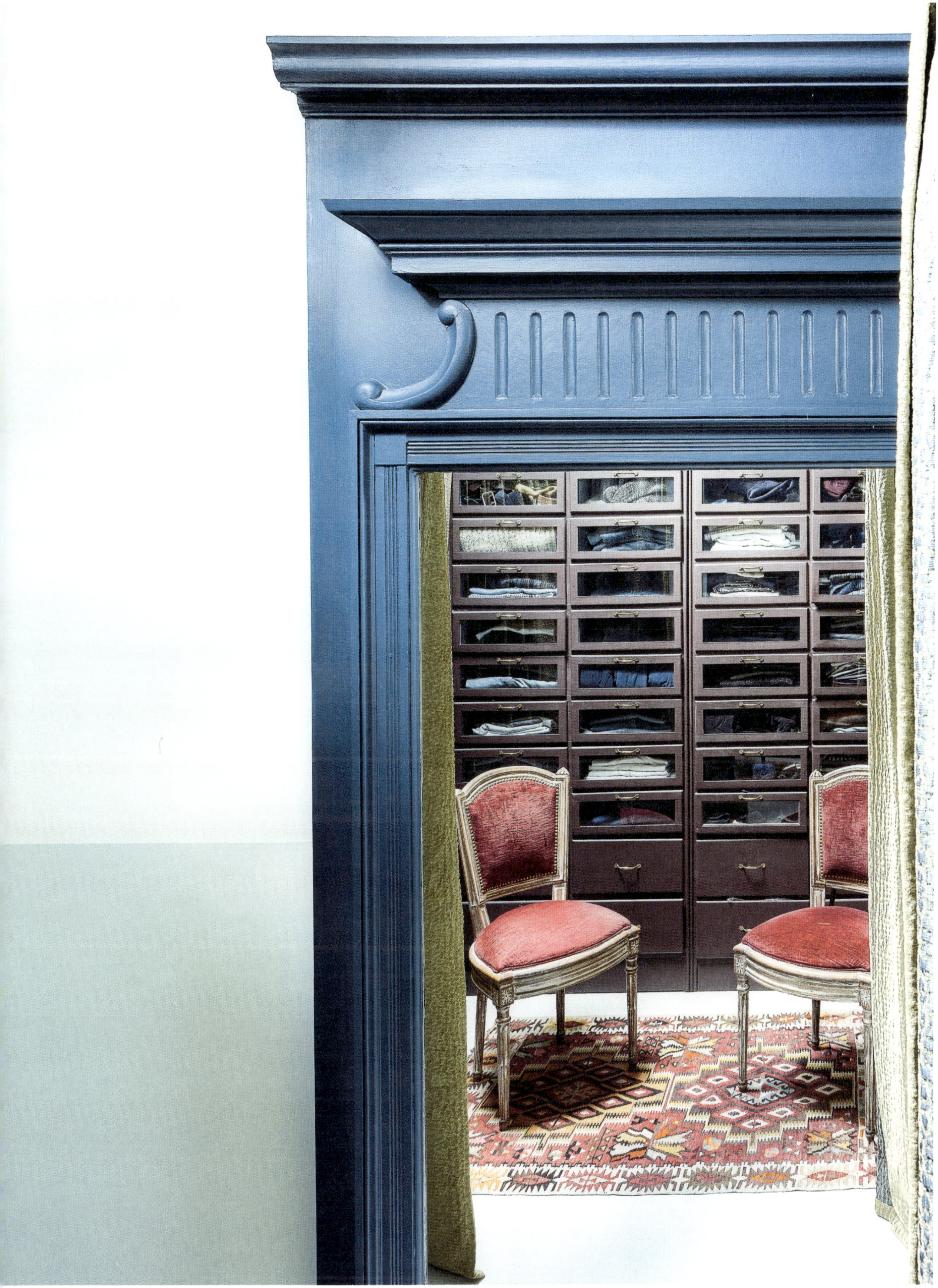

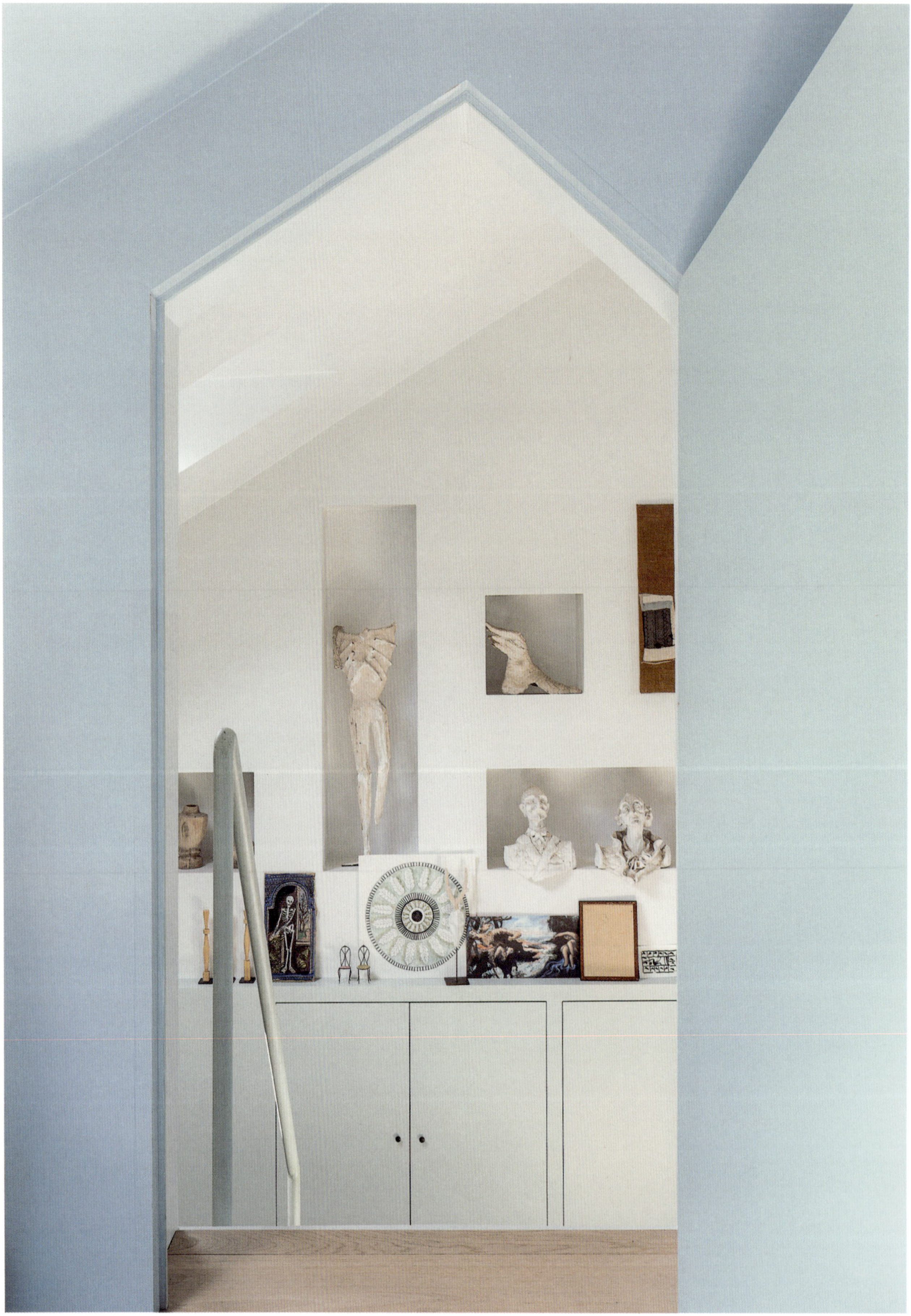

LOFTY IDEAS In Marianne's upstairs studio, personal treasures, sentimental art and collections of loved books form the backdrop for new creative ideas.

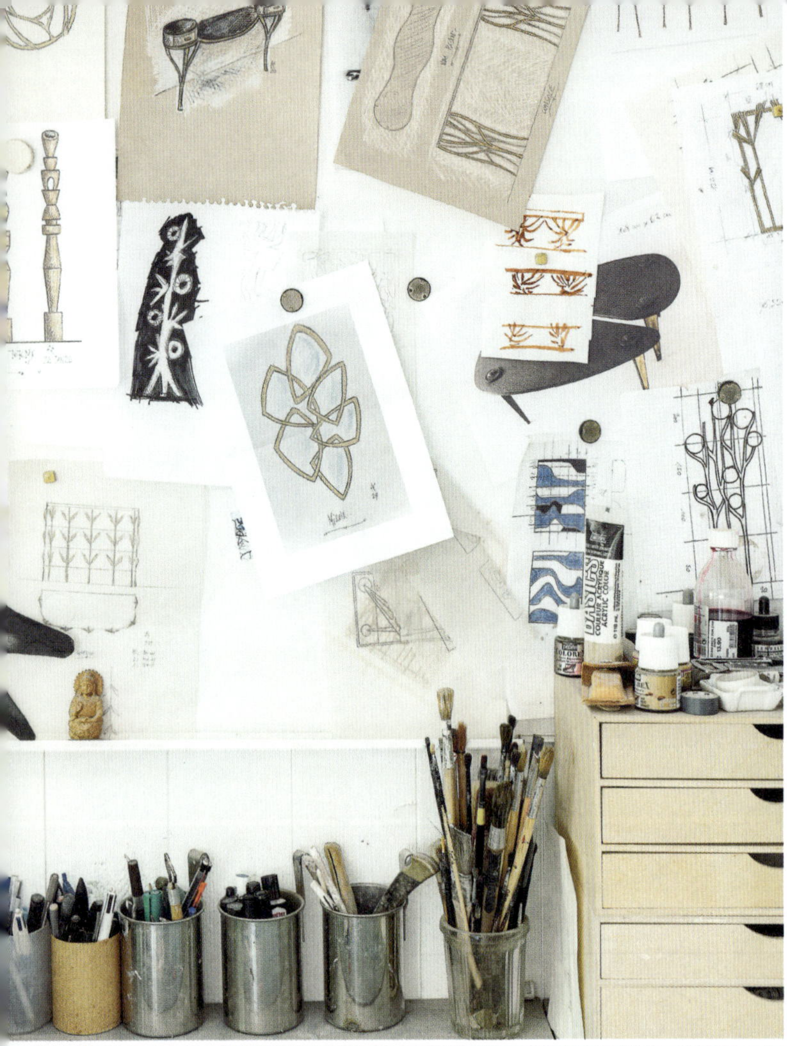
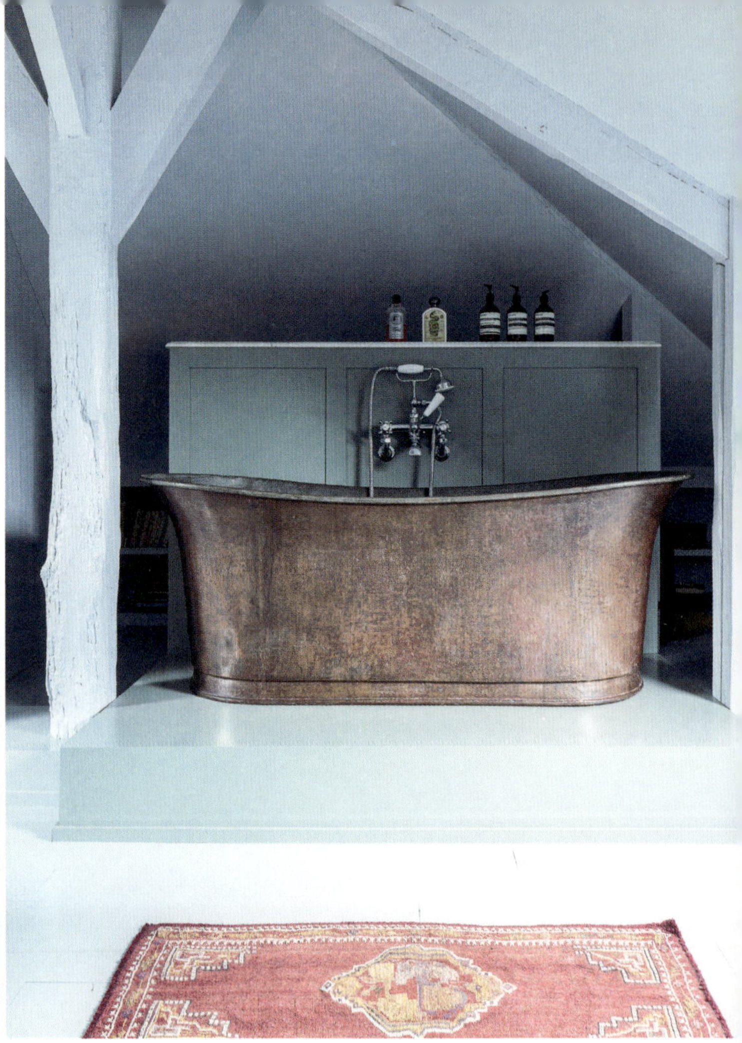
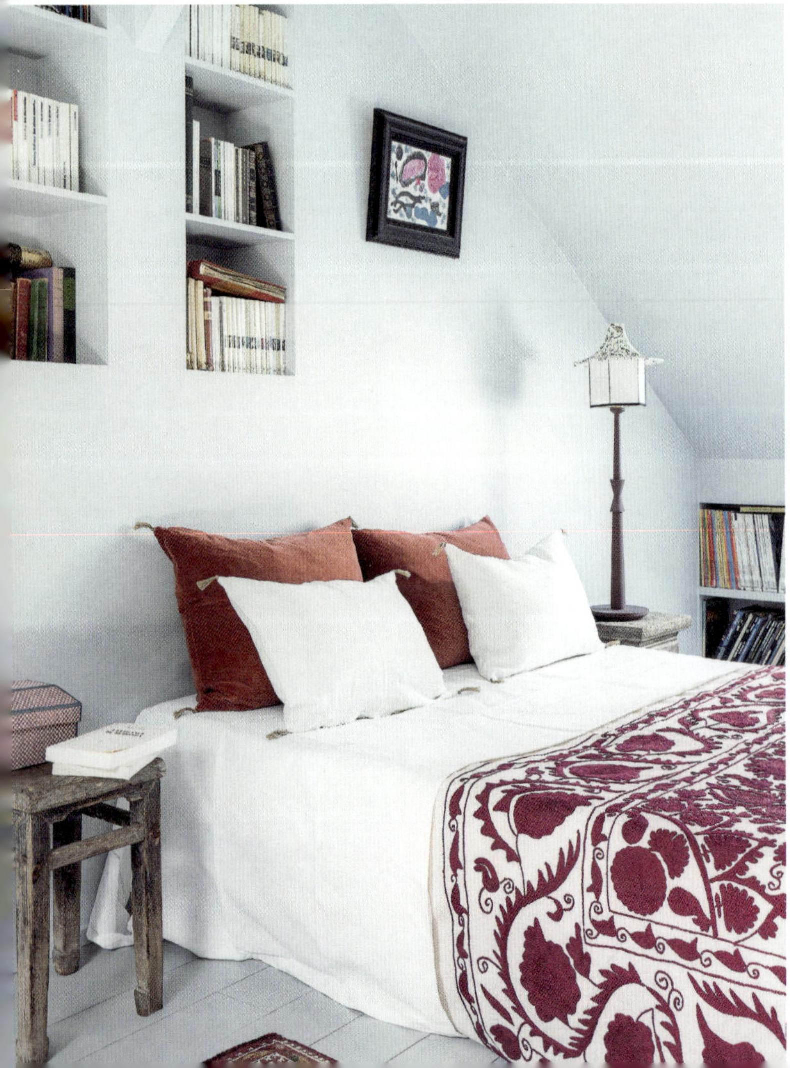
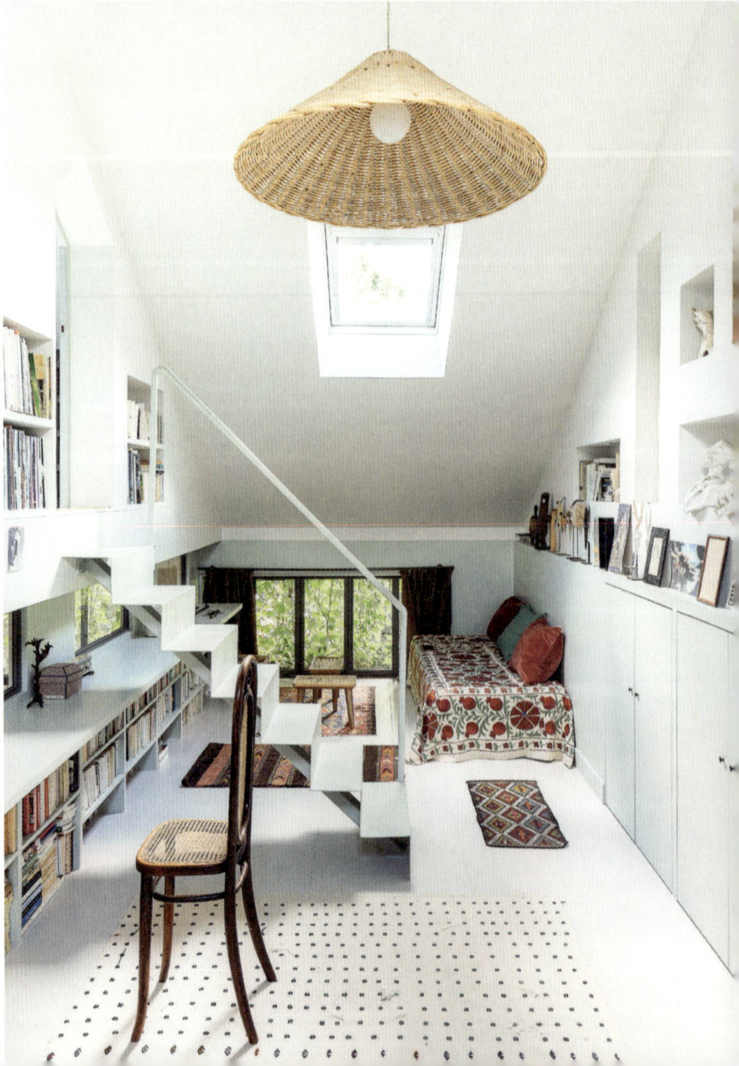

PRIVATE SPACES Franck's secluded garden studio is a hub of creativity. And in the upstairs guest room, a comfortable layered bed and heirloom bathtub provide sanctuary and calm for all who visit (opposite, bottom left and top right).

COUNTRY IDYLL
Tracey Appel / Entrepreneur

TAKING A 19TH-CENTURY MANSION HOUSE AND TURNING IT INTO A RELAXED 21st-century home involved major design goals. For Tracey Appel, it was an opportunity that she couldn't resist. Complete with a glorious confection of castellated towers, trefoil-headed and oriel windows, tall gables, circular turrets and chimneys, the house is set in 5 magical hectares (12 acres), looking out to the English Surrey Hills.

Architect Henry Woodyer was commissioned in 1860 to design the house for Archibald Mathison, on land leased from the Duke of Northumberland. Built in Scottish baronial style and incorporating an element of Gothic, the Victorian country estate was divided into three private homes in 1954. Tracey and her husband David purchased the main residency in 2019, retaining the original entrance and traditional carriage sweep at the front – with gardens on three sides and south-facing views from the loggia where they love to entertain, looking across lawn and woodland.

'I relax as soon as I come through the gates and see the romantic roofline looking across the hills to the west. My favourite time is first thing in the morning, sitting in the kitchen courtyard wrapped in a blanket and sipping tea, or walking the dog, and watching the sunrise – especially beautiful when the mist sits low. I feel at peace here,' says Tracey.

Having lived in a Parisian Haussmann apartment for six years, then returning to the UK and converting several city-meets-country houses for her family, Tracey is no stranger to the alchemy of great design matched with a need for hard work. Her style – a combination of sympathetic restorer meets passionate modernist – is characterized by her love of authentic architecture, brought to life with a mix of antique and contemporary. 'I am obsessed with the contrast and how it can transform a period house. Adding purely old pieces would feel predictable and detract from the beauty of the historical bones – the juxtaposition makes both feel more refined.

'Obtaining permission for the alterations was a lengthy process, but the frustrations were worth it. With such strong architectural details, it was a case of overhauling the workings of the house, then updating the kitchen, bathrooms and decor to reflect our style,' Tracey explains.

Striking new flooring connects spaces with a patina-rich mix of chequerboard marble, parquet, tiled mosaics and comforting carpet. A palette of off-whites, strong

OUTDOOR SPLENDOUR The original Victorian loggia connects to the dining room, living room and snug, making it a favourite place to entertain and relax in all seasons.

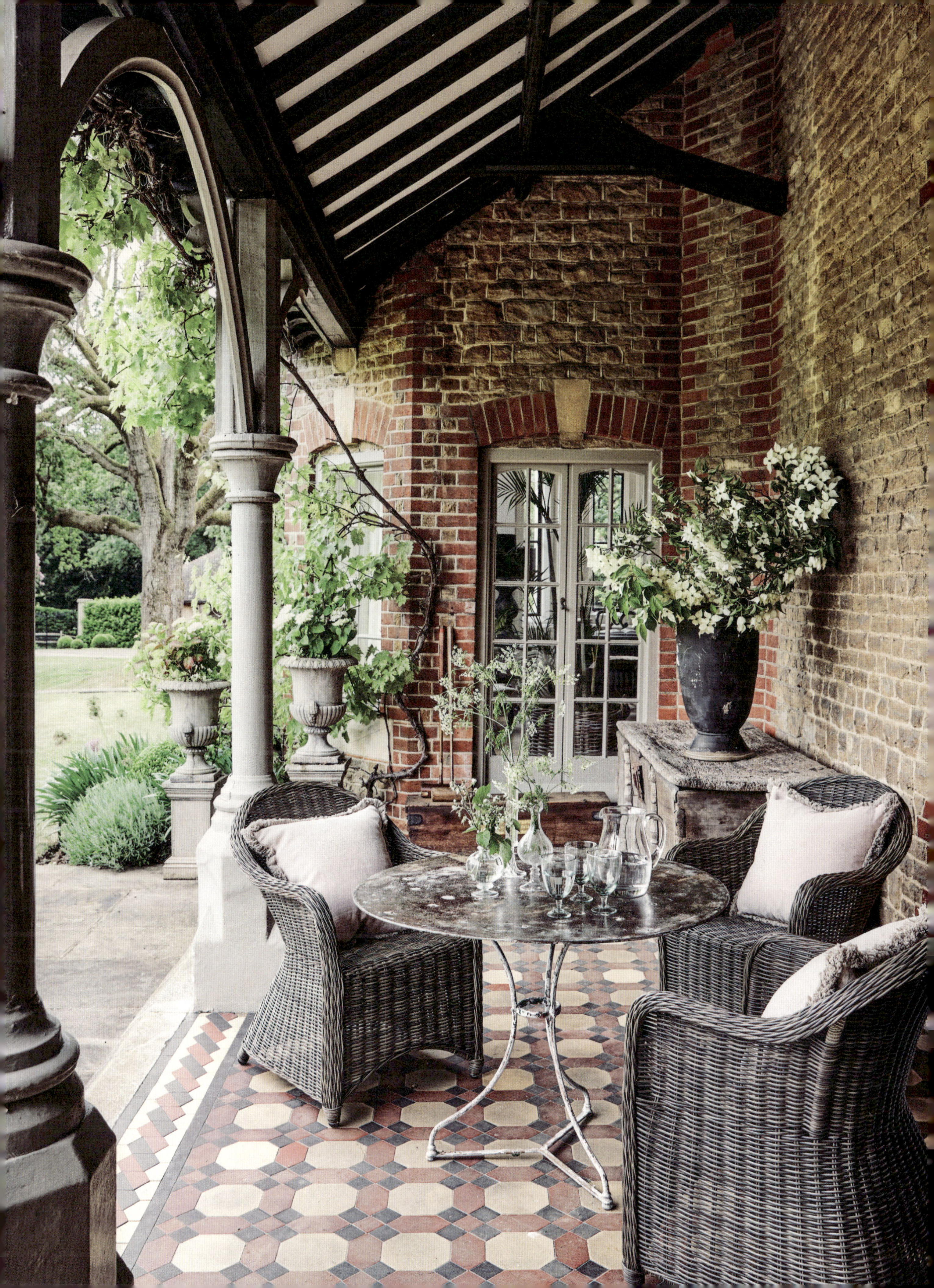

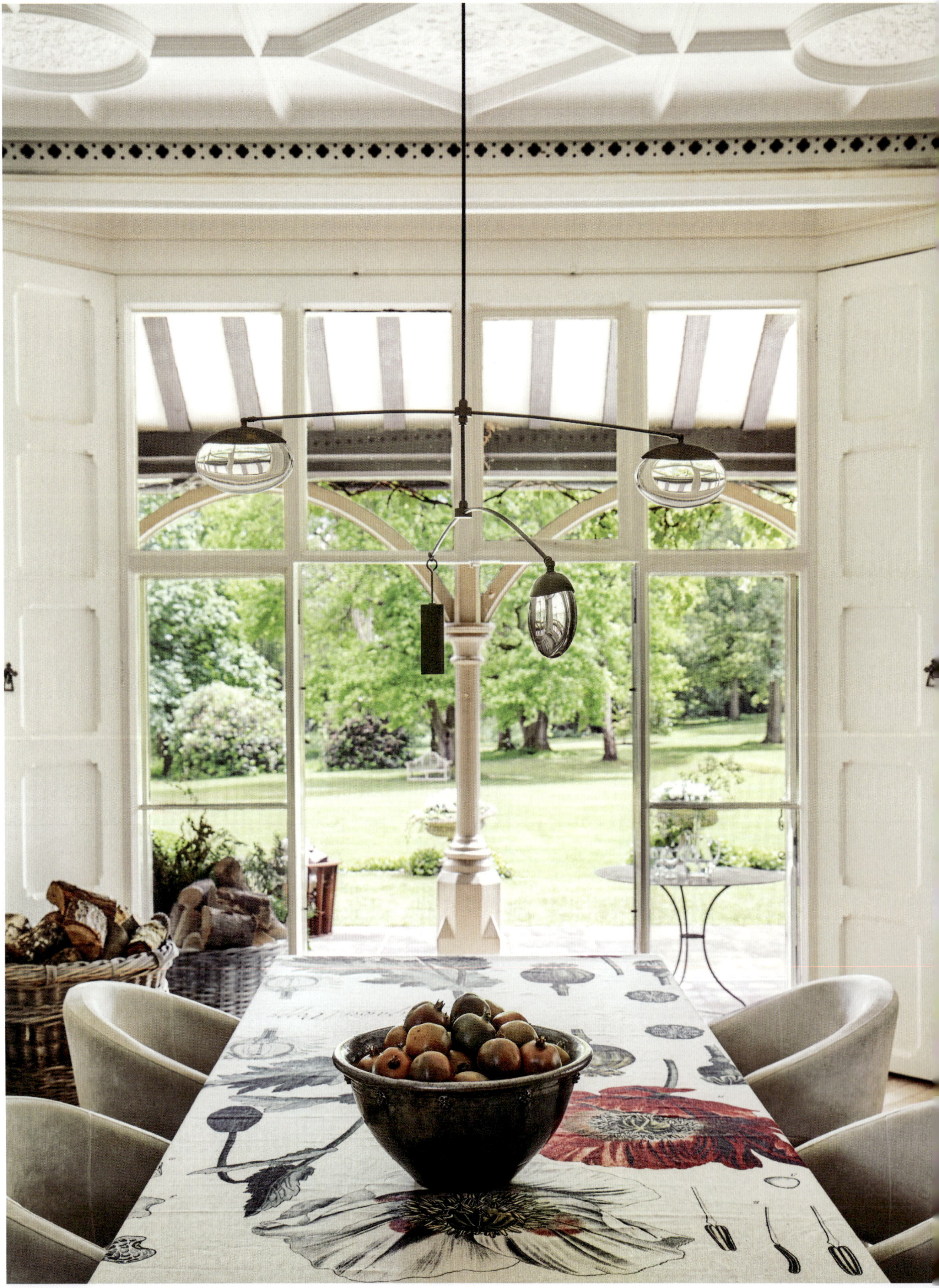

blacks and natural linens adds calm to the formal living room and dining area, where contemporary and handmade furniture is softened with handmade lighting, oversized rugs, painterly tablecloths and elegant sculptures and vignettes. Candles are Tracey's guilty pleasure – and throughout the house, Ernesto by Cire Trudon and Ginger Lime by Dr. Vranjes fill the air with their memorable scent.

Spaces have been thoughtfully remodelled throughout to enhance the feel and flow, and Tracey has ensured each room has a purpose. For example, positioning pieces such as her favourite desk in the less-used formal living room to enjoy the view each day – cozy in winter with fires lit and airy in summer with doors flung open.

The kitchen sits at the heart of the home. More decorative than domestic, elegant choices prevail: rich chocolate, marble-topped cabinetry from Plain English, aged-mirrored walls to reflect the landscape, and an elegant La Cornue range framed with open shelving – home to precious collections of Astier de Villatte and special pieces discovered over time. Balancing opposites, Tracey cleverly combines antique with new, glossy with time-worn, and dark with light. A pair of 19th-century candelabras add drama to the kitchen island, while a welcoming circular table and battered leather chair nod to the relaxed, informal welcome that balances the grandeur throughout.

In the family snug, a backdrop of olive green and soft pinks complements deep sofas, with space for the whole family and dog to cozy up. 'The scale of the rooms has made it easy to optimize comfort – here big is never too big,' notes Tracey. Upstairs, more intimate bathrooms juxtapose contemporary marbled showers with traditional bathtubs and classic tapware, while restful bedrooms add to the sense of escape.

Having owned an interior shop for many years, while working as a designer for private clients, Tracey is well versed in sourcing beautiful finds. Now concentrating on her own projects, her passion for the unusual prevails, but with increasing discernment about what makes the cut. 'Art is a passion – everything from tiny vintage finds to huge modern canvases, along with many abstract pieces commissioned from friend and artist, Sassy Hardwick. Often chosen to complement antique frames I have sourced,' Tracey says.

'Our home is a true reflection of who we are and what interests me in design, but most importantly it is a nurturing, down-to-earth retreat that we love to share.' ✧

OPPOSITES ATTRACT In the dining room, traditional architecture is juxtaposed with a contemporary Gaia pendant from Ochre and an abstract tablecloth from Babylonstoren in South Africa.

WALL TO WALL Original architectural details nod to the history of the house. Drinks cabinet and desk by Sassy Hardwick (opposite, top and bottom left). Large artwork above the sofa by Sara Lee Roberts (above). Bronze resin figure of man sitting cross-legged by Margaret Samuel (opposite, bottom right).

PAGE 168 **BARONIAL SPLENDOUR** A Sienese marble fireplace and Gothic-style panelling in the family snug are offset by cocooning walls painted in 'Heath' from the Paint & Paper Library.

PAGE 169 **LADY IN RED** Hallway painting, *Scarlett* by Sassy Hardwick.

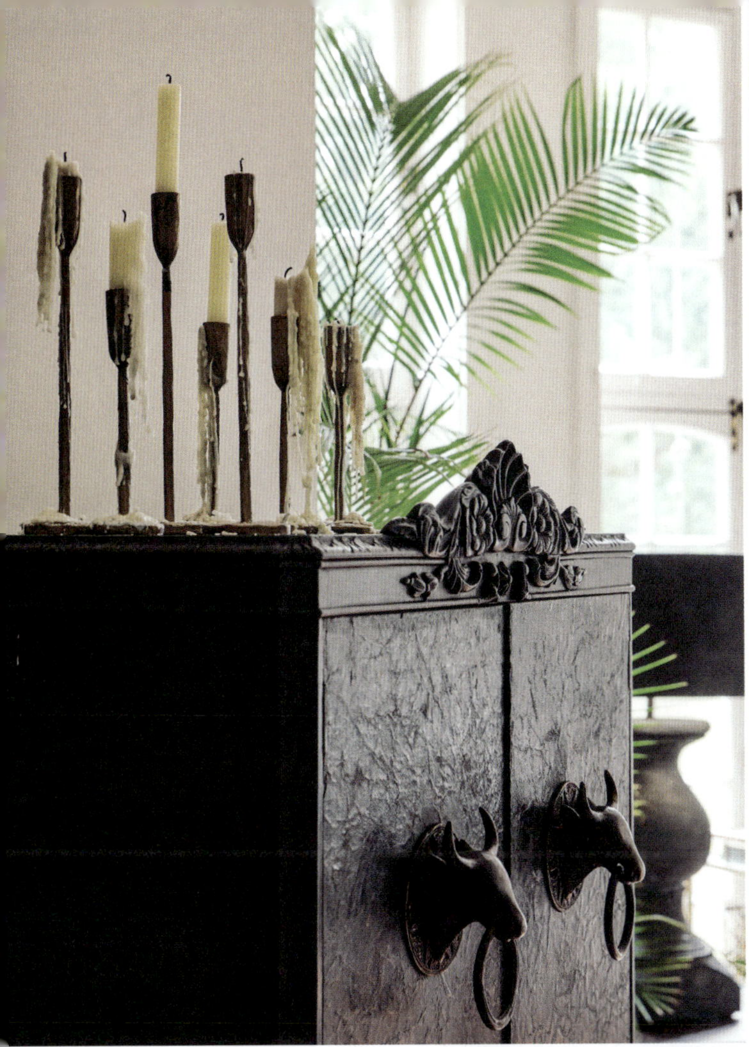
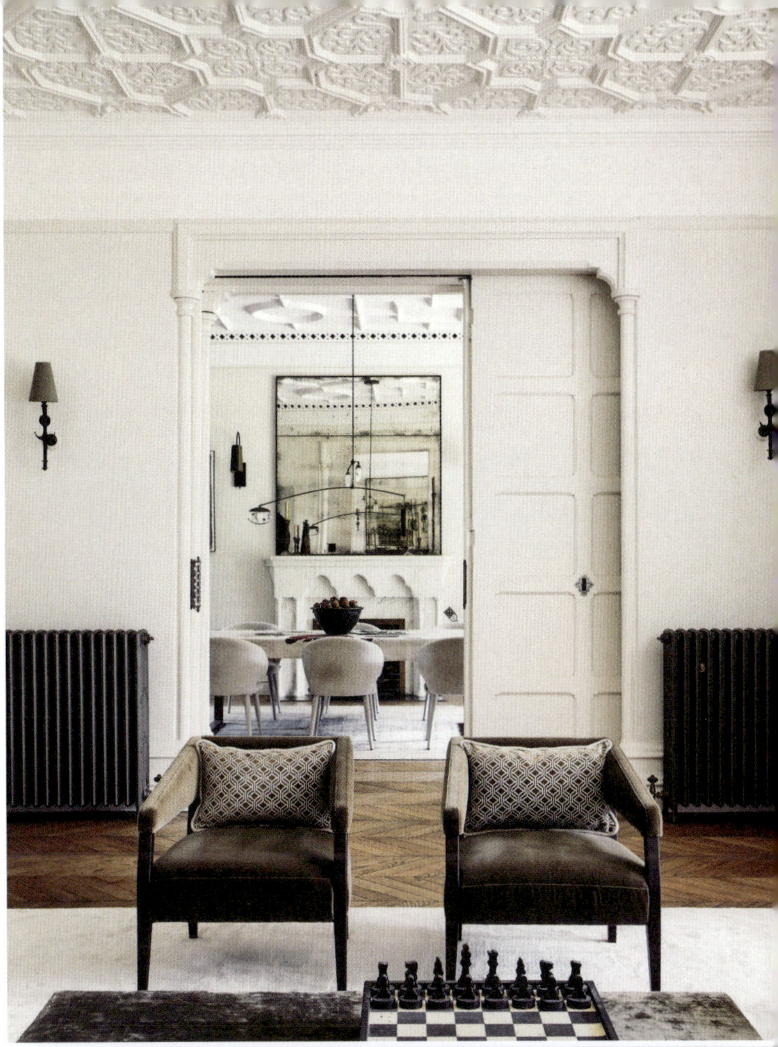
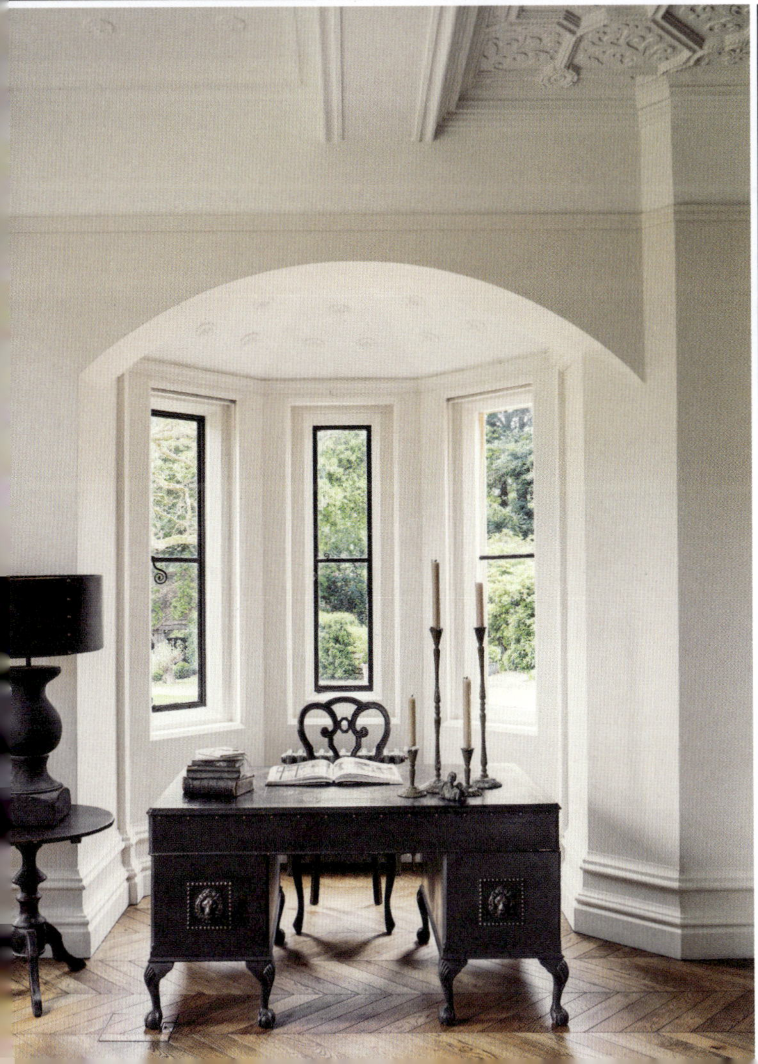
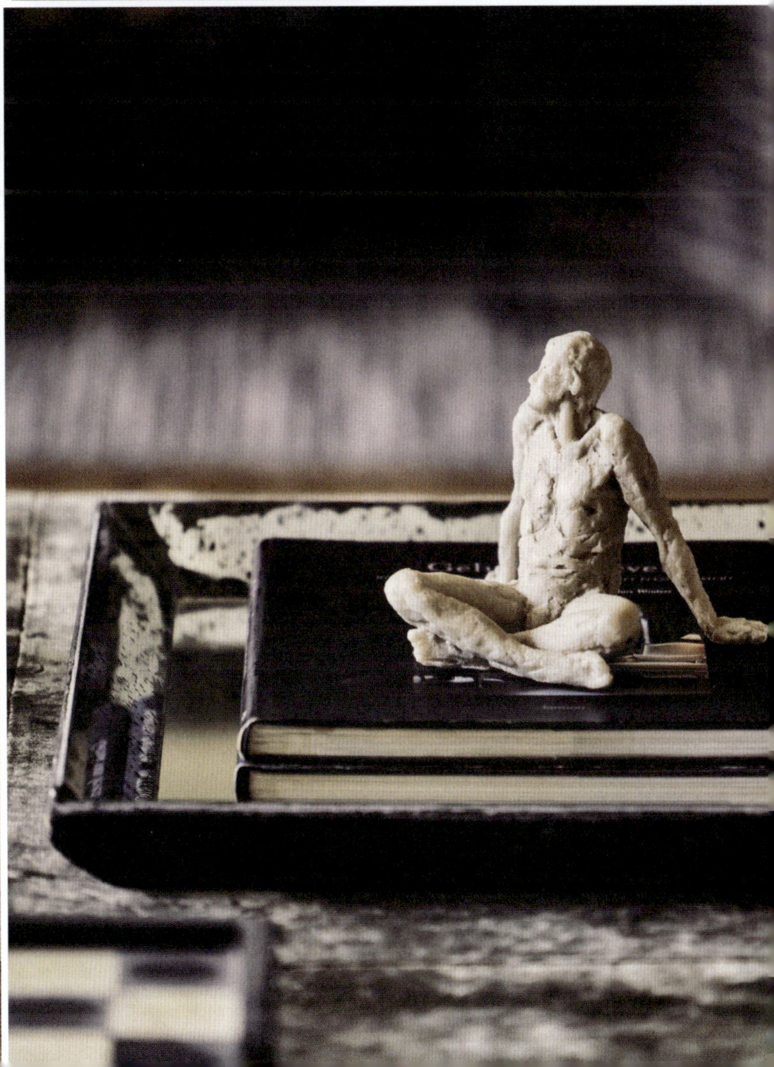

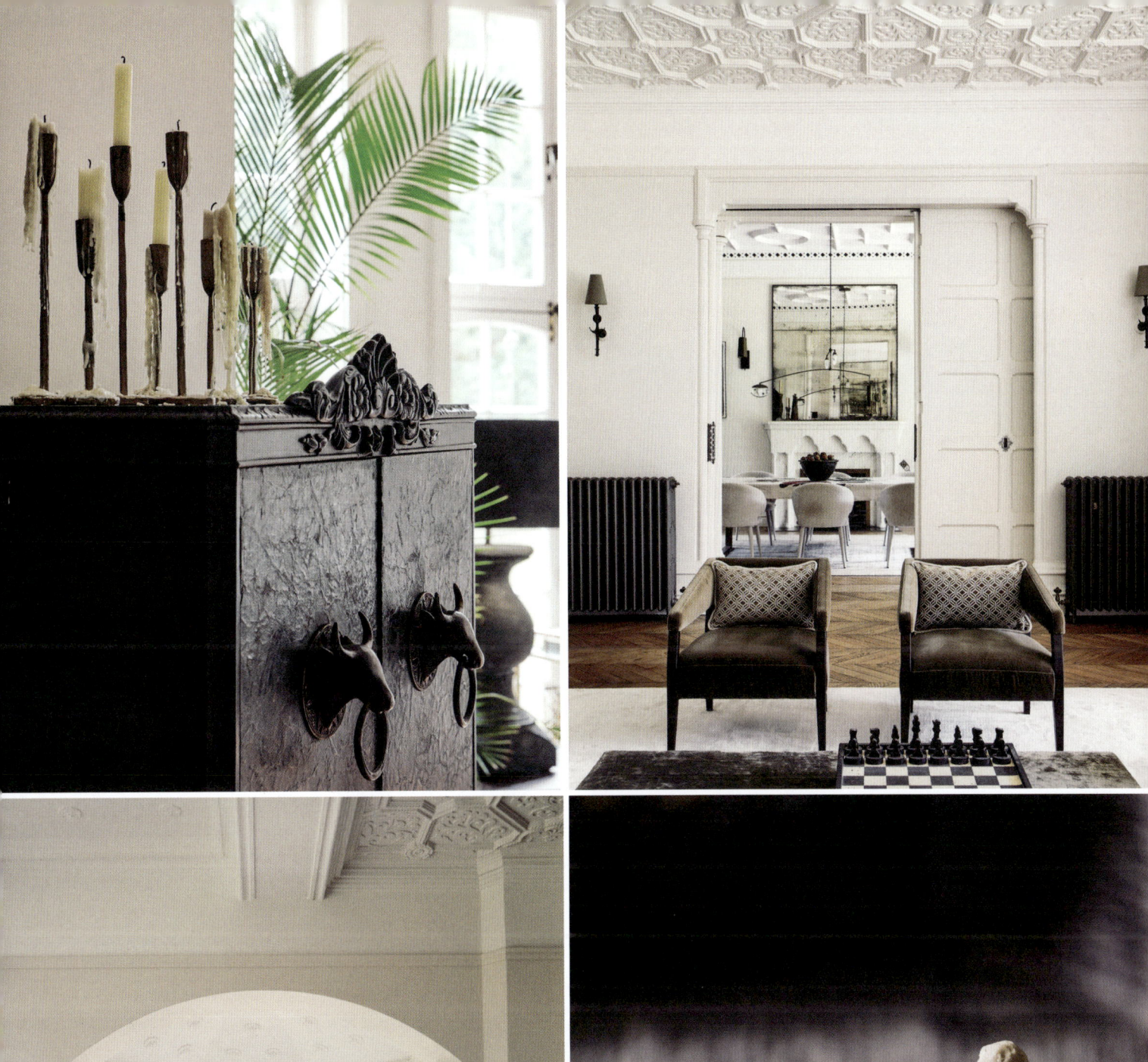

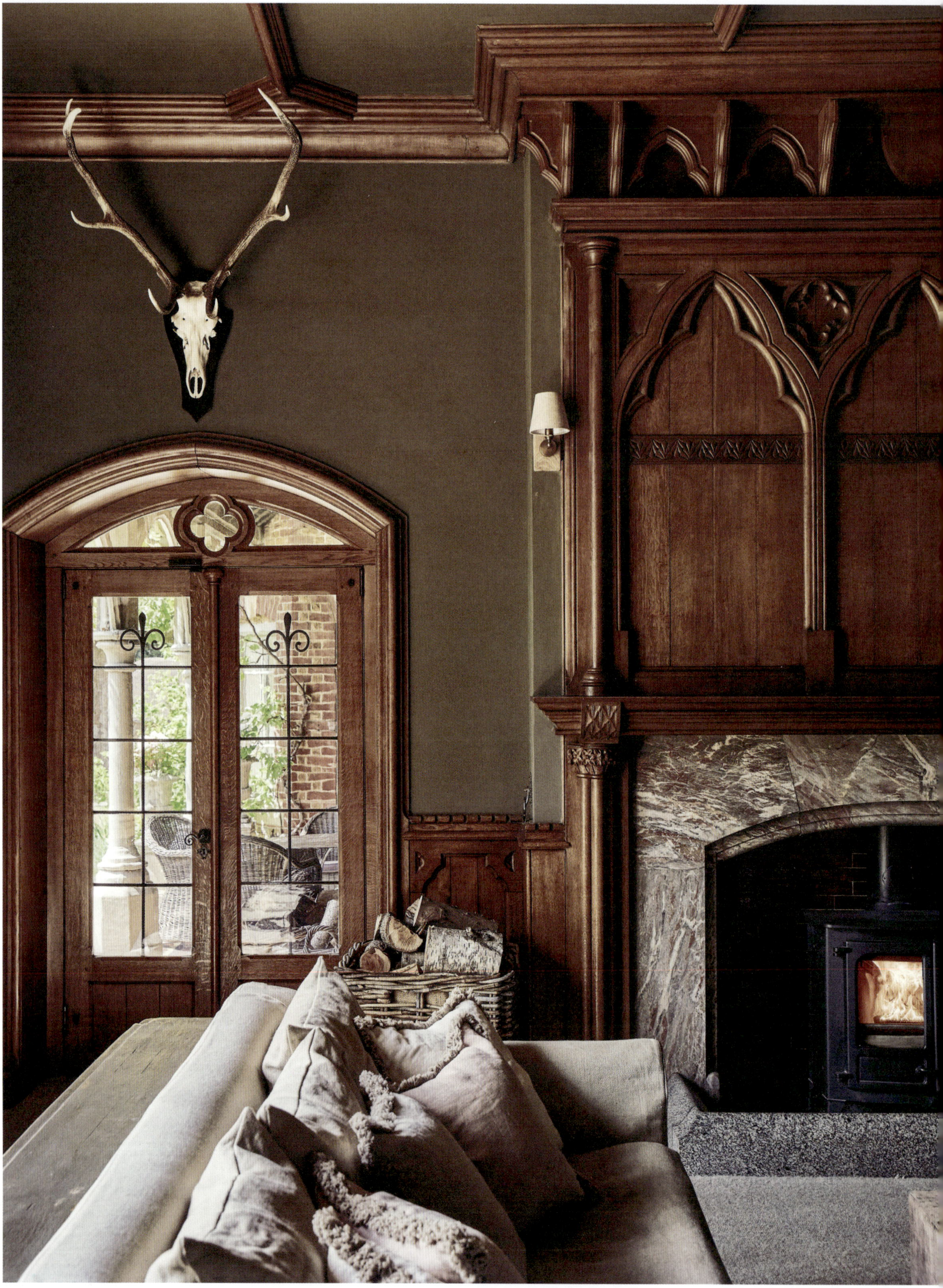

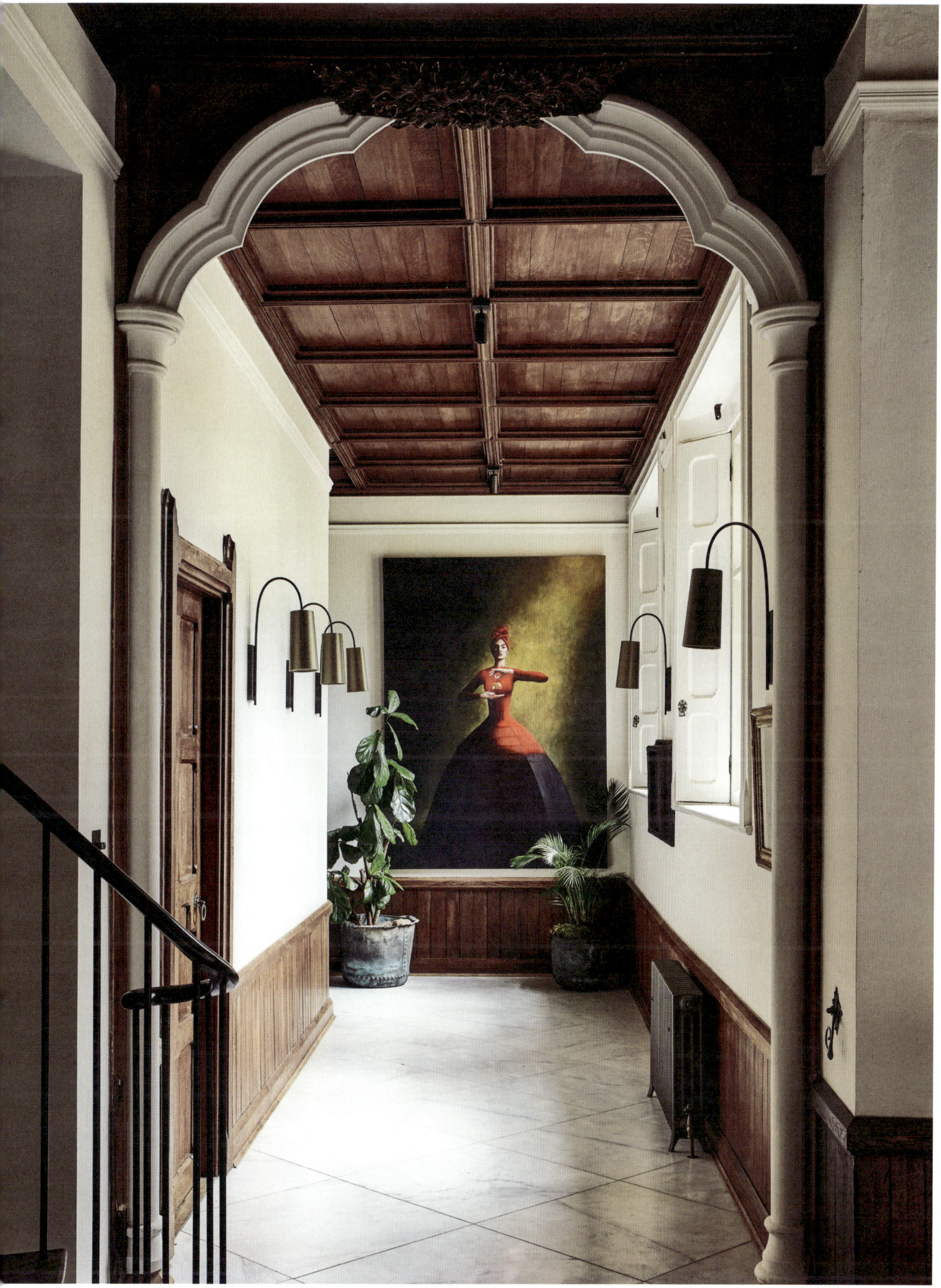

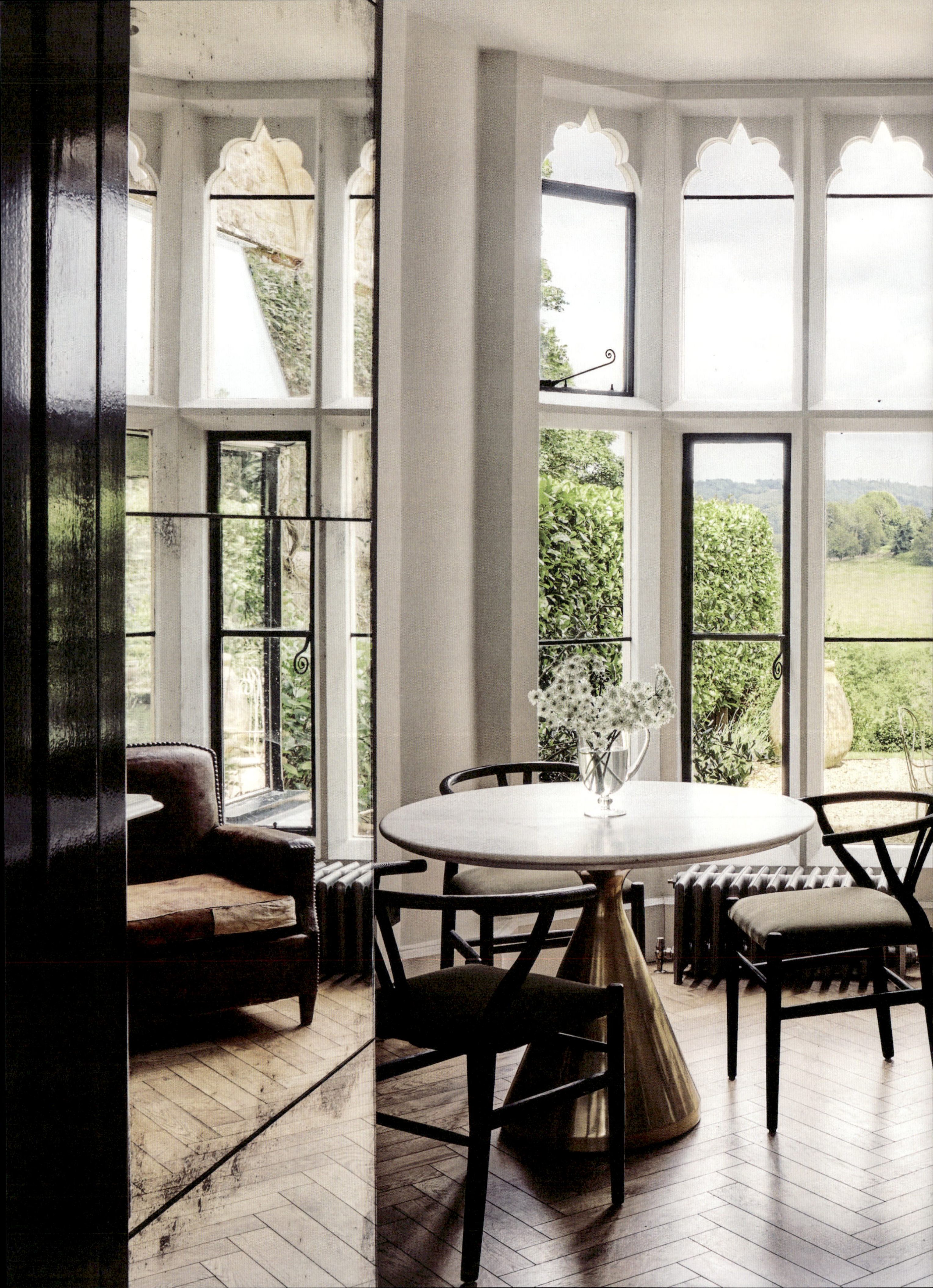

LET THERE BE LIGHT A traditional handmade kitchen by Plain English contrasts a contemporary table from Liang & Eimil and Wishbone chairs from Carl Hansen & Søn. In the outdoor courtyard, rustic French antiques enhance the rural outlook.

EXPRESS YOUR STYLE Collections of Astier de Villatte ceramics are displayed with natural finds, heirloom silver and treasured ceramics. A curved pantry cupboard (opposite) and brass detailing for handles and tapware add to the luxurious feel.

COUNTRY IDYLL 173

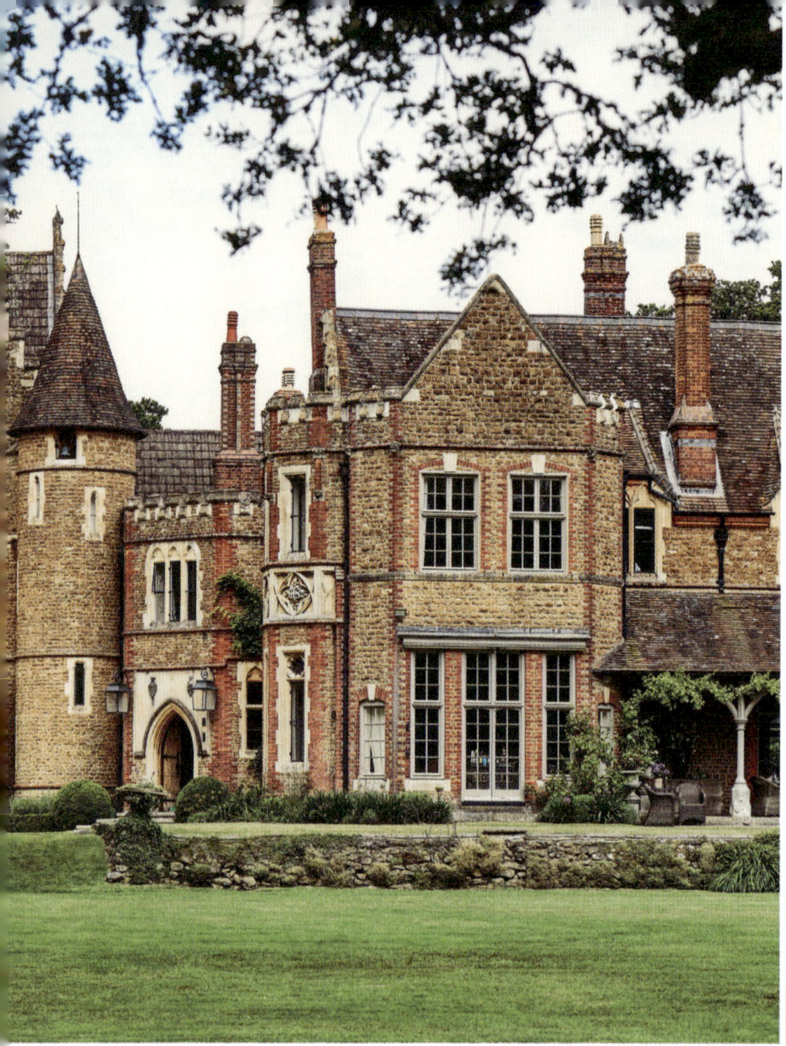

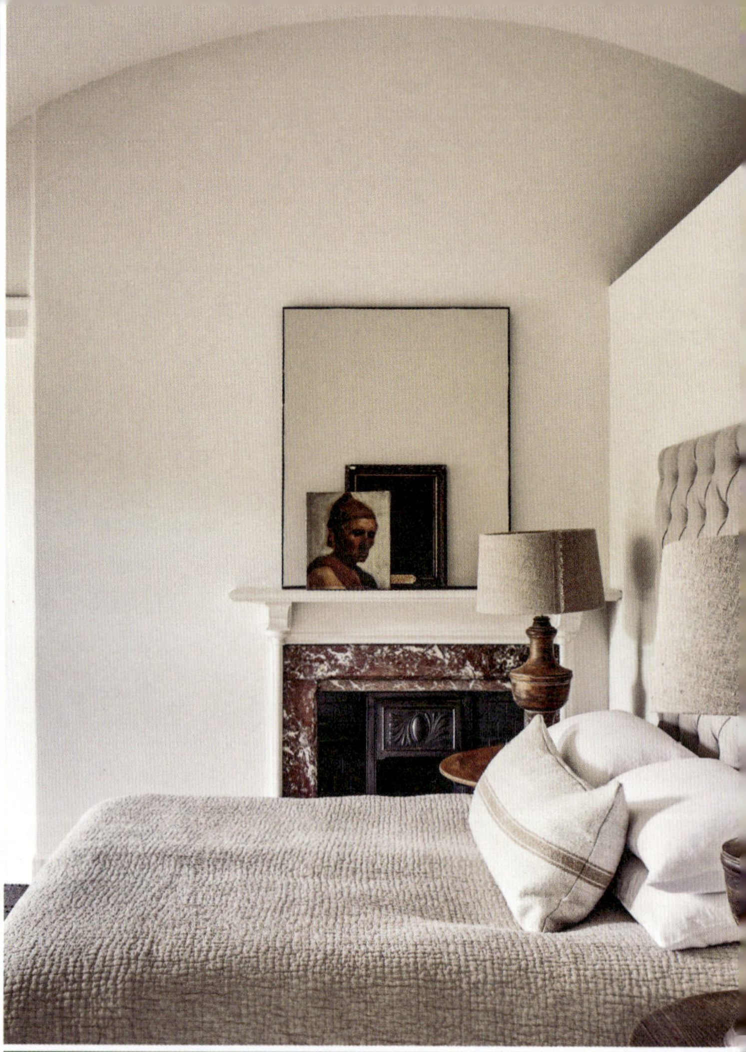

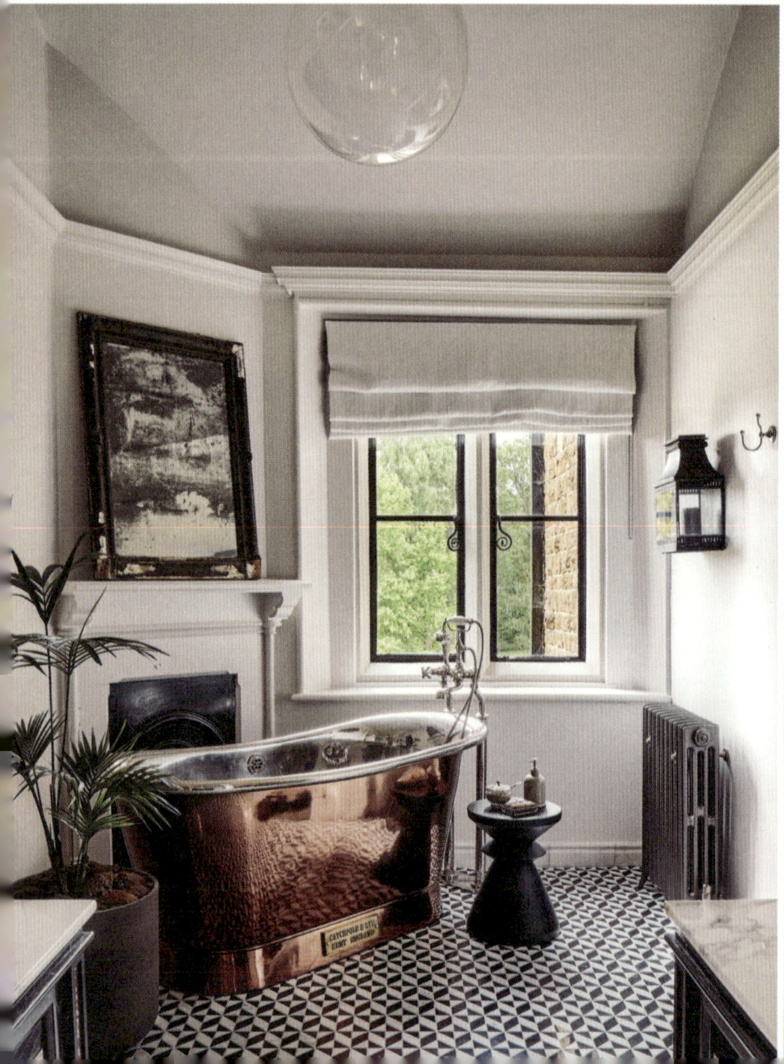

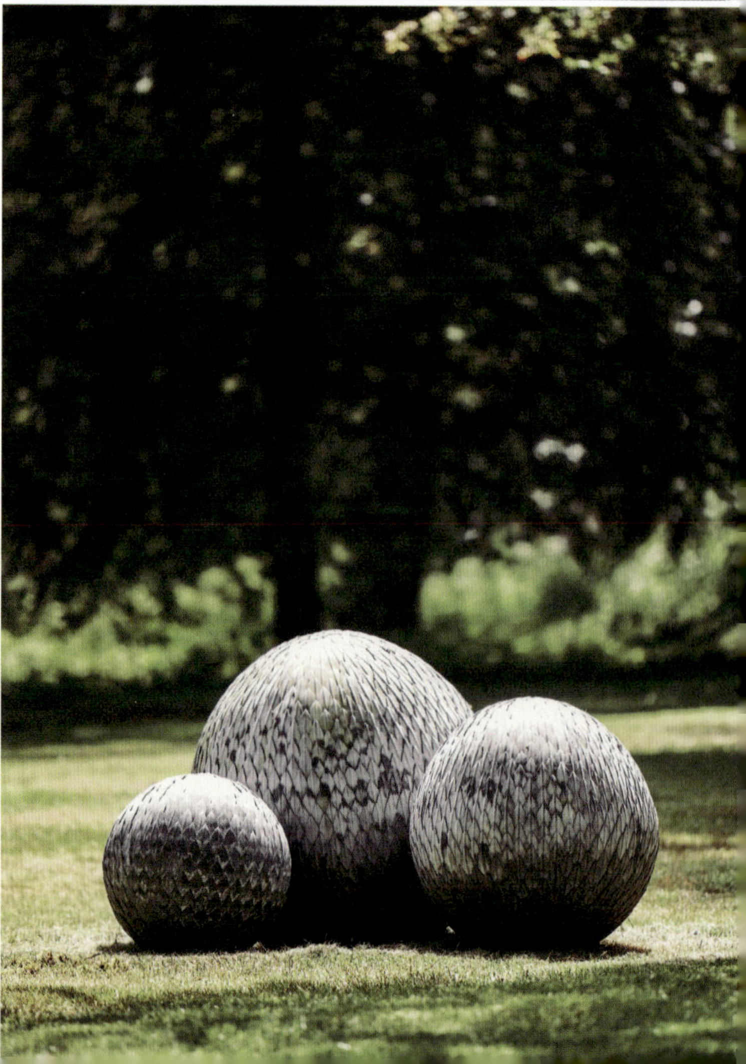

NATURAL EDGE Antique garden pots and sculptural balls introduce a stylish fluidity between the interior and exterior. In the master bedroom and en-suite bathroom, natural linen textures, marble surfaces and a copper bathtub from Catchpole & Rye heighten the feeling of escape.

COUNTRY IDYLL 175

REIMAGINED BAKERY
Bee Osborn / Interior Designer

BEE OSBORN'S PASSION FOR OLD BUILDINGS AND INTERIOR DESIGN HAS SPANNED nearly four decades, with nine renovations of her own and countless client and boutique hotel projects. Her name has become synonymous with the natural and muted, and in the UK with the transformation of historic Cotswold cottages. 'Preserving the heart of these special villages is important to me. If they are not looked after, they will disappear,' says Bee.

Having featured her former home in my book CREATE, it has been wonderful to chart her journey with this cottage, one that honours a deep respect for time-worn materials, authentic processes and a love of home.

Built in the mid-1500s, the Old Bakery had been left to decay, as the previous owners had sadly moved into residential care. Discovered by chance as a result of a road diversion, Bee inadvertently drove through a less well-known Cotswold village and spotted a 'for sale' sign. Curiosity piqued, she couldn't resist looking: 'Clearly falling down, the two-up-two-down cottage was hidden by voracious brambles, but on a plot with huge potential,' says Bee. A few weeks later, heart full, papers signed and with a buyer for her former home, work commenced – and despite arduous planning delays, she completed the transformation within 15 months.

During the build, Bee lived in a customized shepherd's hut, craned in at the start of the project, to avoid expensive rental costs and to be on site to make decisions. Complete with a wood-burning stove, kitchen, shower and outdoor bathing area, the hut was a lifesaver during the build. No longer surrounded by mud, it is set in its own wild meadow garden, nestled next to the cottage – now a fourth bedroom for one of her girls or guest retreat for friends.

The starting point for the renovation was how it would feel. 'I wanted the cottage to feel nurturing and comforting for myself and my partner; and to feel uplifting and welcoming when full of visiting family and friends,' says Bee. 'With three daughters (two now married), it was important to me that we had space to all sit, eat and relax comfortably together, and for the bedrooms to feel like private escapes with their own bathrooms.'

Doubling the original 93-square-metre (1,000-square-foot) space, a series of dilapidated garden buildings were reimagined and now connect with the old

OLD MEETS NEW The new black-painted cottage extension juxtaposes the original 16th-century stone walls. With 2.5-m (8-ft) high, Crittall-style doors, the living area connects seamlessly to the terrace.

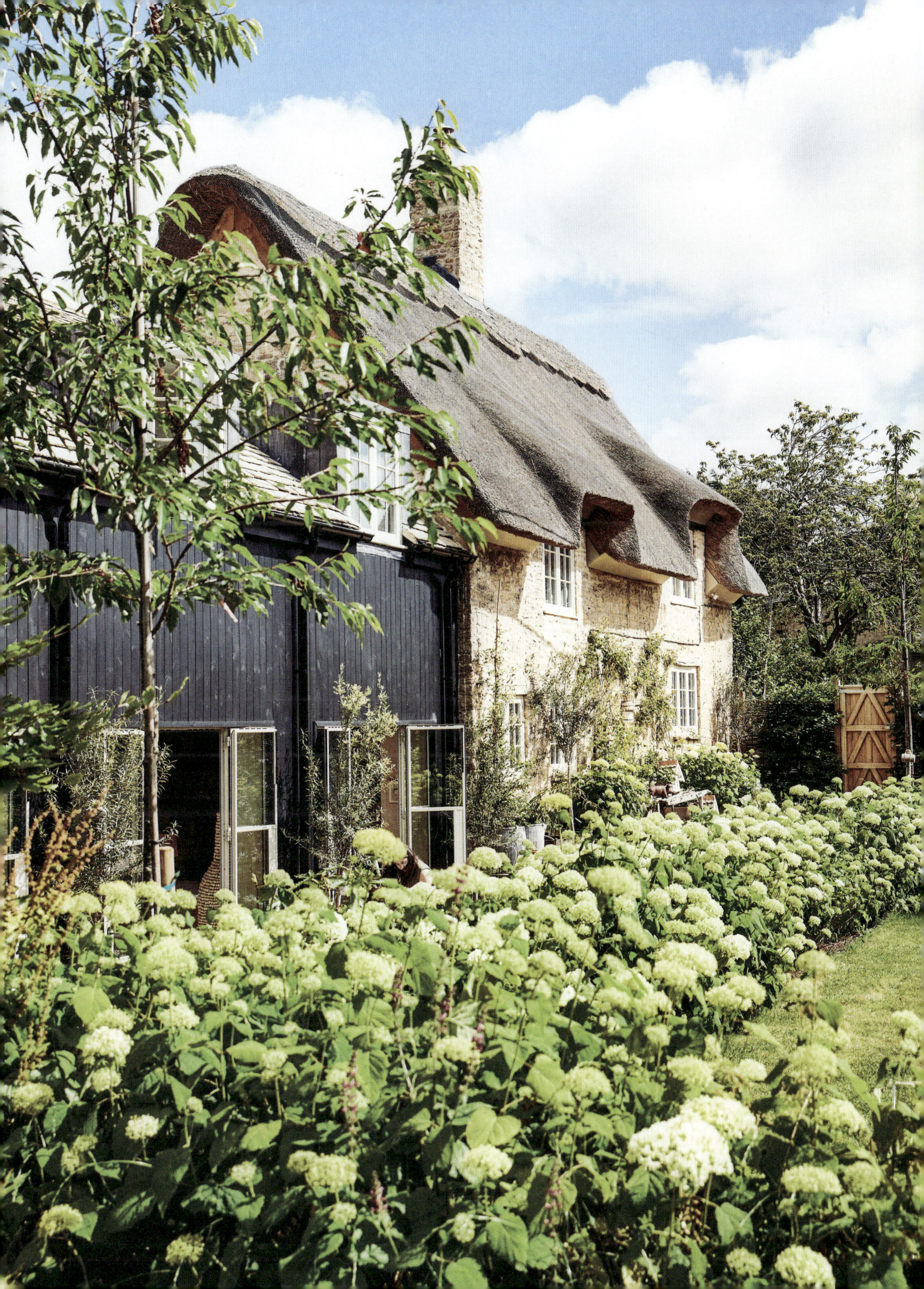

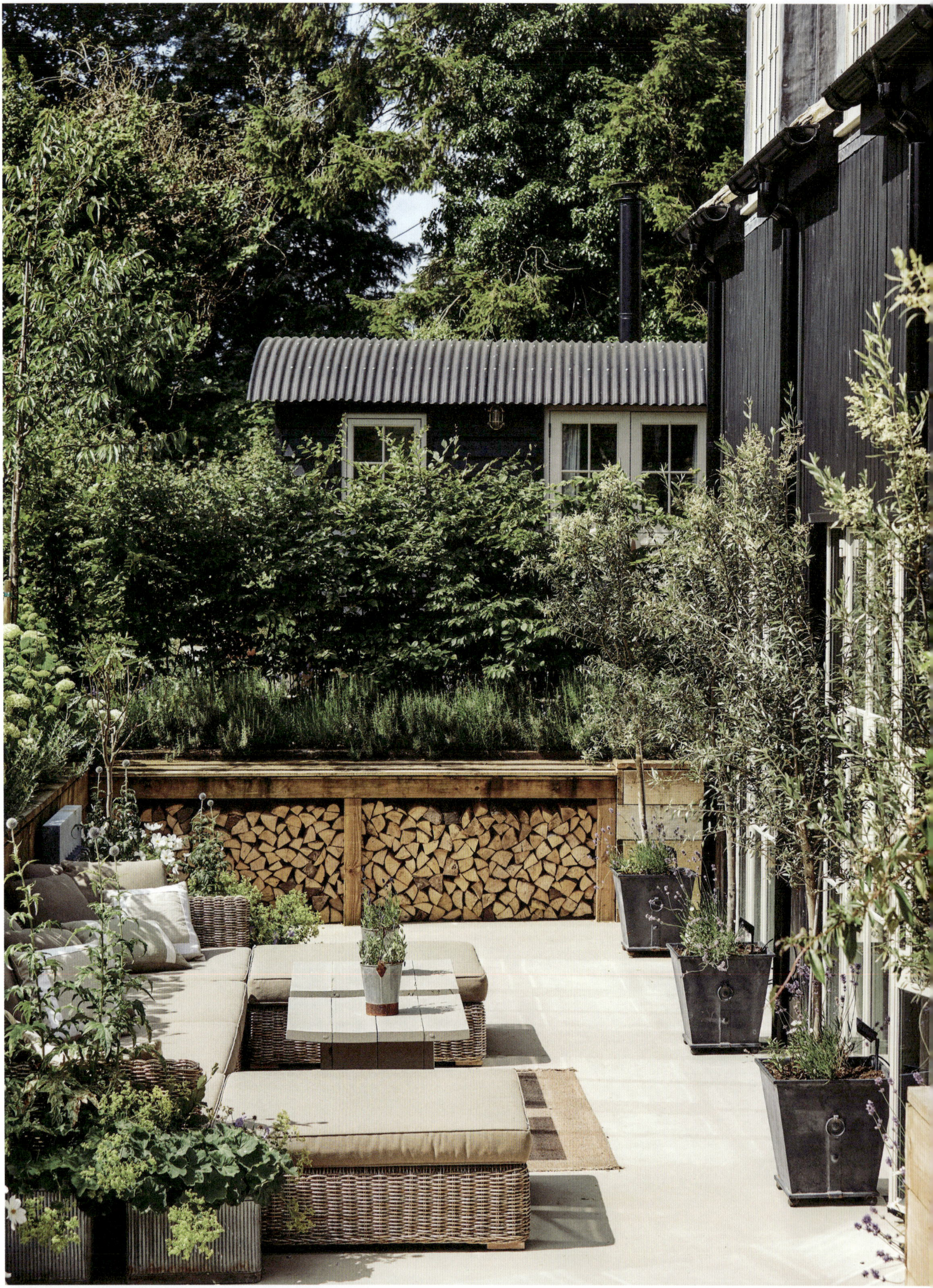

cottage via contemporary, wood-clad elevations, which sit within the parameters of the original stone structure. Excavating down 2m (6½ft), a retaining wall was created along the boundary, laying the foundations for a lofty living room. Framed by Crittall-style doors, the space leads out to a sunken terrace, where comfy furniture adapts easily as a place to sunbathe, rest or dine, surrounded by a beautifully landscaped garden, and Bee's favourite 'Annabelle' hydrangeas.

Inside, reclaimed wood-clad walls dressed in compelling art have added a warm, earthy edge to the main living area, while an inviting sofa and wood-burning stove make it a place where the family loves to hang out. 'I am at my happiest sharing a meal, or enjoying time with my family, so it was important to me that the kitchen and dining area link seamlessly to this space and the garden – you feel very connected to each other and nature,' Bee explains.

'In the original cottage, deep window recesses have been turned into cozy reading nooks,' continues Bee. 'I love the architectural details in the snug – the 16th-century mullion windows, worn beams and open fireplace make it feel very cosseting.'

Throughout, old stone walls have been lovingly brought back to life and are offset by wall finishes in soft lime plaster and reclaimed wood cladding, which adds to the calming, tactile appeal. 'I wanted the new materials to honour the integrity of the cottage, but with a high-low balance of original, expensive and more affordable,' says Bee. 'I am a great believer in making budgets work hard, and by installing simple painted floorboards, I have been able to afford timeless, special brass tapware, which brings me joy every time I touch it.'

Upstairs in the main house, previously cold and draughty vaulted bedrooms have been upgraded to be thermally efficient and cozy; and the creation of a master suite in the new extension has enabled Bee to create a private sanctuary. Layered, textural finds highlight Bee's appreciation of the beautiful and natural and add to the feeling of warmth and character. There are artisanal tables, handmade seagrass lights, weathered timber furniture, woven baskets, beaded sculptures and abundant textiles – many from her collaboration with Zoe Glencross.

'I always believe if you can see something in your mind, you can create it with your hands. It's been a labour of love, but we feel very at home here.' ✧

SHEPHERD'S DELIGHT Designed internally by Bee, the cocooning shepherd's hut by Arbor Shepherd's Huts provided a welcome bolthole during the renovation. It is now a guest retreat, complete with outdoor bathtub.

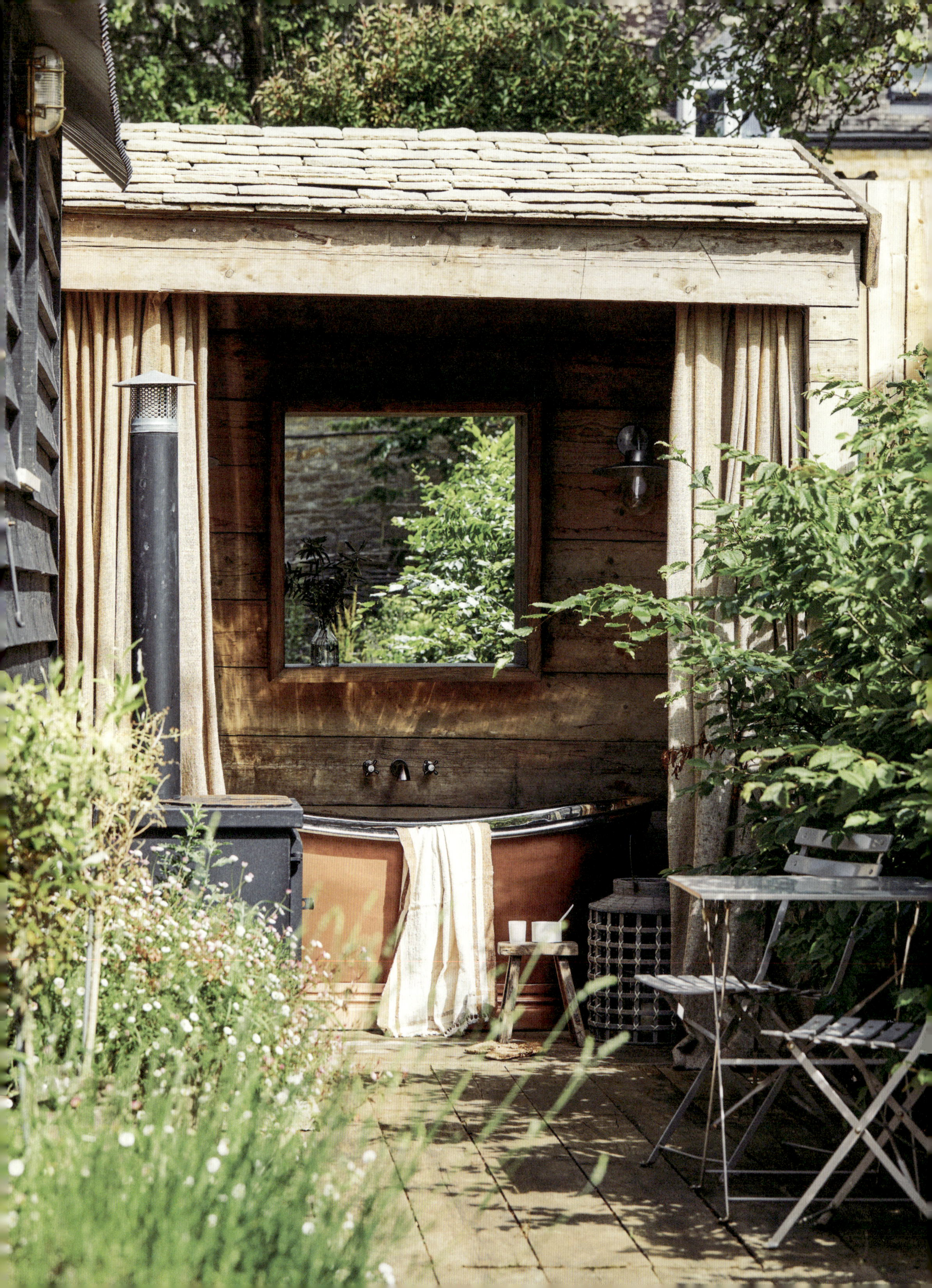

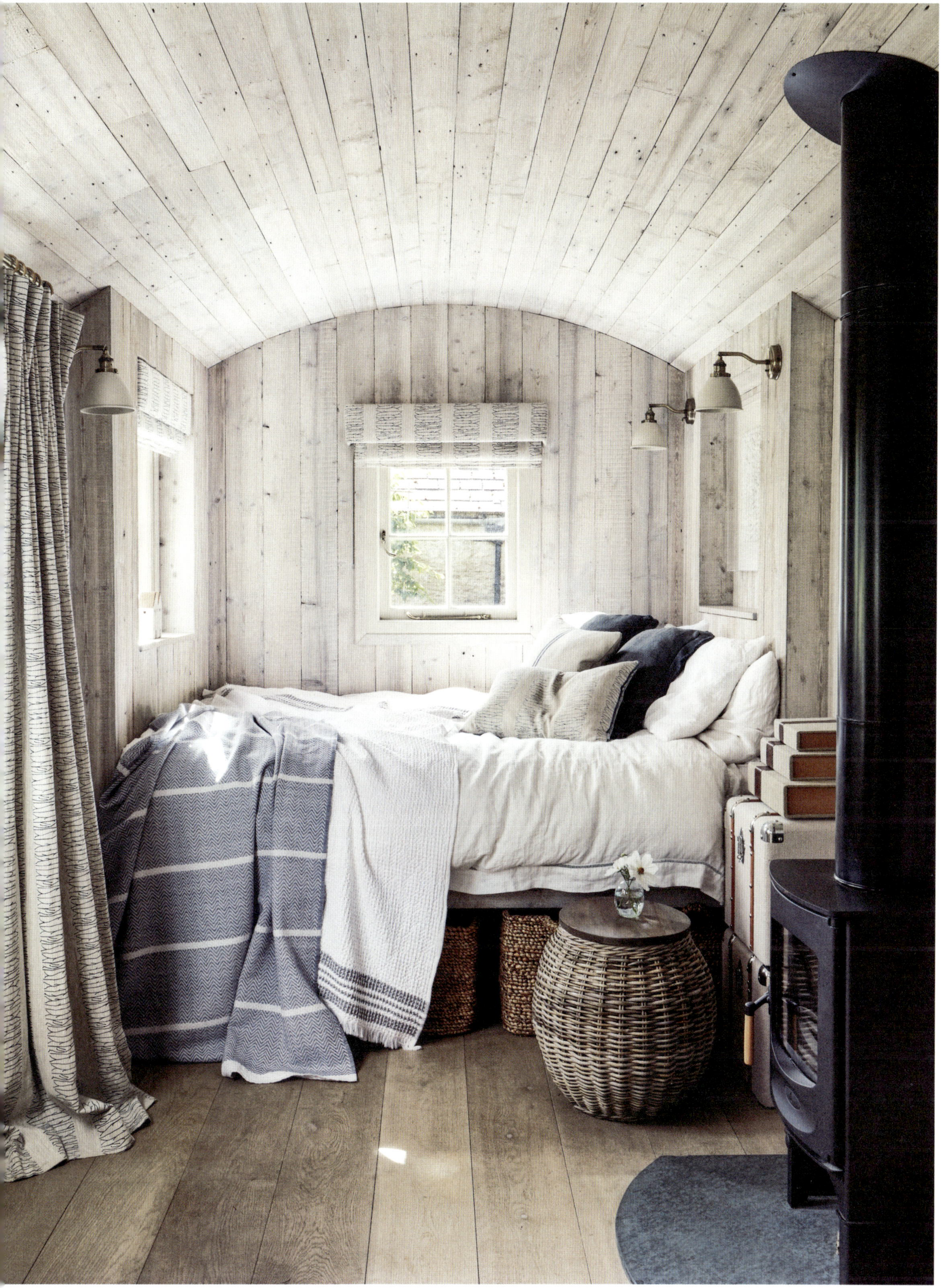

INSIDE OUTSIDE Crittall-style windows and doors frame two sides of the panelled living and kitchen space. The television is cleverly inset behind a wall hanging above the wood-burning stove (opposite, top left). Lamps on the kitchen island by Porta Romana.

182 LIVING

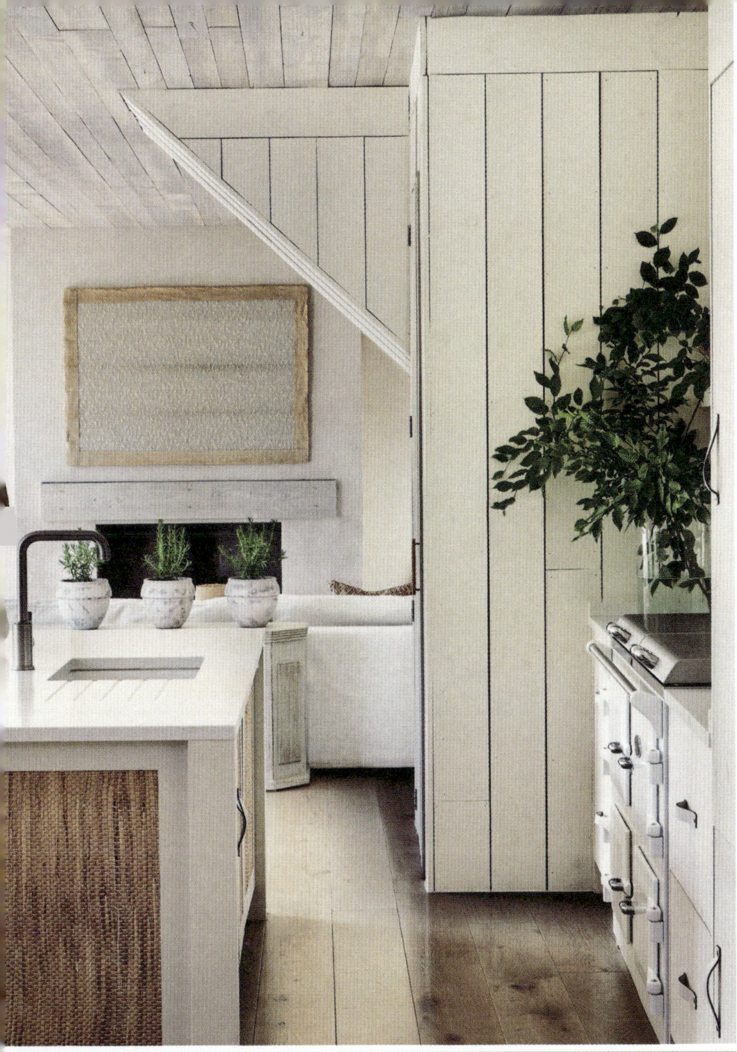

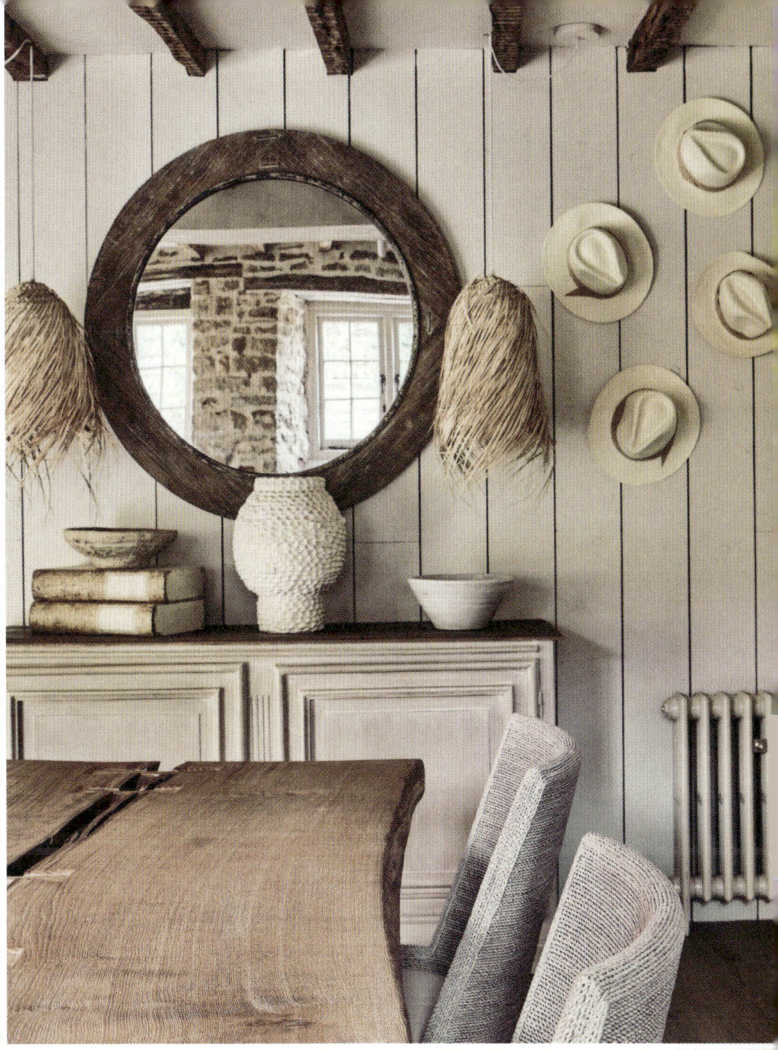

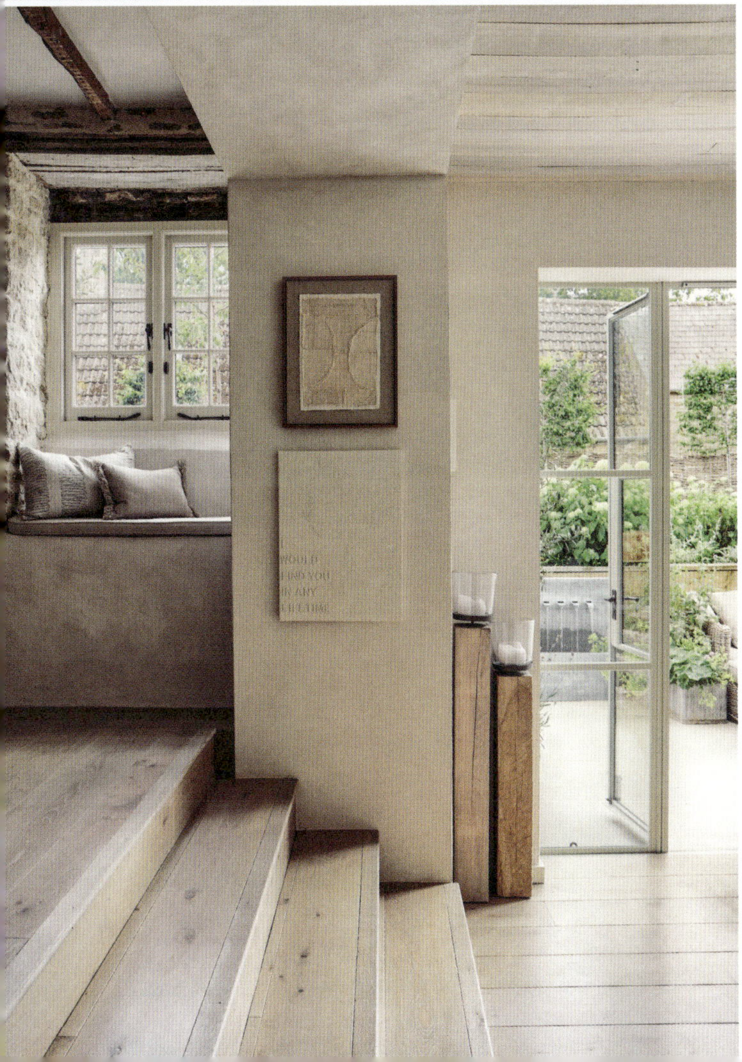

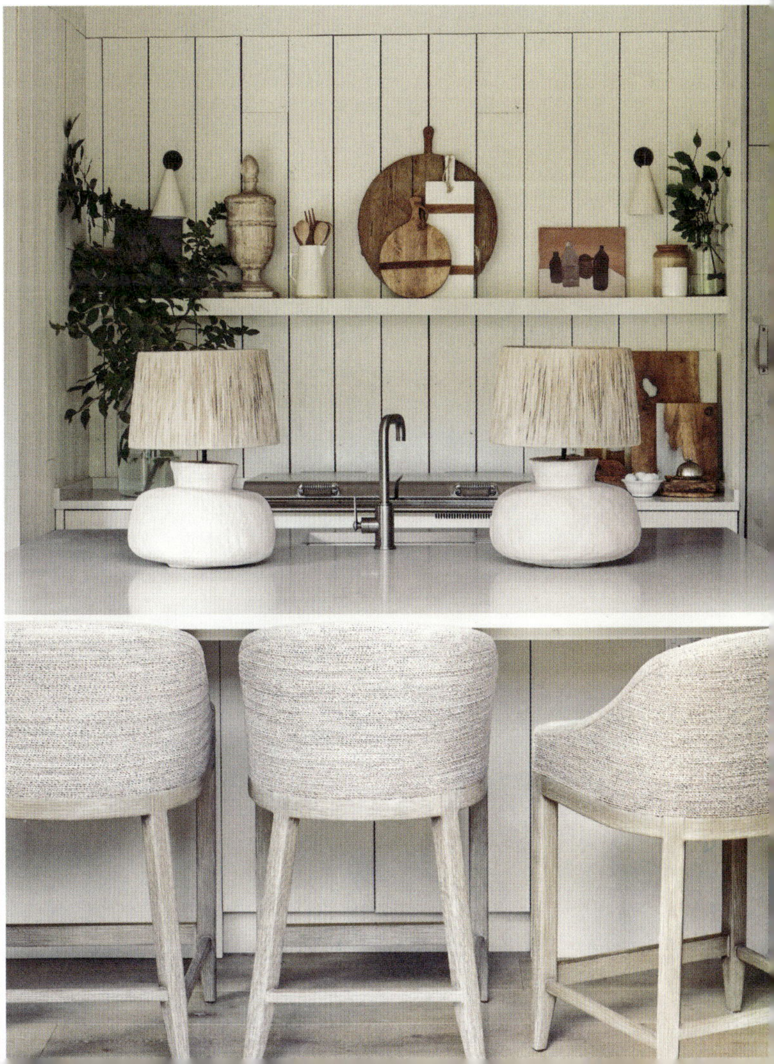

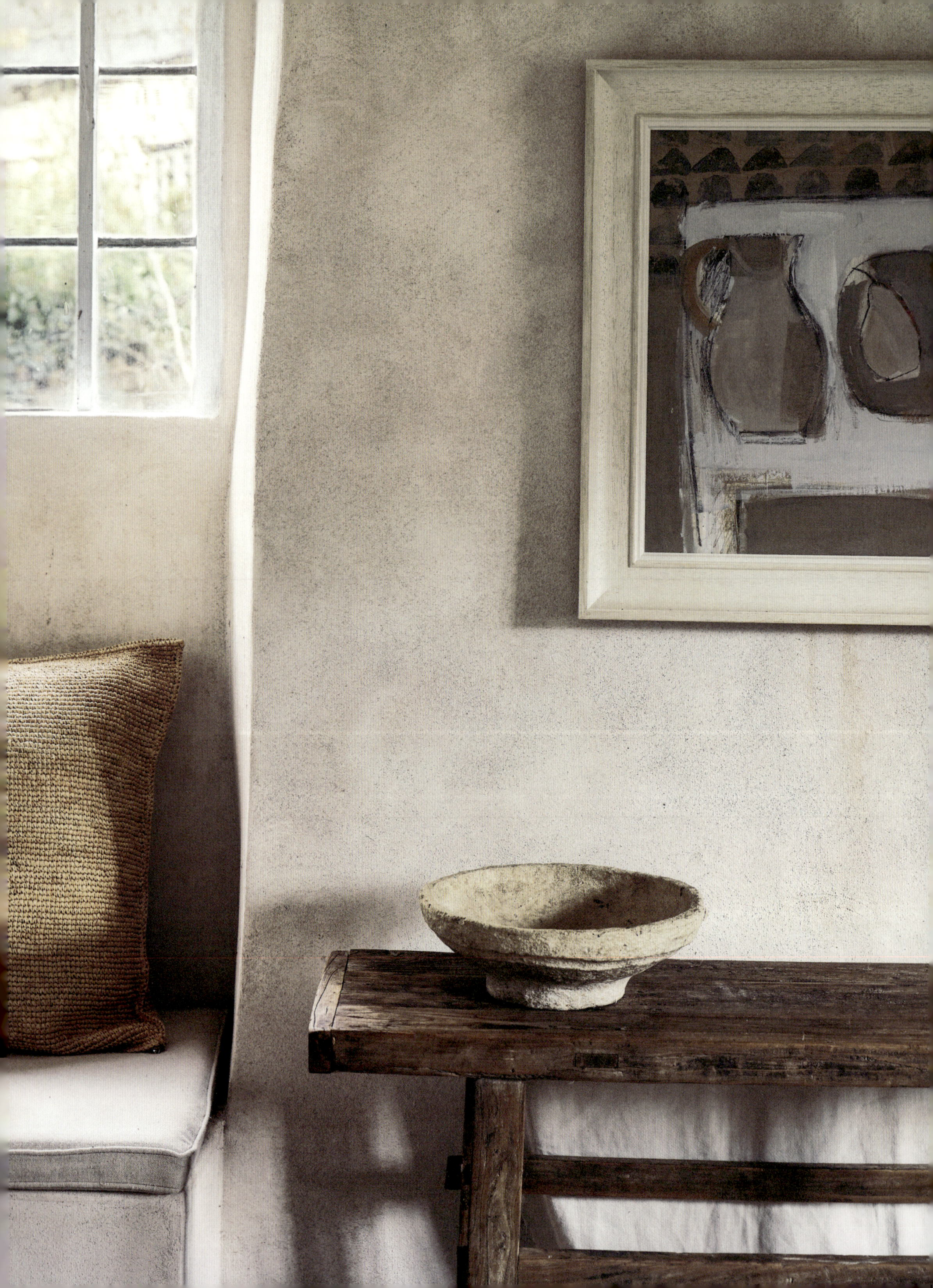

SANCTUARY & PEACE Original architectural details and lime-plastered walls lend a cossetting appeal to the 16th-century snug. Painting by Netta Carey (opposite). The roll-top bathtub in the master bedroom heightens the feeling of comfort. Painting above wood-burning stove from Art Untamed (this page).

PAGES 186–187 VAULTED ELEVATIONS The roof and thatch were restored by Bee to create a luxurious guest retreat. Roll-top bathtub by BC Designs and tapware by Samuel Heath.

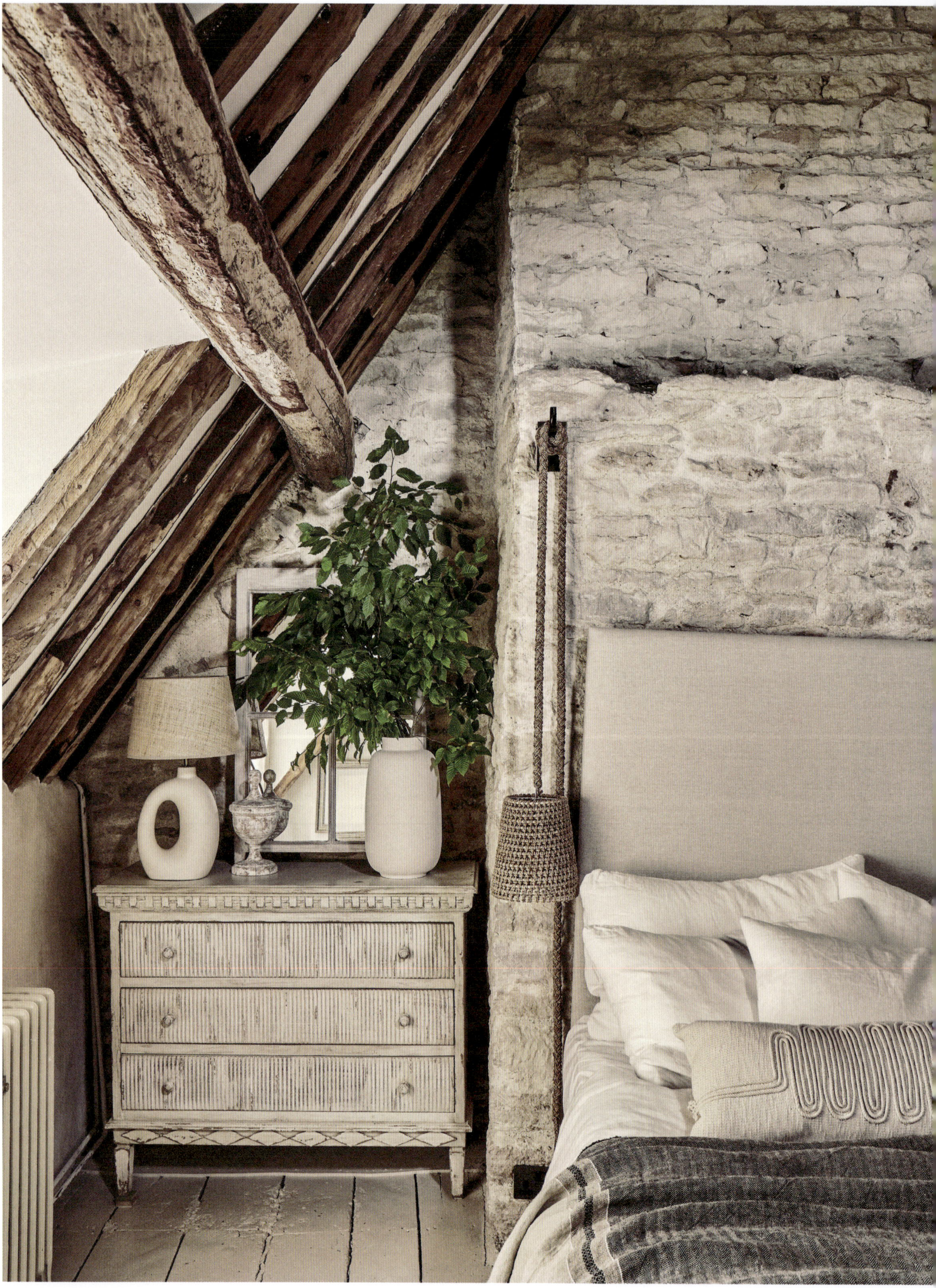

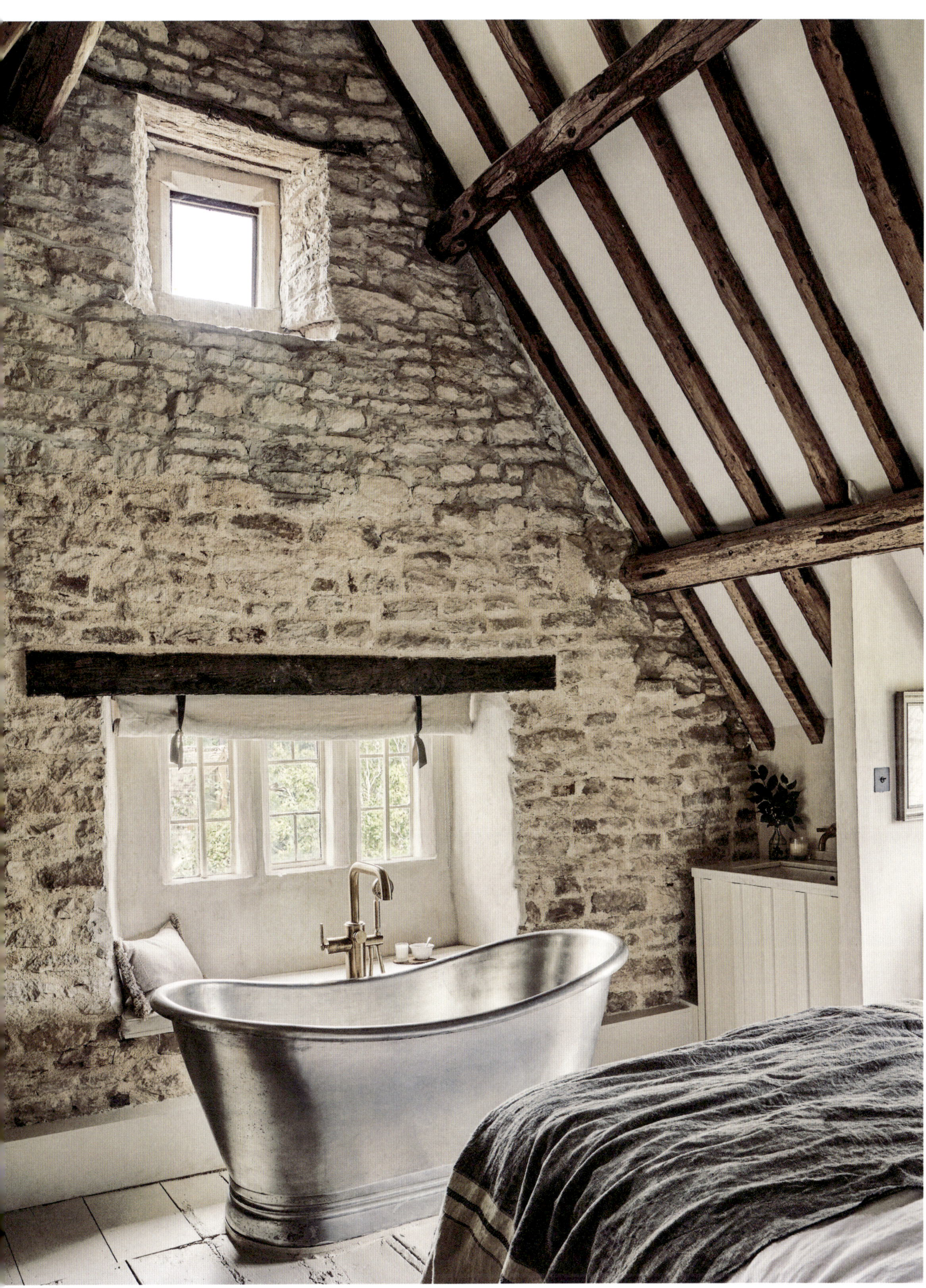

RURAL HAVEN
Maria & Paul Le Mesurier / Furniture Makers

FOR MARIA LE MESURIER, THE MOVE TO THEIR RUSTIC, FAMILY FARMHOUSE IN North Devon has been about balancing two of her greatest needs: being surrounded by nature and being true to herself. Letting go of past childhood trauma and emerging as her authentic self, Maria has created the nurturing sanctuary she had craved – for both herself and her family.

'This house has been a dream for many years,' says Maria. 'We have the best of both worlds – surrounded by open farmland, yet a ten-minute walk to some of the most striking beaches and coastline. You can smell the salt in the air and at night the sound of the sea is very soothing,' she continues. 'It was a long search, but with five children aged 8–22, a budget that had to work hard, and on-site workshop requirements for our business, WoodEdit, everything took time. Discovering this place – the energy, location and house – all felt right.'

The 300-year-old thatched cottage sits at the end of a lane, flanked by wild hedgerows, which are alive with vibrant pink foxgloves, towering cow parsley and fragrant honeysuckle. 'I find nature incredibly inspiring, and the seasonal changes really influence how I layer our home. For me, tall swathes of wildflowers, cut branches or simple vases of rosemary or mint add sculptural detail throughout and bring a deeper symbolism and significance that can help to heal, nurture and inspire,' says Maria. 'It's like having art without the need to fill the walls,' she says. 'As I've got older, I like to keep walls bare. It draws your eye to the whole room and connects spaces to the view and nature,' she explains.

With strong architectural bones already in place, the renovation has focused on the decorative – shifting the aesthetic from white and bright to warm and cocooning. Exercising restraint, Maria used one shade of paint for both the exterior and interior walls: a soft, sandy colour that changes depth throughout. 'I wanted to keep things simple, and as the light shifts, the walls feel like a tonal mix of shades, so there was no need to complicate choices,' says Maria.

'I like to keep backdrops cohesive. Clutter and busy interiors make me uneasy, so hardworking storage, hanging wicker baskets and regular edits ensure spaces feel calm.' Despite a love of the pared back and minimal, Maria successfully balances a need for comfort and warmth with her use of textural, natural materials. 'I gravitate toward authentic, durable foundations in wood, stone, wool, sheepskin, linen and jute.'

NATURAL ELEGANCE Natural materials help Maria to feel grounded and are both stylish and hard-wearing for a family of seven. Simple hedgerow flowers and fallen branches add an earthy decorative appeal.

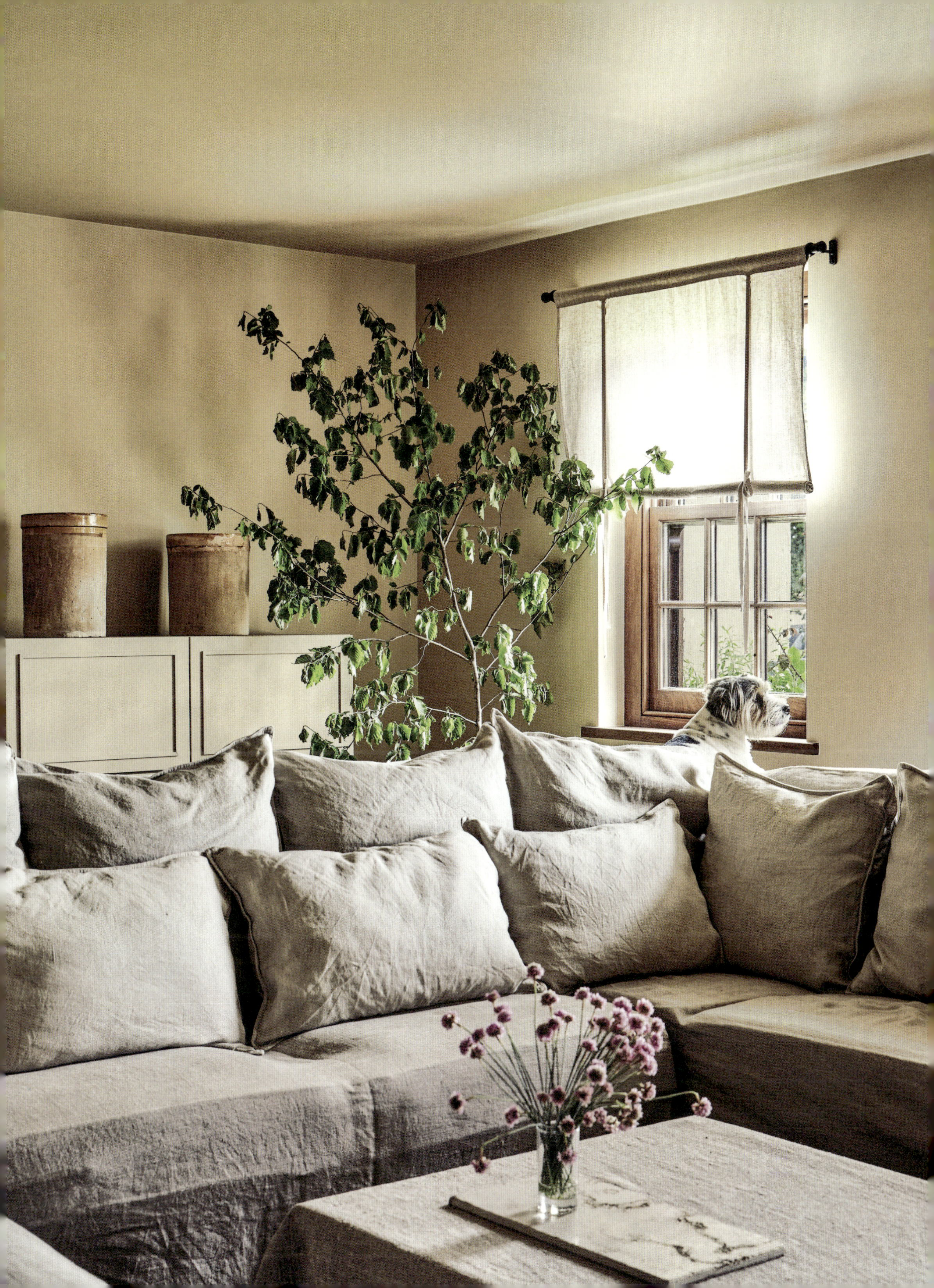

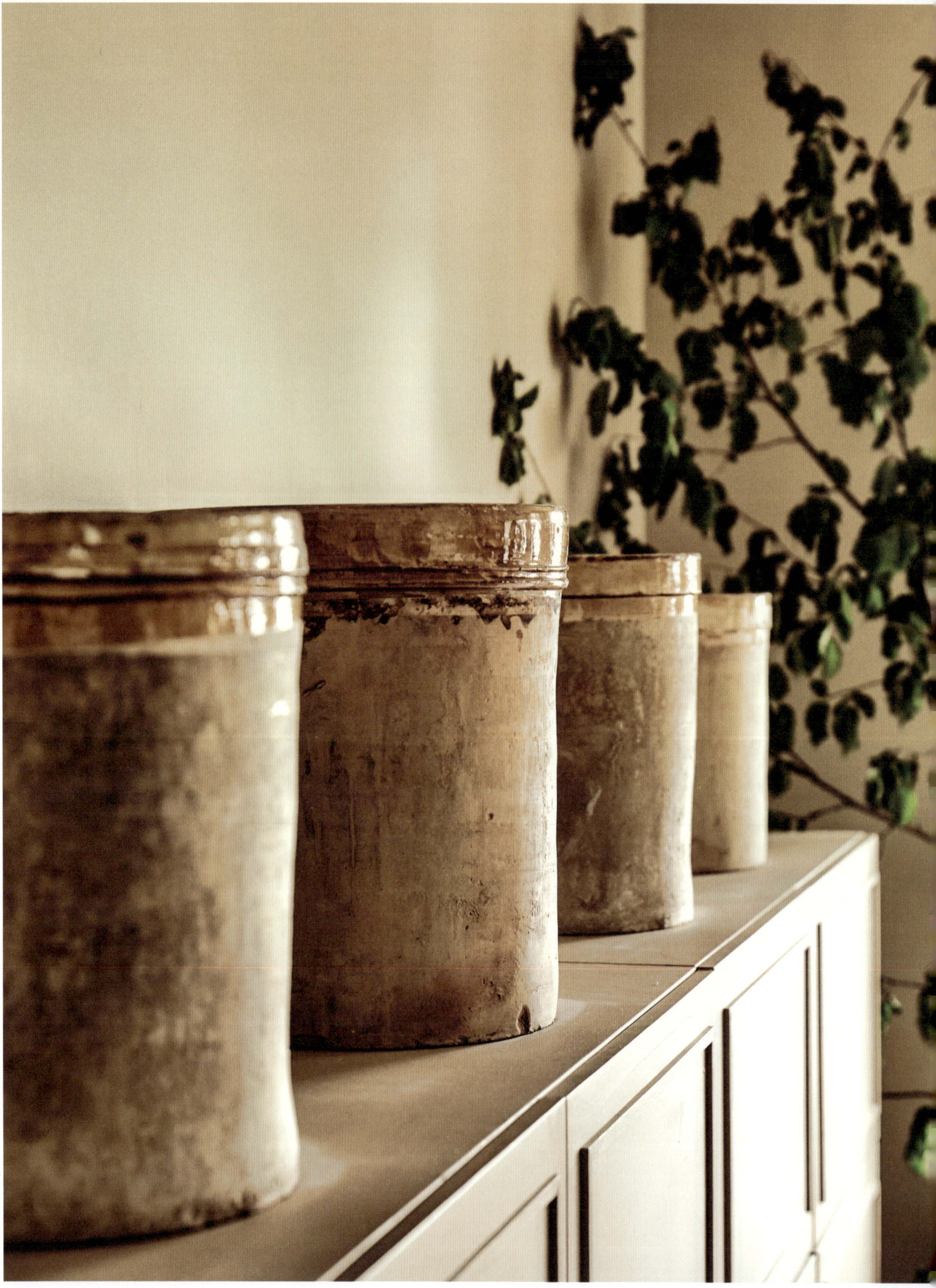

Maria applies the same seasonal wardrobe rules to how she dresses her home – using natural linen sheets to cover their oversized family sofa in spring and summer, then switching to earthier tones in autumn and winter. 'As well as reflecting the season, these materials are extremely durable – I never want home to feel precious, so with a large family it means everyone feels comfortable,' says Maria.

A modernist storage cupboard at the back of the living room amplifies a decorative display of Italian olive pots. With a rich, mustardy glaze and tactile patina, they are part of a wider collection of Italian ceramics that Maria has collected for many years and layered throughout her home. Their graphic shapes and sizes contrast with the low ceilings and cozy proportions of the cottage with an engaging alchemy.

Bathrooms have been updated with timeless stone and contemporary tapware, and new, generously sized walk-in showers and curved bathtubs create a sense of retreat. In the kitchen and dining area, traditional Shaker cabinetry is offset by select contemporary pieces from the couple's WoodEdit collection. These include a clean-lined kitchen island, abundant serving boards and a handmade table and benches that can seat the entire family – and still squeeze in a few more for extended get-togethers.

As creative director for their family business – WoodEdit, a company specializing in simple and timeless furniture – Maria designs each piece, which is then handmade by her husband Paul. Their philosophy is that your home should reflect the essence of who you are. 'The way we live and my desire for things to feel functional, as well as elegant, were the starting point. We couldn't find the everyday pieces we were looking for, such as tables, desks, peg rails, boot racks, radiator covers and wardrobes (closets), so made them ourselves. Everything we sell has been tried and tested at home – as a family of seven, I want things to look great, but they must also be practical.'

The move has provided the peace for Maria to also establish her own business alongside WoodEdit, working as a lifestyle enhancer and helping others to feel better about themselves and their homes, with her podcast encouraging a positive outlook in all areas of life. 'Life is an edit – we can choose what we decide to carry with us and our homes should always be a reflection of that,' she explains. ✧

RUSTIC & RAW Decorative details are kept to a minimum, with Maria's collection of antique Italian pots taking the place of art.

PAGES 192–193 **SIMPLICITY OF FORM** WoodEdit dining furniture enhances the rustic stone walls and slate floors.

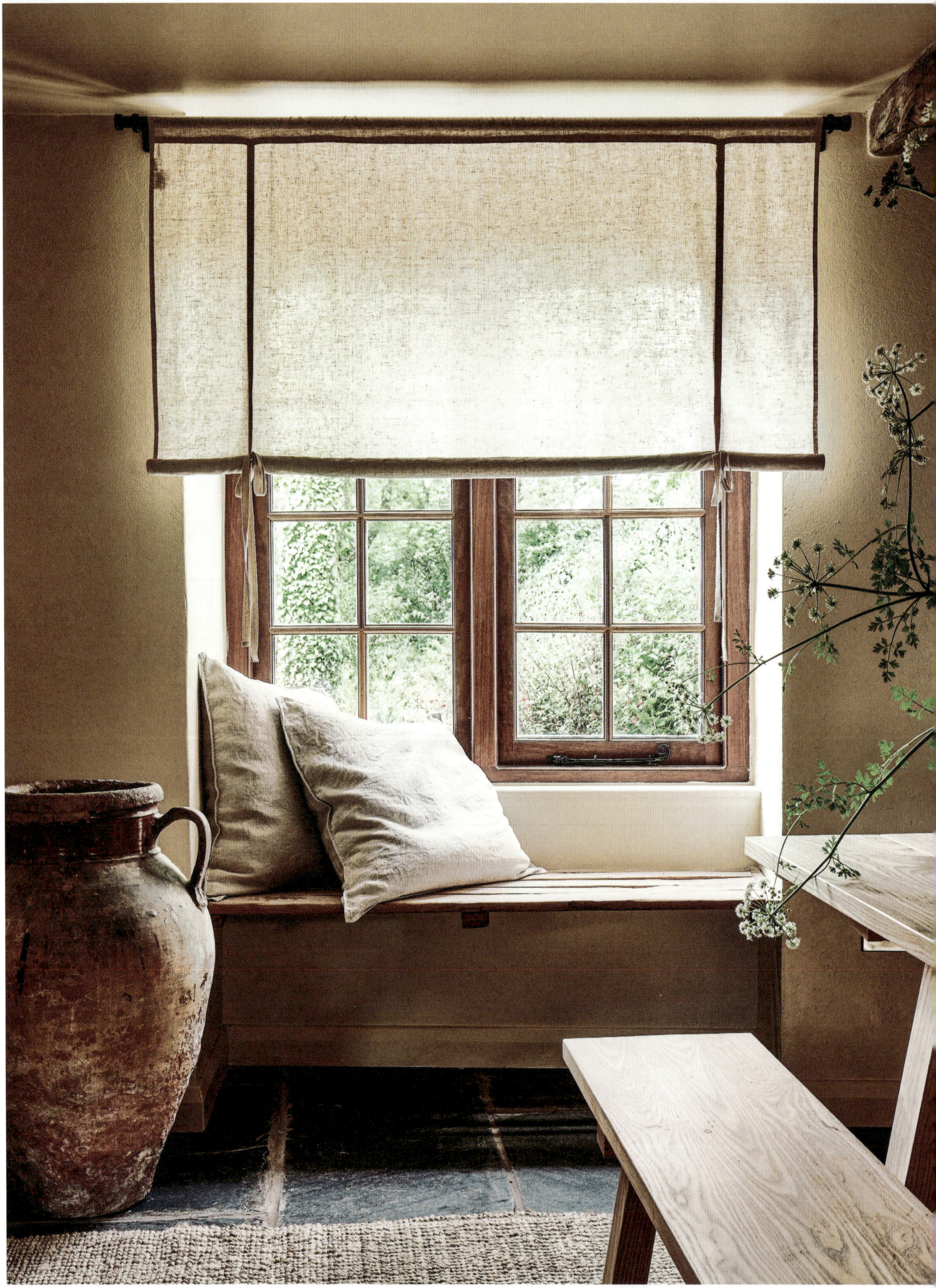

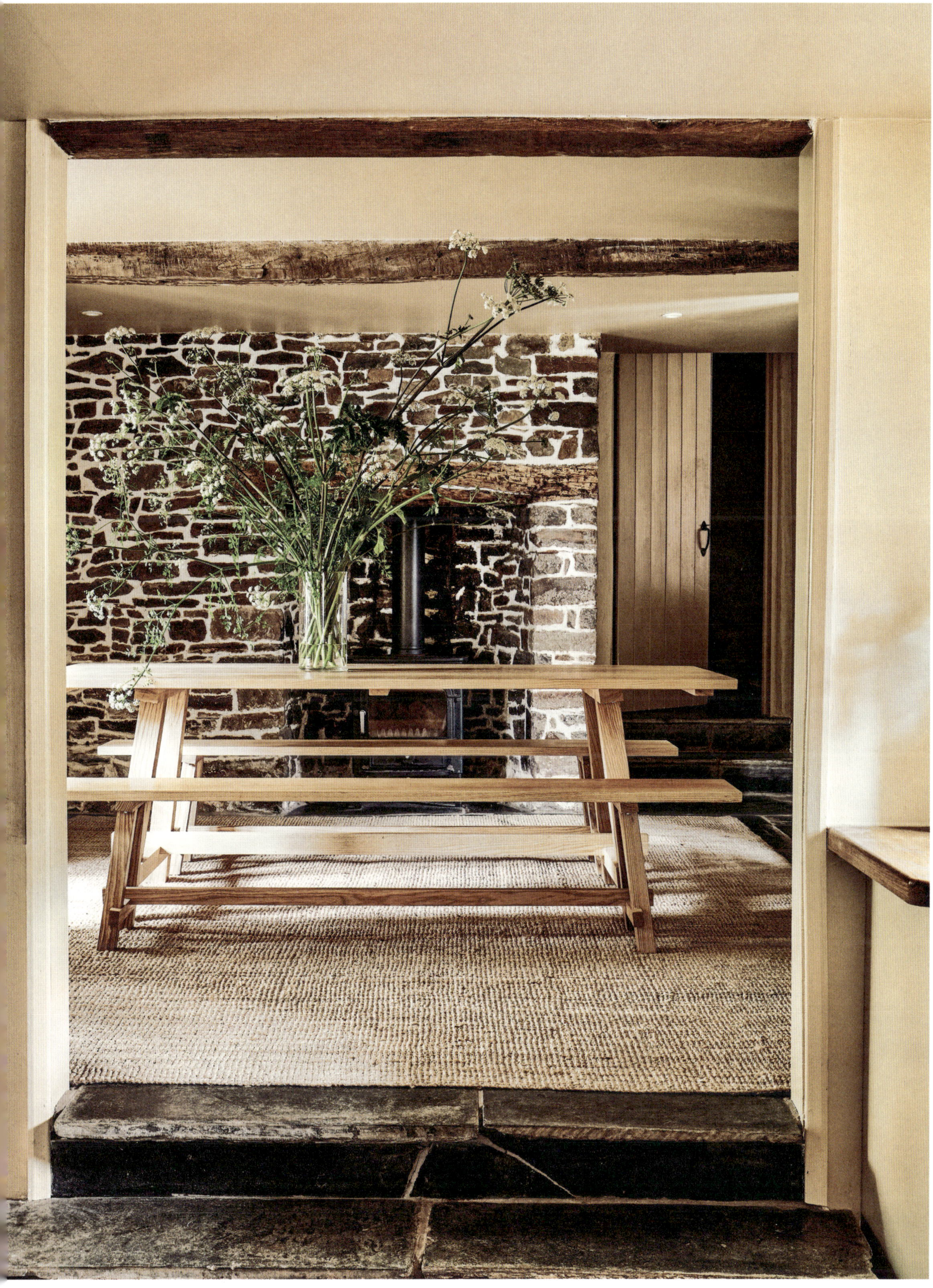

KEEPING IT COZY An inherited kitchen has been painted in gentle hues to match the walls, while natural linen blinds (shades) softly filter the light. The adjacent flower room is alive with vibrant hedgerow cuttings and stacks of WoodEdit cutting boards.

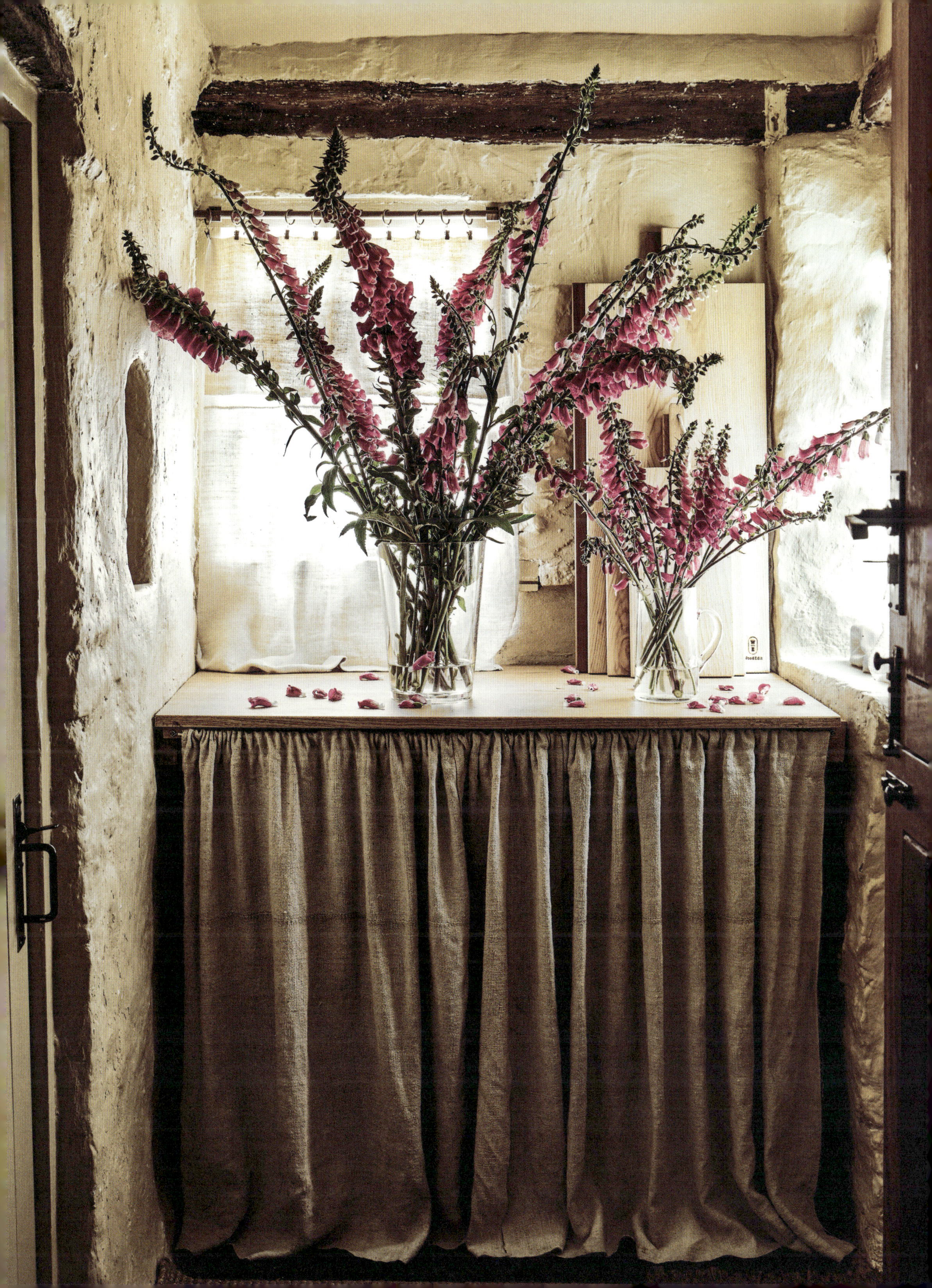

LAYER IT UP In the master bedroom, an inviting bed is dressed in natural linen, soft wool and cozy cashmere layers. And in the family bathroom, a chic, contemporary bathtub adds an indulgent touch to the pared-back interior.

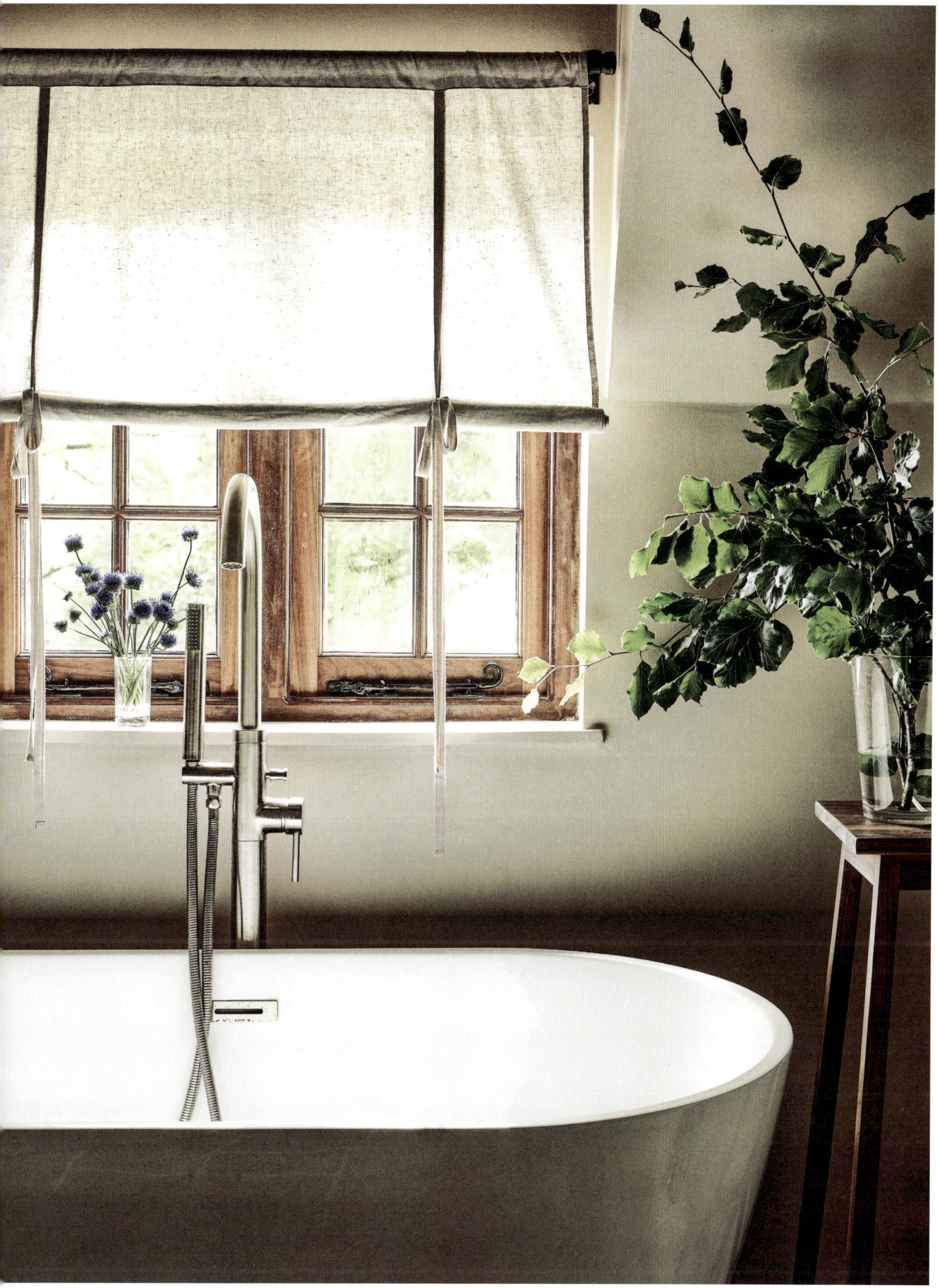

THATCHED CHIC The exterior is painted to match the interior. The slate-roofed extension next to the main house is home to the WoodEdit studio. Woven animal heads sourced by Maria.

RURAL HAVEN 199

VALLEY HIDEAWAY
Tom Cox / Designer

AS CAN HAPPEN WITH MANY GOOD THINGS, THIS PART OF DEVON AND THIS special farmhouse were both discovered by designer Tom Cox through old-fashioned word of mouth. Nestled at the end of a bumpy farm track and set between hills on both sides of a remote valley, it enabled a much-desired relocation from London and the chance to balance home and work.

'I had been looking for a home like this for as long as I can remember,' says Tom. 'With no distractions – the only sounds you hear are the river, or the call of wild animals and birds. I'm very outdoorsy, but here it is also easy to rekindle simple pleasures like listening to the radio, lighting a fire, or in setting a table. The farmhouse is filled with things I love and have collected for years, such as the antique kilim rugs, giant antlers, fishing trophies and all the art. It's a very authentic read of me and it feels comforting to be surrounded by things that are so personal.'

Built into a south-facing hill, this 17th-century, three-bedroom farmhouse, with an adjacent one-bedroom guest cottage (complete with bathroom, tiny kitchen and creative studio), forms part of a larger complex of outhouses and garden areas that Tom has imaginatively brought to life. 'An amazing elderly couple lived here before, and the foundations for the outbuildings and garden had been done exceptionally well,' he explains. Now with an outdoor kitchen, wood-fired bathtub and sun deck all in constant use, along with a sauna and cold-water plunge, it's evident that reset is embraced here – nothing is designed for show. 'I'm happiest in nature. I can get lost outside for hours without seeing a soul, then return to the comfort of home.'

Throughout the space, antiques, gathered objects and art are layered with curatorial precision and wit. Since the farmhouse is Grade II listed, the rooms couldn't be altered, so it was a case of choosing a lead piece and allowing spaces to develop. For the living room, it was a yellow Irish dresser that caught Tom's eye. 'Perfect for my whisky collection and now a favourite corner – sat in the window, with the wood-burning stove blazing and the river rushing by, it's very calming.'

With a natural affinity for pattern and colour, the downstairs snug, painted in Farrow & Ball's 'Oval Room Blue', complements a Delft-blue-tiled fireplace and impressive salmon trophy above. A double Howe chair (where Boo, Tom's dog, is usually found) is offset by a vintage kilim footstool and an antique sofa covered in a favourite Mulberry Home stripe – encouraging all who visit to kick back.

CENTRE STAGE Antique sofa, recovered in a Mulberry Home stripe. Cushions from Ralph Lauren Home. Arrow rug, Yellowstone artwork, and lamp made from an antique tole tea caddy, all Studio HÁM designs.

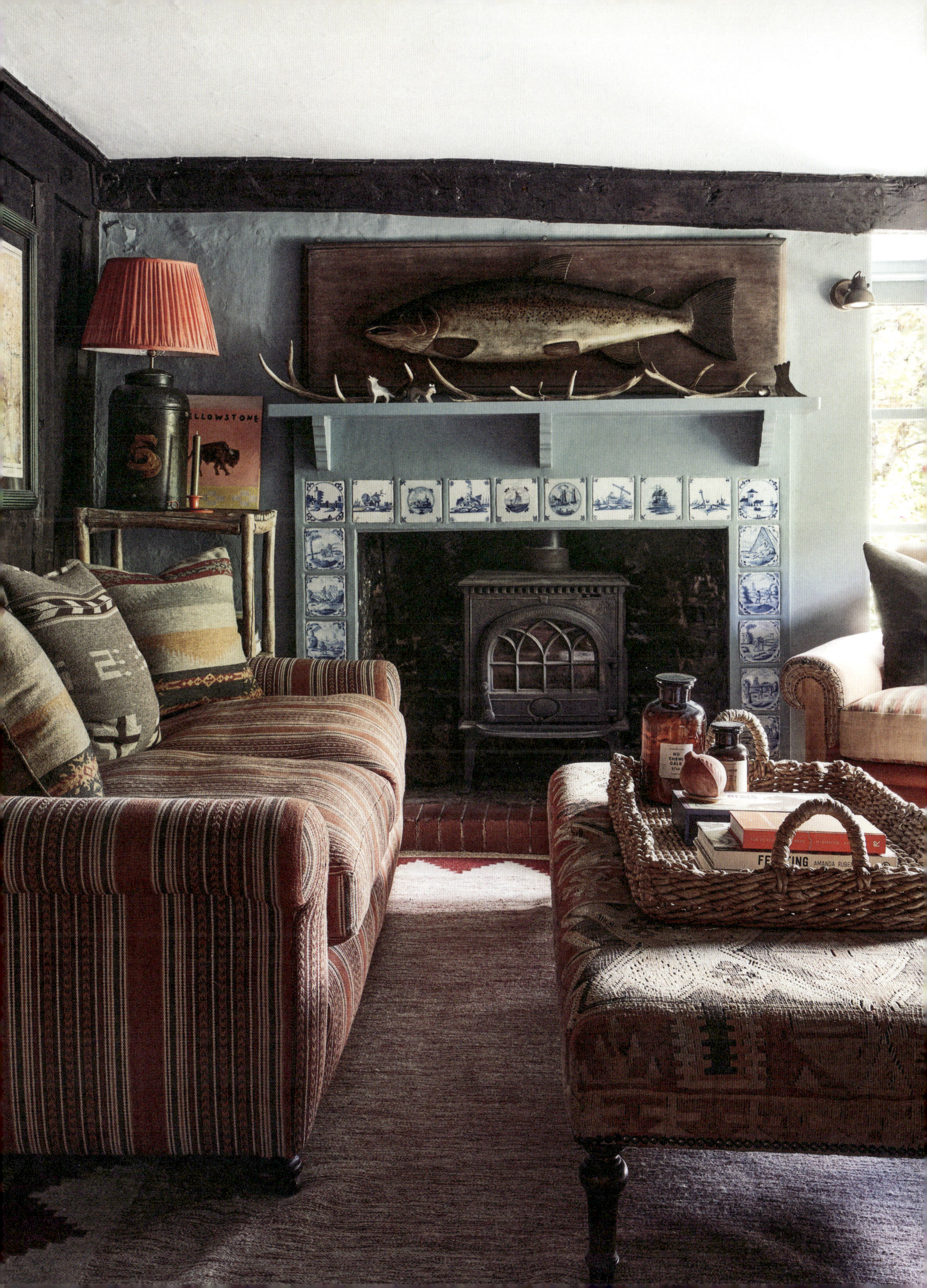

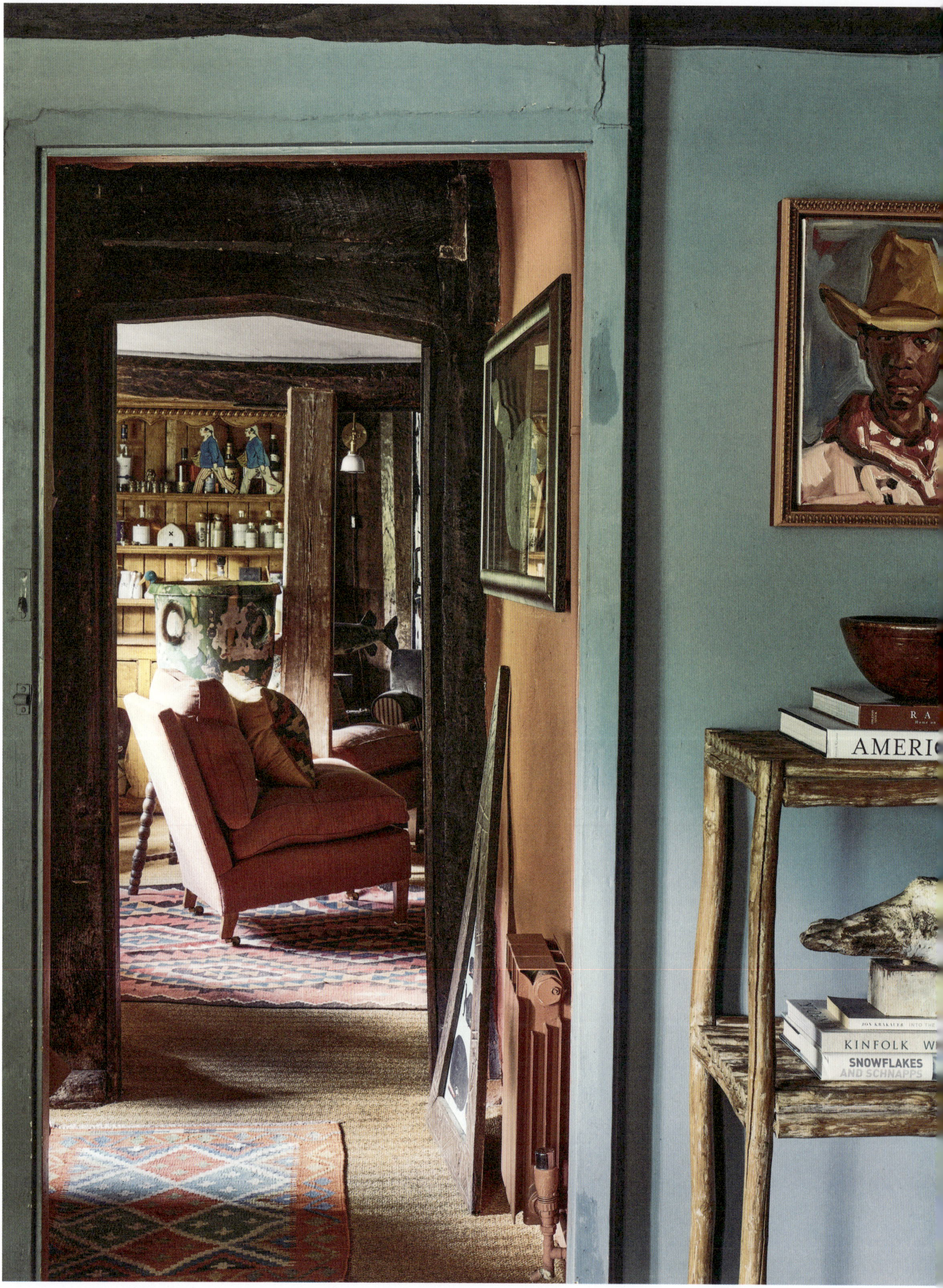
AMERIC
KINFOLK W
SNOWFLAKES
AND SCHNAPPS

'Unwittingly exposed to beautiful things, with parents immersed in the antiques and interiors trade, I have always been quietly obsessed with home and hotel design. I've spent my life holidaying in Devon and Scotland – cold-water swimming, fishing and canoeing; and many summers as an adult in America, living in the outdoors and staying in beautiful cabins. This house echoes a lot of those memories. It's always been about seeking beauty alongside an immersion in nature.'

Tom co-founded HÁM Architecture, Build and Interior Decoration with his parents back in 2011, joined shortly after by his younger sister Kate. A much-loved British success story, HÁM has fostered a reputation as a family of tastemakers – with an in-house team of architects, interior designers and build services, plus an online store, Studio HÁM, selling antiques, art and finishing details, sourced by all the family. With the launch of their own furniture collections, they are now extending their reach across the pond to the US.

Tom's strong sense of style can be seen throughout. Amusingly, with low ceilings and beams, you would think his 6ft 5in physique could be problematic here, but he works it to his advantage, favouring cocooning over lofty, and turning everyday home interactions into sensory ones. Think marble-topped, handmade vanity units, elegant brass tapware, bespoke headboards and tactile furnishings. Along with covetable art walls: everything from the abstract and folksy to the antique and irreverent.

The compact, original kitchen has not been touched, as a new extension is being planned. But with the bright red Aga and welcoming dining table (cut to fit through the door), it's an intimate space where Tom enjoys spending his time. 'I find it hard to switch off, but coming home to the smell of a roast and the radio on, I always breathe a sigh of relief.'

Tom has also introduced his partner to this area, and now, with the arrival of their son, the farmhouse has become even more beloved. 'This place is home to everything I have dreamed of and love.' ✧

LAYER UP Snug walls painted in 'Oval Room Blue' by Farrow & Ball. Entrance hall painted in 'Sang de Boeuf' by Edward Bulmer Natural Paint. The living room beyond is filled with covetable antiques and art sourced by Tom for Studio HÁM.

204 LIVING

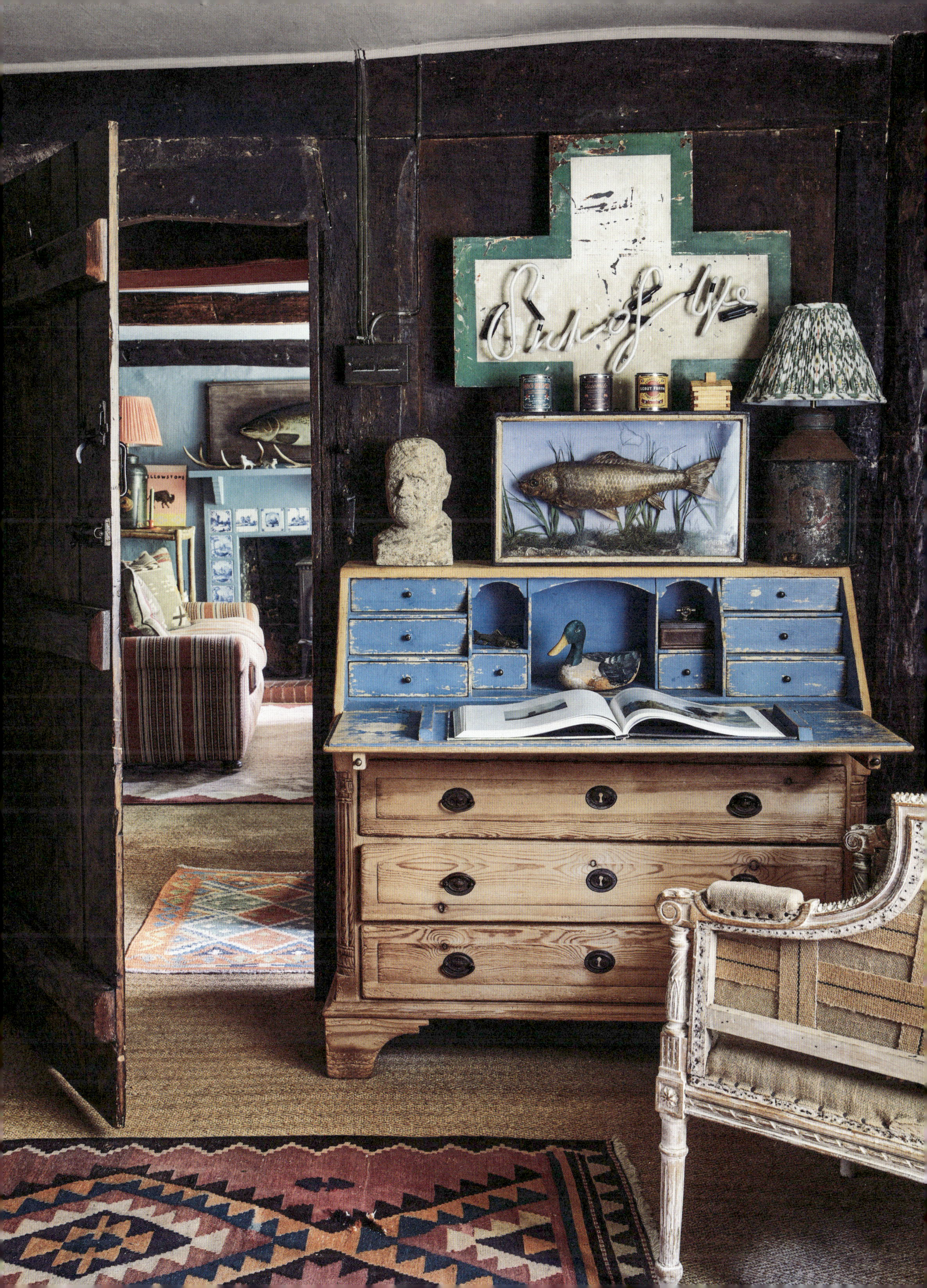

ORIGINAL DETAIL The kitchen retains a cozy, old-world charm, with a bright red Aga, brass tapware and an abundance of vintage finds that add character and warmth. Rush chairs painted with folk art detailing. Artwork all from Studio HÁM bespoke collections (see also pages 204–205).

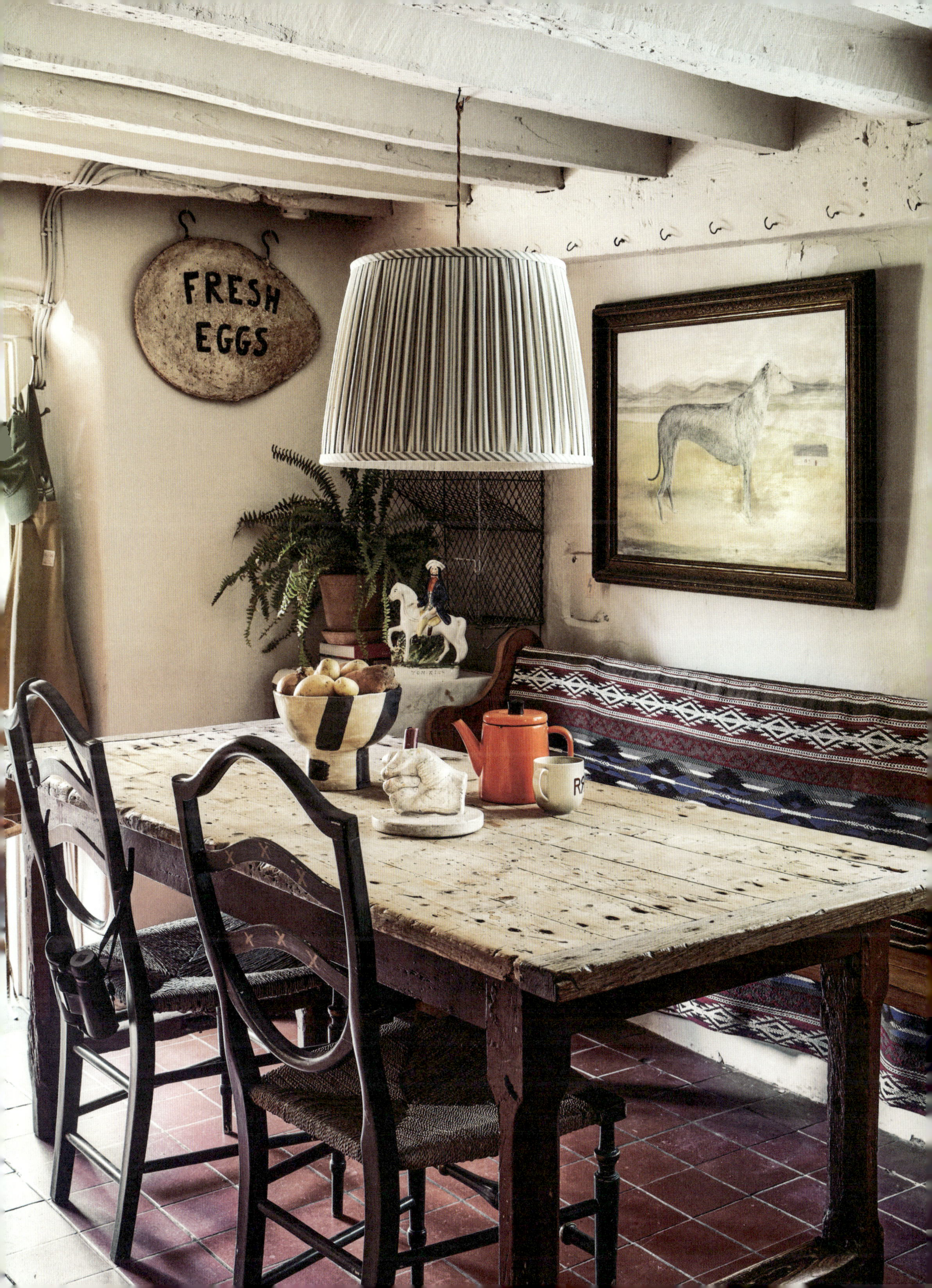
FRESH
EGGS

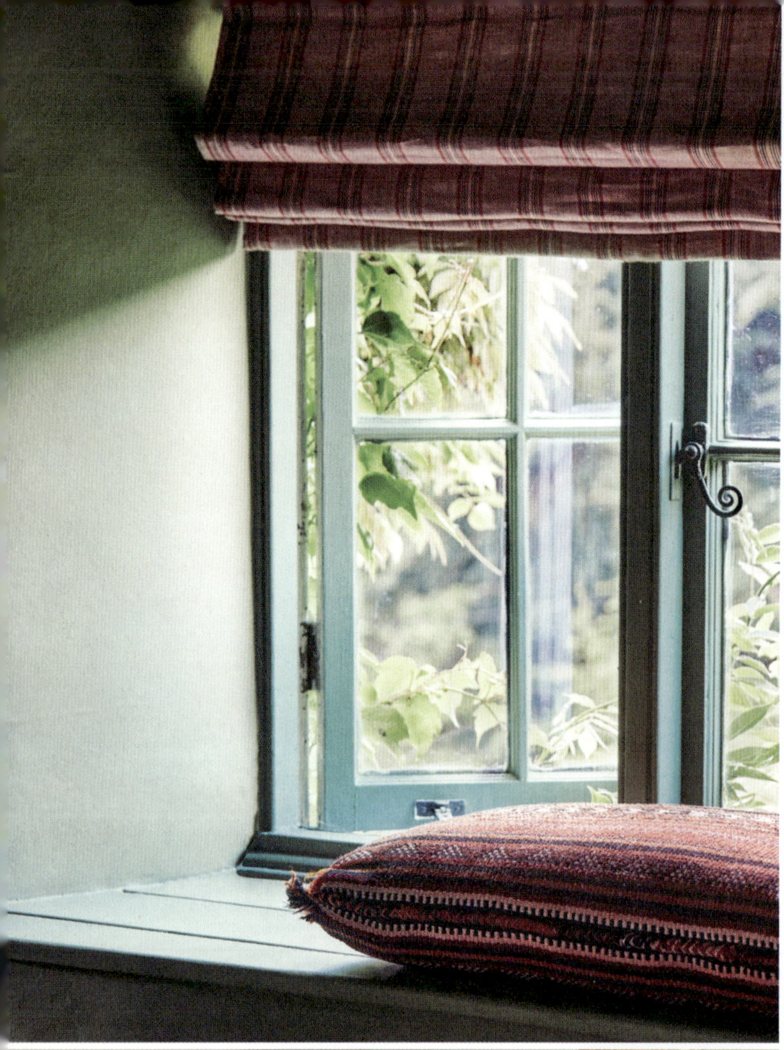
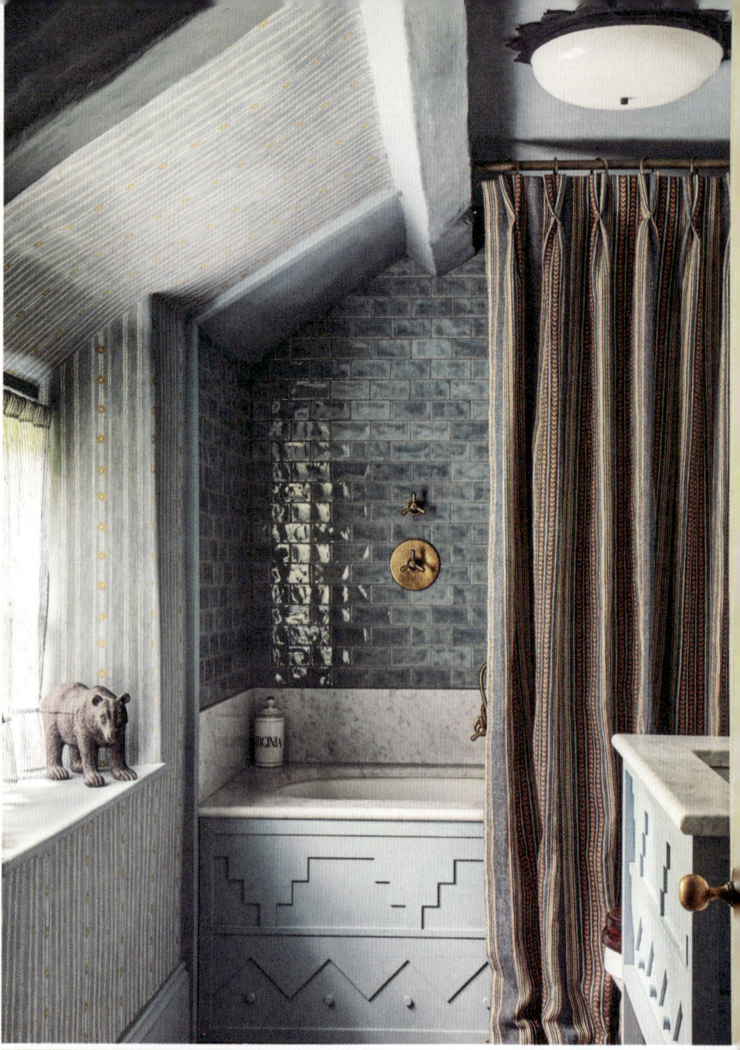
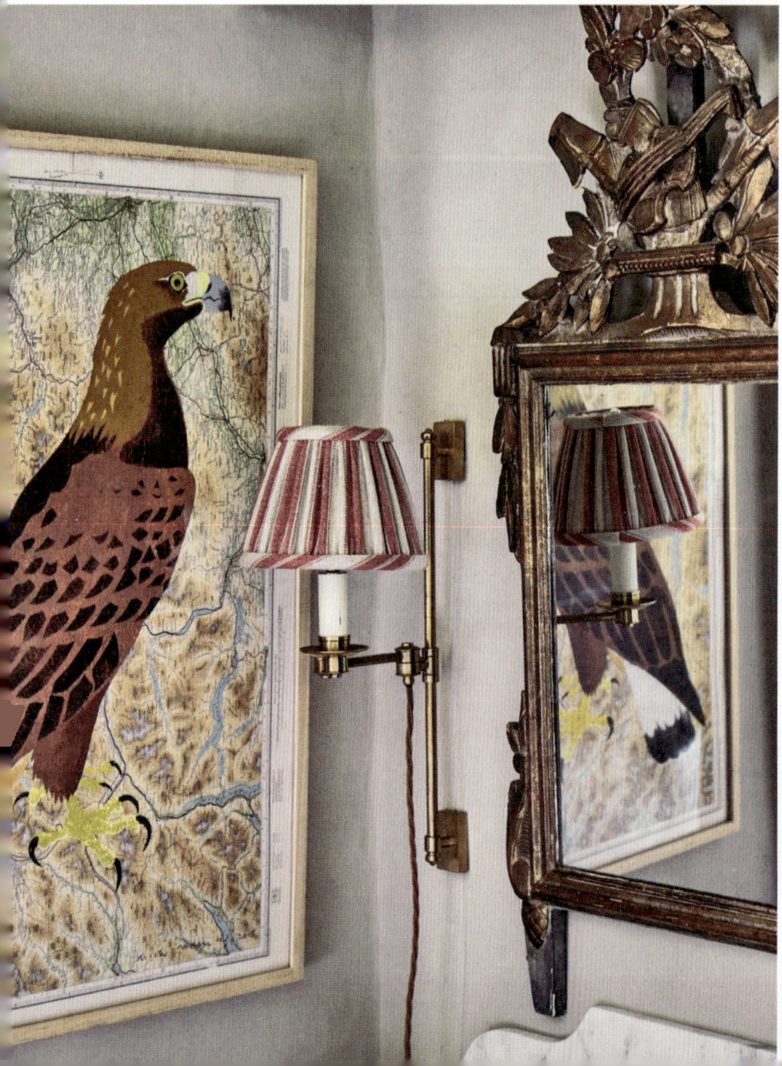
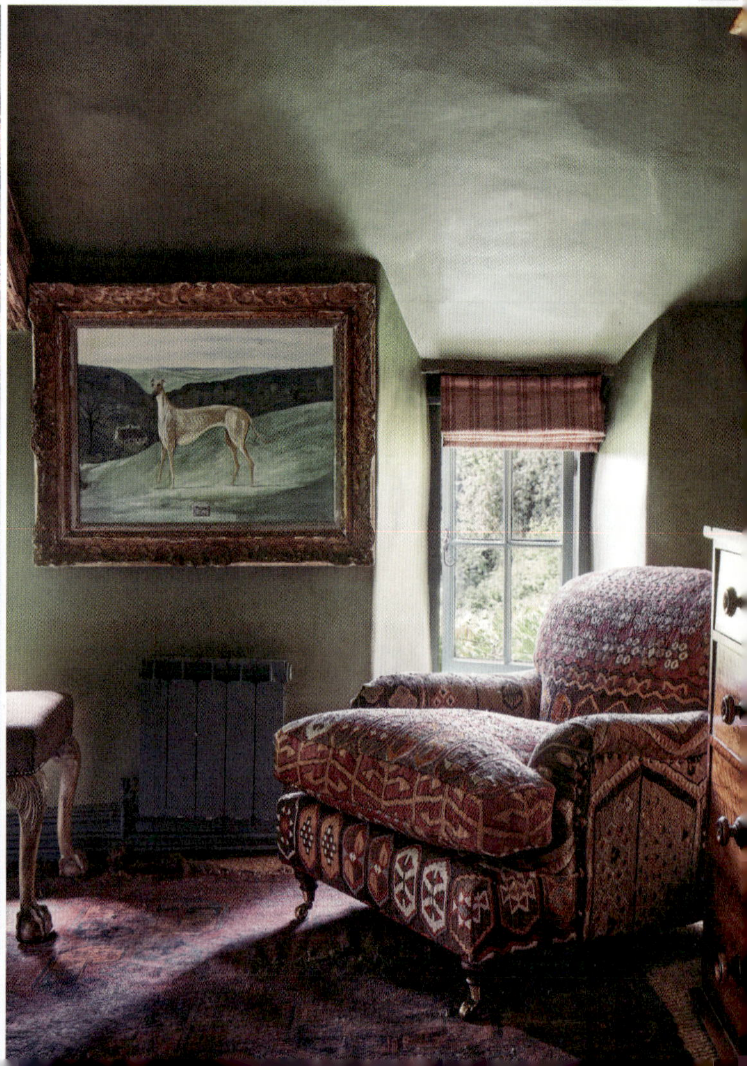

OBJECTS OF AFFECTION Headboard fabric is Kintbury Stripe from the Guy Goodfellow Collection (above). Wall light by bedroom sink, 'Oban Rise and Fall' by Vaughan Designs, and eagle artwork by Mick Manning (opposite, bottom left). Shower curtain in Berber Stripe Fabric, 'Denim', by Mulberry Home (opposite, top right). Cowboy vanity and kilim armchair, both Studio HÁM (opposite, top and bottom right). Blind (shade) fabric, Melcombe Stripe in 'Red', by Colefax and Fowler (opposite, top left and bottom right).

HUTS & HIDEAWAYS In the guest cottage, a cozy bedroom, bathroom and kitchen occupy the ground floor, below Tom's office (see page 212). Headboard and matching wall-light shade fabric, 'Cheyenne', by Güell Lamadrid. Bathroom Exe vanity and Branch mirror, both by Studio HÁM. Bathroom wall lights from Jamb.

PAGE 213 GARDEN RETREAT Bespoke outdoor kitchen customized by Tom and an outdoor bathtub and sauna.

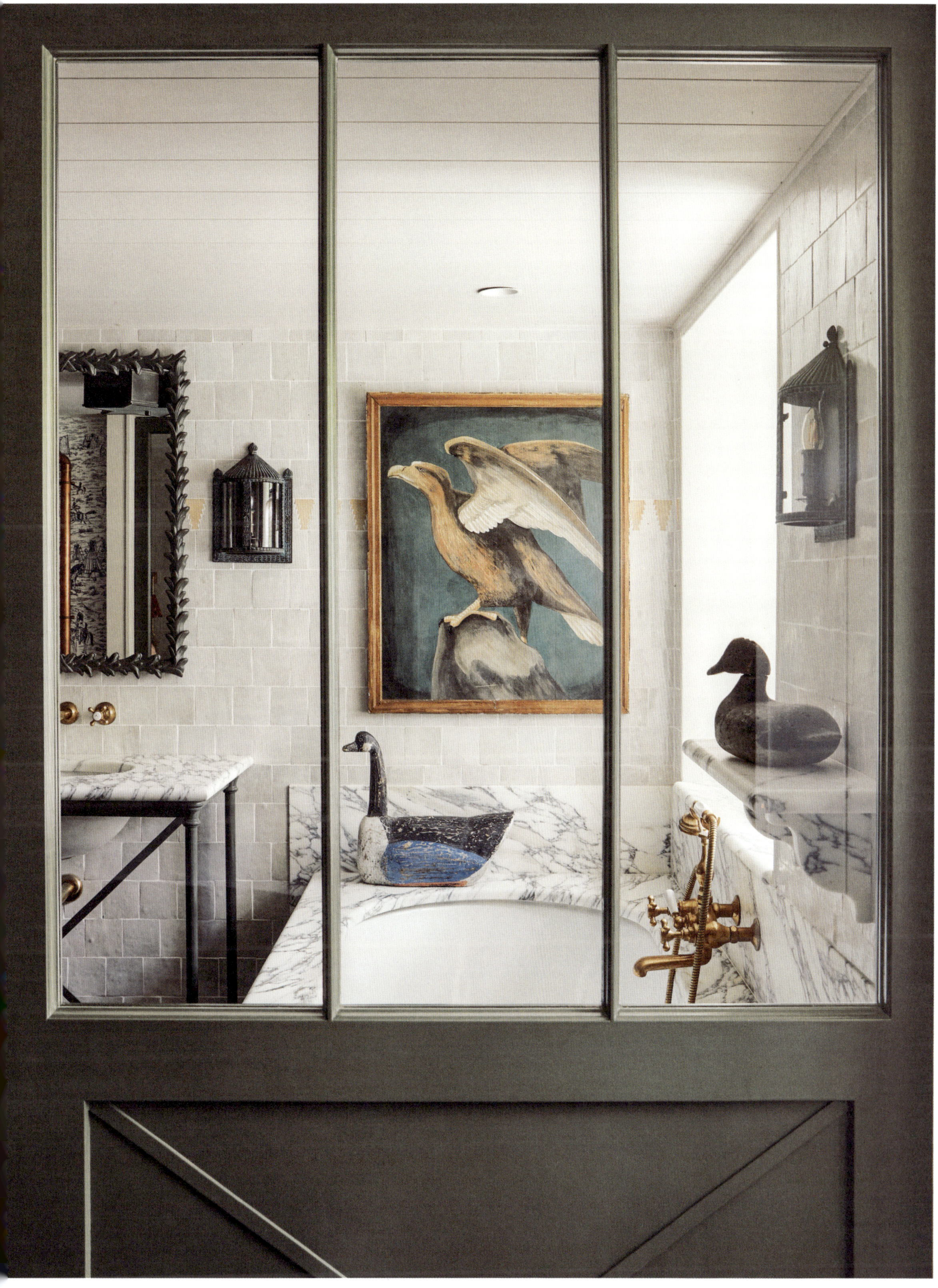

212 LIVING

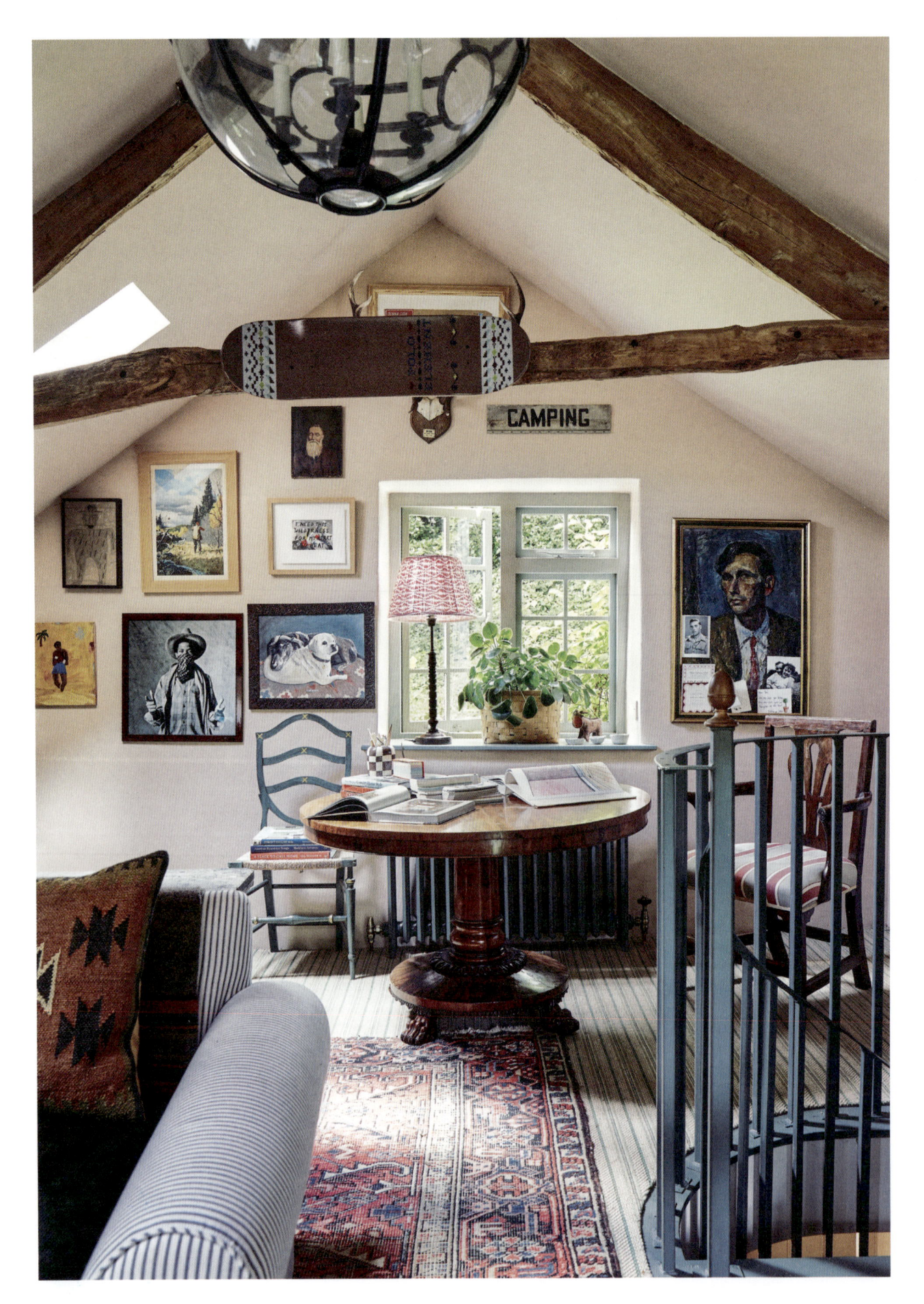

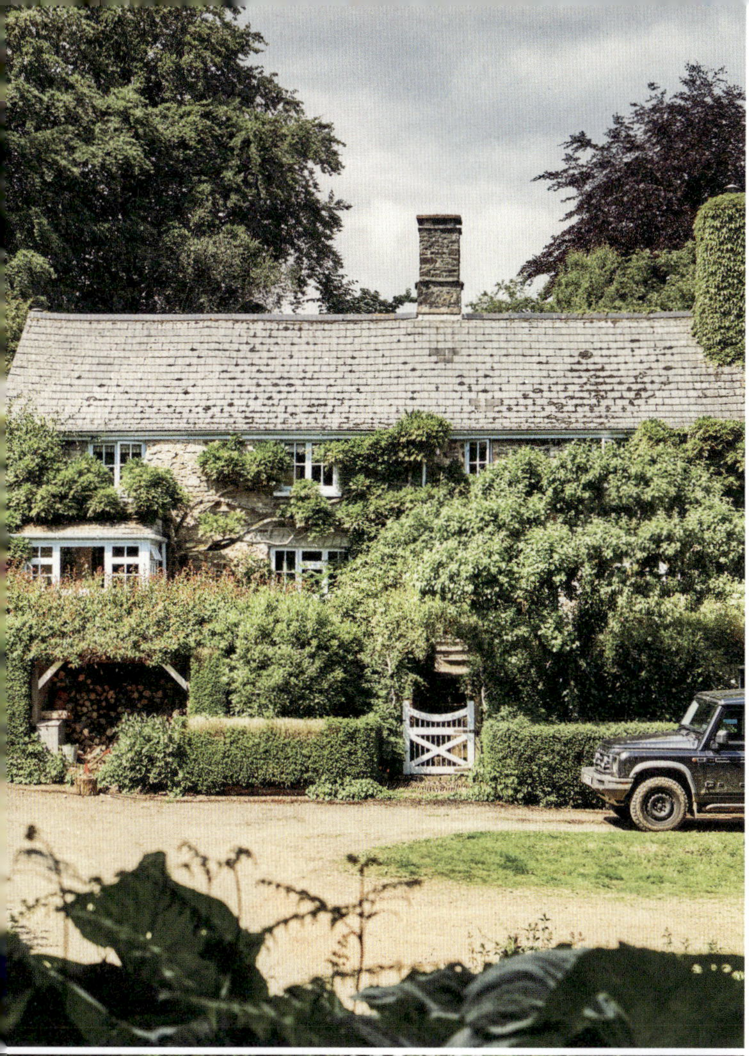

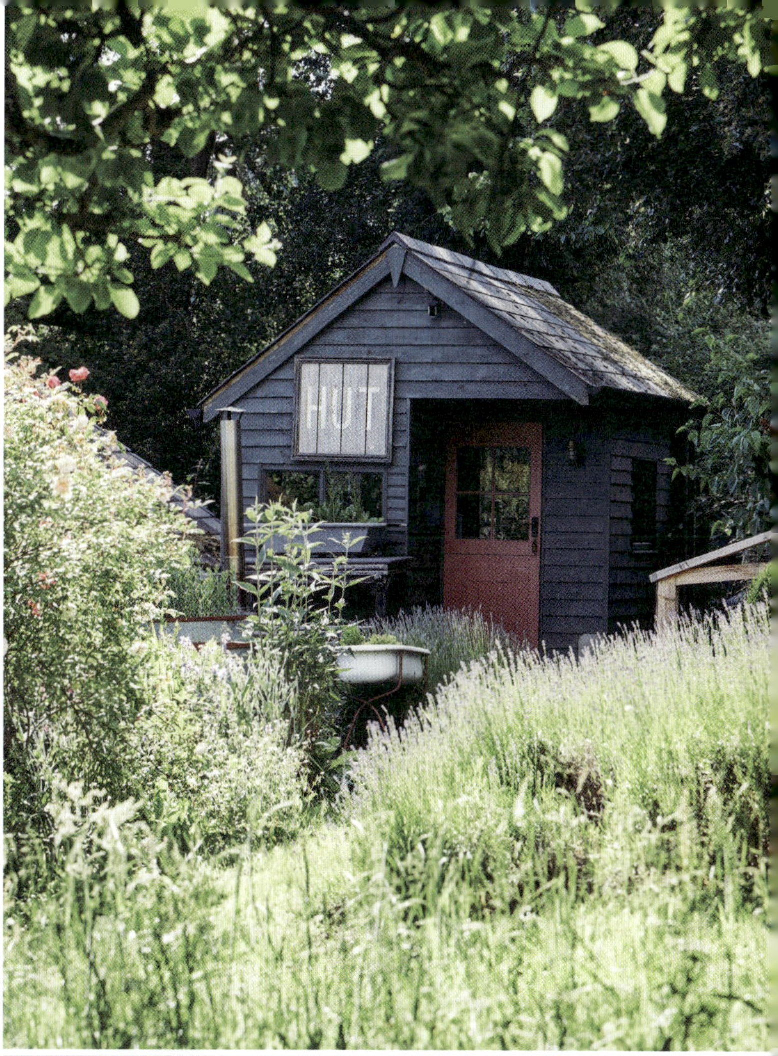
HUT

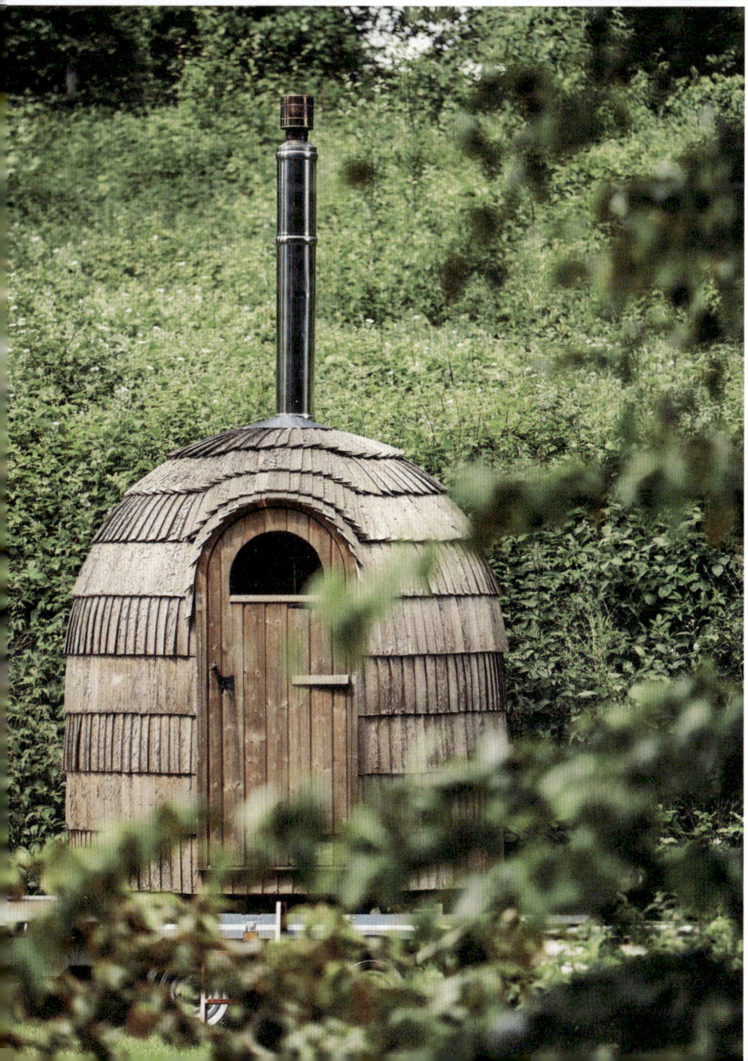

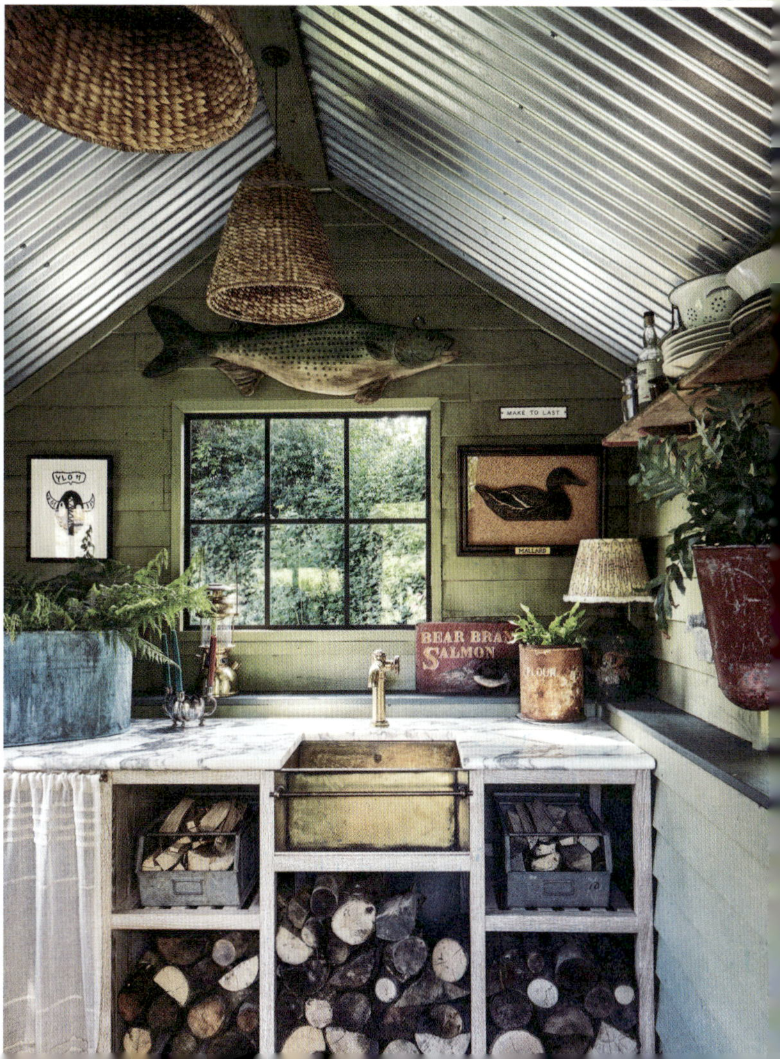

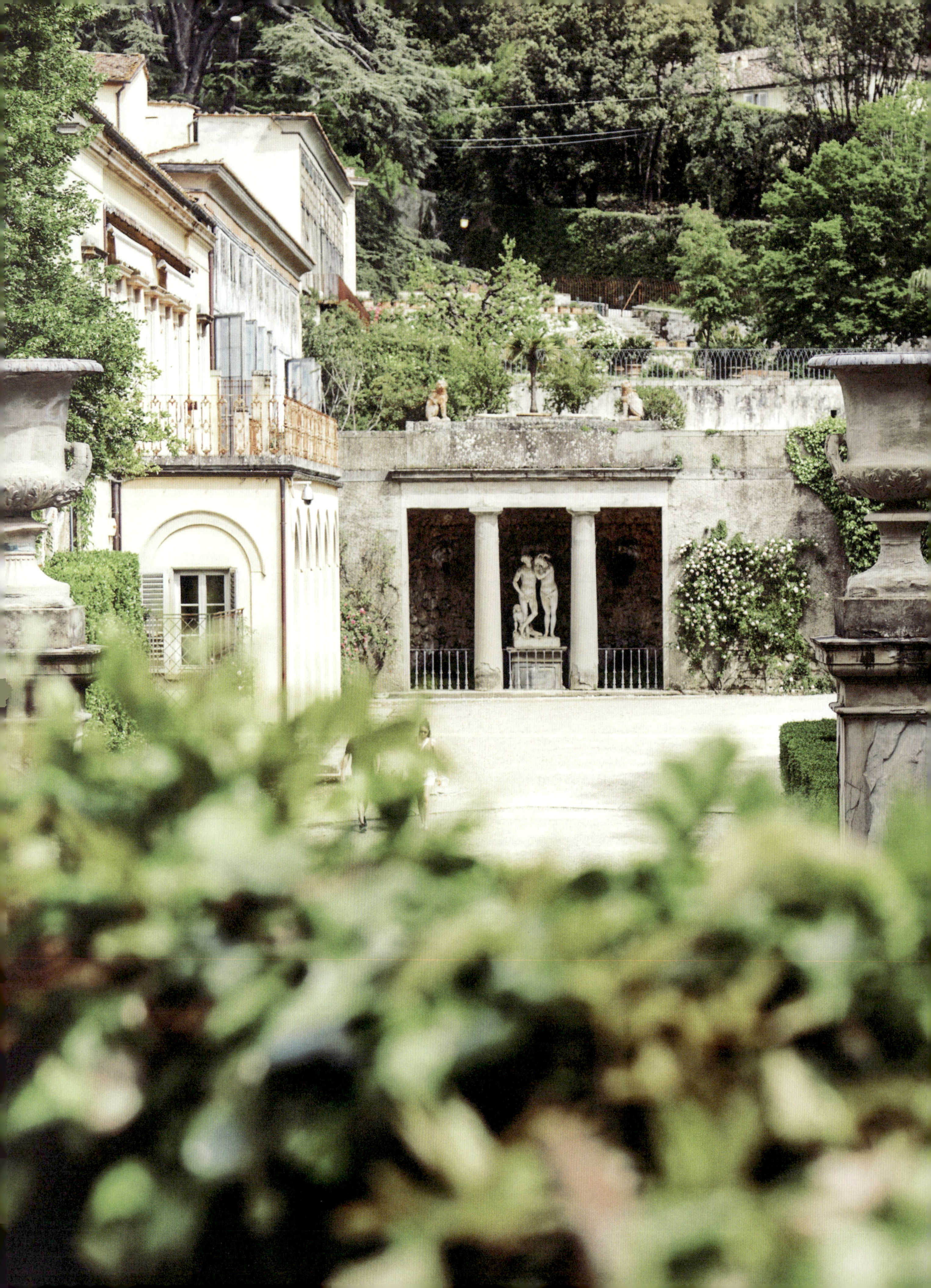

THINGS I LOVE

This is my love list – your favourites most welcome on a postcard!

Places I never want to leave Hotel Costes in Paris; JK Place in Florence and Capri; Le Sirenuse in Positano; Six Senses Laamu in the Maldives; the Experimental hotels in Venice and Menorca; and Hip Hideouts chalets and apartments in Val d'Isère.

Location close to my heart The Dunes in Mawgan Porth, Cornwall. For the house, the beach, Kingsurf Surf School, and the coming together of family and friends.

Museum that captured my imagination Palazzo Fortuny in Venice. If walls could talk.

Houses to visit Charleston Farmhouse and Farleys House in East Sussex, UK; Kettle's Yard in Cambridge, also UK; and Potter's House in Mallorca.

Restaurants to return to Trattoria Al Gatto Nero, on the island of Burano, and Antica Pesa in Rome. Both family-run and firmly etched in my memory.

Creatives who inspire Axel Vervoordt, Ben Pentreath, Diane Keaton, Ilse Crawford, Lidewij Edelkoort, Leanne Ford, Malene Birger, Roman and Williams, Rose Uniacke, Spencer Fung and Studio Oliver Gustav.

Books that have influenced my idea of home *Atmospheres* by Peter Zumthor, *The Poetics of Space* by Gaston Blanchard, *A Frame for Life* by Ilse Crawford, *The Thinking Hand* by Juhani Pallasmaa, *The House in Good Taste* by Elsie de Wolfe, and *Love Notes from The Hollow Tree* by Jarod K. Anderson.

Favourite scents Cire Trudon's Ernesto; Diptyque's Baies and Figue; Astier de Villatte's Grand Chalet.

Garden that left a lasting impression I fell in love with the Boboli Gardens, in Florence, 20 years ago. Discovering they were actually opposite Betty Soldi's studio made shooting her story for this book very special.

Bed must-haves Natural linen sheets – cool in summer, warm in winter – and they get softer and cosier over time. Go-to bedding companies are Piglet In Bed, Libeco, Cultiver and Ellei Home.

Materials of choice Marble and limestone – even with the inevitable chips, they add character that gets better with age. And always wood – for warmth and to ground us. The more gnarly, the better.

Everyday handmade obsessions Vases from Astier de Villatte, small plates from Elvis Robertson, mugs by Nicola Gillis and dinner service from Skye McAlpine.

More time for Love letters, spontaneous road trips with my husband, girlfriend weekends, afternoon wine, long chats, family and friend suppers, slowing down, revving up, accepting imperfections, bubble baths, self-care.

Memories I would give anything to have delayed the inevitable with our darling dog, Purdey. He sat by my side while I wrote this book for two-thirds of the journey before passing away, but his soul is firmly embedded within these pages and our home.

Life lessons The feeling you create at home is up to you. It does not need to be bound by the past; it's simply a decision to choose your own freedom of expression. Love, family and friendship are everything. Staying curious stretches your mind and pushes your creativity. Being kind and true to yourself is the only way to live.

BEATING HEART Betty Soldi's studio garden overlooks the entrance to the Boboli Gardens, which I fell in love with in my thirties on a trip with my husband.

SOURCES I LOVE

ANTIQUES

Anton & K
@antonandkantiques

AU
@anna.unwin

Brownrigg
@brownrigguk

Bunny Williams Home
@bunnywilliamshome

Catherine Waters
@catherinewatersantiques

Chloe Antiques
@chloeantiques

Claire Langley Antiques
@clairelangley_

Decorative Antiques UK
@decorativeantiquesuk

Emma Leschallas Antiques
@emmaleschallas

Eneby home
@enebyhome

Family Founded
@family_founded

Franck Delmarcelle
@franckdelmarcelle

Gaëlle Jézéquel
@gzbadboysantiques

Galerie Half
@galerie_half

Galerie Stéphanie Olivier
@galerie_stephane_olivier

Gallery B·R
@gallery_br_

Gilli Hanna
@gillihanna_antiques

HOWE London
@howelondon

Jamb
@jamb_london

Kabinett & Kammer
@kabinettandkammer

Larusi
@larusirugs

Liz Morris
@lizmorrisdecorativeinteriors

Lorfords Antiques
@lorfordsantiq

Mason & Painter
@masonandpainter

Maison Artefact
@maisonartefact

Max Rollitt
@max_rollitt

Millington and Hope
@millingtonandhope

No1 Lewes
@no1lewes_antiques

Nook Vintage
@nookvintage

Norfolk Decorative
@norfolkdecorative

Old Potato Store
@theoldpotatostore

Pickett's House
@pickettshouse

Puckhaber
@puckhaberdecor

Retrouvius
@retrouvius

Societique
@societique

Streett Marburg
@streett_marburg

Tasha Interiors
@tasha_interiorsuk

The Blacksmith Rupanyup
@theblacksmithrupanyup

The Country Brocante
@thecountrybrocante

The Drill Hall Emporium
@thedrillhallemporium

The Oscar Collective
@theoscarcollective

ARTISTS

Amanda Duggan
@amandadugganstudio

Atelier Bleu
@atelierbleuart

Atherton Green Art
@athertongrnart

Caroline Popham
@carolinepopham

Felicity Keefe
@felicity.keefe

Gergei Erdei
@gergeierdei

Ines Brenneman
@inesbrenneman

Josh Young
@jyoungdesignhouse

Liza Giles
@liza.giles.art

Lizzie Owen
@lizzieowenartist

Lukas
@lukastheillustrator

Mary Norden
@marynorden

Molesworth & Bird
@molesworthandbird

Ness Lockyer
@nesslockyerart

Nicola Heim
@haymwerk

Oyster Bridge & Co
@oysterbridgeandco

Quiet Thunder
@quietthunderco

Ricardo Fontales
@rfontales

Rob Wyn Yates
@robwynyates.studio

Ruby Bateman
@ruby_bateman

Saskia Saunders
@saskia_saunders

Sassy Hardwick
@sassy_hardwick

Spencer Fung
@spencerfung_art

Uli Van Neyghem
@ulivanneyghem

CERAMICS

1690 Store
@1690store

1882 Ltd
@1882ltd

Astier de Villatte
@astierdevillatte

Be Still
@bestillceramics

CJ Abbey
@cj_abbey

Crèadh Ceramics
@creadhceramics

Elvis Robertson
@elvis_robertson_ceramics

Franck Evennou
@franck_evennou

Gavin Houghton
@gavin1966

Ginny Sims Burchard
@ginnysimsceramics

Giuseppe Parrinello
@giuseppeparrinelloceramics

Hannah Tounsend
@hannah_tounsend

Helen Johannessen
@helenjohceramics

Joseph Dupré
@josephduprestudios

Lucille Lewin
@lucillelewin

Martyn Thompson
@martynthompsonstudio

Michael Chandler
@michaelchandlerceramics

Nicola Gillis
@nicolagillis

Penny Spooner
@pennyspoonerceramics

Pollyanna Johnson Ceramics
@pollyannajohnsonceramics

FURNITURE DONATION

Furnishing Futures
@furnishingfutures

GALLERY STORES

Axel Vervoordt Gallery
@axelvervoordt_co

Bard Scotland
@bard.scotland

Cavaliero Finn
@cavalierofinn

Francis Gallery
@francisgallery

Galerie Objets Inanimés
@juliepailhas.objets.inanimes

Guild Gallery
@guildgallery

KALPA Art Living
@kalpaartliving

Maud & Mabel
@maudandmabellondon

New Ashgate Gallery
@newashgate

Object & Thing
@object_thing

Sarah Myerscough
@sarah_myerscough

The New Craftsman Gallery
@newcraftsmangallery

The Shop Floor Project
@theshopfloor

The Stratford Gallery
@the_stratford_gallery

TIWA
@tiwa_select

HANDMADE DECORATIVE

Barnaby Ash & Dru Plumb
@ashandplumb

By Walid
@bywalidlondon

Caroline Zoob
@carolinezoobdesign

Catherine Hammerton
@cathhammerton

Cristina Rebeccani Coretti
@cristina.rebeccani.coretti

Geoffrey Preston
@geoffreyprestonsculpture

Nic Webb
@nicwebb1

Pacha Design
@pachadesignuk

Sandra Tyson
@allfiredup.pottery

HANDMADE FURNITURE

Emma Diaz
@byemmadiaz

Hadeda
@hadeda_co

Matthew Cox
@matthewcoxetc

Nicola Harding & Co
@nicolahardingandco

Pilgrim House
@pilgrim.house

PINCH
@pinch_london

Temper Studio
@temperstudio

WoodEdit
@woodedituk

LIFESTYLE STORES

8 Holland Street
@8hollandstreet

ABC Carpet & Home
@abccarpetandhome

Abigail Ahern
@abigailahern

A G Hendy & Co
@a_g_hendy_co_homestore

Alex Eagle
@alexeaglestudio

Alice In Scandiland
@aliceinscandilandshop

Anthropologie
@anthropologie

Antoinette Poisson
@antoinettepoisson

Atelier AH
@aliheath_uk

Atelier Sukha
@ateliersukha

Baileys Home Store
@baileyshome

Berdoulat
@berdoulat_interior_design

Bettencourt Manor
@bettencourtmanor

Betty Soldi Studio
@bettysoldistudio

Bless Stories
@blessstories_

Buck Mason With Leanne Ford
@leannefordinteriors

Casa González & González
@gonzalezygonzalezstore

Casa Gusto
@getthegusto

Cathy Penton Atelier
@cathypentonatelier

Cowdray Lifestyle
@cowdrayestate

Curated Living
@curated_living

Daylesford Organic
@daylesfordfarm

Deans Court
@deans_court

Dear: Rivington +
@dearrivington_official

Ecoco
@ecoco.com.au

edit58
@edit.58

Frama
@framacph

Freight HHG
@freighthhg

Haus
@haushaslemere

Heathcote General Trader
@heathcotegeneraltrader

Home Stories
@homestoriesnyc

House of Grey
@houseofgreylondon

Imprint House
@imprint_house

John Derian
@johnderian

Katrina Phillips
@katrinaphillipsinteriors

Liberty London
@libertylondon

Lobster and Swan
@lobsterandswan

Maiden Home
@maidenhome

Maison Curate
@maisoncurate

Maison Flâneur
@maison_flaneur

Mason & Painter
@masonandpainter

Malene Birger
@malenebirgers_world

Merci Paris
@merciparis

Nām
@namstore_bath

Nest Home & Café
@nesthomeandcafe

Pentreath & Hall
@pentreathandhall

Petersham Nurseries
@petershamnurseries

Plain Goods
@plaingoodsshop

PORTA
@porta_nyc

Restoration Hardware
@rh.restorationhardware

Rialto
@rialto_shop

Rose Uniacke
@roseuniacke

Rue Verte
@rueverte

RW Guild
@rwguild

Sailors
@sailorsofrye

Sanne Hop
@sannehop

Salubrious Living
@salubrious__living

Sharland England
@sharland_england

Southern Wild Co
@southernwildco

Studio HÁM
@studio.ham

Studio Oliver Gustav
@studiooligervustav

The Curated Store
@the.curatedstore

The Dharma Door
@thedharmadoor

The Edition 94
@theedition94

The Evandale Village Store
@the.evandalevillagestore

The Fig Store
@thefigstore

The General Store Palmwoods
@thegeneralstorepalmwoods

The Hambledon
@thehambledon

The Hub General Store
@thehubgeneralstore

The King and I Design
@thekingandidesign

The Merchant's Table
@the_merchants_table

The Newt
@thenewtinsomerset

The Oakmoor Hare
@theoakmorehare

The Panton Store
@thepantonstore

The Shopkeeper at Tomolly
@tomolly_carcoar

The Society Inc
@thesocietyinc

The Ticking Tent
@thetickingtent

The White Company
@thewhitecompany

Thyme
@thyme.england

Toogood
@t_o_o_g_o_o_d

TROVE By Studio Duggan
@trovebystudioduggan

Vanil
@vanil_ltd

Wattle and Daub Home
@wattleanddaubhome

Wesley & Willis
@wesleyandwillis

SOURCES I LOVE 217

THANK YOU

The saying 'Home is Where the Heart Is' is so true. Wherever you are in your process of creating a cocooning home that makes you feel happy and nurtured, I hope this book will become a well-worn friend that you return to for ideas and encouragement. You are as unique as the home you choose to create, so – no matter how bumpy life can be – pick the path that lights you up and don't lose sight of what is important to you personally. Perfection doesn't exist, but making home a special place to be will be the best gift you can give to yourself.

I firmly believe that to create a home you love you must show up emotionally and creatively on a regular basis, and the same has been true for the making of this book. I would like to thank all the creatives and homeowners featured for sharing this wonderful journey with me. Your stories, style and generosity have filled these pages with inspiration and beauty.

Special thanks to my talented, principal photographer, Brent Darby, for coming with me on this adventure to many different countries and for your patience and commitment to shooting this project with such dedication. Thank you for your gorgeous images and friendship for the past 20 years.

I am also so grateful to Abbie Mellé for her wonderful photography of Satellite Island; Grégory Timsett and Marianne Evennou for capturing Marianne's home so atmospherically; and Rob Mills for so kindly sharing the stunning images of his Australian project, shot by Dan Preston. You have all done me proud, thank you so much.

Huge respect to my publisher, Alison Starling. It has been great to work with you again – thank you for believing in me and this book. Special thanks also to my brilliant extended team at Octopus, including designers Nicky Collings and Juliette Norsworthy; editorial team, Scarlet Furness and Caroline West; production, Katherine Hockley; and press and marketing, Vic Scales, Megan Brown and Erin Brown. Thank you all for your hard work and attention to detail – it has been a joy to create something beautiful together. Many thanks also to Nikki Griffiths for your advice and good humour, Georgia Knowles for bringing to life my graphic ideas for the book, and Sophie Youngs for your fabulous hard work, assisting on Bee's shoot.

Thank you to my dear family and friends, for the help, love and messages while I have gone off-radar again creating this book. I can't tell you how much it has meant.

Finally, a massive thank you to all the readers, retailers and editors who have so kindly bought, stocked and promoted my books. Thank you for coming on another book journey with me and for all the kindness you have shown me with my earlier books, *CURATE* and *CREATE*. That support has made this book a reality, so I am forever grateful, and never take your generosity for granted. Ali x

ABOUT THE AUTHOR

Ali Heath is an interiors expert and her multi-faceted work as an author, journalist, stylist, interior designer and creative consultant has featured in prestigious magazines, books and newspapers all over the world.

Her non-linear career has been defined by listening to her heart, remaining curious and focusing on the things she loves – pivoting from corporate and creative agency worlds to set up her own antiques business, then for the past 20 years following her passion for interiors.

Her first two bestselling books, CURATE and CREATE, were published by Mitchell Beazley in 2021 and 2023, and Ali was also Contributing Editor and Creative Consultant for The White Company's second book, *The Art of Living with White* (Mitchell Beazley, September 2022).

Ali's unique background brings an original perspective, and she is passionate about breaking down the traditional barriers of the interiors industry and creative world – encouraging others to trust in their intuition, find their voice and to believe in their own creativity.

Ali lives in the south of England, but is often travelling, as she seeks out new places and hidden talent. If you're interested in working together, or are interested in collaborating on projects or product designs, you can find her online at:

www.aliheath.co.uk and @aliheath_uk

INDEX

A
ABASK 54
Agas 124, 203, *206*
Alstergren, Kate & Will 62–75
antiques 46, 124, 200, *203*, *216*, *224*
Appel, Tracey 53, 162–75
Armadillo & Co. 79, *112*, 117
Aroundfiveoclock 53
Art Untamed 185
Artìcolo 139
Astier de Villatte ceramics *172*
Atelier AH 46, 53
AU 76, 86

B
B&B Italia *141*
Banchory Farm, Scotland 26
bathrooms 45
   architectural villa 79, *88*
   converted shops 161
   cottage conversion 179, *185*
   farmhouse renovations 191, *196*, *209*, *210*
   Hillside Residence *144*
   mansion house conversion *175*
   outdoor 65, 72, 179, *210*
   Victorian townhouse *123*
Baxter Bourgeois desk *141*
BC Designs 185
bedrooms
   architectural villa *88*
   converted shops 156, *161*
   cottage conversion 179, *185*
   farmhouse renovations *196*, *210*
   Hillside Residence *144*
   mansion house conversion *175*
   Scandi-style cabin *97*
   Victorian townhouse *123*
Birger, Malene *21*, 53
boathouses 62–75
Boboli Gardens, Florence *215*
bonding 54
books 53
brass 46
Brockhoff, Fiona 65

C
Calacatta Viola marble vase *144*
candles 49, 50, *165*
Caratos chairs *141*
Caravane 46, 79
Carey, Netta 185

Carl Hansen & Søn *171*
Catchpole & Rye *175*
ceramics 53, 57, *172*, *191*, *216*
chairs *117*, *139*, *141*, *171*, *206*, *209*
Chalk Path Studios 120
childhood imagination 7, 15
Circular Salutogenic Design 112
Citterio, Antonia *141*
cocktails: Saint-Germain 55
cocooning 12
Colefax and Fowler *209*
Colette kitchen stools, *139*
collections 24, 53, *172*, *191*, *191*, 200
Collinson, Edward *119*
colours 19
   bright & bold *103*
   cool blue *200*, *203*
   natural & earthy 80, *93*, *127*, *188*, *194*, *196*
comfort 19
connection to others 57
connection with home 7–8, 15, 42
consumerism 45
Corsi Garden, Florence 31, 35
cottage conversion 176–87
Covid pandemic 15
Cox, Sebastian 93
Cox, Tom 46, 200–14
crafts 45, 46, 54, 79
creativity 15, 49
   and environment 32, *33*
   and travelling 36, *38*, 39
Crittall-style doors *176*, 179
Crittall-style windows *182*
Cultiver 86
curiosity 15, 21, 24
curtains & blinds 50, 79
   cottage conversion 179
   farmhouse renovations *194*
   Victorian townhouse *115*
curves, effect of 45

D
Dandy ottoman *117*
darkness & shadow 50, *50*, 179
daydreaming 15
daylight 19, 49, *90*
Default Mode Network 15
Deià, Mallorca 100–11
design 15, 18–19, 21, 24
desks *141*, 146

dining rooms
   converted shops *151*
   farmhouse renovations *191*, *203*
   Hillside Residence *139*, *141*
   mansion house conversion *165*
   Scandi-style cabin *97*
dream boards *21*, 21
dreams 15

E
Eckersley Garden Architecture 134
Edward Bulmer Natural Paint 203
Ellipse Collections 117
emotions
   balancing head & heart 16
   connection to home 7–8, 15, 42
   and design principles 18
   vs rational thinking 16
energy, sources of 49, 50
entertaining 54
environment 45, 112
   scents 19, 32, 49
   sounds 18, 31, 32, 49, 65
essential oils 49
Ethnicraft 82, 97
Evennou, Franck 146–61
Evennou, Marianne 53, 146–61
exteriors 19, 31, 35
   architectural villa *76*
   converted shop *127*
   cottage conversion *176*
   farmhouse renovations *188*, *198*
   fisherman's cottage *100*, *110*
   Hillside Residence *134*
   mansion house conversion *162*, *171*, *175*

F
farmhouse renovations 188–99, 200–14
Farrow & Ball 203
feelings 8, 19, 21, 39, 42, 65, 215
fisherman's cottage 100–11
flexibility 19
flooring 93, 115, 124, 137, 162, 179, *191*, 200
Fontales, Nam and Ricardo 21
furniture 32, 45, 46, 82, 97, 115, 149, 191, 217. *see also* individual types

G
GamFratesi *139*
Glencross, Zoe 179
Graham, Romilly 115
gratitude 49
Grey, Christine 119
Grey, Louisa 46, 112–23
GUBI *139*
Güell Lamadrid *210*
Guy Goodfellow Collection *209*

H
hallways
   converted shops *146*, 146, *149*, *155*
   farmhouse renovations *203*
   mansion house conversion *166*
   Victorian townhouse *117*
HÁM Architecture 203
handmade items 45, 46, 54, 93, 165, 191, 215, *217*
Hardwick, Sassy 165, *166*
HAY 97, 115
Heath, Samuel 185
heating 93, 95
Hedegaard, Johannes *129*
Hillside Residence 134–45
Hodgson, Kiki & Chris 90–9
holistic design 112–23
home 12, 15–16, 54
   attachment to 7–8, 39, 42
   as sanctuary 7–8, 24, 65, 93, 115, 144
   and travelling 36, 38–9
   and work 28, 36
House of Grey 79, 119, 123
Husk armchair *141*

I
Ibiza 76–89
ideas 15, 21
imagination 7, 15, 21, 53
indigenous art 137
intimacy 7, 8, 15, 19, 45, 49
intuition 15, 32, 49, *112*

J
Jagged Art *129*
Jarman, Derek 129

K
kilim armchair *209*
King, Sarrita 137

kitchens
   architectural villa 80–3
   converted shops 129, *155*
   cottage conversion *182*
   farmhouse renovations *194, 203, 206, 210*
   Hillside Residence 137, *139*
   mansion house conversion 165, *171, 172*
   Scandi-style cabin 93
   Victorian townhouse 119–20

L
'La Famille Charles' collection *155*
Lamadrid, Güell *210*
Lazzeroni, Roberto *139*
Le Mesurier, Maria & Paul 188–99
Liang & Eimil *171*
light 19, 21, 50
   artificial 50, *115, 120, 139, 141, 210*
   natural 19, 39, 49, 50, *90*
linen 46, 50, 54, 62, 88, *175, 191, 196, 215*
living areas
   converted shops *133, 149, 155*
   farmhouse renovations *203*
   Hillside Residence *141*
   mansion house conversion *166*
   Victorian townhouse *112, 115, 117*
loggias *162*
love 57
Lowe Furniture *141*
Lukas the Illustrator *21*

M
Mallorca 100–11
Manning, Mick *209*
mansion house conversion 162–75
marble 46, *124, 175*
Maslow's hierarchy of needs 15
materials 45
   natural 18, *24*, 45, 46, 88, *93, 137, 144, 175, 188, 196*
   repurposing 45, 46
   sustainable 45, 112
   and temperature 18
   toxin-free 115
meals 54

memories 43
Mills, Rob 134–45
mindfulness 49
mirrors 117, *146, 156*
mood boards 21
Muir, Jane 57
Mulberry Home 46, *200, 209*

N
natural light 19, 39, 49, 50, *90*
natural materials 18, *24*, 45, 46, *137, 144, 175, 188, 196*
   architectural villa 88
   Scandi-style cabin 93
nature 31–2, *33, 35*, 65, *97, 127, 137, 175, 176, 210*
neuroscience 15
new vs old 19
Newman-Morris, Tess 62
nomadic lifestyle 36, 38–9
North Uist 90–9
nostalgia 19

O
Ochre *165*
O'Connor, Ellis *95, 97*
old vs new 19
Osborn, Bee 176–87

P
Paint & Paper Library *166*
patterns *103, 107, 155, 200, 209*
pendant lights *115, 120, 139*
Pentreath & Hall 21
perspective 21, 134
Phillips, Katrina 124–33
photographs for inspiration 21
Pickett, Anna 100–11
Pickett's House *100, 103*
Plain English *171*
plaster 28, *31*, 46, *86, 88, 115, 179, 185*
Popcorn, Faith 15
Popham, Caroline 53
Porta Romana *182*
Portobello Road 124–33
possessions 39
preferred curvature effect 45
priorities 39

R
Ralph Lauren Home *200*
Rams, Dieter 32
rational vs emotional approach 16

reflection 49
Reid, Magnus *107*
relationships 57, 65
relaxation 49, 65
repurposing materials 45, 46
rituals & reflection 49
RMA Architects 134
Roberts, Sarah Lee *166*
Robertson, Elvis 53
Rural Design *90*

S
Sadler, Marc *141*
sage 46, 49
Samuel, Margaret *166*
sanctuary, creating 7–8, 24, 65, *93, 115, 144*
Satellite Island 62–75
Scandi-style cabin 90–9
scents 19, 32, 49
Schiffini *155*
seasonal furnishings *191*
self, sense of 36
sensory reactions 15, 18, 19, 32, 45, 49, 115
shapes, organic 115
shepherds huts *176, 179*
shops, converted 124–33, 146–61
simplicity 24, 53
Sims, Ginny 21
Skye Stone Studios *93*
social skills 57
socializing 54
sofas 45, *79, 115, 133, 137, 141, 166, 200*
Soldi, Betty 28, *31–5, 215*
sounds 18, 31, 32, 49, 65
space and design 19, 21, 24, 179
Space Furniture *139*
Spade chair *117*
spontaneity 53
stone 45, 46, *137, 179, 191, 215*
storage 19, *95, 129, 188, 191*
stoves *90, 95, 176, 179, 182, 185*
Studio Duggan 53
Studio HÁM *200, 203, 206, 209, 210*
styles 18
summerhouses 62–75
suppliers: value alignment 18
sustainability 45, 112

T
table decor 54

tapware 79, *86, 119, 165, 172, 179, 185, 191, 206*
task lighting 50
technology 45, 46, 57
textiles 45, 46, 88
   curtains & blinds 50, *79, 115, 179, 194*
   layering 45, 46, *79, 196*
   linen 46, 50, 54, 62, 88, *175, 191, 196, 215*
   wall hangings *79, 117, 182*
thatched roof *185, 188*
Toogood, Faye *117*
travelling 36, 38–9
Twiggy floor lamp *141*

U
Unwin, Anna 46, 50, 76–89, *115*
Urquiola, Patricia 137, *141*

V
values 18, 39, 45
Vaughan Designs *209*
ventilation 19, 93
Verheyden, Michaël *144*
versatility 53
Victorian townhouse 112–23
views. *see* windows
Vola *119*
Vossel, Keith 15

W
walls *103, 115, 188, 191*
   hangings *79, 117, 182*
   plastered *86, 88, 115, 179, 185*
   whitewashed 62, *76, 79, 93, 103, 124*
   wood cladding *166, 179, 182*
Wills, Samantha 36, 38–9
windows
   converted shops *149, 151*
   cottage conversion *179, 182*
   Hillside Residence *144*
   Scandi-style cabin *90, 93, 97*
   Victorian townhouse *123*
Wishbone chairs *171*
wood 46
WoodEdit *191, 194*
wool 46
work space 28, 36

Z
Zara Home 54

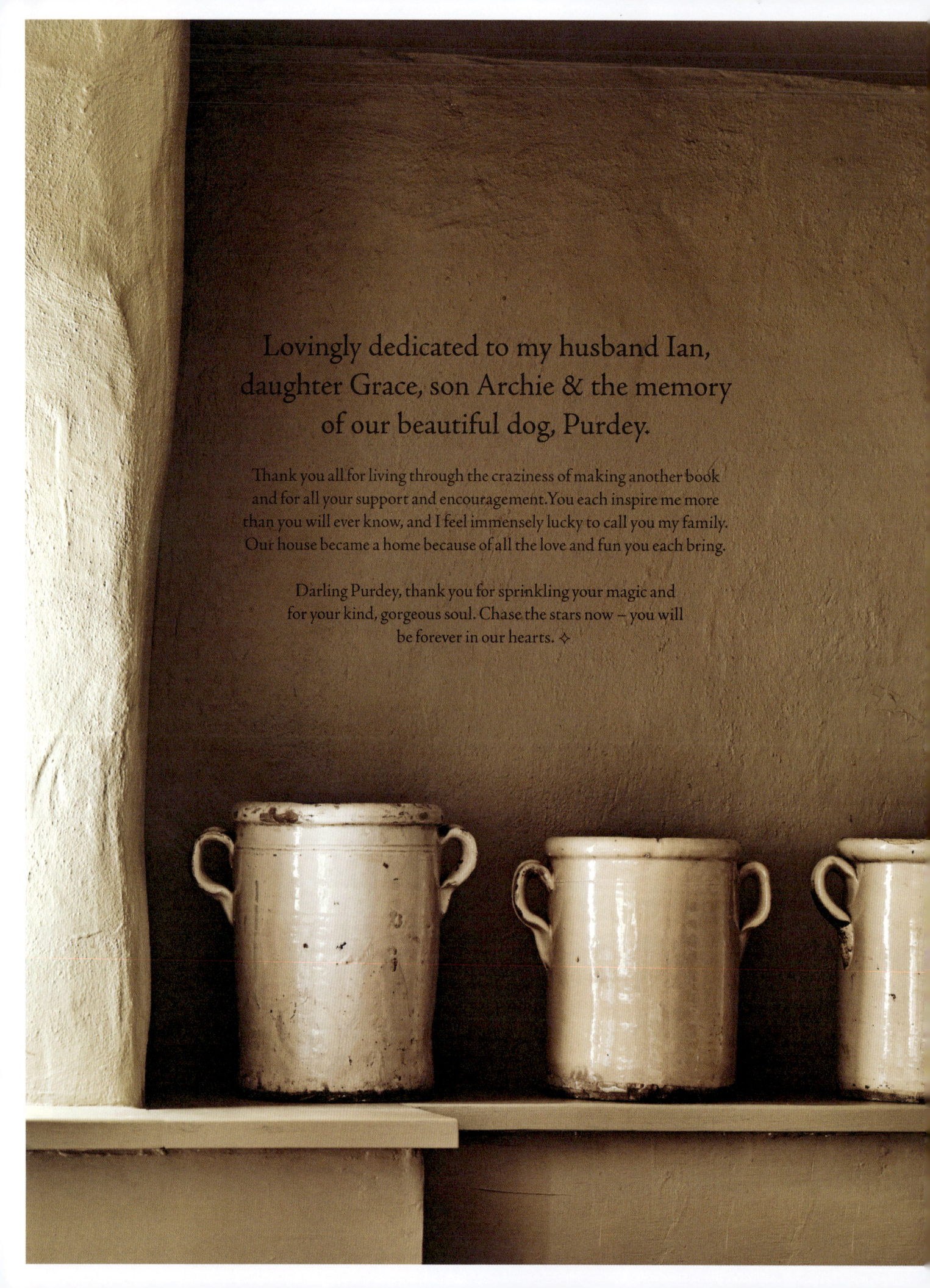

Lovingly dedicated to my husband Ian,
daughter Grace, son Archie & the memory
of our beautiful dog, Purdey.

Thank you all for living through the craziness of making another book
and for all your support and encouragement. You each inspire me more
than you will ever know, and I feel immensely lucky to call you my family.
Our house became a home because of all the love and fun you each bring.

Darling Purdey, thank you for sprinkling your magic and
for your kind, gorgeous soul. Chase the stars now – you will
be forever in our hearts. ✧

HOMEOWNER CREDITS

Ali Heath
aliheath.co.uk @aliheath_uk
Pages: 17, 21, 22–23, 25, 44, 47 (a2, a3, b2, c1), 48, 52 (a3, b1–3, c1–3), 56, 216–217

Amanda Pickett
clarkepickett.com @pickettshouse
Pages: 100–111

Anna Unwin
annaunwin.com @anna.unwin
Pages: 38, 43, 47 (b1, c3), 51, 76–89, back cover

Banchory Farm
banchoryfarm.co.uk @banchory_farm
Page: 26

Bee Osborn
osborninteriors.com @osborninteriors
Pages: Front cover, 13, 176–187

Betty Soldi
bettysoldi.com @bettysoldistudio
Pages: 29, 30, 33, 34, 35, 214

Kate & Will Alstergren
satelliteisland.com.au @satelliteisland
Available to rent.
Pages: 9, 37, 47 (b3), 62–75

Katrina Phillips
@katrinaphillipsinteriors
@katrina-phillips-ltd.myshopify.com
Pages: 124–133

Kiki & Chris Hodgson
no9uist.com @no9uist
Available to rent.
Pages: 90–99

Louisa Grey
houseofgrey.co.uk @houseofgreylondon
Pages: 4, 5, 47 (a1), 112–123

Maria & Paul Le Mesurier
marialemesurier.com @marialemesurier
woodedit.co.uk @woodedituk
Pages: 2, 188–199, 222

Marianne & Franck Evennou
marianne-evennou.com
@marianne_evennou
Pages: 6, 14, 52 (a2), 146–161

Rob Mills
robmills.com.au @robmillsarchitects
Pages: 134–145

Samantha Wills
samanthawills.com @samanthawills

Tom Cox
haminteriors.com @haminteriors
studioham.co.uk @studio.ham
Pages: 47 (c2), 200–213

Tracey Appel
Pages: 52 (a1), 59, 162–175

First published in Great Britain in 2025 by Mitchell Beazley, an imprint of Octopus Publishing Group Ltd, Carmelite House, 50 Victoria Embankment, London EC4Y 0DZ
www.octopusbooks.co.uk
www.octopusbooksusa.com

A Hachette UK Company
www.hachette.co.uk

The authorized representative in the EEA is Hachette Ireland, 8 Castlecourt Centre, Dublin 15, D15 XTP3, Ireland (email: info@hbgi.ie)

Distributed in the US by Hachette Book Group, 1290 Avenue of the Americas, 4th and 5th Floors, New York, NY 10104

Distributed in Canada by Canadian Manda Group, 664 Annette St., Toronto, Ontario, Canada, M6S 2C8

Text & illustrations copyright © Ali Heath 2025
Cover & principal photography © Brent Darby 2025
All other photography © 2025 by the individual photographer. See full credits, right.

All rights reserved. No portion of this book may be reproduced or utilized in any form or by any means, electronic or mechanical, including photocopying, recording or by any information storage and retrieval system, without the prior written permission of the publisher.

Ali Heath asserts the moral right to be identified as the author of this work.

ISBN 978-1-78472-972-1

A CIP catalogue record for this book is available from the British Library.

Printed and bound in China.

MIX
Paper | Supporting responsible forestry
FSC® C008047

Creative Direction & Interior Styling: Ali Heath
Photography: Brent Darby, Grégory Timsit, Abbie Mellé & Dan Preston
Illustrations: Georgia Knowles

Publishing Director: Alison Starling
Art Directors: Juliette Norsworthy & Nicky Collings
Design Assistant: Ella Mclean
Editor: Scarlet Furness
Copy Editor: Caroline West
Senior Production Manager: Katherine Hockley

Photography Credits:
Brent Darby: Cover and all images (except below)
Abbie Mellé: 9, 37, 62–75
Ali Heath: Inside endpapers, 44, 47 (a2), 52 (a3, b3, c2)
Dan Preston: 134–145
Grégory Timsit: 6, 14, 52 (a2), 146–161

Front cover artwork (from left to right):
Katja Leibenath (untitled), *Far Afield* by Netta Carey, *Tangerines* by Georgina Stanley, *Winter White* by Sonia Barton, unnamed, *Lime* by Netta Carey.

Back cover artwork:
Lady in the Park by Norman Miller.

'You will soon find that your joy in your home is growing, and that you have a source of happiness within yourself that you had not suspected.'

ELSIE DE WOLFE

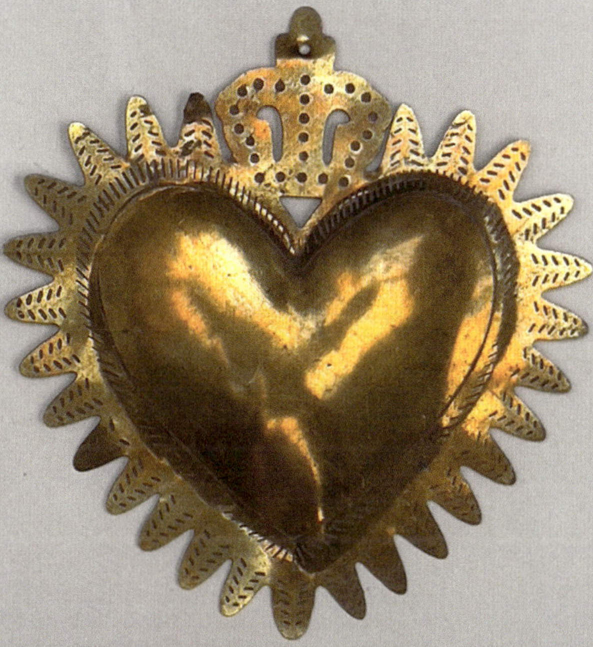